MISSILE

"Here [in *Missile Env...* ...guments that forcefully und... ...futility of government polici... ...on Curtain."

—Walter Cronkite

"It is easy to ... [Dr. Caldicott] has captured the ... ...ds of people around the world. . . . After y... ...eard her speak and shaken her hand, you canno... ...ush aside her message as the emotional outpouring of a fanatic. She speaks from a solid basis of medical experience. She speaks for the victims in a language that all of us should be able to understand."

—Freeman Dyson
The New Yorker

"Helen Caldicott is often described as the mother of the nuclear freeze movement. Anyone who reads *Missile Envy* should demand an end to the nuclear weapons spiral by both the U.S.S.R. and the U.S., who spend more money and time preparing for nuclear war than in its prevention. Hers is the voice of reason in a time of insanity."

—Candice Bergen

"What is unique about this book is that it puts the nuclear arms race in a larger context. It traces connections with the cold war, conventional warfare, intervention, the military industry and the psychological attitudes of the decision makers. Once again Helen Caldicott shows why popular movements are a critical factor in reversing the arms race."

—Randall Forsberg, Director of the
Institute of Defense and Disarmament Studies

BANTAM NEW AGE BOOKS

This important imprint includes books in a variety of fields and disciplines and deals with the search for meaning, growth, and change. They are books that circumscribe our times and our future.

Ask your bookseller for the books you have missed.

BETWEEN HEALTH AND ILLNESS by Barbara B. Brown
THE COSMIC CODE by Heinz R. Pagels
CREATIVE VISUALIZATION by Shakti Gawain
THE DANCING WU LI MASTERS by Gary Zukav
ECOTOPIA by Ernest Callenbach
AN END TO INNOCENCE by Sheldon Kopp
ENTROPY by Jeremy Rifkin with Ted Howard
THE FIRST THREE MINUTES by Steven Weinberg
FOCUSING by Dr. Eugene T. Gendlin
GRIST FOR THE MILL by Ram Dass
THE HEART OF PHILOSOPHY by Jacob Needleman
I CHING: A NEW INTERPRETATION FOR MODERN TIMES by Sam Reifler
IF YOU MEET THE BUDDHA ON THE ROAD, KILL HIM! by Sheldon Kopp
IN SEARCH OF SCHRÖDINGER'S CAT by John Gribbin
INFINITY AND THE MIND by Rudy Rucker
KISS SLEEPING BEAUTY GOODBYE by Madonna Kolbenschlag
THE LIVES OF A CELL by Lewis Thomas
LIVING WITH NUCLEAR WEAPONS by Carnesale/Doty/Hoffman/Huntington/Nye and Sagan
MAGICAL CHILD by Joseph Chilton Pearce
THE MEDUSA AND THE SNAIL by Lewis Thomas
MIND AND NATURE by Gregory Bateson
THE MIND'S I by Douglas R. Hofstadter and Daniel C. Dennett
MISSILE ENVY by Dr. Helen Caldicott
MYSTICISM AND THE NEW PHYSICS by Michael Talbot
NEW RULES by Daniel Yankelovich
NEW TECHNOLOGY COLORING BOOK by Rita Aero and Howard Rheingold
ON HUMAN NATURE by Edward O. Wilson
THE ONE-STRAW REVOLUTION by Masanobu Fukuoka
ORDER OUT OF CHAOS by Ilya Prigogine and Isabelle Stengers
THE PICKPOCKET AND THE SAINT by Sheldon Kopp
PROSPERING WOMAN by Ruth Ross
REENCHANTMENT OF THE WORLD by Morris Berman

SEVEN TOMORROWS by Hawken, Ogilvy, and Schwartz
SPACE-TIME AND BEYOND by Bob Toben and Alan Wolf
THE SPHINX AND THE RAINBOW by David Loye
STALKING THE WILD PENDULUM by Itzhak Bentov
STRESS AND THE ART OF BIOFEEDBACK by Barbara B. Brown
SUPERMIND by Barbara B. Brown
THE TAO OF PHYSICS, Revised Edition, by Fritjof Capra
TO HAVE OR TO BE? by Erich Fromm
THE TURNING POINT by Fritjof Capra
THE WAY OF THE SHAMAN: A Guide to Power and Healing by Michael Harner
ZEN AND THE ART OF MOTORCYCLE MAINTENANCE by Robert M. Pirsig
THE ZEN ENVIRONMENT by Marian Mountain

QUANTITY PURCHASES

Companies, professional groups, churches, clubs, and other organizations may qualify for special terms when ordering 24 or more copies of this title. For information, contact the Special Sales Department, Bantam Books, 666 Fifth Avenue, New York, N.Y. 10103. Phone (800) 223-6834. New York State residents call (212) 765-6500.

MISSILE ENVY

The Arms Race
and Nuclear War

Dr. Helen Caldicott

BANTAM BOOKS

TORONTO · NEW YORK · LONDON · SYDNEY · AUCKLAND

*This low-priced Bantam Book
has been completely reset in a type face
designed for easy reading, and was printed
from new plates. It contains the complete
text of the original hard-cover edition.*
NOT ONE WORD HAS BEEN OMITTED.

MISSILE ENVY

*A Bantam Book / published by arrangement with
William Morrow and Company, Inc.*

PRINTING HISTORY
*William Morrow edition published June 1984
Bantam edition / May 1985*

Grateful acknowledgment is made for permission to reprint the following:
Frontispiece reprinted from Nuclear Weapons: Report of the Secretary General *(Autumn Press, Inc.: 1980, p. 12) with authorization and cooperation of the United Nations. Pictures of burn victims courtesy of Dr. John Constable. Cover of* Aviation Week & Space Technology *courtesy of McGraw-Hill, Inc., Vol. 117, No. 26, December 27, 1982. Action and Reaction Chart reprinted from* Stop Nuclear War! A Handbook *by David P. Barash, Ph.D., and Judith Eve Lipton, M.D. (Grove Press, Inc.: 1982, p. 127). Contracts Chart copyright © 1980 by NARMIC (National Action/Research on the Military Industrial Complex). Foreign Military Sales Chart reprinted from Council on Economic Priorities newsletter, December/January 1981–82. Installations Chart courtesy of Superintendent of Documents, U.S. Government Printing Office, Washington, D.C.*

ISBN 0-553-25080-9

Published simultaneously in the United States and Canada

PRINTED IN THE UNITED STATES OF AMERICA

O   0 9 8 7 6 5 4 3 2 1

Acknowledgments

I wish to thank the following people for their help and support in preparation of the manuscript: Bill Caldicott, Pat Kingsley, Joyce Norman, Jane Wales, Mary Crittendon, Rear Admiral Gene LaRocque (Ret.), Rear Admiral Eugene Carroll (Ret.), Elizabeth Sherman, Gordon Adams, Morton H. Halperin, Dr. Jonathon Fine, Randy Forsberg, and Michael Bedford.

Contents

Introduction   1

Prognosis: How Long Will the Earth Survive?   9

Case History   44

Germs of Conflict: The Third World   84

Physical Examination   114

Pathogenesis: The Pathological Dynamics of the Arms Race   174

The Iron Triangle   215

The Terminal Event   281

Etiology: Missile Envy and Other Psychopathology   308

Therapy   350

Notes   368

Index   387

Examples of ICBM Ranges

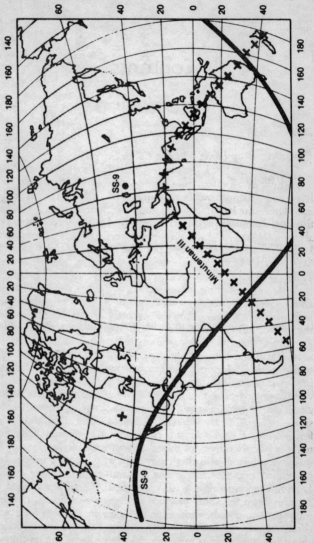

Strategic missiles launched from the USSR or the USA can hit every country in the world excuding only the South Island of New Zealand.

Introduction

I write this book with a tremendous sense of urgency—as a mother, as a pediatrician, and as a woman—aware that we live on a planet that is terminally ill, infected with lethal macrobes (nuclear weapons) that are metastisizing rapidly, the way a cancer spreads in the body. I have been concerned about nuclear war since the time when, as a young teenager, I read Nevil Shute's book *On the Beach*. I lived then in Melbourne, Australia, the scene of the story, and the image of the people of Melbourne giving cyanide to their babies as the radioactive fallout was about to strike has stayed with me all my life. The empty streets of my beloved city, bereft of life, with newspapers blowing vacantly in the wind, signaled the end of human existence.

Since that time, I have never felt protected by the adults around me and have never understood why the governments of the world build more nuclear weapons. When 1 started my first year of medical studies in 1956 at the age of seventeen, I was prompted to speak out about the carcinogenic and mutagenic effects of radioactive fallout from the atmospheric explosions detonated by Russia, America, and England. Unfortunately, I spoke in the refectory at lunchtime, and my male medical colleagues gazed absentmindedly at me, obviously wondering who this crazy lady was, as they proceeded to ignore my comments and continue their poker game. During the remaining years of medical school I managed to suppress my fear and practice a degree of denial—psychic numbing—and only remembered again in 1963 when I was three months pregnant with my first baby. I was worried about bringing a child into a world where he or she might not have the opportunity to enjoy a full life-span without the

1

specter of nuclear war. However, I was so enchanted by the wonder and creativity of birth that we proceeded to have three babies in three years. But always the danger of nuclear war lurked in the background, and I could never really enjoy anything totally without a little voice asking, "How much longer will life continue?"

Being of an intensely curious disposition, I read every article about nuclear weapons that I could find. I was pleased and relieved when the partial test-ban treaty was negotiated and ratified by President John F. Kennedy and Soviet Premier Nikita Khrushchev in August 1963. President Kennedy had already started making some unilateral moves toward the Soviet Union. In June 1963, he made his famous "Strategy of Peace" speech at American University. For the first time, an American President praised the Russians for their sacrifices and bravery during World War II, and he announced a unilateral act—the United States would stop all atmospheric tests and would not resume them unless the USSR did so first. The Russians were apparently so thrilled by this praise that for months after they carried in their wallets clippings of the *Pravda* and *Izvestia* articles reporting the speech. On June 15, Khrushchev responded by welcoming the initiative and announcing a halt to Soviet plans for the production of strategic bombers. Further agreements followed, and a "hotline" agreement was reached on June 20. The Russians were so pleased with this process that they called it the "Policy of Mutual Example." On October 9, Kennedy announced a $250 million wheat sale, and tensions between the Soviet Union and the United States were at an all-time low. On November 22, President Kennedy was assassinated.

I remember being in my sitting room in Canberra, Australia, on a lovely sunny morning when my brother, who works in foreign affairs, came to tell me of the murder. My first thought as I emerged from the shock was, "Will we survive?" Kennedy had sparked a light of hope in the hearts of millions of people around the world, and when he died the light faded. Men on the golf courses in Australia took off their caps and openly wept when they heard the news. Years later, when my husband and I visited Iran in 1974, to our amazement, needlepoint and other pictures of Jack Kennedy adorned almost every shop window in Tehran, Isfahan, and villages in that country. This was not atypical of the respect people felt for him throughout the world. A young President who had his soul scarified by the Cuban missile crisis had reached out to the nuclear adversary to foster a climate of hope and peace in the world.

Then the Vietnam war became the dominant theme in world affairs for the next ten to twelve years. Nuclear war and weapons were forgotten, much to everyone's subconscious relief, for to contemplate nuclear war is to entertain the concept of the end of immortality, not just the idea of death. We need to feel that we leave a part of ourselves behind when we die—our children, a great work, books, buildings, paintings—or that we live on in the spiritual or organic life cycle. Nuclear war obliterates these possibilities. At the same time, the test-ban treaty had moved nuclear testing underground, so out of sight was out of mind, and we all heaved a sigh of relief and proceeded with normal everyday life. Meanwhile, the Kremlin and the Pentagon quietly and unobtrusively continued enlarging and refining their nuclear arsenals.

In 1979, I was asked to join a delegation of Americans visiting the Soviet Union as guests of the Soviet Peace Committee. It was a well-informed group of people, including the journalist Arthur Macy Cox, formerly of the CIA (and an adviser to Paul Warnke during the SALT II negotiations); Everett Mendelson, professor of the history of science at Harvard University; Bill Coffin, formerly of the CIA and fluent in Russian; and Marta Daniels, a Connecticut activist who was highly versed in and articulate on nuclear-weapon strategies. We started off at the lower bureaucratic levels, where we received our daily doses of propaganda *ad nauseam*. We argued vociferously with our Russian hosts when we visited the Atomic Energy Commission and the Ministry for Health, on topics ranging from health and safety measures at nuclear reactors to the storage of radioactive waste and the alleged huge nuclear accident at Sverdlovsk in 1959—an event which nobody could either "remember" or "explain."

As we argued, we obviously demonstrated a sophisticated level of knowledge that was respected, and we were invited to meet high government officials. We noticed that as we moved up the bureaucratic ladder, the people became more knowledgeable and sophisticated and spoke excellent English. In fact, we were embarrassed to observe at the

Institute for Canadian and American Studies that several of our hosts knew more than we did about internal Vermont politics. We had lunch with the prestigious president of the National Academy of Sciences, Alexandrov. At the end of ten days, the red carpet was unrolled, and we met with the two ambassadors who had spent the last seven years negotiating the SALT II treaty. At just that time, we learned that Senator Frank Church had discovered the "Soviet Brigade" in Cuba, and all hell was breaking loose in the Congress of the United States. It was obvious to us and our hosts that SALT II did not stand a chance of being ratified. Nevertheless, Arthur Cox presented to the ambassadors the concept of a bilateral freeze in testing, development, production, and deployment of any new nuclear weapons and delivery systems. They argued for hours about it, made phone calls, ran in and out speaking and consulting with their colleagues, and, finally, at the end of two hours, they said with a sigh, "Well, we'd vote for that with both hands!"

The freeze concept was new to me, as was the extreme state of emergency that the arms race was to present to the world. One night as we were waiting to go to the Moscow Circus, Arthur Cox and I sat in the foyer of a huge Stalinesque hotel in Moscow. He seemed despondent, and I asked him why. He then told me two facts that changed my life.

Cruise Missiles. The United States was about to build and deploy in Europe ground-based, ground-launched missiles. These are small missiles with a jet-propelled engine (designed originally to strap onto the back of a soldier to fly him around like Superman, but it didn't work). They are armed with a hydrogen bomb approximately twenty times larger than the Hiroshima bomb. They fly close to the ground beneath the radar fields, so they are undetectable during flight. They have in their noses a computerized map of the terrain, so they can avoid obstacles by flying up and down the hills and over trees and hedges. They also are equipped with an extremely accurate homing device called TERCOM (terrain contour matching) that gives them almost 100 percent "kill capacity." The most serious problem they present for the purposes of arms control is their invulnerability to detection. They are so small they can be hidden on trucks or in sheds, and it will be impossible to verify their presence let alone whether they contain nuclear or conventional warheads. Because they fly thousands of miles, they are classified as strategic or intercontinental weapons. Previously, all strategic weapons have been so large that their presence can be verified by satellite detection from outer space. Strategic weapons are deployed in land-based intercontinental ballistic missile silos, in large submarines (each of which contains a known number of missiles), or in large intercontinental bombers carrying a known number of bombs. Detection from satellites in outer space is called "national technical means."

Once cruise missiles began to be deployed in Europe in December 1983 (planned host countries are Germany, Italy, Holland, Belgium, and England)—and also on B-52 and B-1 bombers, in submarines, and on surface ships—the means of verification and treaty implementation for strategic weapons was ended. Verification has been the basis upon which the SALT I and SALT II treaties were negotiated. As I write, several hundred cruise missiles have already been placed in a wing of B-52 airplanes (sixteen planes with twelve missiles were deployed at Griffith Air Force Base in Rome, New York, in December 1982 and on the refitted, refurbished battleship *New Jersey)* and are being deployed in England, Italy, and West Germany.

Pershing II Missiles. One hundred eight Pershing II missiles are also to be deployed in West Germany, beginning in December 1983. These are very rapid intercontinental missiles, which can reach Moscow within six to ten minutes of launching, whereas all other land-based intercontinental weapons take thirty minutes to fly from America to Russia or vice versa. Although submarine-launched ballistic missiles fired from the coast of either country may take only ten to fifteen minutes to reach their targets, it is generally considered that we now have thirty minutes, usually, to decide whether or not the computers have failed yet again and have given a false signal of attack (the Pentagon fail-safe system failed 151 times over a recent eighteen-month period), or if the attack is real. However, with a six- to ten-minute lead time, once the radars and satellites have detected the attack, there will be no time for human decision making or input, and a launch-on-warning or a launch-under-attack system will be needed. A computer will then decide whether or not to launch nuclear war. This system will be made even more imperative because the Pershing IIs are deadly accurate and are to be used, according to the new Pentagon five-year war plan, for a decapitation attack on an important component of the Soviet command centers. These weapons have been designed to be used as an integral part of a new form of nuclear war called counterforce or first-strike war, which will be described in subsequent chapters.

At the moment when I learned that our world would be controlled by computers by late 1983 or 1984 and that cruise missiles signal the practical end of arms-control treaties, I knew I would have to leave medicine. This decision was made more obvious by two other experiences in Russia. First, I was impressed by the depth of hardship and suffering undergone by the Russians in World War II—experiences they recounted to us again and again. They lost approximately 20 million people; almost every family was bereft. They told us that 72,000 towns and cities were razed, and Leningrad (probably the most beautiful, majestic city on earth) was under siege by the Germans for three years. Hundreds of thousands of people starved in Leningrad, and we went to a cemetery on the outskirts of the city where 500,000 people are buried in mass graves covered with grass. The cemetery is large, and a long path leads down its center to a distant figure of Mother Russia holding an olive branch. As we walked silently in the bitterly cold, rainy weather, the sounds of Bach's Double Violin Concerto were just audible. Parents were bringing their children to pay homage to their aunts, uncles, and grandparents who died during the war. As we walked back through the rain, I said to Arthur Cox, "Arthur, if there is another war and anyone survives, if they come back here they will say, 'They didn't learn.' "

My other moving experience occurred in Moscow. Red Square seemed to be full of brides. I asked our guide, "What are all these brides doing?" (I love brides), and he said, "Whenever a girl marries, she takes her flowers and puts them on a peace memorial, so that her children will never know war." He also told me as he recounted the deprivations during World War II, "My grandmother has seen people eat people twice in her lifetime."

Toward the end of our stay, we visited the U.S. Embassy in Moscow. We were met by two young men because the ambassador was unavailable that day. They sat us down and proceeded to assail us with figures about nuclear weapons and war-fighting strategy, saying, "If the Russians do this, we will MIRV these missiles and put cruise missiles here, et cetera, et cetera." The diatribe went on for about thirty minutes, and it was obvious that here were two brilliant computerlike minds; but as they talked, the question occurred to me: Do they actually function like human beings, make love, have feelings, or are they robots? As we left, I turned to one of them and said, "Do you think we will survive?" and he said, "What?" Somewhat taken aback, I repeated the question, and he replied, without batting an eyelash, "Of course."

The whole delegation staggered out into the streets of Moscow almost in a state of acute clinical shock. Here we were in Russia, having had long, heated discussions with high-ranking Soviet officials on the topics of nuclear war, weapons, and strategies, always with an overwhelming sense of the tragedy of war and of the unacceptability of allowing a nuclear war to occur. These two young, totally oblivious Americans had just presented to us a cold, immoral analysis of a nuclear war-fighting strategy that could be contemplated as the arms race proceeded. As we wandered down the street in a state of disarray, I realized that Washington was full of young men like these, who have never suffered any real pain, deprivation, starvation, or tragedy, and who have never allowed their emotional or moral reasoning to impinge upon their rational and objective analyses.

The Reverend William Sloane Coffin spoke and sang fluent Russian, and we often left our group and guides and wandered through the city streets and subways, speaking freely with the Russian people. After admiring our jeans and telling us how much they liked America and its music, they universally spoke of their fear of nuclear war.

When I returned from the Soviet Union, I would wander into the labs at Harvard Medical School, which were filled with brilliant young doctors doing experiments on rare and diverse diseases. I would think to myself, "What are they doing that for? We have three years before the world is out of human control; don't they know that?" The fact is that most of them did not. And as I speak around the country, I find that less than 1 percent of American audiences even know what a strategic weapon is. The level of ignorance about the arms race is frightening.

It took me one year to finally decide that I had to leave the day-to-day practice of clinical medicine. Although I loved my forty patients with cystic fibrosis (the most common genetic disease of childhood), I realized that I had a conflict of interest. What was the use of keeping these children alive for another five to twenty years by the application of meticulous and loving medical care, when during this time they could all be vaporized in a nuclear war? Further, as a pediatrician, I also felt a sense of responsibility for all the children—present and future—on the planet.

I went to the door of my chief three times, and three times I walked away, as I thought, "Will I lose my credibility if I leave Harvard? I will cut my ties with Harvard forever, and I love this place." Finally, I opened the door, and when I told him I had to leave, he said, "I know," having understood my conflict for some time. I wandered down the corridor and into the street, feeling as if all my clothing had fallen off and I was naked. I had lost the image of myself as a clever doctor working at Harvard, and I felt like a nobody. I was very depressed and lost for several weeks until the work for our survival absorbed my energy and time.

About a month later, I received a letter from the chief of medicine at Children's Hospital Medical Center, Harvard Medical School, saying she was sorry I had left but that if I ever wished to return, she would reappoint me to my positions at both the hospital and the medical school. Then senior physicians on the faculty at Harvard started coming up to me, saying, "It's because of what you did that I have decided to get involved in Physicians for Social Responsibility." I realized the empathy that doctors have for one another as they recognize the scarifying experience involved in the acquisition of the art and science of medicine. Finally, the dean of a prestigious medical school in New York told me, "You've left medicine to save lives," and I felt vindicated. I learned from that experience that in the future I must do what is right, not because it *feels* right, but because it *is* right.

Prognosis: How Long Will the Earth Survive?

I have described two of the reasons for a sense of urgency about the nuclear arms race and the imminence of nuclear war—cruise missiles and Pershing II missiles. George Kistiakowsky, inventor of the implosion mechanism of one of the first atomic bombs and science adviser to President Eisenhower, felt that we would all be lucky to survive the next ten years. He came to our house in 1979 as one of several scientists to brief presidential candidate Jerry Brown on the nuclear arms race. The new technology they described that afternoon was horrifying, and as he left the house, I asked with a sense of desperation, "George, do you think we will survive?" He looked down and said, "I'll survive my natural life-span; you won't." He was already an old man dying of cancer.

Since then, the situation has deteriorated. In August 1979, President Jimmy Carter issued Presidential Directives 58 and 59. Presidential 58 called on the Defense Department and other agencies to study the capacity of the government, from the President on down, to withstand a nuclear strike. It includes: (1) plans to move military and political leaders out of Washington; (2) hardened silos for personnel and equipment; and (3) creation of a network of command posts for military and civilian leaders in time of war. Presidential 59, or PD59, outlined a war-fighting strategy with a "flexible response" to limited nuclear war, maximizing the potential target structure in the USSR. The prime targets are to be Soviet military and industrial institutions and the country's political leadership. It (1) called for forty thousand targets in the USSR; (2) emphasized the need to target in a timely, redundant, and flexible fashion; and (3) outlined the weapons potentially needed. It described a prolonged nuclear war lasting weeks or months and provided for a "secure strategic reserve": that is, a missile force in reserve, not to be used in the early stages of conflict. This could deter Moscow from launching a major nuclear strike later on.

These directives are still classified as secret. They were issued or leaked to Richard Burt at *The New York Times* just before the Democratic Convention in 1980, but they were not even referred to by the delegates at the convention, even though they represented a radical change in thinking about targeting and nuclear war-fighting doctrines.

The lack of public response to these plans was almost more frightening than the plans themselves. It was obvious from the psychic numbing evident at the Democratic Convention that America had not awakened to the ominous preparations the U.S. government had made for fighting nuclear war. Never before had I seen plans made public for actually fighting a nuclear war. Until then, the deterrence policy of mutually assured destruction (MAD) had stood—massive reciprocal damage to both sides, enough to dissuade each from initiating a nuclear war.

It was obvious from the literature in 1979 that a vast planning network of scientists, industrialists, Pentagon officials, and politicians were involved in producing weapons to fight and win a nuclear war. The scientific developments had been under way for almost a decade, led by the government- and University of California–sponsored weapons laboratories—Los Alamos in New Mexico and Lawrence-Livermore in California—together with Sandia Laboratories in Albuquerque run by Western Electric. Until PD59 was issued in 1979, the MAD strategy called for countervalue nuclear war or destruction of soft targets—cities. But as the accuracy of the missiles and delivery systems increased, it became possible to pinpoint hard targets or missile silos. This strategy is called counterforce nuclear war. (People are soft targets; missiles are hard targets.)

The strategic thinking behind fighting and winning a counterforce nuclear war, from the U.S. vantage point, goes like this:

(1) The Soviet Union has emphasized ground-based strategic weapons, so that 70 percent (5,673 nuclear weapons in 1,398 missiles) of their bombs are land based in silos. About

24 percent are in submarines, and theirs are noisy and easy to detect and track. (They have almost 2,000 nuclear weapons in missile-carrying submarines, but only 15 percent or 300 nuclear weapons are at sea at any one time.) Only about 6 percent of their intercontinental weapons, 290 nuclear bombs, are in old bombers.

(2) The United States has approximately 20 percent (2,140 bombs in 1,040 missiles) of its strategic nuclear weapons based on land, 50 percent (5,152 nuclear weapons) in its noiseless, invulnerable submarines—55 percent or almost 3,000 nuclear weapons are at sea at any one time—and approximately 30 percent or over 3,000 bombs in large intercontinental B-52 bombers.

Hence, the Soviet Union's strategic-weapon arsenal is much more vulnerable to U.S. first strikes, which can only be used effectively against ground-based missiles. The United States already has very accurate "silo-busting weapons" on 300 Minuteman missiles (3 Mark-12A hydrogen bombs per missile). It is on the verge of constructing the MX missile, a huge rocket with 10 independently targeted hydrogen bombs in the nose, each capable of landing on a different silo in a very accurate fashion. Also, the Trident II or D-5 missile is already in production. This missile is to be launched from the Trident submarine. Five subs have been built, with approximately 15 to 20 more planned. Each submarine carries 24 missiles, and each missile delivers 10 hydrogen bombs. (Each trident submarine carries enough weapons to destroy most major cities in the Northern Hemisphere.) Each hydrogen bomb is exceedingly accurate and will be guided to its location from its sea launch by a satellite called NAVSTAR.

The MX and Minuteman take thirty minutes to reach their targets after launching, and Trident II fifteen to thirty minutes, depending upon the location of the submarine. Cruise missiles are also highly accurate although quite slow, taking one to two hours to reach their targets. However, they can be launched from old 747s, B-52s, B-1 bombers, or stealth bombers just off the coast of the USSR, so that planes can evade the anti-aircraft facilities of the USSR.

I stress accuracy because accuracy is an extremely important factor in being able to destroy missile silos. Yield, or size of the explosion, is also important, but you can destroy a missile silo far more effectively with a small, highly accurate hydrogen bomb than with an inaccurate larger hydrogen bomb.

The United States is also working actively on antisubmarine warfare. It is developing tracking stations using extra-low-frequency sonic waves to detect Soviet subs, which are relatively easy to find anyway because they are so noisy. The United States has many sophisticated fast attack submarines designed to destroy Soviet subs. It is also qualitatively more advanced in the area of antisatellite warfare. Eventually such technology may enable the United States to destroy Soviet information satellites in time to prevent Russia from detecting the launch of first-strike U.S. missiles. If the Soviets could detect MX or Trident II launches, they might well launch their missiles first, and the American bombs would hit empty silos.

The scenario of a first-strike war goes like this: The first-strike missiles are launched with a calculated allocation of 2 hydrogen bombs to each Soviet missile silo. The first wave of 1,400 H-bombs will explode in the air just above the missile silos, and a second wave of 1,400 H-bombs will arrive seven seconds later and explode on the ground on top of the missile silos. The jolting and dislocation resulting from this massive show of force will be so severe that although every missile will not necessarily be destroyed, it will have received a severe shakeup and will be incapable of being launched.

At the same time, the air bases in the Soviet Union containing the strategic bombers will have been destroyed along with the Soviet Central Command, Control, and Communication Centers (C^3), many of which are located in major cities, and also the major military installations. The Soviet satellites will be destroyed just before the attack begins, and the submarines will also be destroyed as the first strike takes place.

This is termed a "winnable limited nuclear war," and the doctrine for this sort of war is more clearly enunciated in a new Pentagon five-year war plan, signed by Defense Secretary Caspar Weinberger, which was leaked to Richard Halloran of *The New York Times* in the summer of 1982. It is called the Defense Guidance Plan. Complementary doctrines, called the National Security Decision Document, mandate that the Defense Department will provide a program for implementing President Reagan's nuclear war policy. This is the first policy statement of a U.S. administration to proclaim that U.S. strategic forces must be able to win a protracted nuclear war over a six-month period, at the end of which time the United States will "prevail." (Prevail means having more nuclear weapons at the end of the war than the enemy does.) Such a war will also feature intensive electronic warfare and possibly chemical and biological weapons. The Defense Guidance Plan also calls for nuclear weapons in space, antisubmarine warfare, economic warfare with the Soviet Union, guerrilla warfare in Eastern Europe, and forced intervention in Southeast Asia and the Persian Gulf if necessary, without invitation by U.S. allies. The plan requires the assumed destruction of "nuclear and conventional military forces and industry critical to military power."

To implement this plan, the Reagan administration wants to build 17,000 hydrogen bombs, including 8,000 sea-, ground-, and air-launched cruise missiles, Pershing II missiles, MX and Trident II missiles, and neutron bombs. The United States already has 10,000 strategic hydrogen bombs and the Soviet Union 7,800. Robert McNamara, Secretary of Defense in the sixties, decreed that 200 intercontinental hydrogen bombs would kill up to one third of the Russian people and destroy two thirds of their industry. This number was declared at that time to be an adequate "deterrent."

The Soviet Union does not possess the long-range, highly accurate cruise missiles or quick Pershing II missiles that it can launch from a country adjacent to the U.S. border; it does not have an incredibly accurate land-based missile like the MX or a sophisticated, accurate sea-launched missile like the Trident II. But almost certainly it will develop these if the arms race is not stopped. Soviet Premier Yuri Andropov has recently said that Russia would match the United States weapon system to weapon system as it has always done in the past.

Scientists who have participated in the design of these weapons at the Los Alamos labs say that if there is a first-strike counterforce nuclear war between the superpowers in the next ten or twenty years, a huge quantity of radioactive fallout will be created by the thousands of ground-burst hydrogen bombs. Cubic miles of rock and dirt will be atomized, rendered radioactive, and injected into the stratosphere and troposphere in the mushroom cloud. If most of the other nuclear weapons are used as well, an *On the Beach* syndrome could be created. That means lethal fallout for every human being on earth within weeks to months. Carl Sagan and other scientists have reported that the explosion of 100 megatons on urban centers could induce a "nuclear winter" which could destroy most biological systems on the planet. (The superpower strategic and theater arsenal contains 12,000 megatons.) This medical scenario dictated by first-strike nuclear war is being actively planned by President Reagan and Caspar Weinberger, as well as by the Pentagon. I doubt that these people have ever really considered the medical consequences of their new weapon systems.

The psychological problem related to first-strike nuclear war is very frightening. If the Soviet leaders feel that their weapons are threatened at any instant by a surprise attack, they will respond in the same way that they will respond to the Pershing II missiles in Europe, a launch-on-warning policy. The trouble is that the Soviet detection and computer network is far less sophisticated than that of the United States, and the United States is currently blocking sales of sophisticated technology to the Soviet Union. Problems have been associated with even the relatively sophisticated U.S. computer fail-safe system over the last few years: False alerts have been triggered by a flock of geese that the early-warning system interpreted as a fleet of Soviet missiles, by a rising moon, and by a shower of meteorites. In November 1979, someone plugged a war-games tape into the fail-safe computer, and the machine made a mistake and decided that Russia had really launched a nuclear attack. The whole Western world was put on nuclear alert for six minutes; three U.S. squadrons of planes were armed with nuclear weapons, scrambled, ready to take off; and at the seventh minute the President was to be officially notified, but they could not find him. At that time the mistake was realized, we were fourteen minutes from the moment when the button could have been pressed—and from annihilation. People reassured us that such a mistake would always be detected and that accidental nuclear war could not be initiated in this way, but fourteen minutes is really too close for comfort. The London *Guardian* and the Canadian papers carried headlines reporting the mistake, but *The New York Times* had a tiny article near the obituaries. That was in 1979. The reaction now would probably be more vocal because the media and public have become sensitized in recent years to the dangers of nuclear war. A six-minute lead time with the Pershing II, or a thirty-minute lead time with the paranoid situation of "use 'em or lose 'em" in a threatened first-strike attack, could well induce an accidental nuclear war.

Two men called the National Command Authority (NCA) have been delegated the responsibility for deciding when to launch a nuclear war and whether it is a preemptive first-strike nuclear war, a launch-on-warning nuclear war, or a retaliatory attack. These two men are the President of the United States, Ronald Reagan, and the Secretary of Defense, Caspar Weinberger.

Neither man inspires great confidence. I met for over an hour with President Reagan and his daughter Patti on December 6, 1982. Here is a record of the meeting written immediately after I left the White House.

On December 6, 1982, at 4 P.M., I met with President Reagan and his daughter Patti Davis for seventy-five minutes. I report this meeting because, as a clinician, I was profoundly concerned both by the quality of the information imparted and by a certain lack of background understanding pertaining to crucial issues which I felt the President showed.

He entered the downstairs library of the White House in a somewhat diffident fashion and proceeded to reassure me, as I told him I was nervous being in the presence of the President of the United States of America. We sat around a long table, he at the head and I next to him, with Patti at the other end.

I opened the conversation by saying that he probably didn't know who I was, but he interrupted and said that he knew I was an Australian and I had read *On the Beach* by Nevil Shute when I was young, and that's how I became involved in the issue of nuclear weapons. I then told him that I had been frightened by the incessant buildup in nuclear arms since I was fourteen, and that I began studying medicine in 1956 when I was seventeen and learned about the effects of radiation on cellular mechanisms and genes. At that time, high levels of radioactive fallout were being recorded in the Northern Hemisphere, with strontium-90 and other radioactive elements concentrating in the milk and the deciduous teeth of young children. I told him that I feared to bring my first baby into this nuclear world in 1963, but that I had had three babies because I was selfish and loved children. I also told him that I'm deeply religious and consider what I do to be a spiritual mission.

He replied that he, too, doesn't want nuclear war but that our ways of preventing it differ; he believes in building more bombs. He moved immediately into tactics and strategy and seemed not to be interested in discussing the medical, scientific, or ecological consequences of nuclear war. He said that Russia is stronger than America and wants to take over the world, with Communism dominating, and that Russia already has a base ninety miles off the American coast. He added that the domino theory had proven correct in Southeast Asia. I said that America similarly sees capitalism as the only answer for the world and that the superpowers are mirror images of each other. He said the Russians were evil, Godless communists. I asked him if he thought they were all evil, but he declined to answer. I also asked if he had met a Russian, and he said, "No, but we hear from their émigrés."

I noted that America has Russia ringed by bases in Italy, Greece, Turkey, Britain, France, and other countries, and that many of these bases are equipped with nuclear weapons and missiles. He denied this fact. He then talked about the Russian SS-20 missiles, and when I pointed out that the nuclear balance between NATO and the Warsaw Pact is approximately equal because of the forward-based systems in Britain and Germany together with missiles in American submarines allocated to NATO, he would not accept these facts. He replied that the Russians have submarines, too. I then talked about the Pershing II missile being capable of reaching Moscow from its launching point in West Germany in six to ten minutes, which could induce Russia to adopt a computer-directed launch-on-warning policy. In reply, he noted that the SS-20s could also reach Europe in six minutes. He seemed not to appreciate the strategic significance of the Pershing II missiles threatening part of the Soviet Central Command, Control, and Communication Centers (C^3) in Moscow—as described in the Pentagon Five-Year Defense Guidance Plan, which indicates that they could be used for decapitation of Soviet C^3 centers.

I then talked about Paul Warnke, and he said that Warnke stood for unilateral disarmament.

At one point, Patti interrupted the conversation and said, "Dad, I know that what Dr. Caldicott is saying is correct, because I have a 1982 Pentagon document to prove it." He looked at her and said, "It's a forgery."

I discussed the fact that Russia is ringed by Communist countries hostile to the USSR and that of the six nuclear nations in the world, three (Britain, France, and China), each acting alone, could destroy the Soviet Union as an entity; he denied this, particularly in reference to China because, he said, they lack an adequate delivery system. I replied that the loss of Moscow and Leningrad alone would be a virtual destruction of the USSR, which he did not accept.

He then said, "Talking of saving millions of people, the Russians have a great civil-defense system." I asked him where he got these data from, and he didn't seem to know. I asked if they came from T. K. Jones, and he didn't appear to know who this was. (T. K. Jones is the Deputy Under Secretary of Defense for Research and Engineering, Strategic and Nuclear Forces, in the Pentagon—one of the officials in charge of civil-defense policy, who made the famous statement, "If there are enough shovels to go around, everybody's going to make it.") The President said that Russia has been decentralizing and hardening its industry, and burying it. I replied that for evacuation and civil defense, they have a lousy system of highways, which I had seen, and that none of their civil-defense systems would do any good. I quoted the 1979 CIA report that was highly skeptical of Soviet civil defense.

I told him about the recent Soviet television program during which three American and three Soviet physicians appeared uncensored on national Soviet television for one hour, as they described to 200 million Russian people the medical consequences of nuclear war. I also said that one of the American doctors told the Russians that their civil-defense system was useless. He said that he knows who *they* are. He also said that 200 million Russians could not have watched that program because they don't all have television sets. I replied that I had not known this fact but that I would check it. (I have checked with the U.S. physicians who were on the program and learned that the program was shown twice nationally in a three-day period and that between 100 and 200 million people saw it.)

We talked about the money spent on defense, and he said that Russia has outspent America over the last years. I then told him about the two reports prepared by the CIA on Soviet defense spending, the "Team A Report" and the "Team B Report," and pointed out that he was quoting from the "Team B Report," which had been subsequently shown to be inaccurate. He didn't seem to know the difference between the two reports until I mentioned that the "Team B Report" was prepared under the guidance of George Bush when he was CIA director, and he then said that George's report was the right one.

The President said that a freeze would freeze the Russians into a position of superiority. When I noted that the United States leads in numbers of nuclear weapons, he replied that they are ahead in megatonnage and missiles. I explained that missiles were only the delivery vehicles and that the number of bombs was the important thing to assess.

He said that Russia has violated the ABM treaty, and I said they had deployed only one ABM system around Moscow, which they are allowed by the treaty.

He said the Russians could track U.S. submarines from space by watching the deep wake of the subs. (This is unsubstantiated data, as I found when I later questioned Admiral Noel Gaylor, former Commander-in-Chief, U.S. Forces Pacific.)

I said that America was ahead in killer submarines, but he stated that Russia was. In fact, the Warsaw Pact has 50 and NATO 103, but the NATO subs are substantially superior. He said that the USSR has defied détente and had been building up a huge arms race with nuclear weapons, many tanks and troops. I showed him the data in the manual published by the Center for Defense Information (CDI), run by Rear Admiral Gene LaRocque, U.S. Navy (ret.), which demonstrates that although the Warsaw Pact has 63,000 tanks, NATO deploys over 50 types of antitank weapons and has a total of almost half a million in Europe, and that NATO leads the Warsaw Pact in the total number of ground forces in Europe. He said these data were wrong. He also said that the former high-ranking military officials who run the CDI were not credible. I stated that America had also defied détente by

MIRVing its missiles and that this technology was not outlawed by the SALT I Treaty because at that time only America could MIRV. However, Russia started MIRVing in 1975, and I showed him a CDI graph demonstrating that America leads the Soviet Union in numbers of strategic weapons, both now and during the 1970s; he did not believe the graph.

He said that we have not built a new missile in fifteen years and that Russia is on its fifth generation of new missiles. (America has been continually upgrading and modernizing its missiles during this time and so has not needed to build entirely new ones.)

He told me that the Russians are far advanced in sea power and have built many submarines in the last ten years. He also cited the new, huge USSR submarine class called the Typhoon. I told him that American submarines were noiseless and impossible to track, whereas the Russian subs were mostly old, and all were very noisy and easy to track, and that America carried 5,000 strategic weapons on her submarine fleet while Russia had only 2,000. He seemed not interested.

He replied that the land-based strategic systems were more important than submarine-based weapons because they can be launched and arrive at their targets in thirty minutes. This was to defend his START proposal, which asks the USSR to cut back its land-based systems from 5,000 to 2,500 nuclear warheads (as explained previously, Russia has 70 percent of its strategic warheads on land-based systems whereas only 20 percent of America's strategic weapons are land based, 50 percent are in invulnerable submarines, and 30 percent are in bombers), while allowing America to increase from approximately 2,100 to 2,500 land-based warheads. I replied that submarine-launched ballistic missiles can also reach their targets in thirty minutes or less, but he said the subs are difficult to contact. (The only reason for needing to be in instant contact with submarines would be for a preemptive first-strike attack; otherwise, the submarine-launched strategic weapons are to be used for a retaliatory strike.)

He said that Russia could get to the west coast of Europe in ten days, and that America will continue to maintain a first-use policy of nuclear weapons to deter such an event. He added that we would never use them, to which I replied, "Unless we are losing."

He said the Russian Navy has blockaded and is practicing war games at all the strategically important points on the seas and that this is why America is getting Japan to rearm so that it can defend its territories 1,000 miles out from the islands. I said that the American Navy is far more powerful than the Russian Navy, but he refused to accept this. I also said that if Russia and America fought at sea, it could start a nuclear war. He didn't reply.

I then cited the unilateral moves toward the Soviet Union that President Kennedy made in a speech at American University in June 1963. I talked about Nixon going to China even before diplomatic relations were established and about Sadat's heroic visit to Jerusalem, and I asked, or rather begged, him to go to see Andropov. He replied that just after he had been shot, he had made a move toward Brezhnev by writing a letter to the Soviet leader. The reply, which he said was hard-line, came months later, and he implied that it was no use reaching out to them.

He stressed that America must be strong, and that after World War II, when the United States was the only country with nuclear weapons, it helped its former "enemies" in their postwar recovery and showed restraint during this time. To this I replied that General MacArthur had wanted to use nuclear weapons on China but that President Truman stopped him. But Reagan said the only thing the Russians understand is strength and that their missiles were far better than America's missiles. I told him that almost all the Soviet missiles were liquid-fueled, but he seemed not to understand what that means. (This is antiquated technology, and such missiles require hours for launching. Almost all U.S. strategic missiles are solid-fueled and can be launched almost immediately.)

I assured him that every time I'm interviewed by *Tass* or *Izvestia* I give the Russian reporter's card to the FBI, but he wasn't interested. He seemed continually to have his own agenda, and didn't appear to listen much or to consider seriously my statements or replies.

He then pulled out some papers from a small desk pad on which he had written in longhand. He quoted some material saying that the Freeze Campaign was orchestrated by Russia and that we were KGB dupes. I looked at him and said, "That's from the *Reader's Digest*." He shook his head and said, "No it's not; it's from my intelligence files." If I am not badly mistaken, it was copied straight from the John

Barron article in the October 1982 issue of *Reader's Digest*. He said that Communist and left-wing groups organized the huge June 12, 1982, rally in New York City, alluding to Americans for Democratic Action and others. He implied that we were being manipulated, and I said that he must think we were very unintelligent to allow ourselves to be so manipulated. I told him that I am one of the leaders of the movement, and that I have never met a Communist in it, to which he replied that I might not know I was being manipulated.

I told him that I speak as a citizen of the world, and the whole world is frightened about nuclear war. I then read to him a statement from an eight-year-old girl named Rachel Conn: "I know the big countries of the world think they have to have nuclear weapons to be strong, and that they think they have to have more nuclear weapons than the other countries or else they wouldn't be strong. I think it would be better to be less strong than to blow up the world." He did not respond to this statement, but instead pulled from his pocket a map of Oregon showing the concentric rings of destruction from a nuclear explosion and another map of America showing the location of nuclear weapons facilities. He said these were handed out to primary school students in Oregon and that children should not be frightened in this way. I said maybe not like *that*, but this is the reality of the world in which they live, and children pick up the information anyway from television, as Rachel did. I told him that as a pediatrician, I treat dying children, and that they often have a sixth sense and know when they are going to die—that children intuit the truth and are very intelligent.

At no time during the discussion was there acrimony. I leaped in at many points of the conversation to correct his statements, but he was not receptive at all to what I had to say. In fact, often he seemed not to hear me. At the end of the meeting I felt a great sense of despair, which I'm sure was apparent in my demeanor. I don't think he sensed my concern as he said good-bye and left the room.

I was shocked by this interview. He is not a man of great intelligence, and he lacked both empathy and a deep understanding of the complex subject of nuclear weapons. I am also troubled because he has consistently opposed every arms control treaty in the nuclear age. When he was elected in 1980, his administration walked out on, and suspended work

on, eleven ongoing treaties being negotiated by the superpowers on nuclear weapons. Further, he is an old man, and
old men are prone to obstruction of cerebral vessels by athero-
matous plaques causing small strokes which, without producing obvious damage, may affect the thinking processes.

The Secretary of Defense is the other arm of the NCA.
Caspar Weinberger knew little about nuclear weapons or
arms control before he became Secretary of Defense. Robert
Scheer, *L.A. Times* reporter, interviewed Caspar Weinberger
and George Shultz at Bechtel during the 1980 campaign; both
of them said Scheer could ask about any subject but foreign
policy or defense, because they knew nothing about these
topics. Weinberger is an attorney from California who was
previously Secretary for Health, Education and Welfare, and
was known for severe cutting of social programs to save
money. Unfortunately, he has done the reverse with the
defense budget. He and his President plan to spend $1.8
trillion over the next five years, which will eventually amount
to about $2.5 trillion when cost overruns in production and
other incidentals are included. Over the past thirty-seven
years the United States has spent $2 trillion on defense.
Actually, the Defense Department is inappropriately labeled.
It is really the Department of Offense, or a War Department.
There is no defense against nuclear weapons. If Russia launches
one hundred missiles at one hundred U.S. cities, one hundred missiles will land.

President Reagan and his staff have not inspired confidence around the world. In the early days of his presidency,
the London *Guardian* reported that "cartoons of atomic
explosions, airplanes and warships were used to help President Reagan grasp the options for U.S. military spending.
Visual aids were taken to the White House by Caspar Weinberger, Secretary of Defense."

The authoritative *Armed Forces Journal* tells how Pentagon staff were ordered to revamp the usual tables and graphs
on budget proposals. One chart showed "different size mushroom clouds," the smallest representing the strategic forces
under President Jimmy Carter, and two bigger ones, the
alternatives being discussed by the Reagan administration.
Programs for the tactical air forces were depicted for the
President by "different sizes and shapes of airplanes, a car-
toon rendition of a fighter bomber—one the same size, but

loaded with bombs under its wings, and a third with its nose missing."

Devising the cartoons proved arduous, and Pentagon "action staff" had to work overtime. An informant told the *Journal:* "There were so many revisions, it was difficult to keep track." The visuals, which were more than three feet wide, were vetted by Frank Carlucci, the Deputy Secretary of Defense, before being shown to Reagan. This information was reported in the London *Guardian* in October 1981.

Here are some excerpts from speeches Reagan made in October 1981, when talking about limited nuclear war in Europe, as reported in the *International Herald-Tribune*, October 21, 1981:

> When asked if he thought an exchange in nuclear weapons between the United States and the Soviet Union would be limited or if escalation was inevitable [Reagan replied]: "I honestly don't know. I think again, until someplace—all over the world this is being, research going on, to try and find a defensive weapon. There never has been a weapon that someone hasn't come up with a defense, but it could—and the only defense is, well, you shoot yours and we'll shoot ours, and if you still had that kind of stalemate, I could see where you could have the exchange of tactical weapons against troops in the field without bringing either one of the major powers to pushing the button."

> "The intermediate range—and this is to call your attention to where SALT was so much at fault—is that we have our allies there who don't have an ocean between them, so it doesn't take intercontinental ballistic missiles; it just takes ballistic missiles of the SS-20 type."

I was visiting Europe when he twice commented during news conferences that it would be possible to fight a nuclear war in Europe without pressing a button. This comment frightened the Europeans terribly, and the speeches made front-page headlines throughout Europe. The story had practically no play at all in the press of the United States. The Europeans were convinced that America was planning to fight its nuclear war with the Soviet Union in Europe without involving the continental United States. This, of course, is a misconception because most senior military men say that once a nuclear war started in Europe, within hours or days, a global nuclear holocaust would be triggered between the superpowers. Dr. Desmond Ball, an Australian strategist writing for the International Institute for Strategic Studies in London, estimates that fatalities in a tactical nuclear war in Europe would range from 2 million to 20 million if there were some restraints on the use of nuclear arms, and up to 200 million without restraints. He said that strategic analysts take the view that it is possible to conduct a limited and quite protracted nuclear exchange in such a way that escalation can be controlled and that a war would end before nuclear exchanges reach an all-out level. However, extensive review of the Command, Control, Communications and Intelligence network (C^3I) of the United States shows that about 50 to 100 warheads from the Soviet Union could destroy most of the communication centers, the satellite ground terminals, the early-warning radar facilities, and the very-low-frequency communication stations. In addition, some 10 or 20 high-altitude nuclear detonations could disrupt high-frequency communications. Therefore, because of the vulnerability of the C^3I system, nuclear war could not be limited or controlled. The United States probably has a similar targeting strategy for the Soviet Union. Both C^3I systems are very vulnerable to disruptions.

In this society anybody who contemplates murdering a single individual is considered either mentally unstable or a potential criminal. But people within this administration are making statements about nuclear war that contemplate the death of hundreds of millions of human beings. The same moral and legal restraints should be applied to these people as to ordinary citizens who contemplate the death of only one human being. Following are some of their alarming statements:

"President Reagan, could we survive a nuclear war?"

"It would be a survival of some of your people and some of your facilities, but you could start again."

George Bush, Vice-President of the United States: "If you believe there is no such thing as a nuclear winner, the argument [that nuclear superiority is meaningless] makes sense. I don't believe that."

Frank Carlucci, Deputy Secretary of Defense: "We need more than counterforce. I think the Soviets are developing a nuclear-war-fighting capability, and we are going to have to do the same."

Paul Nitze, arms-control negotiator: "The Kremlin leaders want to achieve military victory in a nuclear war, while assuring the survival, endurance, and core of their party."

Richard Pipes, top presidential adviser on Soviet affairs: "The [nuclear] contest between the superpowers is increasingly turning into a qualitative race whose outcome can yield meaningful superiority." Pipes also said in 1981: "Soviet leaders would have to choose between peacefully changing their Communist system or going to war." He also advised the American people during the same period of time that they had better start preparing themselves psychologically for nuclear war.

Eugene V. Rostow, arms-control chief for the first two years of the Reagan administration: "We are living in a prewar and not a postwar world."

Richard N. Perle, Assistant Secretary of Defense: "I worry less about what would happen in a nuclear exchange than about the effect the nuclear balance has on our willingness to take risks in local situations." Perle has stated publicly several times that he does not believe in arms control between the United States and USSR, yet he is one of the main architects of the START and INF proposals. He said that "cosmetic agreements" on arms control are "in the long run fatal for the democracies of the West. Democracies will not sacrifice to protect their security in the absence of a sense of danger. And every time we create the impression we and the Soviets are cooperating and moderating the competition, we diminish that sense of apprehension." In other words, agreement with the Soviet Union is impossible, and under such circumstances the self-fulfilling prophecy will prevail—we cannot avoid war if we are preparing to fight it.

Charles Kupperman, an employee of the Arms Control and Disarmament Agency: "It is possible for any society to survive a nuclear war." Also: "Nuclear war is a destructive thing, but still in large part a physics problem."

Deputy Under Secretary of Defense James P. Wade, Jr., said before the House Appropriations Committee, "We don't want to fight a nuclear war, a conventional one either, but we must be prepared to do so if such a battle is to be deterred, as we must also be prepared to carry the battle to our adversary's homeland. We must not fear war."

Colin Gray, an Englishman and top arms-control adviser to the Reagan administration, wrote in *Foreign Policy Magazine* in 1980: "The United States should plan to defeat the Soviet Union and do so at a cost that would not prohibit U.S. recovery. Washington should identify war aims that, in the last resort, would contemplate the destruction of Soviet political authority and the emergence of a post-war world order, compatible with Western values."

President Reagan, during the 1982 European trip, said to the Westminster Parliament, London, that with a military buildup combined with diplomatic, economic, and propaganda campaigns, the Soviet Union might collapse into "the ash heap of history."

Laurence Beilenson, a former Hollywood attorney, is a close friend of President Reagan and claims when he was counsel for the Screen Actors Guild in the 1930s, he was responsible for turning Reagan against the Communists. I quote from his book *Survival and Peace in the Nuclear Age:* "For our survival and peace in the nuclear age, what should we do? Realize that whatever we do, nuclear war is likely sooner or later. Prepare the best shelter (civil defense) for our population that money and brains can buy. Go all out to develop an active defense. Know that treaties are a trap and avoid them except in the case of temporary settlement treaties and alliance treaties, and understand that they, too, will be broken. Comprehend that diplomacy is only a patching tool; use it for that purpose, though sparingly, but do not harbor the illusion that diplomacy can do more than patch. Forget SALT. Build up our nuclear deterrent to strive for superiority. In short, employ armed might as our tool of choice for survival and peace.

"Nuclear war, however, is not inevitable. We should devote our utmost endeavor to prevent it by avoidance, as well as deterrence." President Reagan was so impressed with Mr. Beilenson's book that he quoted it in a speech to the War College in 1981.

In October 1983, President Reagan "told a group of congressmen that he had not realized until recently that most of the Soviet Union's nuclear defenses were concentrated in

ambiguous information received from infrared sensors aboard U.S. satellites or from early-warning radar. The false alarms were received by the North American Air Defense Command (NORAD) Headquarters in Colorado. Five of these were serious enough for U.S. bomber and intercontinental missile crews to be placed on alert. Of the other three alerts, one was caused by a war-games tape (previously mentioned) that was fed into a computer in November 1979, and the other two in June 1980 by defective silicon chips in the computer system. There were also an unspecified number of false alarms caused by random failure in computer and communications equipment. Before the June 1980 accidents, specific records of such events were not kept. NORAD spokesmen said such events may happen two to three times a year.

The computer equipment that gives warning of nuclear attack on the United States is acquired in much the same way as the equipment used to process armed services payroll and military leave records. According to Senators Gary Hart and Barry Goldwater, the procedures for procurement of automatic data-processing equipment by the government are "highly regulated, complex, and fragmented." As a result, delays and technical obsolescence are practically guaranteed. This information came from the Goldwater–Hart Report to the Senate Armed Services Committee in November 1980. John Bradley, a former senior test and evaluation engineer, was fired by the Department of Defense in 1979, after he revealed the system's faults. He went over the heads of the Defense Department and complained to the National Security Council that "the Goldwater–Hart Report is a baby-step forward. What we need is a giant-step. The fact is, the computer hardware in this system was obsolete when it was installed, and it is now 10 years old. As for the software, it lacks the ability to take these false alarms, assess them, and come to a positive conclusion within microseconds, instead of having to do it by means of telephone conferences, which eat up vital minutes. It is well within the state of the art for computers to perform this function." He said there are ten false alerts for every one the press is told of. He also said the system is slow, cumbersome, and inaccurate. It fails on an average of once every thirty-five minutes.

In 1979, the General Accounting Office (GAO), the investigating body of Congress, assessed the Worldwide Military

Command and Control System (WIMEX) developed during the sixties. It consisted of 158 different computer systems, operating at 81 separate locations. The GAO concluded that the old system was in bad shape and could not be improved by piecemeal modernization and that a new system was needed. In other words, the system that decides every day whether we and millions of others live or die is in such bad condition that it needs to be replaced. President Reagan has recently decided to spend $18 billion to modernize the C³I system as part of a program to expand and improve the entire U.S. strategic nuclear capability over the next ten years.

Two false alerts occurred in the computer system on June 3 and June 6, 1980. During one of the accidents, about one hundred B-52s armed with nuclear weapons were prepared for takeoff, together with FB-111 airplanes. The crews were ordered to start their engines, and battle-control aircraft were prepared for flight, one of which took off in Hawaii. Silo-based missiles were brought closer to the firing stage as the crews were put on a higher state of alert. This all happened after a duty officer at the Strategic Air Command received computer data indicating that Soviet intercontinental and submarine ballistic missiles were on their way toward the United States. In each instance, officials revealed, President Carter's Airborne Command Post, a modified 747 airplane crammed with communications equipment and based at Andrews Air Force Base, was also prepared for takeoff. In these two accidents, satellite and radar early-warning information was fed into a special NOVA computer built by Data General Corporation at Cheyenne Mountain. Although, in fact, no attack was under way, the computer sent spurious messages to the Strategic Air Command reporting that large numbers of land- and sea-based missiles had been launched. The messages were received in Omaha, and lights immediately began to flash on an electronic map of the Strategic Air Command. Shortly after the alerts began, the officers in Omaha were said to have held a brief "conference" by telephone with officers at Cheyenne Mountain and at the Pentagon Command Center. A Pentagon aide said it took two to three minutes to determine that the computer had malfunctioned, and the alerts were turned off. Subsequently, it was determined that these false alerts were provoked by an electronic component about the size of a dime and worth 46 cents. Although the mistake was discovered within three minutes, it took twenty minutes for the Strategic Forces to resume normal operations.

Assistant Secretary of Defense Thomas Ross declined to discuss the wider implications of the false alarms; specifically, he refused to comment on the suggestion that an alert could set off a series of escalating responses in the United States and the Soviet Union, which could precipitate a nuclear confrontation. "I am going to duck that question," he said. Mr. Ross also declined to disclose whether the United States knew if the Soviet Union had experienced similar mishaps that caused concern in this country. Assistant Secretary of Defense Gerald Dineen said, "I hope that they have as secure a system as we do, that they have the safeguards we do." (As stated before, the sophistication of Soviet technology lags about five years behind that of the United States, and the present policy of the Reagan administration is to ban the sale of sophisticated technology to the Soviet Union.) There is, at this time, no available data about French, British, or Chinese false alerts.

After these near disasters the military concern seemed to be that the computer system was too slow to respond to an attack from the Soviet Union and that American weapons would have been destroyed before they could have been fired. The press voiced little consternation about the fact that, had America launched its nuclear weapons by mistake, the computer error could have provoked a massive Soviet retaliatory nuclear strike on the United States.

Early-warning systems, capable of detecting Soviet nuclear attacks seconds after they are launched, include ground-based radar near the Arctic Circle, infrared satellites that detect missile exhaust, and a new radar in Massachusetts on the coast of Cape Cod (Pave Paws), which detects Soviet submarine-launched rockets. The information collected by these systems is continually fed into computers at the Air Defense Command at Cheyenne Mountain, as well as to the Strategic Air Command in Omaha, the National Military Command Center in the Pentagon, and the Alternate Military Command Center, an underground bunker at Mt. Weather, fifteen miles northwest of Washington. Upon receiving signs that an attack is under way, preparations are immediately started for launching U.S. forces, while officials monitor any new information and decide whether or not to inform the President and other senior officials. But it takes Soviet land-based missiles only thirty minutes to reach the United States and submarine-launched rockets from ten to fifteen minutes.

Recently, adolescent boys have learned how to break into secret computer systems, including the computer system of Los Alamos Labs. They do this for fun and for the intellectual challenge. Probably the idea for the plot in the film *War-Games* was derived from such sport. These young men call themselves hackers. There is some evidence to suggest that the computers that control the nuclear weapons systems may not be immune to such intrusions. An article by Bernard Bereanu, a mathematician, describes the "inherent random behaviour of complex software of Early Warning Systems" and predicts that with the drastic reductions in warning time that will accompany new missile systems, it is only a matter of time before accidental nuclear war occurs.

Electromagnetic Pulse (EMP)

Despite all the talk and calculations about fighting a limited, prolonged, flexible nuclear war or about massive retaliation, both America and Russia are extremely vulnerable. A single Soviet warhead detonated 250 miles above Nebraska could blanket the entire nation with electromagnetic pulse, with peak fields of 50,000 volts per meter, strong enough to shut down all power and communication throughout the country. This pulse would have little effect on human beings, although it would paralyze the United States and throw its armed forces into total confusion.

EMP was first discovered in 1962 when an atomic test, conducted 800 miles southwest of Hawaii and 248 miles above the earth, destroyed most of the electrical and communication systems on the islands. The true significance of this effect was not realized until the seventies, when military engineers discovered that solid-state integrated circuits are a billion times more likely to be destroyed by EMP than primitive vacuum tubes. It is extremely difficult to shield communication systems from such an enormous pulse. Apparently, Soviet manuals and magazine articles are full of references to EMP. To quote: "To achieve surprise in a modern war, high-altitude nuclear explosions can be carried out—to destroy their system of control and communications and to suppress the antimissile and antiradar defense radar system. . . ."

Communication satellites carry more than 70 percent of all long-distance military messages. For some time, the military believed that satellites would be immune to all but a nearby nuclear blast, but in the early seventies physicists discovered that the radiation from a nuclear blast in space travels vast distances and knocks electrons out of a satellite's skin and innards, causing an EMP-type surge. The pulse is clearly different from the terrestrial EMP, but even stronger, about 1 million volts per meter, driven directly into the satellite's electronic heart. A relatively small explosion of two megatons just outside the upper atmosphere at an altitude of 50 to 75 miles would damage an unprotected satellite in geosynchronous orbit 22,300 miles above the earth. The kill range could easily be extended by increasing the size of the bomb.

Actually, an expectation of 50,000 volts per meter on earth might be too little. The Pentagon and some French physicists envision a pulse of about 100,000 volts per meter. If they are correct, the nominal protection the Pentagon has tried to build into communication networks, missiles, radar, and radios would almost certainly be useless; thus, an EMP attack by either country on the other would trip circuit breakers throughout the power grids, silence telephone lines, lobotomize computer memories, and throw the armed forces into disarray. Civilian and military planes alike, their solid-state controls and radios knocked out, would attempt, perhaps unsuccessfully, to make emergency landings. Most of the military would be out of electricity. Emergency backup power would support Cheyenne Mountain in the Colorado Rockies, the nerve center of the North American Air Defense Command, but the super-secret satellites that warn exactly where to expect a rain of Soviet warheads would have been knocked out, and the Defense Command's other eyes, the U.S. early-warning radar, would have been blinded, as predicted in the Soviet manual. Communications with the outside world would be cut off, leaving the nerve center unable to respond. At strategic-bomber bases, B-52 flight crews would find that the planes would not start because the electronic ignition systems would be dead. Even if the President could take off in his airborne command post (hardened against EMP), it is possible that the radio range would be sharply reduced, and the satellites used to relay the President's messages would be out of action.

Theodore B. Taylor, one of the inventors of the miniaturized hydrogen bomb, says there are roughly fifty exotic effects from a nuclear blast, including many types of EMP, gamma radiation, X rays, and electron effects from bomb debris. However, because of classification, he is unable to elaborate on these effects in any great detail.

William Broad, writing in *Science*, says, "Someone standing in an open field would feel no shock, not even a tingling, during an EMP attack. EMP passes harmlessly through human flesh, glass, wood, and plastic, knocking out machines, rather than people." However, someone in contact with or close to a metal object might be shocked or burned. The bigger or longer the object and the better the human connection, the greater the jolt. It would be hazardous to touch a toaster because it plugs into the national power grid, or to iron a shirt, adjust a television, wear headphones hooked up to a home stereo, talk on the telephone, ride a train on miles of metal rails, lean against a chain-link fence, or take a bath (unless the pipes were plastic).

The Department of Defense, in an apparent afterthought, tells of the human threat on the very last page of the EMP manual: "The energy collected in a long wire might cause electrocution or burns," it warns. "Such conditions are not generally expected." Expected or not, such a jolt to a tiny fraction of the U.S. population could represent death or injury to hundreds of thousands or even millions of people.

Broken Arrows (Accidents with Nuclear Weapons)

A nuclear weapon dropped and exploded accidentally by one superpower near the territory of the other could trigger a nuclear war, just as Soviet uncertainty about the Korean jetliner caused that plane to be destroyed. Accidents with nuclear weapons are probably much more frequent than even the unclassified data reveal. Obviously, as the number of nuclear weapons increases, the probability of an accident increases. America has some 30,000 nuclear weapons and the Soviet Union 20,000. Approximately 3 to 10 new hydrogen bombs are made or recycled every day in the United States and probably a similar number in the Soviet Union. In addition, Britain, France, China, and India have nuclear arsenals. According to a Department of Defense unclassified document, there were thirty-two accidents involving nuclear weapons between 1950 and 1980. It is interesting that after the report of a nuclear accident in the spring of 1968, there is not another report until September 1980, when the Titan missile in Damascus, Arkansas, exploded. Obviously, there were accidents between 1968 and 1980, but this information is still classified as secret. During the 1950s, there were nineteen crashes of planes involving nuclear weapons. None of these exploded, but many of them distributed radioactive materials around the site of the crash. During the 1960s, there were twelve more in the unclassified literature. The most serious were as follows:

(1) On January 24, 1961, a B-52 on airborne alert developed structural failure of the right wing over Goldsboro, North Carolina. Two weapons separated from the aircraft during the breakup of the plane at an altitude of 2,000 to 10,000 feet. The bombs were both 24-megaton bombs, which is equivalent to 24 million tons of TNT. The total energy of TNT released during World War II was 3 million tons. One bomb crashed, and five of its six safety catches were triggered. Had that bomb exploded, it would have destroyed much of North Carolina.

(2) On March 14, 1961, the second serious accident involved a B-52 failure near Yuba City, California. All the crew bailed out at 10,000 feet, except for the commander, who stayed with the aircraft to 4,000 feet, steering it away from populated areas. Two nuclear weapons on board were torn from the aircraft on ground impact. Luckily, the high explosives did not detonate.

(3) On January 13, 1964, a B-52 crashed during severe turbulence near Cumberland, Maryland, in isolated mountains. The plane contained two hydrogen bombs.

(4) On December 8, 1964, at Bunker Hill Air Force Base, Indiana, another plane crashed into a B-58 on an icy runway. The B-58 slid off the runway, and its left main landing gear struck a concrete electrical manhole box, igniting the aircraft. Portions of the five nuclear weapons on board burned. The report states that contamination by radioactive material

was limited to the immediate area of the crash and was subsequently removed.

(5) On January 17, 1966, over Palomares, Spain, a B-52 and a KC-135 collided during a routine high-altitude air-refueling operation. Both aircraft crashed. The B-52 carried four nuclear weapons; one was recovered on the ground and another from the sea on April 7, after extensive search and recovery efforts. High-explosive materials from two of the weapons exploded on impact with the ground, releasing large quantities of plutonium. Approximately 1,400 tons of plutonium-contaminated soil and vegetation over 640 acres were scraped up and imported to the United States in 4,827 steel drums, to be dumped straight into the ground at the Savannah River waste-storage facility in South Carolina, where the average rainfall is four inches per month. Plutonium is one of the most carcinogenic, toxic substances known to mankind.

(6) On January 21, 1968, over Thule, Greenland, a B-52 returning from Plattsburgh Air Force Base in New York crashed and burned some seven miles southwest of the runway while approaching the base to land. The bomber carried four nuclear weapons, all of which were destroyed by fire. Radioactive contamination occurred in the area of the crash, which was on the sea ice, and 237,000 cubic feet of plutonium-contaminated ice, snow, and water, with crash debris, were removed to an approved storage site in the United States during a four-month operation.

(7) The last declassified accident occurred in September 1980 at Damascus, Arkansas, when an air force repairman dropped a heavy wrench socket, which rolled off the work platform and fell toward the bottom of a silo. The silo contained a Titan II missile with a 9-megaton warhead. The socket bounced and struck the missile, causing a leak from the pressurized fuel tank. About eight and a half hours after the initial puncture, fuel vapors within the silo ignited and exploded the liquid fuel. One man was killed; twenty other people were injured. The 9-megaton hydrogen bomb was catapulted hundreds of yards away and was found lying in a field next to a grazing cow. Had this weapon exploded, its effect would have been approximately eighty times greater than the Hiroshima bomb.

Four days before the Titan missile accident in Arkansas, a B-52 armed with nuclear weapons caught fire while on a runway at Grand Forks Air Force Base. State emergency officials learned of the accident by intercepting an air force message about a "broken arrow" on the plane. The Pentagon refuses to confirm or deny the accident.

The Stockholm International Peace Research Institute estimates there were 125 U.S. nuclear-weapons accidents, major and minor, between 1945 and 1976, or about one every two and a half months. All the admitted accidents so far have been in the air force, but recently the navy acknowledged the existence of classified documents, dated from March 1973 to March 1978, entitled "Summary of Navy Nuclear Weapons Accidents and Incidents." The documents are hundreds of pages long.

On January 14, 1969, while ammunition was being loaded onto aircraft aboard the U.S.S. *Enterprise*, a bomb accidentally detonated, causing a series of explosions and fires on deck. The carrier, located seventy-five miles south of Pearl Harbor, was believed to have had nuclear weapons on board.

Obviously, more accidents have taken place, and it would seem imperative that this information be declassified so that the people of the world can calculate how many times they have been on the brink of disaster. It is not appropriate for the military to classify such accidents. It is like lying to a cancer patient about the diagnosis, telling the person the doctor knows best, and you shouldn't know anything about your disease or how you might die. The bombs are our bombs, made with our money, and the Pentagon is our department, and the military are our servants.

Location of Nuclear Weapons in the United States

There are 30,000 nuclear weapons in the United States, stored in more than two hundred locations in forty states. Many people are unaware that they live next door to nuclear weapons. The military stores an estimated 1,200 nuclear weapons on at least twelve bases throughout California, and more than half of these are in or near major urban areas. Some are located on active earthquake faults. The navy transports nuclear weapons by truck, barge, and helicopter through heavily populated areas of metropolitan San Francisco, Los Angeles, and other major cities. U.S. military installations often fail to coordinate emergency plans with the local communities and refuse even to acknowledge the presence of nuclear weapons in our cities.

Every day the U.S. government moves hundreds of nuclear weapons. New bombs are first shipped from Pantex, the Department of Energy's assembly plant near Amarillo, Texas. The DOE sends the bombs directly to military deployment sites around the world. Some are delivered overland in unmarked trucks, trains, and recreation vehicles (Winnebagos), but the DOE prefers to send bombs by air, using giant C-141 transport planes.

Once in the hands of the military, the bombs are moved regularly between bases for storage and maintenance. They are often flown by helicopter over densely populated areas. Barges, ships, and aircraft carriers (the latter hold approximately 100 nuclear weapons) regularly steam out of San Francisco Bay from Concord, and out of Long Beach Harbor from the Seal Beach Naval Weapons Station, and transfer weapons to helicopter carriers and other large ships. Officially, the Department of Defense will neither confirm nor deny the presence of nuclear weapons on any ship or aircraft. At a congressional hearing in 1973, Major General Edward B. Giller, the air force's assistant general manager for national security, acknowledged that the Russians probably knew where most of the nuclear weapons were stored. Therefore, the secrecy is maintained only to keep the American people uninformed.

Nuclear weapons in California are stored at three Strategic Air Command bases: Mather Air Force Base near Sacramento, Castle Air Force Base near Merced, and March Air Force Base near Riverside. They are also stored at George Air Force Base near Barstow and at the National Guard unit at the Fresno Air Terminal. In San Diego, home port of 29 percent of the entire U.S. fleet, the navy's nuclear arsenal at the North Island Naval Air Station is situated a mile from downtown, close to the San Diego International Airport. The navy stores nuclear weapons in the middle of San Francisco Bay at the Alameda Naval Air Station—near downtown Oakland and next to one of the world's busiest ports. Nuclear depth charges are probably stored in the navy's anti-submarine-warfare center at Moffett Field, a few miles outside of San Jose. The major nuclear arsenal for northern California is at the Concord Naval Weapons Station, thirteen miles northeast of San Francisco.

Seal Beach Naval Weapons Station is the navy's largest nuclear arsenal in southern California. Originally built on farmland and marsh, the base is now flanked by acres of homes and grammar schools and by Leisure World, a senior-citizen community of ten thousand people. The station consists of molehill-like bunkers, in which the navy stores the weapons. In plain view from the road is a large stack of distinctive nuclear-weapon containers. Trucks haul these containers to and from the docks where large ammunition ships berth. The Seal Beach area has grown so congested that ten airports lie within a twenty-mile radius. There are five layers of air traffic around the base, below 3,000 feet, including the approaches of at least 257,000 aircraft annually. Since the base opened, three planes have crashed into it, including one that left a wide flaming path of jet fuel not far from the nuclear-weapons stockpile. The base was built on the Newport-Inglewood fault, which has the greatest potential for earthquake in the L.A. area. It is thought that some of the weapons stored here are of older design and constitute potentially serious hazards to the surrounding community in the event of accident, earthquake, or fire. Their conventional explosives would be detonated, scattering plutonium over a wide area or, in an extreme case, setting off a nuclear explosion.

Most of the information about the transportation and storage of nuclear weapons in this country is classified. The military also transports high-level radioactive fuel from nuclear submarines along the railways, very often in rail cars that are not marked so people do not know what is contained in them. The military is conducting operations that are extraordinarily unsafe for the public health of the people of this country.

Terrorist Attacks

The Pentagon Five-Year Defense Guidance Plan reflects concern about foreign terrorists trying to steal nuclear weapons: "The existing program and efforts to improve the security of nuclear weapon sites overseas must be sharply accelerated. New methods are being devised to protect nuclear weapons storage facilities in the U.S., Europe and South Korea. Some weapons are small enough to be carried; others must be moved by truck." Colonel Linton of the Defense Nuclear Agency said information had been received that terrorists in Europe might have been planning to break into sites where nuclear artillery shells and other tactical weapons were stored.

There were seventy nuclear-related threats in the United States during the 1970s. The most serious was in 1974 when Boston was threatened with a nuclear explosion, which proved to be a false alarm. A special team of engineers and scientists based in Las Vegas, called the Nuclear Emergency Search Team (NEST), was then assembled to respond to terrorist blackmail and threats. Of course, it would be almost impossible to find a small nuclear weapon in a large city, if the terrorists were clever, because the very small amount of radiation emitted by the plutonium or uranium trigger of the bomb would be practically impossible to detect.

If such a clandestinely placed bomb exploded, it could initiate a nuclear war if the host government was not prewarned of such an event and misinterpreted the source of the attack during the confusion.

Lateral Proliferation of Nuclear Weapons

In 1983, only six countries in the world owned nuclear weapons—the United States, the USSR, Britain, China, France, and India—whereas at that time a total of forty-eight countries could have manufactured nuclear weapons because they were operating either nuclear-power reactors or nuclear-research reactors. A nuclear reactor is a bomb factory; it generates plutonium, which is the trigger for nuclear weapons. Thus a global thermonuclear holocaust could well be triggered by a conflict between two small nations, either of which could have nuclear weapons.

An example: England is a nuclear nation; Argentina is within several months to several years of making its first nuclear weapon. During the Falklands dispute, America reluctantly sided with Britain and Russia with Argentina. Had the war gone badly for either side, it could have become a superpower confrontation, particularly if nuclear weapons had been used by either Britain or Argentina. For instance, if Argentina had destroyed the Falklands with one or two nuclear weapons, Britain probably would have retaliated, and that could have introduced the superpower dynamics. In August 1983, the Reagan administration approved the sale of 143 tons of heavy water to Argentina, even though Argentina has not signed the nonproliferation treaty. Such a move may hasten its bomb program.

Israel, according to the CIA, has many nuclear devices; South Africa, with the help and cooperation of Israel, almost certainly tested a nuclear weapon in September 1979; Colonel Khaddafi of Libya is financing Pakistan's bomb project; South Korea and Taiwan are on the verge of nuclear weapons production. The "hot spots" in the world will obviously be the nuclear trigger points in the future.

As the Third World becomes progressively more deprived of the basic staples of life and America continues to become richer (6 percent of the world's population consuming 42 percent of the world's natural resources), the new nuclear nations of the world will obviously focus their frustration upon the rich. The anger in many Third World countries toward both the United States and the USSR is overt. The anger in Iran was not atypical. In the near future, a small nuclear nation could well threaten to, or actually, destroy New York or Moscow. The source of the weapon may not be apparent, and a nuclear war could be triggered in the confusion.

Military Personnel

Military personnel who handle nuclear weapons are part of the Personnel Reliability Program (PRP). More than 100,000 individuals belong; they must show evidence of emotional stability and good social adjustment, and have no history of alcohol or drug abuse. Physicians routinely assist in the screening process and periodically monitor those selected. On page 323 of the 1979 report of "Hearings Before a Sub-Committee of the Committee on Appropriations of the House of Representatives," these data were reported: In 1975, 5,128 people were removed from access to nuclear weapons because of violations of the PRP; in 1976, 4,966, and in 1977, 4,973, an annual rate exceeding 4 percent. Reasons given for removal in 1977 included alcohol and drug abuse—the primary drug abused was marijuana, but more than 250 people were removed for abuse of drugs like heroin and LSD. In the same year, 1,289 were removed for "significant physical, mental or character trait or aberrant behavior, substantiated by competent medical authorities," which might "prejudice reliable performance of the duties of a particular critical or controlled position." In addition, 828 were disqualified for negligence, 350 for court-martial or civil convictions of a serious nature, and 885 for evidence of "a contemptuous attitude toward the law."

When I was in Phoenix several years ago, I spoke with girls who dated the men who work in the Titan missile silos. Titan missiles contain one hydrogen bomb each, equivalent to nine million tons of TNT. These girls said that their dates frequently took drugs, including LSD, while on duty. Titan missiles can be launched only when two men each insert a key simultaneously into the control board. Each man is armed with a pistol, and one is to shoot the other if he shows signs of abnormal behavior.

Obviously, the Command, Control, and Communications System is so very complex that human errors will be frequent. The equipment is as fallible as those who designed and constructed it. We all make mistakes when we feel well, but mistakes occur with increasing frequency when we have a mild virus infection, such as influenza or a cold, or when we have had a fight with our spouse that morning.

Danger also lurks among seemingly normal military personnel. A retired admiral recently told me that there is no system that is so fail-safe that an intelligent man could not bypass it to initiate a nuclear war if he was really determined. A physician colleague told me that when he was an officer on nuclear submarines, each man was given a special and secret part of the code for launching nuclear missiles, but, as always in the human community, the system broke down when one man would say to the other, "I'm going to the bathroom; my code is so-and-so. Please cover for me." Nuclear weapons can be launched from submarines without their receiving commands from the President or other high officials.

Leaders

Over the last four centuries, seventy-five chiefs of state have led their countries for a total of several centuries while suffering from severe mental disturbances. In this century, at least six English prime ministers and a large number of cabinet ministers were sick while in office. In the United States, Franklin Roosevelt and Woodrow Wilson had advanced atheroma (hardening) of the arteries of the brain during their last months in office, and President Eisenhower had a heart attack, a major operation, and a mild stroke when President. The first U.S. Secretary of Defense, James Forrestal, was frankly delusional when relieved of office. He thought that the sockets of beach umbrellas were wired to record everything he said, and at one point he thought that some planes overhead were Russian bombers.

The characteristic signs of hardening of the cerebral arteries are loss of energy and adaptive capacity, inability to concentrate, lapses of memory, periods of confusion, emotional instability, and irritability. A modern leader is frequently faced with making decisions under extreme emotional stress while suffering from sleep deprivation. If he is already handicapped with the symptoms just described, he will obviously be unable to function adequately. Even healthy people experience severe mental aberrations from prolonged sleep deprivation, for mild to moderate sleep loss leads to the inability to sustain intellectual efforts.

It is interesting that top leaders in the world do not have to submit regularly to routine medical and psychiatric examinations. Airline pilots, who are responsible for, at the most, several hundred lives, are examined every six months. World leaders could now kill hundreds of millions of human beings. I think in the nuclear age it is medically indicated that leaders of nuclear nations be similarly assessed.

Case History

How did we get ourselves embroiled in this potential nuclear disaster? Why are Russia and America such bitter enemies? Why were these bombs built in the first place, and why are they still being made?

I am interested in this enmity between the superpowers because I come from another country, and as a neutral observer, I have been unable to understand the passionate hatred and paranoia harbored by Americans for Communism in general and the Soviet Union in particular. This paranoia is more obvious in the United States than in most other countries of the world. The problem is not really Communism because China, which is the world's largest Communist nation, is now an ally and a major trading partner of the United States. It is the age-old competition between two powerful nations, both seeking supremacy and nationalistic world hegemony.

I react to this seemingly implacable hatred and dislike of Russia with a feeling of intense fear. If in the nuclear age this enmity is carried to its logical conclusion, we will all be destroyed. The roots of the problem must be dissected out from the historical perspective and understood, and then pragmatic and constructive solutions to the disease must be found and implemented as soon as possible.

Often when I finish describing to an American audience the almost unimaginable medical consequences of a nuclear war, the first question is "But what about the Russians?" In a way, this is an appropriate question because if there is to be a nuclear war, it is the Russian bombs that will kill us. But this is not the thought behind the question. That thought is: "They are stronger" or "We can't trust them." Sometimes I think the question is a mechanism of psychic numbing, where the questioner refuses to emotionally integrate the facts I present and the question becomes a symptom of denial: "If I can blame the Russians, I won't have to disintegrate emotionally if I contemplate the end of the earth." A more appropriate response would be: "How can we prevent the Russians from killing us?"

What drives this conflict with the Russians? Why are we locked into this no-win conflict in which ultimately there can be no winners, only losers?

Early Warning Signs

Let us examine the historical context of this dilemma, remembering that, as with a pathological condition in an individual, a nation's pathological reactions are rooted deep in the past. During my ten years of intermittent residence in the United States, I have been trying to understand the nationalistic attitudes of its people.

Just when I develop a sense of security that we share a common understanding about the world, a national crisis like Iran emerges, and I become so perplexed and alarmed by many people's self-righteous, paranoid, warlike sentiments that I want to run away.

Because I also like Americans very much and I know that they are kind, loving people who want desperately to do the "right thing," I decided to review the history of the United States since its inception.

Obviously, the ideology and perspectives of American people have a characteristic logic derived from America's historic expansion and ascendancy to world political and military power.

The Declaration of Independence states that men "are endowed by their Creator with certain unalienable Rights; that among these are Life, Liberty and the pursuit of Happiness . . . whenever any Form of Government becomes destructive to these ends, it is the Right of the People to alter or to abolish it, and to institute new Government, laying its foundation on such principles and organizing its powers in such form, as to them shall seem most likely to effect their Safety and Happiness." Not only was this right stated in the Declaration of Independence, but, indeed, so was "their

duty," when necessary, "to throw off such Government."
Thomas Jefferson summed up the document in 1792 by saying,
"Every man and body of men on earth possesses the right of
self-government." In fact, so pleased were the founding fathers with their new government that they felt all the world
deserved a similar one.

After the framing of the Constitution, Jefferson wrote in
1809, "I am persuaded that no constitution was ever before as
well calculated as ours for extensive empire and self-government."

These sentiments were reinforced by a strong Protestant
religious ethic dating back to the early colonists that God was
always on America's side. Indeed, God was and has been
invoked in every American confrontation—with the French,
the Black Catholics of Latin America, the Infidels in Turkey,
Islam in Asia, and the Atheistic Reds of modern times.

In 1850, Herman Melville wrote, "We Americans are
the peculiar chosen people—the Israel of our time: We bear
the ark of the liberties of the world. God has predestined. . . .
The rest of the nations must be in our rear." And about
the same time, Orestes Brownson wrote that reforming America was a preliminary step in claiming the rightful "hegemony
of the world." So very early in American history, Americans
felt they had the right to determine the fate and political
direction of other nations, whether or not they welcomed
such intervention.

However, despite these idealistic attitudes, America always displayed discrimination toward Latin Americans, whites
in Canada, American Indians, black slaves, and women. In an
unpublished draft of the Declaration of Independence, even
Jefferson was biased toward women—they were honored, but
not included in a commitment to self-determination, and they
were not treated as equal partners in the struggle to fulfill
America's unique mission.

Because of this almost holy sense of mission experienced
by the nation's founders, together with their feelings of great
isolation from the rest of the world, they decided that the past
was essentially bad, and even the future was threatening.
Emerson said, "Whatever is old corrupts, and the past turns
to snakes."

By defying the past and the future and by preserving and
expanding the "present," the American upper classes were

able to control pressure from the lower and middle classes to
change an inequitable political structure. The overriding commitment to an expansionist political economy, shared by all
classes in the society, provided the resources and opportunity
that helped diffuse pressures from within for more equality.

Adam Smith, when writing in 1789 in *The Wealth of
Nations*, propounded the theory of capitalism and its moral
justification. He said that the pursuit of self-interest as a
buyer or seller in the marketplace will ultimately and paradoxi-
cally work for the good of society. That is, through the
invisible hand of the marketplace, everybody will ultimately
achieve everything they desire. When defined differently,
possessive individualism, which is greed, will be the harbin-
ger of future beneficence. This philosophical justification is
logically and morally contradictory and has failed: Some people achieve everything they materially desire, and some do
not.

When the French revolution occurred in the 1780s, America at first enthusiastically supported it in the name of self-
determination. But as soon as it became apparent that the
lower classes were to have equal rights with the upper classes,
that there was a general denunciation of property, and that
French slavery was to be abolished, American support for the
revolution quickly vanished. The French were attacked for
utopianism with the surprising statement: "Empire was the
key to property, and property was the foundation of the good
American presence."

America has always considered itself both expansionist
and the savior of mankind. Driven by this double mission,
the founding fathers, who viewed their country as an endlessly expanding frontier, were motivated by the acquisitive,
possessive individualism of the capitalist ethic. Individualism,
as expressed in the Declaration of Independence, and over-
materialism combined to ensure that empire was the only
way to honor morality and avarice at the same time. Expanding the marketplace enlarged the area of the American form
of freedom in the world. Conversely and expediently, expanding the area of freedom enlarged the marketplace.

Early in the 1800s, the concern over expanding America's
commerce was very strong. Back in 1786, Jefferson had said
that he hoped circumstances would allow the United States to

bring the South American Spanish territories "piece by piece" into an American system. Another commentator viewed Latin America as the key to the "future prosperity, commerce, and security" of the United States. And in 1823, President James Monroe proclaimed the "Monroe Doctrine," to which U.S. interventions in Western Hemisphere nations are usually ascribed.

According to Thomas Boylston Adams, the Monroe Doctrine states clearly that the true policy of the United States is to leave the nations of South America to decide their own destinies, and that the United States would neither interfere itself nor permit any new colonization by any other power.

But for this enlightened policy, Theodore Roosevelt later, in 1904, substituted a proclamation of new imperialism:

"If a nation shows that it knows how to act with decency in industrial and political matters, if it keeps order and pays its obligations, then it need fear no interference from the United States. Brutal wrong-doing, or an impotence which results in a general loosening of the ties of civilized society, may finally require intervention by some civilized nation, and in the Western Hemisphere, the United States cannot ignore this duty."

This statement overlooked the fact that people with diverse views, traditions, habits, and aspirations—not necessarily North American or European—would not be concerned with these admonitions. Any doubts about U.S. intervention anywhere in the Southern Hemisphere Roosevelt dismissed with the remark, "It will show those Dagos that they will have to behave decently. They will be happy if only they will be good."

The expansion of America's frontiers by conquest of the western territories—the annexation of Texas in 1845 and northern Mexico in 1848—was justified for its ultimately beneficent missions. The phrase "manifest destiny" referred to the preordained logic and fate of America's historic role in world history, to civilize and develop a cohesive nation under the mantle of capitalist democracy. Despite cautions by John Quincy Adams about the unrestrained "spirit of aggrandizement," the perspective of Daniel S. Dickinson of New York, who said, "New races are presented for us to civilize, educate and absorb," characterized the expansionist ethic of the times.

In the years prior to the Civil War, the West was opened

through new methods of transportation, offering outlets and incentives for investments. Steam navigation continued its advance, and the land-grant railways encouraged business confidence in the financial gains to be made from the aggressive drive westward. The urge to expand and debates concerning annexation and statehood for the territories occurred, but they were within the context of the growing conflict between "free" versus "slave" states. In 1860, the Confederate secession plunged the country into its most wrenching and cataclysmic internal conflict. The Civil War ultimately pitted the rising industrial class of the North and West against an agrarian aristocratic tradition in the South based on slave labor.

Once slavery was abolished, the progress of industrial capitalism was assured, free from the domination of government affairs that slave owners had perpetrated for more than a generation. A steady stream of European immigrants, enlarging the population by over 7,500,000 from 1850 to 1880, fulfilled the growing needs for a labor supply for American industry. In effect, the growth of industrialism, mechanized production, and national income provided the material basis for further national aggrandizement of the United States.

Advocates of America's future as a world empire, such as John Fiske, Josiah Strong, and Admiral Alfred T. Mahan, saw the future from 1890 as assured. Pressing for increased naval strength, Mahan argued in the popular press that war, far from being the worst resort, functions as a means for the ascension of mankind, exercising right by force according to the power that God ascribes to them. Mahan thus reasserted the moral duty of America to protect its colonial possessions, such as Puerto Rico and the Philippines, and to drive European nations out of the Americas, through the exertion of naval power, as in the Spanish American War. The commercial advantages of such a strategy were considerable but had to be approached from a perspective of responsibility. As a popular philosopher of war and imperialism, Mahan once said, "Peace, indeed, is not adequate to all progress; there are resistances that can be overcome only by explosion."

Power and force were glorified as an intrinsic endowment of national life necessary to counter defiance by evil forces. Such a frame of mind supported the dispatch of marines to Panama to quell an insurrection in 1885 and further

military campaigns to Chile, Peru, and Brazil, to defeat incipient revolutions against semifeudal ruling aristocracies.

In 1880, U.S. capital was heavily involved in the Cuban
economy, particularly in sugar. One American financier wrote
in 1895, "It makes the water come to my mouth when I
think of the state of Cuba as one in our family." America's
investment in Cuba was continually being threatened by
attempts at self-determination and revolution by the people
against Spain. In 1898, America "liberated" Cuba from Spain
in the Spanish American War. It moved into the Congo to
support Belgium and to claim another market for American
goods. The United States divided Samoa with Germany and
Britain in 1887. A U.S. campaign ensued in 1891 to 1892 for
control of Chile and Peru, and America intervened in Brazil
to defeat revolutionaries who opposed economic penetration
by American corporations.

The Monroe Doctrine asserting American supremacy in
its own hemisphere and the Open Door policy of free and
unencumbered trade in China legitimized U.S. economic
and political expansion. The ramifications of these policies for
the militarization of foreign relations have vitally affected
present U.S. relationships with the rest of the world. Under a
false rubric of responsibility and goodwill these attitudes have
created a vast military armada that reaches out to touch every
corner of the world.

The Birth of the American Military-Industrial Complex

The military-industrial complex was spawned before World
War I when linkages were forged between the big steel
companies like Bethlehem and Carnegie and the U.S. Navy.
The superpowers of the "Age of Imperialism"—Great Britain,
France, the United States, Germany, Russia, and Japan—
were all seeking ways to build navies commensurate with
their quests for global advantage. The United States perceived
itself as a nation with political and economic requirements to
compete in a hostile international environment. This was an
era of transition from the "militia" processes of the Civil War
to an integrated military production system designed to meet
the needs of both an expansionist nation and its largest industrial manufacturers. To this end, connections that initiated the

military-industrial complex were made among the captains of industry, admirals of the navy, and politicians. By 1882, the steel-company executives were viewing with keen anticipation the profits and markets to be gained from the construction of armaments.

As the technology in shipbuilding shifted from wooden to steel vessels, new ties were established between the steel industries and government. This mutual dependency totally undercut the traditional laissez-faire dictum separating government and private enterprise. Under these conditions, in the 1880s the characteristics of the modern military-industrial relationship—political deals, kickbacks, cost overruns, favoritism—began to emerge. By 1887, faced with a slump in railroad orders and sinking profits, the steel firms looked increasingly to the U.S. Treasury to bolster their fortunes. Bethlehem Steel, for example, suffered from a declining rail market and the navy's needs for armor were the only outlets that carried it through the Depression of 1894–96. President Cleveland asserted the merits of these military construction programs as a device to help alleviate serious domestic economic problems associated with unemployment and social unrest. Additionally, the navy was more than willing to pay any amount that the industry demanded to get the steel necessary for naval expansion in 1899. According to naval historian Benjamin Franklin Cooling, "The proliferation of defense-related industries became inevitable once American industrial capacity and the needs of security became synonymous in the minds of policy makers and entrepreneurs alike. Each crisis—real or imagined—opened another stage in the process."

Fortified with an imperialistic ideology and the sustaining life of a global "free market," America hobbled into the twentieth century with its working class increasingly prey to severe depressions, which are characteristic of totally unfettered capitalism.

As President Theodore Roosevelt fed the American national ego with his vigorous foreign policy, he boldly proclaimed that the semibarbarous peoples of the world must be disciplined by an international police force for the welfare of mankind. A tireless campaigner for American military and economic strength, Roosevelt succeeded in "taking Panama," as he put it, and subjugating nationals of Central America to construct under slave conditions the Panama Canal for the purposes of U.S. trade access. He once asserted to President Drago of Argentina that only those countries in conformity with certain standards of political and economic behavior could rely on U.S. friendship. In building up the navy, Roosevelt compelled international recognition of America as a significant force.

In addition to its nascent rise as a military and political power to be reckoned with, the U.S. economy recouped after the slumps of the 1890s, largely through the consolidation and integration of the large corporations. A leading role was played by the investment banking houses, notably J. P. Morgan and Company, which dominated the railroad industry and later influenced the creation of the General Electric Company, American Telephone and Telegraph, Western Union, and International Harvester. Eventually, aroused popular outcry against the big trusts mobilized around the candidacy of Woodrow Wilson, who opposed monopolies and favored state interventionism in the public interest.

In foreign policy, Wilson promoted an explicit role for American power: "to prevent revolutions, promote education and advance stable and just governments." Adamantly opposed to popular attempts at revolution, he utilized American military forces to put down rebellions—in China, in Haiti in 1915, and in Mexico in 1917—which advocated communal ownership of productive assets.

The economic and political self-interest of the predominant leaders in the United States succeeded in preventing the kinds of revolutionary changes that had been enshrined as part and parcel of American ideology in the Declaration of Independence!

It seems clear that in its relations with other countries, the United States has pursued an aggressive, often antidemocratic, policy, more intent on opening the doors for resource and labor exploitation than on implanting democratic norms and political practices. Wilson himself abjured the uses of national power on behalf of corporate interests, saying, "It is a very perilous thing to determine the foreign policy of a nation in terms of material interest. It not only is unfair to those with whom you are dealing, but it is degrading as regards your own action."

Regardless of these sentiments, Wilson justified sending

forces to dominate Nicaragua and Mexico, and despite their antidemocratic characters, dubiously distinguished between "good" and "bad" revolutionists. Ironically, this convoluted logic still pertains regarding the U.S. State Department's tolerance for pro-Western "authoritarian" regimes, as distinguished from socialistic "totalitarian" ones.

Wilson's ideas were opposed by Herbert Hoover, who was President from 1929 to 1933. He was a Quaker who considered the Bill of Rights to be "the heart of the Constitution." He opposed the use of force, except in self-defense, and "absolutely disapproved" of global crusades and of Dollar Diplomacy, claiming the latter was "not a part of my conception of international relations." He warned Wilson against destroying revolutions that would only allow the rich to dominate the poor. "We cannot slay an idea or an ideology with machine-guns," he said. "Ideas live in men's minds, in spite of military defeat." Hoover honored his commitment to self-determination. He saw national security as requiring only enough force to prevent any foreign soldier from landing on American soil, for "To maintain forces less than that strength is to destroy national safety, to maintain greater forces is not only economic injury to our people, but a threat against our neighbors, and would be a righteous cause for the ill-will amongst them." Is this not a prophetic statement for today?

Emergence of a Rival

Although the adversarial relationship between Russia and America began during the rule of the czars, it was only after World War I that the United States began to perceive the USSR as the spokesman for a world view that would challenge America's newfound status as a global power.

The two Russian revolutions in 1917 were seen by America as more relevant to World War I and the Germans than to internal Russian events. The first revolution, early in 1917, involved the fall of the czar and his replacement by a liberal democratic regime, which opposed the pro-German imperial Russian court. This was welcomed by America as support for the Allied war efforts. The second revolution, by the Bolsheviks in November 1917, was not understood for what it really was, and Americans seemed to believe that the Bolshevik leaders were merely pro-German agents.

Only after the war was Russian Communism seen as a true political reality. At that time, 1918 to 1920, the Russian civil war was in progress, and America intervened militarily and sent troops to two areas of the Soviet Union: to Arkhangelsk (Archangel) on the White Sea in northern Europe, and to eastern Siberia. They were sent in by President Wilson as part of the Allied war effort against Germany and were thousands of miles from the Russian civil-war battles. Nevertheless, America did invade Russia at the time of her revolution and civil war, and some Russians still have strong feelings about this.

It was difficult for America to accommodate to the new Soviet regime, which, while not declaring war on the United States, was committed by its strongest beliefs and doctrine to the dismantling of the political and social traditions common to the American ethic. This threat was more monstrous in the eyes of Americans than any sort of military feat would have been, because it struck right at the heart of the ideological beliefs of capitalism, free enterprise, and God. It could be viewed as a religious dispute in that Communism denied the existence of God. Communism in unadulterated form really represented the good and well-being of all the people. On the other hand, Americans believed in the Judeo-Christian tradition, which also recognized the quality and goodness of all human beings. Hence, the basic American ethic was almost socialistic in its call for government of the people, by the people, and for the people.

The only differences between the two regimes, theoretically, were that in Russia all people were considered equal and worked for each other's good, organized by a state bureaucracy, which should come from the people, and that there was no recognized God, whereas in America, all people had equal opportunities to look after themselves. There was, however, no built-in mechanism to care for all the people equally, and a belief in God was dominant. One of the historical reasons why the concept of religion was eliminated in Russia involved the corrupt role played by the Church, which had supported the czars during years of gross inequality.

In retrospect, at no time was America even remotely threatened by the Soviet Union. America was a large landmass bordered by two huge oceans on the east and west and by two relatively friendly countries to the north and south.

Over the years, the Soviet ideological ethic became more "a rhetorical exercise than a guide to policy." But another circumstance had concerned and alienated America: the lack of commitment by the new Soviet government to repay debts owed by the czars to the United States.

The American government remained refractory to the new regime for thirteen years until, in 1933, Franklin Roosevelt established formal diplomatic relations between the two countries. The debts were never repaid and were quickly forgotten during the Roosevelt years. During the thirties, Stalin began implementing his repressive policies within Soviet society, murdering millions of his citizens; and by the end of the thirties, the belief and joy and hope in the idealism of Lenin had been extinguished for most in Russia.

At the same time, in 1933, Hitler became chancellor of Germany. From this time until 1938, Hitler and his Brown Shirts instigated the persecution of Jews, which eventually became "the final solution." United States newspapers were supportive of Hitler because of his anti-Bolshevik policies, although he was also anti-Jewish during this time, and only after Kristallnacht in 1938, when the Jews in Berlin were overtly attacked, did they begin reporting the Nazi atrocities.

During this period, also, although official U.S.–Soviet relations improved, Red-baiting and anti-Communism were used by U.S. corporations as an excuse for union busting. Corporations stocked munitions and killed workers in order to end strikes. This technique was among many used by the corporations to destroy the membership and to prevent the growth of unions, so that in 1983 only 20 percent of the American workers were unionized. (In Australia, 75 percent of workers are unionized.)

In 1939, Germany and Russia signed a nonaggression pact, but in June 1941, Russia was invaded without warning by Hitler. Suddenly Russia became a close ally of the United States, and all previous hostilities were dropped or forgotten during those fateful days of World War II. In fact, I remember that when Germany turned its might on Russia, my Australian mother heaved a sigh of relief and said, "Thank God, we're saved."

The First Missile Gap

During the years of World War II, the structure of the world changed. Man learned to fission the atom and capture the energy of the stars. Overnight our concept of good and evil and previously acceptable standards of international behavior suddenly became old-fashioned. In 1939, the physicists Albert Einstein, Leo Szilard, and Edward Teller and the banker Dr. Alexander Sachs wrote a letter to President Roosevelt saying that they believed Hitler was developing nuclear weapons and that America should do the same thing. Roosevelt was convinced by the letter and thereupon instituted the Manhattan Project—the largest scientific project ever undertaken. The operation was run by General Leslie Groves and was the brainchild of a brilliant physicist named Robert Oppenheimer. It was conceived and executed under total secrecy at a private boys' school named Los Alamos deep in the mountains of New Mexico. The project quickly grew to incorporate thousands of brilliant scientists and technicians and was in operation for three years. Apparently the work was challenging and exciting, and Oppenheimer called the problems they faced "technically sweet."

Some months before the bombs were due to be completed, Hitler was defeated and the raison d'être for the nuclear force disappeared. One of the scientists called an emergency meeting to decide what they should do. Oppenheimer did not attend. It was decided that the work should go on, and in a documentary film, *The Day After Trinity*, it was admitted that the scientists could not stop themselves from working on these fascinating technical problems. The fuel for the bombs was made either of highly enriched uranium, which took several years to produce, or of plutonium—the very toxic, carcinogenic, mutagenic, manmade metal produced when uranium fissions in nuclear reactors.

The first bomb, named Trinity or code-named the Gadget, was to be tested in the New Mexico desert at Alamogordo in July 1945. There was great uncertainty about whether the bomb would explode at all and, if it did, what the yield would be. There also was an outside chance that the atmosphere of the world would be rendered critical and the earth enveloped in fire. Despite these calculations, the decision was made to proceed. One astonished junior technician was amazed to hear the brilliant physicist Enrico Fermi taking side bets, as the Gadget was hoisted to the top of its tower, that New Mexico would be incinerated.

The night was wild and stormy with bolts of lightning in the sky, and the scientists were worried that lightning would explode the bomb prematurely or disturb its functions. However, Trinity exploded on time, and as they crouched in their shelters some miles away, they were amazed at what they had done. One said—to paraphrase—the desert suddenly became tiny, as it was filled with a violent blue light. A sound like thunder occurred, which seemed to last forever, and a huge cloud of radioactive debris appeared and hovered overhead, but just at the right time the wind changed and the cloud blew away. The scientists were not contaminated by the fallout. Robert Oppenheimer, on seeing the first atomic explosion of Trinity, quoted the Hindu scripture the Bhagavad Gita, "I am become death, the shatterer of worlds."

That night the scientists held a party to celebrate their success.

The next bomb, code-named Little Boy, equivalent to 13,000 tons of TNT, was dropped from a plane called *Enola Gay* at 8:15 A.M. on August 6, 1945, over a city called Hiroshima. At that time, approximately 100,000 people were killed. The population had responded to an air-raid siren earlier but had emerged from the shelters just before the bomb exploded. Hiroshima disappeared.

People, exposed to heat equal to that of the sun at the instant of explosion, were vaporized and left only their shadows on the pavement behind them. Children were seen running along the streets with their skin falling off their bodies like veils. A woman lay in the gutter with her back totally burned, and as she died, her baby suckled at her breast. A man stood acutely shocked, holding his eyeball in the palm of his hand. Bodies lay in all areas. Tongues were swollen and protruded from the mouths; eyes were eviscerated by the blast and hung on the cheeks. To quote a survivor: "In one small space amidst a pile of bricks, a young woman's head faced towards me, and a look of innocent beauty still remained on her face."

That night the scientists held another party, but one man described his feelings as the party commenced. He said he could not go because he was so depressed and was physically nauseated. He commented that when the scientists were planning and designing the bombs, they never calculated people as matter. In other words, they had not extrapolated their calculations to determine how the enormous forces they had unleashed would affect the human body, although bombs were designed to kill people.

Some people survived Hiroshima and ran away to the only Christian center in Japan, a very old port called Nagasaki. They arrived just in time for the second atomic bomb, code-named Fat Man. Some 50,000 people were killed instantly. The Atomic Age had begun.

Roosevelt died some months before the bombs were used, and Harry Truman came to office with little knowledge of foreign affairs. Just before Roosevelt died, Szilard, Einstein, and others had written a letter to the President, advising him that the bomb should not be used on population centers. The letter lay unopened on his desk when Truman acceded and was not read until after the war. By the time the bombs were dropped, the Japanese had already opened peace negotiations through the Soviet Union, but although the American government knew about these peace initiatives, it still went ahead. Truman said of the Russians on the eve of the first atomic test, "If it explodes as I think it will, I'll certainly have a hammer on those boys."

Why were those bombs used? It is said that they saved 500,000 American lives that would otherwise have been lost during the invasion of Japan—obviously a fallacious argument because of the ignored peace proposal. At the same time, Russia, a professed ally which had shouldered an enormous burden during World War II, was being branded as an enemy by the American President. Was it because of the incipient hostility toward the Soviet Union held by a few hard-line anti-Communists close to the seat of power and by other influential individuals? America lost 400,000 servicemen during World War II, and the Soviet Union lost, as I said, 20 million people—both civilian and military.

Americans had been told during World War II that Russian–American collaboration assured the future peace, but this was obviously not to be so.

Only after the end of the war did the behavior of the Soviet Union become overtly suspect. It left in the Warsaw

Pact countries modern mechanized military units. Even though their equipment was inferior to that of the Western armies, this threatened the Europeans and the Americans. But it represented little change from previous Russian policy. For centuries it had been the custom of Russian rulers to maintain in being, even in time of peace, ground forces much larger than necessary.

Superimposed on this seeming threat was the fact that the Russian troops were often brutal in the countries they overran. Although inexcusable, this could be seen as a reaction to the sheer brutality they had suffered under the Nazis. It soon became clear that democracy was not to be practiced in the occupied countries. Incidentally, these countries— Hungary, Bulgaria, Rumania, Poland, and Czechoslovakia— had not been democratic states before occupation. In addition, the Soviet government remained secretive and inscrutable and continued to issue propaganda statements about the destruction of capitalism. American anxiety increased.

At the end of the war, America was the only nuclear nation on earth and still had one bomb in its arsenal. At this time, there was one clumsy attempt to internationalize nuclear energy, "which failed." This was called the Baruch Plan, named after a wealthy businessman, Bernard Baruch, but initially conceived by the Secretary of State, Dean Acheson, and the chairman of the Atomic Energy Commission, David Lilienthal. It was as follows:

A proposed International Development Council would receive the nuclear warheads from America only if the Soviet Union immediately relinquished control of its uranium mines and production facilities to an international authority. Meanwhile, America could continue making bombs and conducting research on new weapons until it was satisfied with the international procedures for inspection and control. A nation that failed to abide by the agreement would receive punishment at the behest of the U.N. Security Council, which was dominated by the United States. Russia would also have to surrender its veto power. Russia rejected this plan, which was obviously designed not to succeed.

Because Russia rejected the plan, it was deemed reasonable for the United States to continue building nuclear weapons.

The anti-Russian feeling immediately after the war seemed to be almost as intense as the anti-Nazi feeling had been—as if a direct transference had occurred from one enemy onto another country, which had been a close ally. In 1946, Eugene Rostow (recently director of the Reagan Arms Control and Disarmament Agency) circulated a memo among people at the Office of Strategic Services, proposing that Stalin be given an ultimatum—democratize your society or we will obliterate your cities with nuclear weapons.

Before World War II, Russia had been seen by America as a revolutionary political force. After the war, it became the traditional great military power poised on the edge of America's newly acquired sphere of political-military interest in Europe.

At the end of the war the United States was left with a huge military superstructure and an expanded apparatus for military planning. With Germany and Japan defeated, a new military opponent seemed necessary in order to maintain the American military status quo. The Soviet Union became the obvious candidate. The Soviet leaders, partially confused by American pro-Soviet support during the wartime years and Western agreement to extension of Soviet borders after the war, thought that American forces would probably withdraw from the European continent when the war was over and felt that they could penetrate the European vacuum that would result. They had not intended to do this by force but rather by allying themselves with the French and Italian Communist parties, by exploiting Soviet military-control powers in Berlin and Vienna, and by penetrating the Western labor unions' intellectual and student movements. However, their dreams of political takeover in Western Europe were frustrated by the Marshall Plan, which from 1947 to 1948 helped restore the shattered Western European economy. It is postulated that the crackdown in Czechoslovakia and the Berlin blockade in 1948 were essentially defensive in nature—attempts by Moscow to play its last political cards in anticipation of a new division of power on the European continent. It is entirely possible that had the Marshall Plan been continued on a strong economic and political basis for European recovery, Stalin would have been forced to concentrate on economic recovery within the Eastern Bloc countries. Instead, America saw this international tension as the forerunner of war, conditioned as it already was by anti-Soviet thinking, and thus the North Atlantic Treaty Organization (NATO) was established in

49. This was a military alliance, which obviously increased
e tensions within Europe.

By indulging in the nuclear fantasy of strength, America
d sown the seeds for its own suicide. It had initiated the
clear arms race, and Russia, wanting to be a viable
perpower, followed. Until Russia developed a large deliver-
le nuclear arsenal, America was totally invulnerable. Today it
n be virtually obliterated within several hours.

The Arms Race Begins

By 1949, Russia had learned the secret of atomic fission
d had exploded its first atomic bomb. That same year
merica "lost" China to the Communist revolution of Mao.
is Chinese revolution was blamed on the Russians, al-
ough it had nothing to do with the Soviet Union. Rather, it
as an internal civil war, supported by a majority of its 600
illion people. Throughout the Chinese revolution, the only
ajor American reporting came from a brilliant young man,
H. White, a *Time* correspondent in China. Henry B. Luce,
e owner of *Time* magazine, had been born in China to
issionary parents. At no time in his life could he accept the
hinese Communist revolution. Most dispatches that T. H.
hite sent back to *Time* were altered or totally changed by
ice. He reviled the revolution and supported Chiang Kai-
ek, the deposed leader of China. Consequently, America
ceived a totally incorrect message about the happenings in
hina, and thus began the Two China policy, which led to
ch bitter acrimony between two major powers of the world,
e Republic of China and the United States of America.

Also in 1949 the General Advisory Committee, chaired
 Robert Oppenheimer, met to decide whether America
ould proceed with the construction of a hydrogen bomb,
e brainchild of Edward Teller. The committee recommended
ainst it, on the grounds that there were no limits to its
structiveness and it would endanger humanity. Teller pushed
r his "super bomb" and prevailed against Oppenheimer,
d Truman decided on a crash H-bomb program. The first
-bomb was exploded on Eniwetok atoll in 1952. An im-
oved model was detonated at Bikini in 1954.

In 1950, soon after the explosion of the first Russian
omic bomb, another source of conflict emerged, the war in

Korea. This was viewed by the United States as an attack b
the Red Army across international borders, although it was,
fact, a conflict inspired overwhelmingly by local problem
related to the Manchurian–Korean area.

By 1951, in addition to having many more nuclear wea]
ons than the Soviet Union, America had Russia ringed by a
bases in Greenland, Iceland, Okinawa, Japan, Alaska, Spai
Saudi Arabia, Tunisia, Morocco, and Turkey. Planes fro
these locations could all deliver nuclear weapons. The Unite
States had cut back military manpower, but the Soviets had
huge standing army of 6 million by 1955—probably in r
sponse to the U.S. nuclear arsenal. Early in NATO history,
conscious decision was made that it was cheaper to deplo
nuclear weapons than men—hence, the obvious dispari
between the two sides. Also, NATO from the beginning h
always maintained the right to use nuclear weapons first
provoked by political or conventional military consideration
This doctrine is known as "first use." In 1954, a decision w
made to include West Germany in NATO and to rearm
This upset Russia because of its recent conflict with German
At that time, Russia announced the formation of the Warsa
Pact. Both pacts are military alliances.

Once the Russians got the bomb in 1949, the U.
military assumed that if the Soviets had the bomb and tl
necessary delivery mechanism, they would use it if necessary
worst case analysis.

The Eye of the Beholder

The American statesman George Kennan says:

When a military planner selects another country as the leading hypothetical opponent of his own
country—the opponent against whom military preparations and operations are theoretically being
directed—the discipline of his profession obliges
him to endow that opponent with extreme hostility
and the most formidable of capabilities. In this way,
not only is there created, for planning purposes, the
image of the totally inhuman and totally malevolent
adversary, but this image is reconjured daily, week
after week, month after month, year after year, until

it takes on every feature of flesh and blood and becomes the daily companion of those who cultivate it, so that any attempt on anyone's part to deny its reality appears as an act of treason or frivolity. In this way, the planner's hypothesis becomes imperceptibly the politicians' and journalists' reality, upon which a great deal of American policy and of American military efforts come to be based.

But the "enemy image" that a nation adopts is fickle and transitory. To give recent and relevant examples: In 1942, Americans responded to a poll by using these adjectives to describe the German–Japanese enemy—warlike, treacherous, and cruel. None of these adjectives appeared in describing the Russian allies. By 1966, the mainland Chinese were warlike, treacherous, and sly, but these words had disappeared from language describing the Germans and Japanese; indeed, *they* were seen as hardworking allies. Now the Russians had become warlike and treacherous. In American eyes, the "bloodthirsty, cruel, treacherous, slant-eyed, buck-toothed little Japs of World War II have become a highly cultivated, charming, industrious and thoroughly attractive people." Similarly, since 1966, the attitude toward the Chinese has also moved in this direction, yet they are still hard-line Communists armed with nuclear weapons.

In this connection, it is interesting to note how the American Revolution and subsequent Civil War, so fraught with positive values for their participants, were viewed by the European community at that time. Europe seemed to be as suspicious of the United States as the United States is now of the Soviet Union. As the historian Henry Steele Commager writes: "Republicanism, democracy, constitutionalism, and social equality challenged Old World monarchies and class societies."

After the United States proclaimed the Monroe Doctrine, which excluded European influence from South and Central America, Metternich, a powerful Austrian statesman, said: "These United States have suddenly left a sphere too narrow for their ambition, and have astonished Europe by a new act of revolt, more unprovoked, fully as audacious, and no less dangerous than the former [against Britain]. They have distinctly and exactly announced their intention to set not only power against power, but, to express it more exactly, altar against altar. In their indecent declarations, they have cast blame and scorn on the institutions of Europe most worthy of respect. In permitting themselves these unprovoked attacks, in fostering revolutions wherever they show themselves, in regretting those which have failed, and extending a helping hand to those which seem to prosper, they lend new strength to the apostles of sedition, and re-animate the courage of every conspirator."

A leading British journal of the time, *Blackwood's Edinburough Magazine,* commented on Lincoln's Emancipation Proclamation: "Monstrous, reckless, devilish . . . It proves . . . [that] rather than lose their trade and customs the North would league itself with Beelzebub and seek to make a hell of half a continent."

So the present enemy image is the Soviet Union, and the American nuclear arms race has reinforced itself by suspicions, inadequate information, and an enemy image. Jerome Wiesner, president emeritus of MIT, former science adviser to President Kennedy, said recently, "For years, America has been holding an arms race with itself."

The War Blows Hot and Cold

Since 1945, American perceptions of the Soviet Union have been determined largely by internal domestic affairs, often divorced from the reality of international events. The intensity of the Cold War has fluctuated ever since 1945.

The period 1945 to 1952 was one of intense Cold War rivalry. President Truman, not well versed in international affairs, was open to manipulation. Harry Hopkins, a trusted adviser, was sent by Truman to Moscow in 1945 and found Stalin to be a reasonable man, interested in cooperation and even willing to compromise on Poland. James Byrnes, Secretary of State, while in Moscow in late 1945, negotiated a compromise with Stalin over Eastern Europe, and won agreement for a U.N. Atomic Energy Commission. Diplomacy with Russia was obviously possible.

But a faction of old hard-liners in the State Department who were notoriously pompous, anti-Semitic, tolerant of Hitler and ultrareactionary, persuaded Truman to adopt a hard-line posture toward the Soviet Union. Their attitude was reinforced by some liberals in labor unions who sought to gain respectability against some of their more radical opponents, and by those liberal politicians who saw a strong anti-Soviet stand as an opportunity to placate more conservative politicians. In addition, an adversarial posture toward Russia promulgated high military budgets, which were thought to be conducive to postwar economic recovery. All these factors combined to create an ideological offensive against the Soviet Union.

Between the years 1952 and 1957, the American people elected a President who was more moderate in his interpretation of the Soviet threat. Eisenhower was also fiscally conservative and was not prone to vast increases in weapons expenditures. Although John Foster Dulles, Secretary of State, was a zealous anti-Communist, he seemed more hostile to the Chinese than to the Russians. By mid-1958, he became more flexible as he explored partial American military disengagement in Europe and seemed to endorse reduction of tensions with the Russians.

From 1957 to 1963 the American right wing mobilized because it was increasingly frustrated by Eisenhower's policies. Its "Gaither Report" described a fallacious missile gap between the United States and the USSR. Former Army Chief of Staff Maxwell Taylor wrote a book, *Uncertain Trumpet*, calling for a buildup of conventional arms, and Henry Kissinger produced a study advocating limited nuclear war. Ambitious Democratic presidential contenders who were attracted to this anti-Soviet rhetoric were Stuart Symington, John Kennedy, Lyndon Johnson, and Hubert Humphrey. They used it to criticize Eisenhower's complacency. Upon his election, President Kennedy increased the defense budget, supported the Special Forces, encouraged insurgency warfare around the world, and intimated he would welcome a confrontation with the Soviet Union. He was assisted by the verbally belligerent Nikita Khrushchev, who sought to maintain control over Eastern Europe and attempted to curry favor with newly independent nations in the Third World. But Russia was far behind in military strength.

After the Cuban missile crisis, Kennedy did reach out toward the Soviet Union and negotiated a partial test-ban treaty. But both Kennedy and Johnson were determined not to be seen by the American right wing as "soft on Communism," so they escalated a nationalistic struggle in Vietnam into a major confrontation with China and Russia, which was not welcomed by either country. China is an old enemy of Vietnam, and Russia did everything it could to bring the war to an end. The Soviets also negotiated SALT I and the ABM Treaty during this terribly traumatic time, even as America secretly bombed Cambodia, breaking international law.

From 1968 to 1978 Nixon and Ford were more secure domestically in their anti-Communist stance and therefore less inclined to play the domestic anti-Soviet line. They were pragmatic about international big-power politics, and they recognized China and established détente with the Soviet Union. During this era, the defense budget, as a percentage of the GNP, fell. Tensions between the superpowers relaxed.

Then from 1978 on, during the Carter administration, the Committee on the Present Danger mobilized to counteract the effects of détente—again influencing a liberal Democratic administration to develop hard-line anti-Soviet policies. President Reagan, contrary to most previous Republican administrations, has continued and even exaggerated the anti-Soviet stand.

The Reality of the Soviet Threat

The Soviet "menace" has been used by Democratic administrations since 1945 to bolster their more progressive domestic policies and to support themselves against attack from right-wing Republicans who disapprove of liberal social programs. Thus the Soviet threat has assumed a magical political quality that placates the right wing and allows liberals to be liberal at home. It has also been used extensively by the armed forces to promote interservice rivalry and by the military-industrial complex to support military and economic growth.

So successful was this self-fulfilling enemy image that between 1949 and 1968 not a single military appropriations bill was denied in the House or Senate.

In 1950, the United States had 300 nuclear bombs on 300 airplanes—the only nuclear weapons in the world. By 1953, the United States had several thousand nuclear weapons and the USSR 300.

In 1955, at the Soviet Air Show, the Russians repeatedly

flew 10 Bear bombers past the reviewing stand. Because of this trick, American officials thought Russia had many more planes than they actually had, and estimated they could build 600 by the year 1957. In response to this misperception, the United States expanded its bomber force to 600 B-52s and 1,400 B-47s. In fact, the Soviet Union has never had more than 150 long-range bombers.

By 1960, the Soviet Union had acquired the means to deliver nuclear weapons to the United States. It had 150 intercontinental bombers and 500 short-range bombers that could reach Western Europe. It also had about 10 intercontinental ballistic missiles (ICBMs). At the same time, President Kennedy campaigned in 1960 on a fictitious missile gap, claiming that the Soviet Union had many more nuclear weapons and missiles than did the United States. Consequently, by 1962, although the USSR had 50 to 100 ICBMs and fewer than 200 long-range bombers, America had built 50 ICBMs, 80 submarine-based Polaris missiles, 90 Thor and Jupiter nuclear missiles placed in Europe, 1,700 long-range bombers, and 300 carrier-based and about 1,000 supersonic land-based fighters, all carrying nuclear weapons.

Despite the fact that President Kennedy learned from a spy satellite soon after his election that the missile gap was fallacious, in 1963 the Defense Department decided to build 1,000 new intercontinental missiles called Minutemen, 650 submarine-launched Polaris missiles, and more than 1,000 long-range bombers. At this time, the Russians had fewer than 150 long-range bombers and 300 intercontinental ballistic missiles.

The arms race has continued in this fashion until the present time. The chart on page 68 illustrates that on only three occasions has the Soviet Union surpassed the United States in nuclear weapons developments, one of which—the antiballistic missile system—did not work.

So, between 1960 and 1967, the main force of the invulnerable U.S. missiles was deployed both on land and at sea in the submarines. At that time, the Soviet Union was relying only on its few intercontinental bombers and about 300 vulnerable intercontinental ballistic missiles. However, in 1965, partly as a response to the Cuban missile crisis, the Soviet Union began developing missiles that were placed in reinforced-steel underground silos that were invulnerable in the event of a large-scale nuclear war. Over the period from 1965 to 1971, the Soviet Union deployed 1,400 intercontinental ballistic missiles in hardened silos and began deploying submarine-based missiles within range of the United States—62 strategic submarines between 1967 and 1977. It has only been within the last fifteen years or so that United States cities have become vulnerable to a Russian missile strike that could take place within thirty minutes after launching. This is because the United States failed to stop the arms race in 1960, when it started deploying its first intercontinental ballistic missiles.

By 1970, around the time of the SALT I negotiations, America had learned to MIRV its missiles. *MIRV* stands for multiple independently targetable reentry vehicles—a vehicle is a hydrogen bomb, and several hydrogen bombs were placed within each missile, each capable of landing separately on a different target. This greatly increased the number of nuclear weapons that the United States could deliver on the Soviet Union. Because only America knew how to MIRV, MIRVing was not outlawed during the SALT I negotiations. Although it is frequently claimed that the Soviet Union had

Action	Initiated by	Date	Reaction by	Date
Sustained nuclear chain reaction	U.S.	1942	U.S.S.R.	1946
Atomic bomb	U.S.	1945	U.S.S.R.	1949
Intercontinental bomber	U.S.	1948	U.S.S.R.	1955
International military pact (U.S. NATO: U.S.S.R. Warsaw Pact)	U.S.	1949	U.S.S.R.	1955
Tactical nuclear weapons deployed in Europe	U.S.	1954	U.S.S.R.	1957
Nuclear powered submarine	U.S.	1955	U.S.S.R.	1959
ICBM	U.S.S.R.	1957	U.S.	1958
Satellite launching	U.S.S.R	1957	U.S.	1958
Supersonic bomber	U.S.	1960	U.S.S.R.	1975
Submarine-launched ballistic missile	U.S.	1960	U.S.S.R.	1968
Solid fuel missiles	U.S.	1960	U.S.S.R.	1968
Accelerated ICBM build-up	U.S.	1961	U.S.S.R.	1966
Multiple reentry vehicles (MRVs)	U.S.	1964	U.S.S.R.	1968
Penetration aids on missiles	U.S.	1964	U.S.S.R.	none yet
ABM system	U.S.S.R.	1968	U.S.	1972
High-speed warheads	U.S.	1970	U.S.S.R.	1975
MIRVs	U.S.	1970	U.S.S.R.	1975
Computerized missile guidance	U.S.	1970	U.S.S.R.	1975
Neutron bombs	U.S.	1981	U.S.S.R.	none yet
Long-range cruise missiles	U.S.	198?	U.S.S.R.	none yet

surpassed the United States in the arms race during the seventies, actually the reverse is true. During this time, the United States added 5,250 warheads to its missiles, and the Soviet Union, only beginning to MIRV in 1975, added 4,560. The Soviets have finished MIRVing their land-based missiles but will only complete MIRVing the submarine missiles by 1985.

During the 1960s, Theodore Taylor, a brilliant physicist, developed a method of miniaturizing nuclear weapons. As a result, the United States decided to nuclearize all forms of conventional weapons—torpedoes, land mines, surface-to-surface and surface-to-air missiles—even small nuclear weapons in artillery casings (called Davy Crocketts) that men could carry on their shoulders. And from 1950 to the present, large numbers of tactical nuclear weapons (weapons used in local battlefield conditions as opposed to intercontinental strategic weapons on rockets) were deployed throughout the world. It was decided in the fifties that it was cheaper to deploy nuclear weapons than troops in Europe. Consequently, there are approximately 6,000 short-range tactical nuclear weapons deployed in West Germany very close to the border of East Germany. Because they are so close to the front line, should Russia invade West Germany, military doctrine prescribes: Use 'em or lose 'em. In fact, NATO doctrine has for many years included a policy of first use. If NATO is losing a conventional war with the Soviet Union, it will use tactical nuclear weapons first to stop invading Soviet tanks, the theory being that Russia would not be so crazy as to retaliate with a nuclear weapon and start nuclear war. To quote Morton Halperin, former Assistant Secretary of Defense, "The NATO doctrine is that we will fight with conventional forces until we are losing, then we will fight with tactical nuclear weapons until we are losing, and then we will blow up the world." Soviet policy is exactly the reverse. It claims it will not be the first to use nuclear weapons, but should one be used against it, it will retaliate with its whole arsenal.

Over the years, Cold War politics and enemy image have been used to justify the momentum of the nuclear arms race, which was partly engendered by the sweet technological problems inherent in designing nuclear weapons and delivery systems, by the huge amount of money involved, which was transferred from the people's taxes to government grants and private industrial corporations, and by private and public scientific research and development labs. Sir Solly Zuckerman, a British scientist who was involved in the Manhattan Project, identifies scientists as the driving force behind the arms race. Politicians obviously used the Communist menace to enhance their political prestige and power, and historically at every election and at appropriations time for nuclear weapons, the Russian menace has been dragged out of the closet to justify either personal or political ambitions or new weapons development.

A parallel dynamic that has always operated is the interservice rivalry between army, navy, and air force.

Relationships between the superpowers are now almost totally controlled by military thinking—political considerations have in effect ceased to exist. Consequently, the Pentagon and the Secretary of Defense seem to determine the direction of international affairs. Just as the weapons are invented, so political doctrines and rationales for their use are devised. Political thinking always lags five to ten years behind scientific development. In a way, politicians are almost innocent bystanders as they watch the mad technological momentum emanating from the minds of the scientists, who always assume the worst possible case for Russian motivations and weapons developments. Over the years, the strategic doctrine of American nuclear thinking has changed to accommodate the new weapons systems.

The Collapse of Détente*

The Cold War came to an end as détente was established by a hawkish Republican president in the early 1970s. President Nixon and his Secretary of State, Henry Kissinger, also established diplomatic relationships with China, a long-time bitter enemy.

Nixon moved to end the Cold War with the Soviet Union soon after his inauguration in 1969. SALT I was negotiated with the Soviet Union and ratified in 1972, together with the Anti-Ballistic Missile Treaty at the Moscow Summit in 1972. As has been mentioned, the United States had just

---

*Information for this section was taken from *Russian Roulette* by Arthur Macy Cox, and from *With Enough Shovels* by Robert Scheer.

learned to MIRV missiles, and because the Russians could not do it, it was decided that MIRVing should not be included in the SALT I treaty. The United States continued to increase its arsenal of nuclear warheads by MIRVing its missiles, and the Soviet Union began to catch up only when it learned to MIRV in 1975. This situation has created an enormous bilateral momentum in the arms race, and Kissinger has said that he lived to rue the day that MIRVing was not outlawed in SALT I.

Following Nixon's resignation, President Gerald Ford and General Secretary Leonid Brezhnev met in Vladivostok in November 1974 to establish, for the first time, a limit on all strategic weapons systems, which would extend for ten years. At that time, Russia agreed that it would not include in the strategic balance French and British strategic forces or U.S. medium-range nuclear bombers (or forward-based systems) in Europe and Asia. This was a quid pro quo for Russia's being awarded Most Favored Nation status in U.S. trade. But Senator Henry "Scoop" Jackson, Democrat from Washington and one of the most powerful men in the U.S. Senate in military affairs and national security, disapproved of the SALT I treaty and falsely suggested that it gave the Soviet Union a strategic advantage. He moved quickly to destroy the pending U.S.–Soviet trade bill by attaching the Jackson–Vanick Amendment to the bill. The amendment called for withholding Most Favored Nation status from the Soviet Union unless it granted the right of emigration to its Jewish citizens. In December 1974, Congress was persuaded by Jackson and his young staffer Richard Perle to vote for the amendment. The Soviet Union immediately rejected the amendment because it said it would not submit in its internal affairs to manipulation and humiliation by the United States. Subsequently, Jewish emigration fell from 35,000 to less than 10,000 per year, and Russia lost the trade bill it so desperately desired. And in response to the U.S. forward-based systems and the British and French strategic forces, the Soviet Union announced that it would modernize its medium-range SS-4 and SS-5 missiles targeted on Europe. This Jackson–Vanick Amendment remains a source of friction between the superpowers to this day. Senator Jackson was a longtime advocate of both U.S. military superiority and the Boeing Corporation, which manufactures the B-52 bomber, the Minuteman missile, the cruise missile, and the Trident submarine. Only by establishing good trade relationships with the Soviet Union can the United States ever hope to defuse tensions between the superpowers.

During the years of détente a group of neo-Conservative Democrats, the Coalition for a Democratic Majority, always rejected the détente concept. They were hawks who preferred to compete with Russia by building more hydrogen bombs and missiles, rather than by reducing tensions and weapons. Among them were Henry Jackson, Daniel Patrick Moynihan, Ben Wattenberg, Eugene Rostow, Norman Podhoretz (editor of *Commentary*), and Irving Kristol (editor of *The Public Interest*).

President Ford's Secretary of Defense, James Schlesinger, was another hawk who had been highly critical of SALT I because it gave the Russians greater "throw weight." He said that because the Russian missiles were bigger and heavier than those of the United States, the Russians' were superior. But the United States has always chosen to build smaller, more accurate missiles than the Soviet Union, because accuracy increases killing power and because, at that time, America was far advanced in MIRVing. A Schlesinger report to Congress in 1974 audaciously compared the American military arsenal—the most lethal in history—to that of impotent Britain in the thirties, and used Neville Chamberlain, with his pathetic performance in Munich, as an example of appeasement which the United States might have to follow in dealing with the Soviet Union. This totally inappropriate position became a regular theme song of the hawks during the seventies and into the Reagan presidency.

In November 1975, when George Bush, with no previous intelligence experience, was appointed head of the CIA, the hawks saw their chance. Bush quickly appointed a hand-picked committee called "Team B" to compare U.S.–Soviet military spending—although the CIA already had "Team A," a group of professional intelligence officers who were paid to work on this question in an unbiased way. Team B was stacked with hawks, all of whom are now appointees in the Reagan administration. The committee was chaired by Richard Pipes, a Polish immigrant and a professor of eighteenth-century Russian history at Harvard, later to be Soviet specialist on the Reagan National Security Council, and a notorious

Soviet hard-liner. Other members were Paul Nitze, now chief of the U.S. delegation to talks on intermediate range nuclear weapons in Geneva (which were ended in December 1983 by a Soviet walkout); William R. van Cleave, later head of the Reagan Transition Team for the Department of Defense; Paul D. Wolfowitz, now chief of policy planning in the State Department; Seymour Weiss; Daniel O. Graham, retired army lieutenant general and former director of the Defense Intelligence Agency, now serving on a National Strategy Committee of the American Security Council, a private lobby advocating increased defense spending and Cold War policies; Foy D. Kohler, a think-tank associate of General Graham; Thomas Wolfe, a specialist on Soviet military affairs at the RAND Corporation, a think tank substantially funded by the U.S. Air Force; John W. Vogt, Jr., retired air force general; and Jasper A. Welch, Jr., air force brigadier general, assistant chief of staff, who has helped prepare SALT positions for the Joint Chiefs of Staff.

The team used new evidence and a reinterpretation of old information to produce a revised estimate of Soviet military spending, which was published in October 1976. The still-classified report showed that Soviet military spending, as a percentage of gross national product, had increased from between 6 percent to 8 percent to between 11 percent to 13 percent, while the United States was at 6 percent. This "increased spending" was apparently overwhelming proof for Team B that Russia was ahead in the strategic nuclear race.

It is important here to understand how the CIA had been estimating Soviet military spending. For example, the United States captures a Soviet tank and gives it to Chrysler to estimate how much it would cost to build such a tank. Of course, such U.S. estimates are totally meaningless in ruble values. The CIA also estimates Soviet military pay as equivalent to American military pay, although Russia pays its soldiers a mere pittance compared to what American soldiers receive. That means every time the American military receives a pay raise, estimates of Soviet military spending increase.

What the new estimates really showed was that an error had been allowed to stand for years in previous CIA estimates and that, in fact, the Russians were far less efficient at producing weapons than had previously been thought. (America has known for years the size of the USSR conventional and nuclear arsenals.) In order to place these new figures in perspective, it is necessary to understand that the Soviet gross national product is half that of the United States. Consequently, Soviet–American expenditure levels are approximately equal, allowing for all contingencies I have just discussed. And no mention was made of NATO–Warsaw Pact spending. For example, in 1971 and 1972 the NATO allies outspent the Soviets' Eastern European allies by five to one.

The Team B report, which is still classified, concluded that Russia had rejected the notion of parity and mutually assured destruction (MAD) and was aiming instead for nuclear superiority. This erroneous conclusion was derived solely from the false estimate of increased defense spending. (Another conclusion reached by the Team B people was that the Soviet Union expected not only to survive but to win a nuclear war.)

According to General Daniel Graham, a Team B spokesman, in order to fight and win a nuclear war, one needs adequate civil defense. Studies on Soviet civil defense had been performed by T. K. Jones, now Deputy Under Secretary of Defense for Research and Engineering, Strategic and Nuclear Forces, in the Reagan administration. Before he worked in the Defense Department, he was employed at Boeing and had extensively studied the Soviet civil-defense manuals, which enthusiastically suggested twenty to thirty designs for digging holes in the ground where people could shelter from nuclear attack. One design advocated digging a hole for one person and covering it with two doors and three feet of dirt. T. K. Jones had also practiced covering factory machinery with dirt and then detonating large TNT explosions above the machinery. From these experiments he had deduced that the Russians could protect much of their industrial plant from the effects of nuclear war. T. K. (as he likes to be called) also estimated Soviet nuclear war casualties by theoretically spacing the Russian people equidistant from one another over the whole Soviet subcontinent and then dropping bombs on the selected military and civilian targets. These data have been interpreted by Richard Pipes to mean that the Russian civil-defense program would permit "acceptable" casualties of about 20 million, which, as he likes to point out, is similar to the numbers of their dead in World War II. He concluded that because this had happened before, they could well tolerate a repeat scenario in a nuclear war. Pipes estimates the current probability of nuclear war as 40 percent. (Jones estimates that recovery from nuclear war could occur within about four years.)

The whole Reagan nuclear rearmament program is based upon the assumptions of Team B and T. K. Jones. This is why the President repeats again and again that the Soviet Union has engaged in a massive military buildup over the last decade, that they are preparing to fight and win a nuclear war, and that we have to catch up.

The Team A–Team B process was to end in February 1977, but when Jimmy Carter was elected President in 1976, the Team B report was leaked to the *Boston Globe*. George Bush, head of the CIA, in an unprecedented interview with *The New York Times*, said the Soviet military buildup was much greater than previously had been assumed by the CIA. (Former CIA directors had always refused to be interviewed by the press concerning top-secret national intelligence reports.) Herbert Scoville, Jr., a former CIA deputy director for science and technology, said, "I think this whole thing was clearly an attempt to leave a legacy for the new Administration, which would be very hard to reverse. . . . Now that the integrity of the estimating process has been questioned, it is extremely difficult for the CIA regulars to stand up to the pressure of a biased point of view when the people at the top want to prove something."

The Committee on the Present Danger

In 1976, Secretary of State Henry Kissinger found himself surrounded by tough, dedicated hawks in the Pentagon, in the Arms Control and Disarmament Agency (ACDA), and in the Senate Armed Services Committee. Some of the hawks were Henry Jackson, his assistant Richard Perle, Paul Nitze, Eugene Rostow, Fred Ikle, director of ACDA, and John Lehman, deputy director of ACDA. Because James Schlesinger, former Secretary of Defense, was working with Henry Jackson to destroy the SALT II concept based on the Vladivostok agreement, President Ford fired Schlesinger.

After his dismissal, Schlesinger met with Eugene Rostow and Paul Nitze, and together they decided that a private national committee was needed to influence public opinion about the "danger" of détente and the need to increase U.S. military power. Thus, the Committee on the Present Danger was born at a luncheon at the Metropolitan Club in Washington in March 1976. The main leaders of the committee were Paul Nitze and Eugene Rostow (Rostow was later appointed head of the Arms Control and Disarmament Agency by President Reagan). Both were old-time hawks. Nitze's involvement with these issues began in 1950, when he drafted a document, NSC-68, commissioned by the Department of Defense and Department of State. This report contrasted the "Soviet desire for world domination with the U.S. desire for an environment in which free societies could exist and flourish." It compared Russian global intentions to the totalitarianism and aggressiveness of Nazi Germany, even though they were different social systems in different historical periods. NSC-68 was never officially adopted by the Truman administration, but it is generally regarded as a crucial turning point in American policy because it provided a rationale for two major transformations. It called for programs that would triple the defense budget, and it gave the American people a special interpretation of the Soviet threat. Paul Nitze also was a most influential member of the Gaither Committee, established in 1957 by President Dwight D. Eisenhower. This group's report concluded that by 1959 the Soviets would have a sufficient ICBM force to destroy the U.S. strategic bombers—this claim that the Soviets would win the race was known as the fictitious missile gap. Nitze also said during the Berlin Blockade in 1959 that the United States should evacuate its cities and put the Strategic Air Command on full alert.

Many of the people on the Committee on the Present Danger were transferred into the Reagan administration after his election. They were all strident critics of SALT II, and they defeated this agreement. Some of the members of the committee were: Henry Fowler, former Secretary of the Treasury under Johnson; Lane Kirkland, president of the AFL–CIO; David Packard, former Deputy Secretary of Defense under Nixon; Paul Nitze, negotiator for intermediate nuclear forces in Europe; Eugene Rostow, former head of the Arms Control and Disarmament Agency; Richard Allen, former National Security Adviser to President Reagan; Richard Pipes, former Adviser on Soviet Affairs to President Reagan; Jeffrey

Kemp of the National Security Council; Fred Ikle, Under
secretary of Defense for Policy, and his deputy, R. G. Stillwell;
Richard Perle, Assistant Secretary of Defense for International Security Policy; William van Cleave from the General
Advisory Committee; William Casey, head of the CIA; John
Lehman, Secretary of the Navy; Jeane Kirkpatrick, Ambassador to the United Nations; Colin Gray, Arms Control Agency
Advisory Committee; George Shultz, Secretary of State and a
founding member of the Committee on the Present Danger;
and W. Allen Wallis, top assistant to Secretary Shultz.

After President Carter was elected, in the spirit of unity,
he attempted to bring the right and left factions of the Demo-
ratic party together. In trying to placate Henry Jackson, he
was persuaded to send a proposal to the Soviet Union in 1977
that undermined the Vladivostok–SALT II agreement. Cy-
us Vance, Secretary of State, delivered the proposal to the
Soviet Union. It was grossly inequitable and called for deep
cuts in the Soviet ICBM forces (70 percent of its strategic
nuclear weapons are land-based ICBMs) and did not call for
deep cuts in strategic bombers and submarine missiles, where
the United States had a clear advantage. It also called for a
ban on Soviet Backfire bombers, which the Pentagon had
previously classified as medium-range and had not included
in the SALT II agreement. This new proposal reclassified
them as long-range strategic bombers. America now claimed
the Backfire could reach the United States from the Soviet
Union, although it was known that the Backfire could not
return to Russia because it only had enough fuel to fly one
way. The new proposal also allowed the United States to
continue developing cruise missiles. Both of these new conditions contradicted the Vladivostok proposals. William Hyland,
one of Kissinger's staff, said that he knew the Soviets would
never accept such an unfair proposal. Brezhnev was very
disturbed by this overtly unilateral proposal and rejected it.

President Carter was personally deeply committed to
eliminating nuclear weapons. During his term in office, he
frequently called for détente and a reduction of nuclear weapons combined with a ban on direct or indirect military intervention in the world, a freeze on further modernization of
weapons, and a comprehensive test-ban treaty. Indeed, in his
inaugural address, he called for elimination of all nuclear
weapons.

But unfortunately, during the Carter presidency, th
Soviets made détente and Carter's commitments difficult b
airlifting Cuban troops to Angola and Ethiopia (these Cuba
troops support and protect Gulf Oil facilities in Angola); b
supporting intervention in South Yemen and the invasion c
Cambodia by Vietnam; and, finally, by invading Afghanistan
Of course, the Committee on the Present Danger capitalize
on these actions.

All these events should, in fact, have spurred America t
negotiate even harder with the Soviet Union, for throughou
this time Brezhnev was promoting a freeze on further mod
ernization and a complete test-ban treaty. Indeed, in Jul
1980, the Russians agreed to on-site inspection during negoti
ations on the complete test-ban treaty.

But the U.S. hawks were not at all in favor of a freeze o
a complete test-ban treaty and wished to continue buildin
the MX, Trident II missiles, cruise missiles, Pershing I
missiles, and the strategic B-1 and stealth bombers. The
believed in the exotic fantasy put forth by Team B—that th
Soviets were planning to fight and win a nuclear war and tha
the only way we could prevent this was to regain America
nuclear "superiority." (Throughout the SALT II negotiations
however, and even now, it is agreed by both superpower
that there is at present strategic parity or equality.)

Throughout the Carter administration, the Committe
on the Present Danger and another like-minded think tan
called the American Security Council, propagandized thei
new doctrines of: (1) a huge buildup of Soviet military power
(2) the Soviet drive for world conquest, and (3) the Sovie
doctrine of fighting and winning a nuclear war.

The American Security Council boasted a national mem
bership of 230,000 and formed a coalition called Peace Throug
Strength, to which 42 percent of the elected members of th
House and Senate belonged. This council then produce
several films that were frightening depictions of Soviet mili
tary strength, full of lies and half-truths, one of which, *Th
Price of Peace and Freedom*, was shown on two hundred loca
TV stations and viewed by fifty million Americans. One of th
arguments presented was that the Soviets never abide b
their treaties. In fact, there have been sixteen treaties o
nuclear weapons negotiated between the Soviet Union an
the United States. Despite alleged infringements on bot

sides, there have been no proven substantial violations by either party. The American Security Council was and is funded by millions of dollars—from private individuals, military-industrial corporations, and others. This film and others it has produced influenced millions of Americans to change their mind about détente late in the seventies. The common refrain from many well-intentioned people was now: "But you can't trust the Russians" and "The Russians are ahead." Even intelligent and moderately well-informed journalists and TV and radio interviewers were convinced by this brilliant propaganda exercise.

President Carter, unfortunately, lost his way on nuclear weapons, as he accepted advice from "Scoop" Jackson and his National Security Adviser, Zbigniew Brzezinski, who briefed him every day on world affairs. He was also obviously influenced by the pressure exerted by the Committee on the Present Danger. Cyrus Vance and Paul Warnke eventually left the administration in disgust. The hawks worked hand in hand with Brzezinski, who worked closely with Richard Burt, a *New York Times* reporter and a well-known Washington hawk, and past assistant director of the Institute for Strategic Studies in London. Burt frequently wrote stories that were fed to him straight from the Pentagon, with little or no critical journalistic comment or search for the truth. Once I called him after he produced a verbatim report on the meeting of the Committee on the Present Danger. I told him the data in his article were biased and untrue, and he replied, "Madam, when you have a similar meeting, we will report that." So Physicians for Social Responsibility organized a conference in New York on the medical consequences of nuclear war, using Cyrus Vance as a moderator. Vance had just resigned as Secretary of State and spoke movingly about his concerns of nuclear war. Neither Mr. Burt nor *The New York Times* covered this unique event. However, it was attended by Jonathan Schell, who afterward wrote his book *The Fate of the Earth*. Mr. Burt is now Assistant Secretary of Defense for President Reagan. During the five days preceding the Reagan election, *The New York Times* published five full-page articles by Burt about the antiquated, rusting, useless U.S. military force. These articles, I am sure, played some part in Reagan's victory.

In 1978, President Carter and Chairman Brezhnev signed

the SALT II treaty in Vienna. But during the subsequent SALT hearings before the Senate Foreign Relations Committee, Senator Frank Church "discovered" the Soviet troop brigade in Cuba. The CIA later admitted that these troops had been in place since 1962, but the atmosphere in the Senate became so charged with emotion that Church had sounded the death knell of SALT II. Soon thereafter, Russia invaded Afghanistan following the tortuous year of the Iranian hostage crisis, and the American public, almost in relief, immediately transferred its frustration and anger from Iran onto the reliable and time-trusted enemy Russia. SALT II was over. It was never ratified by the United States Senate. The hawks had won.

The European Factor

At the same time that SALT II was born and died, other events were occurring. Between the years 1969 and 1972, Willy Brandt, in West Germany, developed a policy of Ostpolitik. As a result of this policy, a nonaggression pact was initiated and signed between West Germany and the Soviet Union; West Germany recognized East Germany as a separate state; West Germany established diplomatic relations with Poland and Czechoslovakia; and a four-power agreement was signed in Berlin. This reduced East–West tension enormously, and the West German fear of a Soviet invasion virtually disappeared.

As these events took place, Senator Mike Mansfield, sensing the atmosphere of reduced tension in West Germany, advised that the number of U.S. troops be reduced in West Germany. This suggestion, however, badly frightened the Russians, who saw the void thus created being filled by a buildup of German soldiers. Haunted by the memories of twenty million World War II dead, they initiated talks on Mutual and Balanced Force Reductions, insisting that together with Soviet and U.S. troop reductions, German troops must also be reduced; but for various technical reasons the negotiations have never borne fruit.

Instead, the U.S. forces mysteriously were strengthened, and the U.S. contribution to NATO increased to $80 million per year. In order to justify the buildup of troops and money, America issued warnings of a Soviet blitzkrieg—although at no time during the Cold War has Russia ever indicated that it would risk nuclear holocaust by invading West Germany.

During these years, American scientists had developed the neutron bomb (a modified hydrogen bomb), which killed people with intense radiation while producing a smaller blast effect than an ordinary hydrogen bomb. The radiation would be used to penetrate and stop Russian tanks, which were expected to be used in a blitzkrieg on West Germany. Helmut Schmidt was persuaded by the United States to accept the bomb, much to his discomfort, and revulsion was exhibited by an outraged European public. The neutron bomb is considered by the U.S. and NATO military officials as a usable first step if conventional battle lines fail. It therefore must be considered a possible trigger for nuclear war.

Schmidt was also troubled in 1977 by some of his advisers, and some American strategic weapons experts who were in Bonn at the time, who told him that he could no longer rely on American support for German security. One of these Americans was Fred Ikle, the present Under Secretary of Defense for Policy.

So in October 1977, Schmidt countered these U.S. threats and innuendos by delivering a speech at the International Institute for Strategic Studies in London, where in the context of the modernization and replacement by Russia of its twenty-year-old intermediate range SS-4 and SS-5 missiles by SS-20 missiles, he suggested that the West rectify the nuclear balance in Europe.

The NATO high command met this request in mid-1978 by recommending NATO deployment of long-range missiles in Europe that could strike at the Soviet Union. There was consternation in Germany that this move could threaten détente, which had enabled millions of East and West Germans to visit and call each other more frequently than in the previous decade, and had allowed West German exports to Eastern Bloc countries to triple.

In September 1979, Kissinger gave a speech in Brussels, announcing that Europe should no longer rely on the U.S. strategic umbrella because the United States would not risk destruction of its civilization to protect Western Europe. Therefore, America had to develop the capability to fight small-theater nuclear wars, implying that a U.S.–Soviet nuclear war could be fought on European–Soviet ground, excluding American territorial involvement. This scared the hell out of the Europeans. He left out the obvious facts that such missiles would be U.S.-controlled and that Russia would obviously retaliate against the United States should they be used.

Schmidt then recommended that other NATO nations, not just West Germany, accept these new American missiles. These nations were Italy, Holland, Belgium, and England. The missiles chosen, cruise and Pershing II, were very controversial during the SALT II negotiations, and so were put under temporary control in a protocol to SALT II, which was to last until December 31, 1981.

On October 6, 1979, Chairman Brezhnev, speaking in East Berlin, announced that the Soviet Union would dismantle an unspecified number of its medium-range missiles in Europe and remove 1,000 tanks and one Soviet division from East Germany if NATO would agree to forgo its decision to deploy new missiles in Europe and would enter into immediate negotiations with Russia. Brzezinski immediately dismissed the proposal as propaganda, although Brezhnev indeed carried through with his promise and removed the troops and tanks. A few months later, Brezhnev also offered to freeze all further deployment of SS-20s in return for negotiations. This offer was also rejected.

On December 12, 1979, a two-track decision was made to deploy a total of 464 ground-launched cruise missiles and 108 Pershing II missiles. (These are both first-strike weapons and part of the new war-fighting strategy; the ground-launched cruise missiles signal the end of arms control agreements and the Pershing IIs signal the beginning of launch-on-warning systems.) The cruise missiles were to be distributed in the countries previously listed, but the 108 Pershing II missiles would be placed only in West Germany. The deployment of the missiles was made contingent on ongoing arms-control talks. The Americans also promised to remove from Europe 1,000 of the 7,000 old tactical nuclear weapons already deployed. This was done in 1980.

The NATO decision sparked a fear in Europe that had been latent for the first thirty-five years of the nuclear age. Somehow, Europeans had been content to feel secure under the nuclear umbrella, but they now realized that the United States was probably ready to fight its nuclear war in the

European theater. This fear was compounded by well-publicized pronouncements by Reagan administration officials that America could fight and win a nuclear war. The President himself announced that nuclear war could be fought in Europe without pressing the button. It was obvious to the European public that there were no moderates in this new government, only hard-line hawks who hated the Russians and who agreed with the President when he said that the Russians reserve the right to lie, cheat, and clearly steal, and are the forces of evil in the modern world. The U.S. defense budget also signaled planned spending of $1.5 trillion over the next five years to build up a nuclear arsenal designed to fight and "win" a nuclear war.

The European public erupted with anger and indignation in 1981 and 1982. Huge marches were organized in most capital cities, and governments crumbled under the political pressures exerted by their people.

President Carter left office as he had entered: warning about the threat of nuclear war. In his inaugural address, he had said he wished to eliminate nuclear weapons from the face of the earth, and in his farewell speech, he said that a nuclear war would last a long afternoon with the equivalent of a World War II every second. He was a good man, but misguided and misled, and not strong enough to avoid being outmaneuvered by the hawks—a handful of hostile men who had gained enormous power in a political vacuum created by the lack of knowledge and widespread apathy of the vast American electorate. This situation must be reversed.

Germs of Conflict:
The Third World

President Reagan keeps talking about Soviet expansionism throughout the world. At the time of this writing, there are 161 nations in the world. The United States has supplied weapons to 130, and the Soviet Union has significant influence in 19. In fact, 1958 was the high point in global Soviet influence. At that time, 31 percent of the world's population and 9 percent of the world's gross national product—outside the Soviet Union—were under Soviet influence. But by 1970, Russia influenced only 6 percent of the world's population and 5 percent of the gross national product. Since the sixties, it had "lost" China, Egypt, India, Indonesia, and Iraq. The only time it has used large numbers of Soviet troops outside its own territory, excluding the Warsaw Pact nations, has been in Afghanistan.

Because Americans display such a revulsion toward Russian international and internal policies, it is important that Americans understand not only their own early history but also their more recent history. Frequently the American press has misrepresented events in foreign countries, so that it has been difficult for the American public to know the truth about international affairs. Incorrect or adulterated reporting has had a serious effect upon American public opinion, which in turn has often distorted American foreign policy. As we have seen, this happened with Germany in the 1930s and with China in the 1940s.

Recent U.S. Interventions in Latin America

In the name of the Monroe Doctrine, terrible events have occurred in Central and South America. Since the 1917

Russian revolution, movements for self-determination in Latin America have usually been labeled "Communist," and so any U.S. intervention is justified in the name of anti-Communism. To maintain its economic power, the United States trains client military personnel at some 150 bases and training schools and sends mobile units and advisers to serve on an in-country basis. This training has placed great weight on ideological conditioning. In addition to the ideological cement of this (dogmatically anti-Communist) world view, U.S. military training has purposefully helped build a network of personal relationships between the United States and Latin American military cadres. This tie has been further consolidated by military aid from the wealthier power, as well as by cooperative maneuvers and logistical training. Over 200,000 Latin American military personnel have been trained in the United States, and since 1949, over 35,000 Latin American officers have trained in the School for the Americas alone, a school identified in Latin America by its historic function as the "school of coups." Thus, the United States has exercised enormous influence in the military organizations of these client states.

An integral part of the U.S. military establishment is the CIA. It operates clandestinely, so a large portion of its activities are unknown to the public. The total number of cases of CIA involvement in active subversion of established governments (and attempts at political murder) run into the hundreds or even thousands. For example, in Brazil in 1964, "the CIA was able to bribe its journalists, subsidize its politicians, conspire with military factions, infiltrate and subvert the labor movement, and engage in extensive propaganda campaigns—in short, it could virtually disregard the sovereignty of this large and theoretically independent country. The catch, of course, is that Brazil was not an independent country—U.S. penetration was already enormous by the 1960's. . . . The Brazilian military and much of its economy were already 'denationalized' with strong ties and dependency relations to the United States; and U.S. business had a substantial presence in Brazil. . . . It was hard to separate U.S. business and CIA activities in Brazil before 1964." CIA intervention in Brazil occurred with "weapons on a huge scale, together with bribery, black propaganda, and practically open conspiracy with military officers, and massive institutional subversion." This was a prime factor in the military coup in Brazil in 1964.

Another power that is used by the United States for covert activity in other countries is the U.S. National Security Agency. It employs 40,000 military and 50,000 civilian personnel, and it deploys an enormous array of electronic gadgetry to monitor communications all over the globe, gathering information on any activity it considers subversive.

Argentina

In March 1976, Argentina was taken over by military rulers. Since that time, 15,000 to 20,000 citizens have disappeared after arrests by security forces. The government imprisoned hundreds without charges and restricted hundreds more by house arrest or by severe limitations on their movements. Human conditions continued to worsen. There was censorship of the media. Thousands of clandestine cemeteries have been found, in some of which more than 1,000 victims have been buried since 1976. And yet President Reagan wanted to certify Argentina for financial support. Stories about ordinary middle-class people being removed from their families in the middle of the night, taken out in helicopters, and dropped into the sea were common. Grieving mothers tried to pressure the government to determine the whereabouts of their loved ones, to no avail. Physicians from Argentina came to American hospitals to work and were still so intimidated that they could hardly talk about what happened at home without being fearful for their lives. In December 1983, the people of Argentina elected a new government led by Raúl Alfonsín—the first civilian president in seven years. He is prosecuting, interrogating, and jailing former military leaders for their crimes.

Chile

In 1970 a physician called Salvador Allende was elected president in Chile by democratic vote. During his campaign he had promised to nationalize the Chilean economy and end the exploitation of Chile by foreign capital. Chile had been under repressive regimes in the past, but now Allende would help his people with education, health care, and food for all. The United States and the CIA, along with IT&T and Pepsi-

Cola, saw this as a threat to their vital interests. These agencies together with President Nixon, Henry Kissinger, Richard Helms, and General Brown, Chairman of the Joint Chiefs of Staff, organized a destabilization campaign that stirred discontent among the people and the labor unions. A vast press campaign was coordinated via CIA connections in Europe and Latin America, linking Allende to the Soviet Union and concluding that he posed a direct threat to "democracy and freedom" in the Western Hemisphere. The CIA began a series of covert propaganda actions and support for terrorist activities, which lasted from 1970 to 1973, designed to stir discontent and fear among the Chilean people. This led to a coup d'état in September 1973 when the Chilean military overthrew Allende, and the Chilean president died, assassinated by the military. The international banks were coordinated to reduce their credit facilities to Chile from $300 million to $17 million. Direct American investment fell from $1 billion in 1969 to less than $100 million in 1972. The Swiss banks played a key role in this economic strangulation of Chile. Since that time, Chile has been ruled by a repressive military dictator, General Pinochet—supported by the government of the United States. Tens of thousands of people have been tortured and killed (the torture techniques taught by the CIA at the International Police Academy in Panama), and the wealth of the country remains in the hands of a few. One million people have fled Chile— 10 percent of its population. The junta has been supported by the Chase Manhattan Bank, Bank of America, First National City Bank, Irving Trust, and Bankers Trust. Other American corporations in Chile are Dow Chemical, IT&T, General Motors, General Electric, Textron, Dodge, and General Tire and Rubber Company. To quote Gabriel García Márquez, Nobel Prize winner in Literature, 1982: "A promethean President, entrenched in his burning palace, died fighting an entire army alone."

Cuba

In 1959, Fidel Castro overthrew Cuban dictator Fulgencio Batista. Batista, with recognized ties to organized crime, had ruled that country for twenty-five years and had supported the economic monopoly of the American corporations. At the time of the revolution, most of the Cuban people were illiterate and malnourished, and diseases such as hookworm, malaria, and tuberculosis were endemic. Since the revolution, almost all the Cuban people have become literate, the endemic diseases have been eradicated, and health care is uniformly good. Indeed, during the Carter administration, the U.S. Surgeon General traveled to Cuba to investigate its health-care system, which was functioning so efficiently. It is true that Cuba is a Communist country.

After the revolution, because of loss of large capital investments by Americans, the U.S. government petulantly refused to establish relations with Cuba. It imposed a total blockade on trade, so that Cuba had to turn to other countries for economic support. It was literally pushed into the hands of the Soviet Union and has subsequently had to endure enormous hardships in trade and economic well-being. No ship that travels to Cuba can dock in an American port; consequently, many European countries are loath to trade with Cuba because it is economically inefficient. Had America been more open and receptive to Cuba just after the revolution, it might well have influenced the course that country has taken over the last twenty-five years. Instead, the United States has tried on many occasions to destroy the Castro regime; the most famous was the ill-conceived Bay of Pigs invasion, orchestrated by the CIA and Cuban exiles from Florida. In reality, the Cubans have performed miracles with their people in the last twenty-five years, but their rigid political system has been exacerbated by their mandatory relationship with the Soviet Union. It is interesting to speculate how Americans would have reacted if a foreign power had tried to unseat its new government soon after its own revolution.

El Salvador

Ever since the Spanish conquest of this region in 1524, a powerful minority has dispossessed the vulnerable majority of native Indians from their lands and resources and has exploited their labor. The original Spanish conquest itself was violent, and the various forms of oppression imposed since then have been consistently enforced by violence. The colonial conquerors in El Salvador and Guatemala have exacted tribute, imposed forced labor, resorted to debt peonage, enslaved native peoples, bought African slaves, and exercised brutal retaliation against any who resisted. Physical independence from Spain in 1821 brought no relief to the oppressed. On the contrary, it gave a freer hand to the landholding elite of El Salvador and Guatemala.

In 1881 under U.S. and European pressure, the government of El Salvador abolished all communal forms of land tenure and paved the way for the wholesale expulsion of peasants from their land and consolidated vast tracts of land in the hands of coffee magnates. Coffee became the major export crop in El Salvador. It dominated the economy by the turn of the century, making up 76 percent of the exports by 1901 and remaining the primary export ever since, reaching 95.5 percent in 1931. The wealthy elite owned the coffee crops. When the world coffee market collapsed in 1931, resulting in loss of employment on the coffee plantations, thousands of peasants rose in rebellion against a system that had methodically denied them all sources of livelihood. In 1932, Salvadoran security forces working for the rich killed some 30,000 peasants, further bolstering the power of the wealthy.

At the present time, privileges of the wealthy in El Salvador are maintained. The population is 4.8 million; 2 percent, dominated by fourteen families, own 60 percent of the most fertile land and produce coffee, cotton, sugar, and beets for export; 90 percent of the people own 22 percent of the land. In 1971, six families held as much land as 80 percent of the rural population. The number of rural families possessing no land at all increased from 30,000 in 1961 to 167,000 in 1975. The symptoms of this desperate pervasive poverty are ramshackle housing and spindly legged, malnourished children. Infant mortality is 60 percent. The average caloric intake is the lowest in Latin America, 40 percent below the recommended minimum. Ninety percent of the people earn less than $100 per year.

Approximately 40,000 civilians have been murdered in El Salvador since 1979.

Refugees number 800,000—20 percent of that country's population. In El Salvador, doctors, nurses, and health-care workers, as well as the patient on the table, were shot down in cold blood by soldiers in operating rooms. The Salvadoran

Army entered the National University, which includes the nation's only medical school, and killed students, occupied buildings, and ransacked and destroyed equipment, libraries, and records. Thirty percent to 40 percent of the nation's physicians have left the country. The military controls the availability of blood, and El Salvador is the only nation in which food aid is distributed by the government, and the country is ruled under emergency decrees that permit the detention of people not suspected of any crime, and the use of confessions extracted under torture.

There are virtually no prisoners of war, and, contrary to the Geneva Conventions of 1949, most prisoners have been executed. All legal and judicial safeguards that guarantee rights and due process have been suspended by the military.

Health care is treated as a subversive activity by the El Salvador government. Well-documented evidence shows the overwhelming majority of violent deaths have been perpetrated by the military government and right-wing paramilitary death squads, and clandestine guerrilla movements have inevitably arisen because the government does not permit nonviolent political opposition. The present U.S. administration insists that the fundamental problem in Central America is the threat of Soviet or Cuban domination in the area. In fact, the problems are poverty and the helplessness of millions of human beings, and many people in Latin America have joined the struggle for independence. Most of them are Christians; a few are Communists. They are seeking justice and self-determination.

The United States has approximately $100 million invested in El Salvador at this time. Some of the main corporations are Texas Instruments, Chevron, Phelps Dodge, Kimberly-Clark, Texaco, and Crown Zellerbach. Since World War II, the United States, through its Military Assistance Program (MAP) and its Office of the Public Safety (OPS), has provided extensive training to Salvadoran military and police officers in the many forms of counterinsurgency along with a thorough indoctrination in anti-Communism and has supplied military and police equipment. Since October 1979, the United States has supplied more than $100 million in lethal military equipment to bolster the threatened military government, more than six times the military aid provided during the previous twenty-nine years. In 1981, a so-called free election was held. However, the left did not participate, because to do so would have been suicidal, and a right-wing government was elected. The country's most feared killer, D'Aubuisson, was one of the leaders who emerged from the rigged election. Amnesty International has declared that El Salvador practices gross violation of human rights. Yet the Reagan administration, every six months, declares that human rights continue to improve, as it sends more and more military equipment that is openly acknowledged to be used by the death squads.

Guatemala

In 1944, a nonviolent revolution occurred, led by students supported by the urban middle classes, which overthrew the despotic Guatemalan President Jorge Ubico. For the first time in four centuries, major social reforms were instituted that reversed the oppression of the poor, ended forced labor, encouraged union organization and social-security measures, and redistributed land from the great wealthy plantations to rural peasants.

But most of the country—500,000 acres of the most fertile land—was owned by a Boston-based company, United Fruit. This company had penetrated Central America in the late nineteenth century and came to own directly or indirectly Guatemala's only Atlantic port, the major railroads in Costa Rica and in Honduras, and nearly 900 miles of railroad in Guatemala and El Salvador. It established an immense network of plantations in Honduras, Costa Rica, Nicaragua, Panama, Jamaica, and the Dominican Republic.

The plantations contributed directly to the U.S. market and made little or no contributions to local economies. United Fruit enjoyed a variety of tax exemptions and profit remittances. This company wreaked social and political havoc in these countries. The wages paid were minimal and almost all the workers' money was spent in company-owned workshops. This company and others throughout Central America were closely allied with arch-conservative landlords and the military.

In 1954, the newly elected President Jacobo Arbenz Guzmán took measures to expropriate 387,000 acres of land owned by United Fruit, land that was not under cultivation at the time, and offered the company compensation commensurate with United Fruit's declared tax value of the land. But

United Fruit had consistently undervalued its property in order to reduce its already insignificant tax liability. At the same time, the peasant laborers were to form a union to help improve wages and working conditions. Secretary of State John Foster Dulles, whose law firm had prepared the United Fruit Company contracts with Guatemala in the 1930s, began a campaign to smear the reformed government as part of the international Communist conspiracy. His brother, Allen Dulles was director of the CIA. The United Fruit Company launched a massive public-relations and political campaign in the United States, accusing the Arbenz Guzmán government of being Communists. Listed as supporters in this effort, among others, were Claude Pepper, Mike Mansfield, Henry Cabot Lodge, President Eisenhower, John and Allen Dulles, Arthur Hays Sulzberger of *The New York Times*, and journalists from the *Miami Herald*, *Christian Science Monitor*, *San Francisco Chronicle*, UPI, *Time*, and *Newsweek*. The CIA planted Soviet arms in adjacent Nicaragua, with the support of that country's dictator, Anastasio Somoza, to make it seem that Russia was involved. The CIA organized and financed from the neighboring Honduras a military coup, which overthrew Arbenz Guzmán and replaced him with a U.S.-trained Guatemalan army officer, Carlos Castillo Armas. Some months later, the United Fruit Company itself gradually disintegrated and disappeared. Under the rule of Castillo Armas, trade unions and political parties were abolished. Eight hundred campesinos (peasants) were killed in the first two months, and there were 9,000 political arrests in the first year.

In 1966, guerrilla resistance arose again but was put down by the puppet government with the aid of U.S. intervention, which provided military and police training, a large influx of weapons, military advisers, and $6 million in military aid to the Guatemalan armed forces. The violence was so excessive that a 1980 State Department report concluded, "To eliminate a few hundred guerrillas, the government killed perhaps 10,000 Guatemalan peasants." The Guatemalan government has since ruled with such terror that President Jimmy Carter suspended military assistance because of inadequate attention to human rights in that country. At this time, Guatemala has a population of 7.2 million, of which 65 percent are rural. Only 2.1 percent of the landowners hold 72.2 percent of the land, on which they grow crops almost exclusively for export, while 91.4 percent of the land-owners hold 21.9 percent of the land.

Some 80,000 civilians have been murdered since 1954. Recently, a report in *The New York Times* described hideous murders by government soldiers using rusty machetes. They hacked and killed children, pregnant women, and babies. They pick up children by the feet and smash their heads against a wall or tie ropes around their necks and strangle them. Children are thrown in the air and bayoneted. On March 23, 1982, General Romeo Lucas García, the president, was replaced by General José Efraín Ríos Montt, a born-again Christian who is reported to have been systematically killing peasants in rural areas, using the army. He is quoted as having said, "We have no scorched earth policy. We have a policy of scorched Communists." Recently, Rabbi Arthur Hertzberg, vice-president of the World Jewish Congress, described Guatemala as a "charnel house." President Reagan said that he thinks Ríos Montt's government has been "getting a bum rap."

The United States instituted this form of despotic government in 1954 and supports Ríos Montt and supplies him with helicopters and other military equipment, all in the name of anti-Communism. Fifty thousand to 80,000 peasants fled that country in 1982 alone.

Nicaragua

In Nicaragua, America has firmly supported the rule of the Somozas since 1930. Anastasio Somoza Debayle once told Luís Echeverria, then president of Mexico, "You should envy me. I have no problems. All I have to do is what Washington wants me to do." The United States has exploited and controlled Nicaragua since the 1850s, when an American investment group, led by Cornelius Vanderbilt, instituted a transit system across Nicaragua. The United States was once also interested in establishing a canal across that country and in protecting mining and banking interests. As a result, U.S. Marines landed in Nicaragua in 1909. After establishing a government satisfactory to the United States, they withdrew in 1910, but reinvaded in 1912 to quell a rebellion. A treaty giving the United States exclusive rights to any canal across the country was forced on Nicaragua. New York banking interests gained control of the Bank of Nicaragua and the nation's railroads. They exploited the coffee export trade; they manipulated currency at the expense of the poor and to the advantage of the rich, profiting themselves. A U.S. Marine detachment of at least one hundred occupied Nicaragua until 1925 and returned in 1926 to remain until 1933. They departed only after setting up the National Guard under the control of Somoza's father, who eliminated a people's movement by murdering its leader, Augusto Sandino. The United States has consistently supported the Somozas, even though they did not protect democratic freedoms, hold elections, or free the economy from the dynasty's stranglehold. In 1979, the people of Nicaragua—businessmen, church leaders, students, middle-class, and left-wing—rose up against this dictator, who owned and controlled practically all the wealth and corporations of that country. With great sacrifice of civilian lives at the hands of Somoza's national guards, the revolution prevailed and a nationalistic government, with the general support of most of the people, assumed power. They called themselves Sandinistas, after their dead hero. By 1981, the country had achieved self-sufficiency in food production; health and medical care was available to the rural poor; illiteracy had been reduced from 50 percent to 12 percent; and land was being distributed to formerly landless peasants. There was a high degree of democratic participation at the local level, and representatives were elected to a national governing council. Churches, out of their concern for the poor, supported this revolution. However, soon after the revolution, the country found itself terribly in debt because Somoza in exile had removed hundreds of millions of dollars from Nicaragua to banks in Florida. President Carter was to have supported the new government with several hundred million dollars, but refused to send a final $15 million because the U.S. government said Nicaragua was aiding a rebellion in El Salvador. The Reagan administration continued the cutoff, even though it admitted that Nicaragua had stopped aiding the Salvadoran insurgents. Since then it has advanced a variety of explanations for a policy of unremitting hostility that is, in fact, based on Nicaragua's left-wing politics and behavior. Is it left-wing to want to feed and educate the majority of the people? Nicaragua established economic relationships with

France, Sweden, Finland, and Brazil. Because it got no support from the United States, it had to go to the Soviet Union for financial support. There was no other avenue open to it.

Now the CIA is arming and training Somozan supporters in Florida and in Honduras, and it has more than 150 agents based in Honduras and dozens more in neighboring countries. A recent American visitor to Honduras says that country is teeming with American troops. The CIA is conducting the largest covert operation mounted in nearly a decade, which involves indirectly an attempt to overthrow the Nicaraguan government. It supplied money and military equipment to paramilitary groups fighting under the banner of the Nicaraguan Democratic Front, a coalition of Nicaraguan exile groups intent on toppling the Sandinistas, and had enlisted the aid of Argentina and Israel to support these Nicaraguans being trained in Honduras. The United States is also arming the military in Honduras to the tune of $3.1 million, and has conducted a huge military training exercise called Big Pine II involving 6,000 U.S. troops from August 1983 to January 1984. In January 1984, an unpublished report of the House Armed Services Committee stated that the United States has taken advantage of this exercise to create "a substantial semipermanent military capability" in Honduras, with construction of airstrips, housing, radar facilities, ocean piers, roads, and an eleven-mile-long tank trap. Honduras has been a remarkable area of stability in Central America for many years, a true democracy which had an election as recently as 1980, when it elected its first civilian president in a decade. However, such support of the military by the United States is almost certain to destabilize this small country. The Nicaraguan Democratic Front makes frequent forays into Nicaragua, and there are at present an estimated 4,000 to 10,000 counterrevolutionaries supported and organized by the United States operating inside the country, conducting guerrilla warfare. What are the ethics of the United States when it intervenes in a covert way to destroy a government attained by a majority revolution of its people? The countries of Colombia, Mexico, Panama, and Venezuela, which have offered to help mediate the problems in Nicaragua, have been rejected by the United States—as well as a six-point peace plan proposed by the Sandinista government and an offer by Fidel Castro for a bilateral removal of all foreign troops from the territory.

*   *   *

In an address before the General Assembly of the United Nations on October 7, 1981, Daniel Ortega Saavedra of Nicaragua referred to the history of U.S. aggression:

> The emergence of the Monroe Doctrine, America for the Americans, was to represent the aggressive will of Yankee expansionism on the continent, and from 1840 onwards our people were no longer to benefit from the influence of those ideals of democracy and freedom, but rather to suffer interference, threats, the imposition of treaties contrary to the sovereignty of our countries . . . blackmail with the presence of the United States fleet in our territorial waters, military interventions, the landing of Marines and the imposition of corrupt governments and one-sided economic treaties. More than 784 acts hostile to the right of our countries to sovereignty have occurred on our continent since that time, and more than 100 of them since 1960.
>
> Why were our countries insulted, invaded, and humiliated on more than 200 occasions from 1840 to 1917? Under what pretext, since at the time there was not a single socialist state in the world and the Czar ruled over all the Russians? Treaties and loans were imposed on us; we were invaded; we were given the status of protectorates under the same thesis of national security, which was first called the Monroe Doctrine. . . .
>
> How can we explain the numerous acts of aggression and interference and the landings that occurred between 1917 and 1954 in Latin America, when there was still no Cuban revolution and Cuba could not be accused of interference . . .?
>
> The United States did not take over Cuba and Puerto Rico in 1898 . . . to save Caribbean territories from the influence of the Soviet Union since the latter was not yet in existence.
>
> The United States did not land Marines in Vera Cruz, Haiti and Nicaragua, nor did it from 1903 onwards arm the most formidable Naval force ever seen in Caribbean waters to resolve the East–West

conflict to its own benefit. It was simply defending the interests of its territorial expansionism, the interests of its financiers and its bankers, of those business tycoons, who were beginning to beset Latin America.

This history is well-chronicled. It is clear that the Soviet–Cuban Communist expansionism is only an excuse for the preordained economic expansionism of the United States of America. It is obvious that the military assists such expansionism. The threat of the Nicaraguan revolution is a threat to U.S. economic interests.

What is happening to human beings in many of these countries of Central and South America is not dissimilar to the atrocities that occurred in Hitler's Germany. Yet their governments are still eligible for support by the United States because they are "anti-Communist." So was Hitler. . . .

American Intervention in the Eastern Hemisphere

Iran

In 1953, President Eisenhower, at the urging of his Secretary of State, John Foster Dulles, gave the signal to launch a CIA coup in Iran that overthrew a much-beloved premier, Mohammed Mossadegh, because he had nationalized the British oil companies. The CIA reinstated the shah on the Peacock Throne after returning him from exile. The people in Iran never accepted the autocratic shah with his hated secret police (SAVAK), and they always resented America for removing their beloved premier. This resentment culminated with the overthrow of the shah and the taking of fifty-two American hostages. The bitterness engendered could well have thrust the United States and the USSR into a superpower confrontation. The patriotic fervor created among many Americans during those months of the hostage crisis was frightening, indeed, from a neutral perspective. Indeed, I saw a young messenger walking through the halls of the Children's Hospital at Harvard, wearing a T-shirt that read "Nuke Iran." Most Americans did not know or understand the reason for the Iranian people's resentment. I had visited

Iran in 1974 to see my brother who was a diplomat, and I had seen the boiling resentment toward the shah at that time.

Vietnam and Cambodia

In a ten-year undeclared war, America sent half a million soldiers into Vietnam and bombarded the country with three times the tonnage of bombs dropped on Germany and Japan in World War II. There were approximately 2 million casualties. Chemical warfare was practiced, using Agent Orange as a defoliant over hundreds of thousands of acres of Vietnamese territory. A by-product of Agent Orange is dioxin, one of the most carcinogenic and mutagenic substances known. The effect of the defoliant has been to make a virtual desert of some of the most lush tropical forests in the world. Napalm was also used on thousands of innocent men, women, and children.

In 1969, Henry Kissinger and Richard Nixon authorized the secret bombing of Cambodia. B-52s bombed "boxes," areas of land half a mile wide by three miles long, to root out nonexistent North Vietnamese bases. The secret war in Cambodia continued for just under four years, and at one stage, the number of B-52 sorties was as high as eighty-one a day, whereas in Vietnam the maximum had been sixty a day. The total tonnage of bombs dropped was 539,129, almost half of them in the last six months of the war. (During World War II, only 160,000 tons of bombs were dropped on Japan.) Thousands of square miles of densely populated fertile areas of Cambodia were blackened, and hundreds of thousands of people were killed. Also as a result of the massive bombings, most of the ancient irrigation system was destroyed, and most of the rice-growing areas of this country fell into ruin.

The United States also allowed Prince Sihanouk to be deposed. Thus, in 1969, began the destruction of a beautiful, peaceful country held together by a delicate coalition of forces guided and directed by the clever and intensely nationalistic Sihanouk.

The United States then supported the government of Lon Nol, a very weak and ineffectual ruler. He was opposed by the Chinese-backed Pol Pot who armed and trained hordes of young adolescent soldiers in the name of Communism. During and after the secret bombing of Cambodia, Pol Pot and his young soldiers murdered hundreds of thousands of

Cambodians. They committed the most frightful atrocities against their people, nailing old women against houses and then burning the houses, slaughtering children and anybody who seemed to have an education. Almost three million people died during those years of the war; a whole civilization was almost destroyed. Relief came only after the invasion of that country by an ancient enemy, Vietnam, which displaced the Pol Pot regime. To this day, Pol Pot is supported by China; and Vietnam, because of lack of American financial support after the war, has had to rely totally on the Soviet Union. Hence, America recognizes only Pol Pot in the United Nations, despite the fact that he is a despotic murderer and war criminal.

America also supplies moral, political, and economic support to the oppressive regime of apartheid in South Africa, which separates husband from wife and forces people to live in subhuman conditions in the meanest parts of a very rich country just because they are black.

I have not covered the past activities of America in Taiwan and South Korea, as well as in Greece, Spain, and many other countries. The history of these interventions is similar to many of the stories just told.

Soviet Interventions

Afghanistan

Since the nineteenth century, the Afghan monarchy had maintained order in a society riddled with deep ethnic, tribal, and religious diversity. The rulers had also maintained a policy of international nonalignment, and in return, the Soviet Union had left the Afghans alone. In 1973, Prime Minister Mohammad Daud staged a coup and overthrew his cousin, Zahir Shah. Daud's regime became corrupt and cruel. He was courted by the shah of Iran, who wished to extend his influence throughout the Persian Gulf. Daud accepted the shah's hated SAVAK—secret police—to help him "root out Communist influence" from the Afghan civilian and military service.

The Communists consisted of two rival groups, which until that time had posed no threat to the stability of the country. One faction originally had supported Daud, but he eventually lost Communist support. The Soviet Union was unhappy that the shah, with American influence, was invited to participate in Afghan affairs and was distressed by his vehement opposition to the Communists. It and the Communist party of India worked to unite the opposing factions. Daud moved closer to the Washington–Tehran axis, which really alarmed the Soviet Union, as it saw its southern border in danger of becoming destabilized.

Daud, in a clumsy attempt to overthrow the Communists, inadvertently instigated a coup in April 1978, which brought a Marxist–Leninist government to power. Russia, the CIA, and SAVAK were all taken by surprise. Once the coup was accomplished, the Russians were obliged to support the new government. Hafizullah Amin became the leader, but he consistently ignored Soviet advice as he moved too fast to force an impoverished and illiterate agrarian society into the twentieth century. Amin also began to develop close associations with the United States through Ambassador Adolph Dubs.

Russia tried to get rid of Amin in September 1979, when the rift between them became irreparable, but the wrong man was killed. Amin now assumed complete control. Russia eventually, in December 1979, had Amin and his family killed, replacing him with Babrak Karmal and invading Afghanistan with 85,000 troops in order to bring "stability" to the southern Russian border. In so doing, it aroused the wrath of the world. It was the first time Russia had moved its troops beyond its borders and those of the Warsaw Pact nations since 1945.

The Soviets continue to be plagued by rivalry between the two Communist groups, and there is evidence that one of the factions is cooperating with the Afghan rebels fighting the invading army. Senator Birch Bayh was chairman of the committee that approved CIA aid to the rebels through Pakistan.

Obviously, Russia did not invade Afghanistan because it needed oil from the Persian Gulf; it is the largest producer of oil in the world today. Russia invaded when its stable, nonaligned neighbor was destabilized by the 1978 coup, and by the disturbing influence of the shah and the CIA. It was confronted by a Communist but pro-American country on its southern border, just as America had been confronted with a pro-Soviet regime in Cuba some twenty years earlier, and had responded with the Bay of Pigs invasion. Apparently both the Soviet military command and Soviet intelligence argued against military intervention, since it was a no-win situation militarily and politically. The Kremlin overruled the military and KGB advice and took defensive action in response to an unacceptable challenge to strategic Soviet interests in an area of vital concern. Soon after the invasion an all-party committee of the British House of Commons concluded: "The Soviet Union did not go into Afghanistan earlier because the Afghan regime prior to 1978 had been stable, even though not Marxist. Once the Communist regime had been established, the USSR had the double incentive of ideological commitment to the maintenance of Communist gains, in line with the Brezhnev doctrine, plus the desire to restore stability on its borders."

At this time, it is unknown how many people have been killed, and there may be 3 million refugees in Pakistan, according to the Pakistani government, although some people would say this estimate is too high. There are 100,000 Soviet troops in Afghanistan. The Soviet Union is having a difficult time maintaining order among these troops, since many of them are unhappy with their role there. They are also dying of endemic hepatitis, and apparently they are freely using drugs. There has been some evidence that the Soviet Union has been using mycotoxins (yellow rain) on the Afghan people. However, these data have only come from the U.S. State Department and have not, at this time, been verified by the United Nations or any other independent agency.

Unfortunately, Russia invaded Afghanistan just at the time of high anxiety in the United States generated by the hostage situation in Iran. The anger, indignation, and frustration of the American people toward Iran was projected immediately onto the Soviet Union and its illegal invasion of Afghanistan.

Poland

During 1980, a new union movement, called Solidarity, developed in Poland. Workers all over Poland rushed to join—ten million of the eleven million in the labor force. The government eventually capitulated to all their demands—the right to form independent unions, the right to strike, reduced censorship, and access to state-controlled television and radio for the unions and the church. They were developing freedom of speech and other freedoms and had an enormous consensus throughout the country under the leadership of Lech Walesa.

But Poland was terribly in debt as a result of Prime Minister Edward Gierek's cavalier economic attitude over the preceding ten years. Food became scarce, and even soap was difficult to obtain. New mothers were discharged from the hospital prematurely for fear their babies might become infected because there were insufficient supplies of soap for the doctors to wash adequately. As a result, the movement got out of control, and Walesa was not able to moderate some of the more militant people within the unions. Finally the militants called for a national referendum on the future of the Communist government in Poland and the reexamination of Poland's military alliance with the Soviet Union. The whole world wondered what the Soviet Union would do with this challenge coming from one of its Warsaw Pact countries, but Russia knew that if it invaded Poland, all hell would break loose, possibly instigating a U.S.–Soviet confrontation. Since, in the nuclear age, this is not politically indicated, the Polish government itself outlawed Solidarity, and by the end of 1982 had almost destroyed it. During this uprising by the union, there was some bloodshed—and the death of the spirit of liberation. I identify with the Polish people because my maiden name is Broinowski.

Russia thus violated the Helsinki Declaration of 1975 in which the East and West coupled recognition of the existing frontiers of the Warsaw Pact nations with the agreement that all signatories adhere to basic concepts of human rights. It is obvious that Russia can never feel secure when it has to disenfranchise its Warsaw Pact allies by destroying their yearnings for self-government and human rights.

It is true that events in Poland have been tragic, and that events in Hungary, Czechoslovakia, and other Warsaw Pact countries have caused consternation in the West as well as internal bitterness. It is also true that the war in Afghanistan is an immoral war and the intervention by the Soviet Union is illegal. By the same criteria, it is also true that the massacres, the genocidal activities, and the repression practiced by governments in Central and South America and supported by the United States of America are also illegal and immoral. Most Third World countries and other Western countries resent both Russia and America for their economic and/or military intervention. It is time that the superpowers, as they posture for bilateral nuclear disarmament, agree to sign a treaty in which they promise not to intervene in other countries in the world. This would mean that the United States would have to pull out its multinational corporations from around the world, and could not suppress or subvert people in other countries; the Soviet Union would have to stop "supporting" or, conversely, "repressing" national revolutions around the world.

Only if this happens will the world be safe from annihilation, since it is time the Third World and Western countries rose up and demanded that the superpowers start behaving themselves. To this end Canadian Prime Minister Pierre Trudeau has initiated an international cooperative effort to produce real and constructive arms control. Obviously, the nuclear forces on both sides serve to support and bolster the conventional forces that are used by the superpowers to subvert and monopolize small countries for their own ends.

We have looked at American misperceptions of the USSR. It is also important for America to understand how the Russian leaders view the world. The Soviet Union is the only Communist country surrounded by hostile Communist nations—China and the Warsaw Pact countries. Obviously, if Russia invaded Western Europe, the Warsaw Pact allies would hardly move rapidly to support its offensive efforts and would in fact probably fight against it. There are five large nuclear nations in the world, four of which have their weapons targeted on Soviet cities. Each could destroy Russia as a viable entity. It is as if Canada were China, Mexico were NATO—including the British and French nuclear forces—and Russia were about to deploy Pershing IIs and cruise missiles in Mexico. The Soviet leaders at this time have every cause to be realistically frightened and perhaps a little paranoid. (I was interested to discover during my visit to Russia that they are more afraid of China than they are of America.) I would suggest that if there was less belligerency, the Soviet Union might feel freer to moderate its tough posture within Poland. While present conditions prevail, however, should one Warsaw Pact country fall to free expression, the others will obviously also fall. If moves could be made to reassure Russia that it is safe from Western or Chinese aggression, perhaps it might well moderate its stand in Poland as, indeed, it has to a certain extent in Hungary.

One of the reasons the South Korean plane was destroyed was Soviet paranoia induced by a new U.S. military posture in the North Pacific. This article from *The Nation* describes the dynamics of this policy:

Where Flight 7 Flew

TENSIONS IN THE NORTH PACIFIC

WALDEN BELLO AND PETER HAYES

"This region, I believe, is most probably where we shall witness confrontation with the Soviet Union," Adm. Robert Long, then chief of the U.S. Pacific Command, told a Japanese reporter a few months ago. In the aftermath of the September 1 downing of a South Korean commercial airliner by a Soviet fighter, Long's words have taken on an unintended immediacy.

Northeast Asia, where the tragic incident occurred, is one of the world's most militarized areas. Soviet and U.S. forces there are in a state of tense confrontation. The South Korean plane flew close to the Soviet naval base at Petropavlovsk, on the Kamchatka Peninsula, home port for the Northwest Pacific nuclear-missile submarine fleet. It was shot down over Sakhalin Island, site of several important Soviet communications and aircraft facilities, after allegedly being mistaken for an American RC-135 spy plane.

In recent years both the Soviet Union and the United States have engaged in major military buildups in the area. The Russians have deployed about one-third of their 250 SS-20 theater nuclear missiles and the same proportion of their new long-range Backfire bombers. According to Adm. Nataoishi Sakonjo of Japan, an expert on defense policy in the region, Soviet missiles and aircraft are deployed primarily for use in the event of a ground war with the People's Republic of China. Reagan Administration propaganda to the contrary notwithstanding, their purpose appears to be largely defensive.

Perhaps the most accurate assessment of the balance of forces in Northeast Asia was provided by former Defense Secretary Harold Brown, who wrote in his recently published *Thinking About National Security* that the U.S.-Japan-China alliance "must truly be a nightmare to the Soviets and the modest cooperative steps [taken by the three nations from] 1975–80 have . . . tilted the politico-military balance against the Soviets to a degree that significantly exceeds the advantages accruing to them from their substantial build-up in the region during the late 1960's and 1970's."

Indeed, over the past three years, the Reagan Administration's arms escalation has been the prime cause of instability in the region. The thrust of the Pentagon's strategy is to pit the Navy, the only U.S. service that enjoys clear-cut superiority over its Soviet counterpart, against the Soviet fleet in an area where the Russians are geographically highly vulnerable.

The United States now periodically deploys several aircraft carrier task forces in the area; before this Administration, only a single carrier task force was assigned to it. U.S. battle groups hold regular exercises in the Northwest Pacific just off the Sea of Okhotsk and in the Sea of Japan. The Seventh Fleet, which patrols the western Pacific and the Indian Ocean, is stronger than it has been in years, having been augmented by the battleship New Jersey (temporarily on gunboat diplomacy duty off Central America), which has been refitted with cruise missiles, and by America's newest nuclear-powered carrier, the 90,000-ton Carl Vinson. The ships of the U.S. Pacific Command, which includes those of the Third Fleet in the eastern Pacific, now make up almost half the Navy's forces.

The Navy's moves cannot be divorced from its longstanding obsession with outstripping the "upstart"

Soviet fleet under Adm. Sergei Gorshkov. During the years immediately after the Vietnam War, the Navy's expansion plans were frustrated by a popular mood of antimilitarism, budgetary constraints and skepticism on the part of civilian authorities. But when Ronald Reagan, a longtime favorite of the service, became President, the Navy's views became policy.

The harmony between the Navy brass and the Administration has produced the "Lehman Doctrine," named after Secretary of the Navy John Lehman, a former consultant to Boeing and a member of the Navy Reserve, who has called for the "achievement of outright maritime supremacy." In order to attain that goal, the Navy will expand to a 600-ship fleet, including fifteen aircraft carriers and four recommissioned World War II battleships armed with cruise missiles. To make the Soviet Union an "isolated island," as Lehman put it, the Navy's primary mission has been shifted from a defensive one of protecting vital sea lanes to an offensive one of "force projection" against the Soviet fleet and Soviet coastal targets [see James A. Nathan, "Return of the Great White Fleet," *The Nation*, March 5].

By increasing its presence in the home waters of the Soviet Pacific fleet, the Navy hopes to dissuade the Russian naval command from sending substantial task forces out of port, enabling the U.S. fleet to exercise unchallenged control over the Pacific and Indian Oceans.

The strategy of confrontation is, of course, backed up by contingency plans for dealing with any "incidents" that occur in the area. Such incidents are an ever-present possibility in the Northwest Pacific, where the two opposing fleets boldly venture into each other's training maneuvers.

Under U.S. naval doctrine, it is preferable to outmaneuver and overwhelm the enemy in one location than to fight it all over the high seas. Such a strategy gives the United States the edge in the Pacific: the Soviet fleet's main area of operation is the almost landlocked Sea of Japan, where its maneuverability is limited. The five narrow straits that lead to the open Pacific can be easily mined, blockaded or bombed. U.S. battle groups, by contrast, have the immense advantage of operating in the open seas, supported by land-based aircraft launched from Japan and South Korea. As the Joint Chiefs of Staff point out in their last "defense posture" statement, a major U.S. "advantage is the ability of American forces—including those in Japan and Korea—to bottle up the Soviets' Pacific fleet at Vladivostok."

What Harold Brown calls the Russians' strategic "nightmare" would become reality in a battle in the Sea of Japan or the Sea of Okhotsk. Two U.S. carrier battle groups assigned to the Seventh Fleet would be arrayed against only one small Soviet carrier, which is designed for antisubmarine warfare, in the Northwest Pacific, forcing the Russians to rely on cruise-missile firing ships, submarines and land-based aircraft.

The Seventh Fleet and the Air Force and Marine air units based in Japan and South Korea have about 440 aircraft available for use in offensive operations against the Russians. When the U.S.-equipped air forces of Japan and South Korea are included, the balance of power tips against the Russians. Even though they enjoy numerical superiority, their planes are inferior to those of the United States. The Bear heavy bomber, boasts one American admiral, "would not get within 1,000 miles" of a U.S. battle group. It is unlikely that the long-range Backfire bombers would be able to penetrate the screen of U.S. interceptors and fighter-bombers. And the Russians have nothing to match the *enfant terrible* of the U.S. offensive force: the ultramodern F-16, which is capable of carrying nuclear weapons. A squadron of F-16s is now based in South Korea, and another will soon be deployed in Misawa, in northern Japan.

In short, the Soviet Pacific fleet would get little help from air power, which is the decisive factor in modern naval conflicts. The two other tactical arms of the Soviet fleet—its missile-firing surface ships and its submarines—would have to break through the mined or blockaded straits leading out of the Sea of Japan, and the noisy Soviet submarines would have to contend with U.S. antisubmarine forces, which a former Navy Secretary has described as "awesome."

To support its independent capabilities, the United States is strengthening its military alliances with Japan, South Korea and China:

§ The United States and Japan have planned joint twenty-four-hour patrols in three of the straits leading out of the Sea of Japan, and Japan has promised to join the United States in mining or blockading those "choke points" in the event of war.

§ To place North Korea, a Soviet ally, on the defensive, the United States has upgraded South Korea's defense status to the equivalent of the European theater's—that is, from a "significant interest area" to a "vital interest area"—and has indicated its intention to deploy neutron bombs on the Korean peninsula. The Pentagon has advocated linking the United States to Japan and South Korea in a "triangular alliance," which would permit military operations that are not possible under present bilateral pacts—for example, the mining of the strategically important Tsushima Strait.

§ The United States is integrating China into its war plans. In addition to urging a "continuing program of military-to-military contacts and prudent assistance in defensive weaponry," Defense Secretary Caspar Weinberger's "Defense Guidance" for 1985–89 calls for U.S. "logistical support" for "Chinese military maneuvers to tie down the Soviets' Pacific Fleet, tactical air squadrons, and its approximately 50 army divisions on the Sino-Soviet border" in the event of war.

Those initiatives have brought tensions in the area to flash point. The Navy brass's desire to put Admiral Gorshkov in his place and the Reagan Administration's ill-disguised belief in the feasibility of a "limited war" could prove to be an explosive combination.

The destabilizing effect of the limited-war doctrine that guides contingency planning at the Pentagon should not be discounted. As then-Assistant Secretary of Defense for International Security Affairs Francis West put it last year in Congressional hearings on "seapower projection":

> A strategy of global flexibility does not necessarily mean simultaneous, intense conflict worldwide. Quite the opposite. It means assessing the opponent's strength on the entire global chessboard, assessing the capabilities of theater criticalities, and assigning moves and countermoves designed to terminate the conflict speedily and with minimum escalation, while protecting the interests of the United States and its allies.

West based that strategy on the assumption that the Soviet Union "is a mature global superpower in the 1980s." The problem, of course, is that the Russians have stated time and again that a limited war—either conventional or nuclear—with the United States is not possible. It would quickly escalate to global war. Moreover, the lessons of the 1905 Battle of Tsushima, when the Czar's Baltic fleet went down before the guns of the imperial Japanese Navy in the strait, which leads into the Sea of Japan, are deeply ingrained in the minds of Soviet commanders.

It is important to place the shooting down of the South Korean passenger plane in the context of the rapid escalation of the arms race, largely promoted by the United States, in the Northeast Asia-Northwest Pacific region. Perhaps that tragic affair will serve to draw public attention to the buildup and provoke second thoughts in the Pentagon and the Navy among the adherents of pre-emptive strikes and limited war.

International Conventional Arms Trade

A concomitant of the constant wars and insurrections between and within Third World countries, much of it the result of superpower actions, is the growing arms trade. Many Third World countries that cannot afford food, medical care, or education for their people are buying enormous quantities of sophisticated weapons. Russia and America are the leading "salesmen" and sell arms to friend and foe alike. During the period from 1974 to 1981, the United States made Third World arms sales that exceeded those of the USSR by about $9.1 billion. But in nominal terms, the Soviet Union and the United States are very close in Third World arms sales. France is the third major conventional arms seller, followed by the United Kingdom, West Germany, and Italy.

Over a recent four-year period, the Soviets outnumbered the United States in sheer numbers of weapons delivered. Also, the major European suppliers have become serious competitors for arms markets in every region of the Third World, particularly in Latin America. Of course, numbers may not compensate for quality or levels of sophistication in the weapons actually delivered to a particular region. Well-trained personnel using top-quality equipment may, in the end, prove to be more important in a nation's ability to wage successful conventional war than the sheer magnitude of conventional weapons in its inventory.

Since Ronald Reagan entered the White House in 1981, international arms sales have increased enormously. In 1982 alone, orders totaled $21 billion. To give some idea of the rapid increase: Total sales during the four-year Carter administration were only a few billion dollars less than the total transfers made by the United States for the twenty years from 1950 to 1970. President Reagan has greatly increased this yet again with a 30 percent increase in fiscal 1982 over fiscal 1981.

In America, arms bazaars are held several times a year. Here the latest weapons—missiles, tanks, guns, planes—are on display, often adorned with bikini-clad girls draped across the missiles. Sheiks and arms buyers from all over the world walk

Top 25 FMS Contractors, FY 1980
(in thousands of dollars)

	1980	1979[1] (Rank)
1. General Dynamics Corp.	$ 992,958	$ 517,998 (2)
2. Northrop Corp.	859,401	472,282 (3)
3. United Technologies Corp.	749,047	249,048 (5)
4. McDonnell Douglas Corp.	471,238	638,853 (1)
5. Raytheon Co.	435,468	132,113 (8)
6. Sam Whan Corp.	266,306	*
7. FMC Corp.	232,933	65,267 (20)
8. Hani Development Co. Ltd. and Al Mabani Joint Venture	217,558	*
9. Harsco Corp.	205,393	70,508 (19)
10. Chrysler Corp.	197,089	*
11. General Electric Co.	175,597	101,442 (13)
12. Mi Ryung Construction Co. Ltd.	171,340	*
13. Lockheed Corp.	148,536	141,812 (7)
14. General Agencies and Sam Whan Joint Venture	144,306	*
15. Westinghouse Electric Corp.	140,101	85,266 (15)
16. Boeing Co.	131,542	*
17. Saudi Maintenance Co. Ltd.	128,834	*
18. General Motors Corp.	109,071	50,692 (25)
19. Teledyne Inc.	108,541	53,237 (23)
20. Hughes Aircraft Co.	95,533	86,423 (14)
21. Textron, Inc.	81,960	109,158 (10)
22. American Telephone and Telegraph Co.	78,773	61,832 (21)
23. Sperry Corp.	72,705	75,138 (16)
24. Rockwell International Corp.	59,327	*
25. Hyundai Construction Co. Ltd.	58,338	290,486 (4)
Total, Top 25 Companies	$6,331,895	$3,984,775
Total FMS Awards	$8,157,571	$5,329,876

*Not among top 25 FMS contractors during FY 1979.
Source: "Foreign Military Sales, Top 25 Companies and Their Subsidiaries Ranked According to Net Value of Military Prime Contract Awards," for Fiscal Years 1979 and 1980. Chrysler contracts for FY 1979 are from the DoD Public Affairs division.

among the displays, while salesmen from weapons industries and Pentagon military officers pour inviting words into their ears.

President Reagan has also proposed dropping restrictions on arms sales to Argentina, Guatemala, Pakistan, Ecuador, Venezuela, and Brazil. President Carter barred military sales to these countries because of their poor record in human rights. In 1981, $25 million "Aid Packages" were sent with congressional approval to the El Salvador military, and Reagan proposed another $25 million for fiscal 1982. If this is added to the $10 million in military aid from the Carter administration, the total amounts to $60 million in fiscal 1981 and 1982—four times the value of all U.S. arms sales to El Salvador from 1950 to 1980. Reagan proposed $110 million for 1983.

Obviously, the major motivation behind the enormous growth in arms sales in the United States and other Western nations is profit. Probably a similar motivation exists for the Soviet Union, which, although it operates from a nonprofit system, has a balance-of-payments problem. But for a world to become more and more dependent on arms sales which will lead to death and destruction, and could lead to nuclear war, when two thirds of the children are malnourished and starving, is evil and immoral. Approximately half (fifty-two) of all national governments in developing countries are now under military domination. Forty-nine of these fifty-two practice citizen repression under law, and forty show a consistent pattern of extreme repression, including torture. The United States provides military support to twenty-seven of these countries, but both superpowers, as well as other nations, export weapons to repressive regimes.

The discrimination between conventional and nuclear weapons is less and less distinct. The sea-skimming radar-guided French Exocet missile, which destroyed a British ship in the Falklands, is an example. Technologically sophisticated weapons are indiscriminate in the violence they cause. For example, fragmentation bombs made of plastic, which cannot be identified in a human body by X ray, and cluster bombs are sent to Israel by the United States. During the sixties, the number of military deaths worldwide equaled the number of civilian deaths in war. But in the last ten years, three civilians have died for each soldier. As Ruth Leger Sivard says, "It is no longer the men who fight, but rather those for whom they are fighting who become the main victims of war." There have been sixty-five major wars fought since 1960, on the territory of forty-nine countries, which represent two thirds of the world's population and 40 percent of its land area. In these twenty-three years more than 10,700,000 people have been killed. Many of these countries will soon be able to fight with nuclear weapons because, by 1981, fifty-four nations owned research or nuclear power reactors, which are essentially bomb factories. They produce plutonium as a by-product of nuclear fission, and plutonium is the fuel for nuclear weapons.

Physical Examination

Introduction

When the Korean jetliner was shot down on September 1, 1983, the tenuous relationship that had existed between Russia and America was sabotaged. Not only were the people of the world distraught at the news of such an inhumane act, but President Reagan used the occasion to further increase the American people's feelings of hostility toward the Soviet Union.

The White House acknowledged several weeks after the tragedy that U.S. intelligence had evidence confirming that the Russians still thought they were tracking a KC-135 spy plane when they shot down the passenger jet. Despite this knowledge, President Reagan, in addressing the United Nations, called the Russian leaders barbarians.

Since that time, international events have continued to push the world toward the nuclear abyss. The presence of the U.S. "peacekeeping" force in Lebanon had exacerbated the animosity and tensions that had existed for centuries between feuding sects. The U.S. Marines had been used to support the Christian Phalange government of President Amin Gemayel, a government that is not representative of the majority of Lebanese people.

On October 23, 1983, 240 young American men were killed by a suicidal car bomber while they slept. Since that dreadful event, President Reagan has reaffirmed his commitment to play a major role in the direction of that fateful country, and to that end, he has negotiated an agreement with Israel for increased military cooperation.

The Reagan administration decided to confront the Syrian government in Lebanon because it is supported by Soviet troops and military technology. Lebanon has thus become a site for political superpower confrontation, with U.S. Marines placed fifty miles from Syria and the Soviet troops.

These marines are part of the Rapid Deployment Force which is armed to fight in the "integrated battlefield" (simultaneous use of conventional, biological, chemical, and nuclear weapons). There are 7,000 Syrian troops in Lebanon. The Syrians are equipped with Soviet "smart" missiles (similar to the French Exocet missile that sank the British ship in the Falklands). Two U.S. aircraft carriers and one battleship, the *New Jersey*, all armed with nuclear weapons, are patrolling off the Lebanese coast. What will President Reagan do if the Syrians use a Soviet missile to sink an American nuclear-armed ship?

Several days after the marines were killed in Lebanon, America invaded the tiny island of Grenada, with a population equivalent to the capacity of the Rose Bowl. By this act of war, the United States violated international law, while at the same time deeply offending the people of England. Grenada is a member of the British Commonwealth, as is Australia. This event aroused instant jubilation and a flush of patriotism among the U.S. population as they finally felt a sense of vindication and self-righteousness for the first time since their humiliating defeat in Vietnam.

Such patriotic fervor induced by the combined effects of the victory in Grenada and mourning for the marines in Lebanon is dangerous indeed. I felt an increasing sense of anxiety as I traveled the United States in the weeks following these events, observing the flags flying at half-mast. This is the stuff that wars are made of. In the wake of these symbolic events, coupled with the latent animosity toward Russia engendered by the Korean plane tragedy, thousands of young men rushed to join the marines. Never before had I seen so many men in uniform flying in civilian airplanes and milling around in airports, nor had I seen so many military planes taking off from civilian airports.

Any war in the world—Lebanon, Iran and Iraq, Central America, or Grenada—could flare into a superpower confrontation and nuclear war. What the American people must rapidly comprehend is that war can no longer be fought. War is anachronistic in the nuclear age. We must understand in our hearts and minds what Albert Einstein meant when he said, "The splitting of the atom has changed everything save man's mode of thinking; thus we drift toward unparalleled catastrophe."

At the same time that these international events were unfolding, the INF talks in Geneva failed, as the unilateral U.S. zero-option proposal was rejected by the Russians. The cruise and Pershing II missiles began to be deployed in Britain, Italy, and West Germany, and the Russians walked out of the INF talks. One week later, the Russians also announced they were withdrawing from the START talks. As they pulled out, they said they would deploy medium-range missiles in East Germany and Czechoslovakia, and submarine-based missiles off the Atlantic coast—missiles that could hit Washington six to ten minutes after launching (to match the Pershing II missiles). The Reagan administration seemed surprised by these moves despite the fact that Russia had announced months before that should cruise and Pershing II deployment proceed, they would retaliate with similar measures and would withdraw from the talks. Reagan's position had been that the Russians would only negotiate if America played from a position of strength. And so continues the deadly arms race, fueled by macho men who do not understand conflict resolution. Averell Harriman, former U.S. ambassador to Moscow, labels the Reagan administration with "three years of nuclear irresponsibility." He says that "negotiations have been treated as a forum for propaganda, an occasion for invective, a mask to cover new deployments and as an arena to gain advantage—rather than as a path to human survival on this planet."

George Kennan said that never before had the U.S. –Soviet relationship been at a lower ebb and the risk of nuclear war higher.

Because of the serious potential for superpower confrontation in the Middle East, the Persian Gulf, and Central America, together with the qualitative increase in the arms race and the disastrous relationship between the superpowers, 1984 promises to be one of the most frightening years in the history of the world.

It has been my experience that as I became more and more concerned about nuclear war, I developed a hunger for concrete facts about the arms race, so I could maintain my credibility and develop an ability to debate with any person who believed in deterrence, *Star Wars* defense, winnable nuclear war, and/or the arms race.

This chapter outlines basic information about present and future weapons and the C^3I system.

There are approximately 50,000 nuclear weapons in the world today. America and its allies own 31,000. (About 26,000 U.S. nuclear weapons are in the active inventory and 4,000 more are in inactive storage.) Russia owns 20,000; China, 225 to 300; India, 102; Israel, 200, according to CIA estimates; South Africa has probably tested 1. By the year 2000, it is predicted that Egypt, Saudi Arabia, Iraq, Iran, Pakistan, South Korea, Taiwan, the Philippines, Japan, Mexico, Brazil, Argentina, West Germany, Sweden, Italy, Spain, Canada, and Australia could have nuclear weapons.

Nuclear war between the superpowers could occur at any time, triggered by computer accident or by design, as the Cold War escalates. It would take between thirty minutes and several hours to complete. One billion people would be dead with one billion more seriously injured, since there is no defense against strategic intercontinental nuclear weapons. President Reagan, in his third year of office, started to revive the idea of constructing defensive measures against nuclear war. He called this the "Buck Rogers" idea, and he devised the plan after talking to one of his chief advisers on nuclear weapons, Edward Teller. Teller's system, called High Frontier, reflects a "third generation" of nuclear weapons, the first having been atomic bombs and the second hydrogen bombs, for which he was responsible. This system would operate from platforms in space from which laser beams, including X-ray beams, generated by nuclear explosions in space would be focused on Russian missiles and warheads as they zoom by at twenty times the speed of sound. In a full-scale nuclear war, up to 7,500 Soviet nuclear warheads would have to be destroyed in such a manner, all within a period of minutes. Other people advocate laser and particle beams (directed energy), which would need to be focused on each incoming warhead for many seconds, depending upon the energy level, to achieve the desired debilitating effect, but the X-ray beam would be instantaneous. However, the warheads can be protected from such destruction by shielding, spinning, or decoys. According to critics, 100 percent destruction of incoming warheads would be impossible to achieve; so even if only 70 bombs or 1 percent of the 7,500 escape destruction, and if they are targeted properly, it would be sufficient to destroy the seventy major cities in the United States.

Both the United States and the USSR have been working on this space-based, antimissile technology, but both are at least twenty years from achieving any practical application. Further, this new strategy openly violates the Anti-Ballistic Missile Treaty and a 1967 agreement not to deploy weapons of mass destruction in space. Moreover, the Soviet Union views a massive missile defense effort along with a buildup of new and more accurate cruise and ballistic missiles as preparation by the United States for a first-strike nuclear war. The Soviet response will be to work harder on defensive mechanisms, which may never work, and it will generate new offensive systems to overcome the new U.S. defense.

Obviously, this new Reagan-Teller strategy does not attempt to define protection for Europe. Russia could simply use short-, medium-, or intermediate-range tactical nuclear weapons to destroy Europe, weapons that do not need to travel through space to reach their targets. Incidentally, an article in *Science* magazine, November 1982, quotes Hans Bethe, Nobel laureate and longtime colleague of Teller during the Manhattan Project: "Everybody recognizes that Teller, more than anyone else, contributed ideas at every stage of the hydrogen bomb program, and this fact should never be obscured; but, 9 out of 10 of Teller's ideas are useless. He needs men with more judgment, even if they be less gifted, to select the 10th idea, which often is a stroke of genius." It is incredible to me that Teller should now be a member of the White House Science and Advisory Committee, advising President Reagan on nuclear weapons. Teller was one of the main architects of the arms race, and he destroyed Robert Oppenheimer in a vindictive competition, so that Teller could build his "super" or hydrogen bomb.

Submarines. America maintains half its strategic warheads, that is, 5,152 hydrogen warheads, on 34 invulnerable submarines. Fifty-five percent of the submarines (18 to 20 submarines) are at sea at any one time. That means that almost 3,000 hydrogen warheads are targeted from under the sea on the Soviet Union at all times. Because America has two long, uninterrupted coastlines and an additional submarine base in Scotland, it has greater access to port facilities and global oceans than does the Soviet Union. Just one Poseidon submarine with 16 MIRVed missiles, each fitted with 10 hydrogen warheads, can destroy 160 separate targets—most large and medium-size cities in the Soviet Union. There are only 218 cities with populations of 100,000 or more in the country. The 160 bombs that the Poseidon carries have a total explosive yield of 6.4 megatons, greater than that of all the munitions fired in World War II (and still this megatonnage is a few thousandths of the megatonnage in either the U.S. or Soviet arsenals). Because of their staying power under water, the U.S. submarines could wage a protracted nuclear attack on Russia lasting as long as three months.

The Russians have 62 modern submarines carrying strategic nuclear weapons. These submarines are smaller, noisier, and easier to track than the U.S. submarines. Only 15 percent are maintained at sea at any one time because the USSR lacks midocean stations and an extensive coastline, so they must rely on the long transit time from their very few all-year ports. The Soviet submarines carry almost 2,000 nuclear weapons, but because so few are at sea, only about 300 nuclear weapons are targeted on the United States from the sea. These missiles take from fifteen to thirty minutes from launch to hit coastal U.S. targets (less than ICBMs because of their "lower trajectory" and because of the shorter distance they have to travel).

Strategic Bombers. America has 263 B-52 bombers, which, although they are twenty or more years old, have been constantly refitted and upgraded with new armaments and millions of dollars' worth of antiradar and missile-baffling devices.

Although they are high-speed jet aircraft, the planes will not arrive at the targets until after the U.S. missiles, which have a thirty-minute transit time, have destroyed the Soviet air-defense bases, radars, and communication systems. Thus bombers will be used for "post-attack reconnaissance." They will drop hydrogen bombs on the few remaining undamaged targets. Altogether, the United States has 323 operational strategic bombers, with others in reserve, and 250 in storage. These planes carry a total of more than 3,000 large hydrogen bombs and missiles. One of the great advantages possessed by the United States is its 600 KC-135 aerial tankers used to refuel the bombers in midair and extend their range, whereas the USSR has only 30 such long-range tankers. America will soon add new KC-10 tankers to its arsenal and re-engine 300 KC-135 tankers.

Russia has 145 to 150 old bombers, two thirds of which are still propeller-driven. These planes carry 290 large hydrogen bombs. The paucity of Russian bombers is a result of a short-sighted and rigid military and political bureaucracy, reflecting the dominance of the army and its land-based missile command.

Land-Based Missiles. The Soviet Union has concentrated on land-based systems—70 percent of its warheads are land-based, 24 percent are submarine-based, and 6 percent are in old bombers.

It has 1,398 ICBMs (intercontinental ballistic missiles). Seven years ago, it had 1,600. (The discrepancy between 1,398 now and 1,600 seven years ago is because 200 old-style warheads were dismantled.) These missiles carry 5,673 nuclear bombs. These bombs are bigger than the American bombs, but the missiles are less accurate and their systems more clumsy. Ninety-six percent of Russian ICBMs are old-fashioned and liquid-fueled, and their warheads are large, in part, to compensate for inaccuracy. Beyond this, liquid-fueled rockets take many hours to be readied for launch, and therefore many of the Russian missiles are as yet unsuitable for quick launch-on-warning strategy.

America has 1,040 land-based missiles containing 2,140 hydrogen bombs. All but 40 of these missiles are fueled with solid propellant and can be launched against the Soviet Union, should it try to strike first, within the thirty-minute flight time of the Soviet missiles, a plan known as launch-on-warning. Therefore, the Russian missiles would hit empty silos. The U.S. ICBM force maintains an alert rate of 98 percent, whereas the Soviet Union ICBM alert rate is probably much lower. It is now possible to launch U.S. ICBMs from an airborne command post if, during a nuclear war, the ground command centers are destroyed.

President Reagan is fond of showing charts demonstrating the large numbers and larger sizes (called throw-weight) of Soviet missiles. The American missiles, in comparison, seem to be fewer, smaller, and "older" in design. This always suggests to me that the American officials suffer from a case of acute missile envy. In fact, America has continually modified and improved its existing missiles, a policy that has proven to be cheaper, while Russia has introduced entirely new models each time it has wished to upgrade its missiles. For instance, the United States modified the Minuteman II missile with a very accurate Mark 12A warhead that costs $155 million, while Russia had to design three new missiles (SS-17, SS-18, and SS-19) at an estimated cost of $28.5 billion, to attempt the same thing. Further, American missiles are much smaller than Soviet missiles because years ago America learned how to miniaturize hydrogen bombs, that is, to make small bombs with the same yield as larger ones, while Russia still has not perfected this technique. Either the President does not understand these issues or he is intentionally misrepresenting the facts.

Tactical Nuclear Weapons

The other nuclear weapons are tactical, to be dropped from airplanes, used in land mines, artillery, and surface-to-surface or surface-to-air missiles. The United States has a total of approximately 20,000 tactical weapons: 6,000 in Europe (many near the front lines of East and West Germany), 700 land-based in Korea, 1,000 elsewhere in Asia, and as many as 5,000 other forward-based tactical nuclear weapons aboard aircraft carriers, missile cruisers, and other surface ships. The United States has 400 fighter bombers in Europe, which can deliver nuclear weapons on all Warsaw Pact countries, and 180 medium-range Pershing 1A missiles based in West

Germany. It also deploys nuclear weapons at over 200 sites in 11 countries outside the United States: Belgium, Canada, Greece, Guam, Italy, the Netherlands, the Philippines, South Korea, Turkey, Britain, and West Germany.

France and Britain together have more than 500 nuclear bombs, which they can explode on the USSR, including 18 French intermediate-range missiles, 34 French strategic bombers, and 5 French nuclear submarines, each equipped with 16 missiles. According to the Stockholm International Peace Research Institute's "worst case analysis," by 1990 Britain and France could possess 1,600 warheads—an increase of more than 500 percent.

For twenty years, the Soviet Union had approximately 600 SS-4 and SS-5 medium-range missiles, of which about 200 SS-5s now remain. The United States decided not to counter these with its own ground-based intermediate-range missiles but rather to use strategic missiles on submarines allocated to NATO in the Mediterranean, and bombs in forward-based planes placed in Britain. In 1977, that balance shifted when the SS-20 began to be deployed by Russia. The 369 medium-range SS-20 missiles are mobile and more threatening, it is claimed, because they are each MIRVed with 3 warheads. One third of these have been placed along the Sino–Soviet border, aimed at China, Japan, and Korea, and two thirds—that is, 246 missiles having 750 warheads—are on the European frontier.

President Reagan and his team discriminate against SS-20s, SS-4s, and SS-5s by saying they can threaten Western Europe, but Europe has no medium-range missiles with which to threaten the Soviet Union. Yet the 10,000 U.S. *strategic* weapons deployed in the United States and on submarines could reach Russia within minutes to hours; and Russia, if it wished, could target its strategic missiles on Europe. Thus a new and patently *artificial* distinction between *tactical*, medium-range European weapons and *strategic* weapons is being made.

The Reagan proposal on Intermediate Range Nuclear Forces (INF) totally ignores all the U.S., British, and French bombs that can hit the USSR and demands that Russia remove all its SS-4s, SS-5s, and SS-20s, including those targeted on China. (These were excluded in a modified U.S. proposal late in 1983.) This is called the zero-zero option.

Richard Perle, staffperson of the late Henry Jackson, who engineered the Jackson-Vanick Amendment and who helped destroy the SALT II treaty, drafted, promoted, and defended the U.S. proposal at the INF talks. In the summer of 1982, Paul Nitze and Yuri Kvitsinsky, the INF negotiators, proposed that the Soviet Union reduce its three-warheaded SS-20s to 75 in exchange for 300 single-warheaded cruise missiles and no Pershing II deployment. This was called the Walk in the Woods proposal. The State Department, the White House, the Pentagon, and the Joint Chiefs of Staff were favorably inclined. Perle, who was on vacation at the time, returned to sabotage this informal agreement by demanding that America be free to deploy some Pershing IIs. Before the talks resumed, word got to Moscow that Washington had rejected the compromise, and the proposal collapsed. I consider the INF proposal to be a very short-sighted, tunnel-visioned, and a rather unintelligent view of the European situation, which is bound for failure. If the Reagan administration were serious in its intent to reach a negotiated proposal on intermediate-range weapons, it would have included American forward-based systems in the airplanes, American missiles in the NATO submarines, and the French and British forces. A bomb is a bomb is a bomb, and to the Russians it will not matter where the hydrogen bombs originate when they explode on their cities. America could lose 90 percent of its nuclear bombs and still be able to destroy the Soviet Union several times over—if, indeed, that would be the conscious intention of a country whose Constitution is deeply rooted in the Judeo-Christian tradition.

It is thought that the Soviet Union maintains approximately 12,000 tactical warheads within the Warsaw Pact countries and within the USSR itself. Three thousand of these tactical weapons are maintained for European use. (A nuclear bomb is also called a warhead or a weapon; a missile is a rocket that delivers the bomb.)

START Talks. In 1982, President Reagan made a proposal to the Soviet Union called the Strategic Arms Reduction Talks (START) which addresses only the strategic weapons and ignores the tens of thousands of tactical nuclear warheads. In this proposal he called for an equal level between the superpowers of 2,500 land-based nuclear bombs, with a total of

5,000 strategic-missile weapons on both sides. The trouble is that the Soviet Union, because it has concentrated on land-based bombs, has 70 percent or 5,673 of its strategic weapons on land, so under this proposal it would have to disassemble more than half its land-based force. The United States has 2,140 land-based warheads and would, in fact, be allowed to build more under this proposal. Because the United States also has 5,152 nuclear bombs in its submarines (the Soviet Union has only 1,970), America will obviously have to dismantle approximately 2,000 of its antiquated submarine weapons. Reagan says that both sides only have 7,500 strategic weapons. He counts only land- and submarine-based missile warheads, but he has ignored the fact that America has more than 3,000 hydrogen bombs on strategic airplanes, while Russia has over 300 bombs in its strategic planes. Also excluded are the 1,700 tactical, or so-called Euro-strategic, nuclear weapons, which could be flown from Europe to Russia in a short period of time.

The START proposal does not include cruise missiles (each armed with a single warhead), almost 8,000 of which are to be deployed by the United States—and cruise missiles are considered strategic weapons by Defense Secretary Weinberger. The proposal also implies that for Russia to be legitimately equal to America, it must make a huge investment in building a new submarine fleet to compensate for the loss of its ground-based bombs and missiles implicit in the treaty.

Late in 1983, the administration, in order to placate the almost universal mandate from the American people (86 percent in October 1983 wanted a bilateral nuclear weapons freeze), offered a "builddown" proposal—dismantle two old nuclear weapons for each new one. This still allows for the modernization program, and is totally consistent with the Defense Guidance Plan's winnable nuclear war. Both the START and Builddown proposals are unfair and totally unacceptable for the Soviet Union, designed for failure, as is the INF proposal. Both of these proposals were designed to a large degree by the people from the Committee on the Present Danger. When will the American President approach arms control talks with a serious intent and motivation? Both superpowers go to war in their arms control talks, each wanting to come out stronger than the other. This macho zero-sum game mentality is anachronistic, self-defeating, and ultimately suicidal in the nuclear age. In fact, years of arms control talks have only legitimized new generations of nuclear weapons by both superpowers.

Conventional Weapons

Both the Soviet Union and the United States spend about 80 percent of their military budgets on conventional weapons and about 20 percent on nuclear armaments. It is often said that the Soviet Union is stronger than America in conventional arms. Let us again look at the facts.

Troops. NATO has a total of 5.9 million troops, the Warsaw Pact nations 4.8 million, and China 4 million. Russia deploys 1 million troops on the Chinese border. In 1980, Secretary of Defense Harold Brown described the manpower situation as follows: "In the central region of Europe, a rough numerical balance exists between the immediately available non-nuclear forces of NATO (including France) and those of the Warsaw Pact."

Tanks. NATO has 29,000 tanks; China has 11,600; the Warsaw Pact nations have 63,000 in place in Europe. A war between Russia and NATO could well involve China, and Russia would then have an impossible two-front war to fight, which would almost certainly quickly become nuclear. NATO deploys about 500,000 antitank weapons, most of which are precision-guided, heat-seeking, extremely accurate devices (called "smart weapons"). Such weapons destroyed many Israeli tanks in the Yom Kippur War in 1973, and it was the Exocet smart missile that sank the British ship in the Falklands. Because these antitank weapons are extremely efficient, the numerical superiority of the Warsaw Pact tanks becomes meaningless. Many people therefore believe that tactical nuclear weapons in Europe are totally unnecessary and that a Soviet invasion could easily be stopped.

Potential Use of Superpower Conventional Forces

Let us now examine the total conventional forces of the superpowers and their uses. Randall Forsberg's analysis shows that of the total U.S. conventional forces, half are allocated to help Western Europe if there is a war with Russia. This hardware includes the army's armored and mechanized divisions, heavily equipped with tanks and artillery that require an extensive road network and industrial infrastructure. The U.S. Navy sends seagoing convoys to Western Europe with supplies of tanks, artillery, ammunition, and oil. To prevent the U.S. and NATO forces from being able to replenish supplies during a U.S.–USSR war in Europe, the USSR has developed a very large force of antiship submarines designed to sink the supply convoys during such a war. In response to this Soviet submarine force, the United States and its allies have, of course, developed extensive antisubmarine-warfare capabilities, which form the main part of the "sea control" component of the navy. This equipment includes: (1) attack submarines—to destroy other submarines; (2) antisubmarine patrol aircraft; and (3) surface ships—cruisers, destroyers, and frigates, which escort the convoys and provide antisubmarine and antiaircraft point defense in case Soviet submarines and antiaircraft penetrate the outer barriers of the convoy's defenses.

The antisubmarine-warfare system is also being designed and built to be used against Soviet strategic submarines (those carrying strategic nuclear missiles).

The other half of the U.S. conventional forces is designed to fight in Third World countries rather than to defend Western Europe against the Soviet Union. These forces include the marines and the army's infantry, airborne, and air assault (helicopter) divisions. In comparison to the European divisions, these ground troops are equipped more lightly and can fight in difficult mountainous, desert, or jungle terrain, where there are few roads. They are ill-prepared to fight against Soviet tanks but are well-prepared to fight against the weaker and more poorly equipped forces of developing countries (Vietnam, Cambodia, El Salvador, Nicaragua).

The navy has a considerable investment in these missions.

Its "power projection forces" are designed to project or to use U.S. military power in distant parts of the world. These forces are organized around two kinds of ships:

Aircraft carriers are large floating airfields with a crew of 5,000 men and carry 70 to 90 military aircraft, including 60 fighter and attack planes. The attack planes are designed to bomb shore-based targets or naval targets, and the fighter planes will be used to fight off enemy aircraft. The United States owns 13 such heavy aircraft carriers; the Soviet Union has none. Each carrier is surrounded by groups of surface ships to give the carrier antiaircraft and antisubmarine defense. The carriers are also supported by "underway replenishment ships," and these ships also have their own escorts to provide antiaircraft and antisubmarine defense. Therefore, each carrier with the ability to place up to 90 planes in any remote region of the world takes with it a task force of 8 to 10 ships, built at a total cost of $10 billion to $15 billion. Because it is the wealthiest nation in the world, the United States is the only country that can operate a fleet of aircraft carriers with modern supersonic aircraft.

The amphibious assault ship can land marines and their equipment. As with aircraft carriers, these assault ships give the United States the ability to sit offshore and launch ground troops onto a beach in an attack on a country that may not have enough popular support for the United States to use a ground base or harbor. The carriers can support such an assault by aerial bombing. The United States has 12 amphibious assault ships, which are the size of small carriers and carry a total of 20,000 troops. They weigh 40,000 tons and carry 30 helicopters and 8 vertical takeoff and landing (VTOL) planes. The United States also has another 55 amphibious landing ships. Each weighs more than 10,000 tons and carries 25,000 marines. (That is a total of 45,000 marines.)

The two largest amphibious ships possessed by the USSR are the Ivan Rogov class, which displace 11,000 tons and are one-fourth the size of the biggest U.S. assault ships. These are the only Russian ships that can project troops overseas. All the others are smaller and possess only limited combat capability. These small ships are designed to operate in the landlocked seas near the Soviet Union—the Baltic and Mediterranean seas, the Sea of China, and the Sea of Okhotsk. Altogether the Soviets have 100 landing craft. In theory, these ships could carry the total number of Soviet Naval Infantry (marines)—14,500. Since the Soviet Union does not own large carriers and large amphibious assault ships, it cannot launch a large-scale successful attack as can the United States against a developing nation in South Asia, Africa, or Latin America.

To make up for its deficit vis-à-vis the United States, Russia has recently started building smaller carriers, the Kiev class, of which there are now 3. About half the size of U.S. amphibious assault ships, they carry 23 helicopters and 12 vertical takeoff and landing planes, which fly at subsonic speeds. We presume these carriers are to be used mainly for antisubmarine warfare.

The Soviet Union thus has far less offensive power-projection capability than the United States, which is free to intervene militarily in any part of the world (the Americas, Africa, Southeast Asia), while large-scale Soviet military operations tend to be overt and constrained to areas contiguous to Soviet borders (Iran, Afghanistan, North Korea). Since about one third of the Soviet ground and air capabilities are oriented to Europe and one third are deployed along the long Chinese border and in other Far East sites, the 100,000 men in Afghanistan had to be taken from other fronts. The USSR, in short, does not maintain any swing forces for large-scale intervention in the Third World. Instead, Russia supports nationalist, socialist, and Communist revolutions in developing countries only through the flow of funds, arms, and training.

Of course, this type of small-scale indirect intervention is paralleled by military aid and arms supplied from the West to the Third World. The United States has a longer history of major direct intervention in developing countries, for example Korea and Vietnam, which both involved approximately 500,000 troops. The Soviet Union, which has traditionally been prepared to intervene on a relatively large scale only in Eastern Europe (Hungary in 1956 and Czechoslovakia in 1968) took an unprecedented step by intervening in Afghanistan.

Ending the whole arms race will obviously be the only way to prevent the Soviet Union from obtaining such a worldwide capability in the future.

Power Projection

   Many Americans tell me about Soviet expansionism as a justification for any sort of U.S. military behavior, but let us look at the facts. Outside Eastern Europe and possibly Afghanistan, Russia has no foreign military bases in the same sense that the United States maintains foreign military bases. Russia controls none of these foreign military facilities and is merely allowed access by the host country. It must ask permission to use these stations, and there are very few Soviet forces permanently or even regularly stationed there. Even those nations closest to the Soviet Union, such as Cuba, Vietnam, and South Yemen, have stated that they would not allow Soviet bases on their soil. Indeed, Soviet access is limited to seven nations: Afghanistan, Angola, Cuba, Ethiopia, South Yemen, Syria, and North Vietnam. The number of personnel is extremely small in each—fewer than 3,000, except that North Vietnam has 4,500. On the other hand, America controls most of its foreign bases and pays rent for them to the tune of hundreds of millions of dollars (often in the form of foreign military aid). It enjoys unhampered use of the facilities and frequently maintains large military forces and equipment on the bases. America runs 359 large military installations around the world in twenty-one foreign countries and eight U.S. territories, plus hundreds of smaller military installations in many other countries.

   This huge number of U.S. bases has been developed over the years following World War II, but the number has

INSTALLATIONS

	Army	Navy	Marine Corps	Air Force	Total
U.S. TERRITORIES					
Canton & Enderbury Is.				2	2
Gilbert & Ellice Is.				2	2
Guam		9		1	10
Johnston Atoll				1	1
Midway Islands		1			1
Puerto Rico	2	5		1	8
Trust Terr. of Pac. Isl.	1			1	2
Wake Island				1	1
Total U.S. Territories	3	15		9	27

FOREIGN AREAS				
Antigua		1		1
Australia		1	1	2
Bermuda		3		3
Belgium	1			1
Canada		1		1
Cuba		1		1
Diego Garcia		1		1
Germany, Federal Rep. of	176		11	187
Greenland			2	2
Greece		2	2	4
Iceland		1		1
Italy	2	5	2	9
Japan	14	10	4	3	31
Korea, Republic of	36		4	40
Netherlands			1	1
Panama	1	3	2	6
Portugal			1	1
Philippines		8	3	11
Spain		3	3	6
Turkey	1		6	7
United Kingdom	1	4	13	18
Total Foreign Areas	232	44	4	54	334

increased from 323 ten years ago to 359 today. These bases
are and will be used as part of the American power projection
around the world. The location and number of bases are
illustrated in the chart above. The number of American
personnel maintained at these bases is extremely large in
most instances.

Let us take the Philippines as a typical example. This
country is the headquarters of the Thirteenth Air Force at
Clark Air Force Base, which is the logistical hub of the U.S.
military air traffic in the western Pacific, and a nuclear submarine facility. Subic Naval Base in the Philippines is a major
ship-repair facility for the Seventh Fleet. Seven other military installations perform important military communications
and surveillance functions. These bases support more than
15,400 military personnel, supplemented by 9,000 Seventh
Fleet sailors in port at any one time. The bases cover 192,000
acres of arable land, so important to the malnourished people
of the Philippines. This base complex is "a state within a
state," and Clark Air Force Base is larger than the whole
state of Singapore.

Clark was established eighty years ago by General Arthur MacArthur (Douglas's father), chief of the then colonial army that subjugated the Philippines. MacArthur said at that time, "Its strategic position is unexcelled by that of any other position on the globe. It affords a means of protecting American interests which, with the very least output of physical power, has the effect of a commanding position in itself to retard hostile action." In the intervening years, these bases have been used as springboards for U.S. military intervention in Korea between 1950 and 1953, in the Quemoy–Matsu area of China in 1958, and in Vietnam and Cambodia between 1965 and 1975. They have also served as staging areas for U.S. displays of force and military war-game exercises in many parts of East Asia, South Asia, and East Africa.

The Philippines is governed by a dictator, Ferdinand Marcos, and his powerful wife, Imelda, both backed up and supported by the United States. They live lavishly, spend enormous amounts of their country's money on art, showcase medical facilities, and big parties, while the majority of their people live in a state of abject poverty and malnutrition. Their regime is widely regarded as among the world's worst human-rights violators. American troops take their R & R here. Consequently, approximately 3,000 women and girls, some of whom have not yet reached their teens, become receptacles for their pleasures. A whole culture of prostitution and degradation has been established. An additional 12,000 prostitutes service the 9,000 sailors of the Seventh Fleet.

The Pentagon has admitted on numerous occasions that "there is no identifiable external threat to the Philippines," but the bases have recently acquired a special significance because of their possible role in the Pentagon's secret 1984–88 Defense Guidance Plan, which outlines American ability to fight a protracted conventional or nuclear war on different fronts throughout the world at the same time. Because of the Philippines' strategic location, the bases serve the following functions in U.S. interventionist strategy:

(1) As the logistical center for the deployment of naval nuclear arms units in the Indian Ocean, and as a jumping-off point and training center for parts of the Rapid Deployment Force (now called the Central Command), designed for intervention and war in the Middle East.

(2) To project U.S. military power to the mainland of Southeast Asia.

(3) For critical backup of U.S. forces in South Korea.

(4) To deploy naval units and fighter bombers to East Africa and to serve as an alternative supply line to Israel if there are hostilities in the Middle East.

Early in 1983, the United States agreed to give the Philippines $900 million as rent for the bases. Most of this money will be given in the form of military aid to Marcos. The U.S. Foreign Assistance Act of 1961 as amended, section 502B, states that "no security assistance may be provided to any country, the government of which engages in a consistent pattern of gross violations of internationally recognized human rights." Also, part of the U.S. bases agreement signed under the Marcos regime allows the United States to conduct intelligence activities virtually anywhere in the Philippines for U.S. security needs.

Other Examples of U.S. Foreign Bases

In July 1983 the United States paid Greece $500 million in military assistance for the right to maintain more than two dozen military facilities in that country (only 4 are part of the 359 major bases previously mentioned), despite the fact that Prime Minister Papandreou had promised in his 1981 campaign to remove U.S. bases from Greece. Nevertheless, this agreement called for removal of these bases within five years. The facilities consist of two large anchorages, airfields, weapons depots, radar stations, communications centers, and intelligence-gathering outposts. They greatly facilitate the U.S. presence in the eastern Mediterranean and serve as listening posts for southeastern Europe, the Middle East, North Africa, the Black Sea, and beyond.

Australia is also an unwitting host to 20 to 30 U.S. military installations put there without the knowledge of the Australian people. (Only 2 are part of the 359 mentioned earlier.)

Obviously, the U.S. bases expose all of these twenty-one countries to Soviet attack in the event of nuclear war. By signing so-called defense agreements with the United States, these countries have, in fact, signed mutual suicide pacts—not what most people in the nuclear age would call defense.

One of the saddest examples of the abuse of the host country is the saga of the Marshall Islands. These Pacific islands were allocated to the United States after World War II as a U.N. trust territory. The U.N. trusteeship agreement allows the United States in its administration of the islands to bypass the U.N. General Assembly and report directly to the Security Council, where America retains veto power.

The U.N. mandate directed the United States to develop the islands toward self-sufficiency and to "protect the inhabitants against the loss of their lands and resources."

During a twelve-year atmospheric nuclear testing program, America exploded sixty-six hydrogen and atomic bombs over the Marshall Islands, and six islands were blown off the face of the earth, while many others were rendered radiologically uninhabitable by the fallout.

During the fifties, the CIA operated a secret counterinsurgency base on Saipan, one of the islands, training Chinese Nationalists to retake the Chinese mainland, and since the early 1960s, the Kwajalein group of islands has been used to test all the U.S. long-range intercontinental ballistic missiles. Once the islanders were self-sufficient, living off their fish, coconuts, and other produce, and enjoying their own culture. Now they are dependent upon America for 90 percent of their resources. There have been efforts by these people to move toward independence, but America always quashes them. Military Civic Action Teams are used to promote "friendship," but as Roger Gale, former director of Friends of Micronesia, said, "An interesting pattern developed. Army engineering teams became responsible for civic action in the Marshalls, where anti-ballistic missile testing is done. Navy Seabees work in the Carolines, where naval port facilities and marine training sites are planned, and air force teams operate in the Marianas where reconstruction of World War II air bases on Tinian and Saipan are in the cards."

The United States has also been working to ensure military control of Micronesia. In 1973, Secretary of State Henry Kissinger directed the CIA to "assess the possibility of exerting covert influence on key elements of the Micronesian independence movement where necessary to support U.S. strategic objectives."

The island of Palau is a matriarchal society where the women receive the landholdings and choose the tribal chiefs.

Despite the fact that the United States has been teaching the ideals of democracy to the people of Palau for thirty years, it is actively undermining the world's first nuclear-free independent constitution in Palau. This has been passed by popular plebiscite on three different occasions by large majorities. Instead, the United States is pushing for the Compact of Free Association, which calls for extension of an airstrip, use of 32,000 acres for jungle warfare and guerrilla training, and the use of beach areas for landing tanks and other equipment. The pact also demands freedom of activity for off-duty soldiers, storage and ocean dumping of nuclear waste, and storage of nuclear weapons. The women of Palau are leading the battle against this invidious development.

Naval Commander David Burt said during a 1976 visit to Palau, "There are millions of people in Japan and only fourteen thousand in Palau. It may be necessary to sacrifice the fourteen thousand."

Many people from the Kwajalein atoll have been displaced from their islands, and eight thousand people are packed onto a tiny seventy-eight-acre island called Ebeye amid appalling sanitary conditions so that America can operate its Kwajalein missile range—which is a convenient 4,200 miles from California's Vandenburg Air Force Base—to test the MX and other exotic delivery systems. MIT and Draper Labs, where the guidance systems of the missiles are designed, have a direct telephone line to the Kwajalein missile range. The military has severely restricted the access of these people to a nine-thousand-square-mile lagoon, which they used to use for fishing, and to their ninety-three islands, which they used for agricultural purposes.

In 1978, more than 50 percent of the Ebeye population was under fourteen years of age; yet there is no high school on the island, whereas the Kwajalein high school, three miles away, is for American children only. The indigenous parents who want an education for their children must send them hundreds or thousands of miles away to schools in Majuro, Guam, or other parts of Micronesia at great personal expense, but these people are destitute. All the food is imported to this island, and the prices are 100 percent higher than for inexpensive food on Kwajalein. These people have very few recreational facilities—a volleyball and basketball court and one baseball field for eight thousand people. In contrast, three thousand Americans on the main island of Kwajalein have a golf course, bowling alley, basketball and handball courts, baseball fields, swimming pools, free movies, and other amenities. The Marshallese are employed in low-paying jobs to serve the Americans as maids, gardeners, cooks, and so forth, and they must have passes, issued in limited numbers, to travel to their own islands for such purposes as banking or airline business.

Sanitary conditions are appalling, and raw sewage is flushed into the Ebeye lagoon, where pollution levels are 25,000 times higher than the level set as safe by the World Health Organization. In 1963, a severe polio epidemic occurred on Ebeye and other Marshall Islands. More than 190 people became severely paralyzed at a time when polio vaccines had been available in the United States for eight years. Dr. Konrad Kotrady, a Brookhaven National Laboratory resident physician on Kwajalein, told a U.S. congressional committee investigating the problems of Ebeye: "The picture I would like to paint for Kwajalein regarding Ebeye's health care system is that Kwajalein [U.S. administration] has an attitude of indifference and apathy to what occurs on Ebeye. The Army's position was summed up for me one day when a high-level command officer at Kwajalein remarked that the sole purpose of the Army at Kwajalein is to test missile systems. They have no concern for the Marshallese and [it] is not of any importance to their being at Kwajalein Missile Range." U.S. Representative John Seiberling said, in August 1982, "I think the actions of the military are hardly becoming of a nation that is a great power. Here we have a bunch of people who are our wards. We are occupying their land and are denying them the right to peacefully assemble and petition for redress of grievances that our Constitution guarantees to our own citizens, and yet we are in their country. I think it's a pretty sad spectacle." The Marshallese made the following statement to the U.N. in 1956: "Land means a great deal to the Marshallese. It means more than just a place where you can plant your food crops and build your houses; or a place where you can bury your dead. It is the very life of the people. Take away their land and their spirits go also."

On October 20, 1982, the Kwajalein islanders signed an agreement with the U.S. Department of Defense to extend the Kwajalein Missile Range (KMR) agreement through to

September 1985. The negotiations brought changes of (1) reducing the maximum term of lease for KMR from fifty to thirty years, (2) establishment of a $10 million fund to improve living conditions on Ebeye over the next three years, and (3) a return to unrestricted use of six other islands in the atoll.

Despite America's overt support and manipulation of right-wing dictatorships for its own ends, President Reagan, when he was in London in June 1982, introduced a new American plan, called Project Democracy, which was designed to promote "democracy" around the world. It will cost $85 million and will be administered by the U.S. Information Agency. Charles Wick, who illegally taped telephone conversations for the first three years of the Reagan administration, is the director of the U.S. Information Agency. It was to have been coordinated by William Clark, former National Security Adviser, who is extraordinarily ignorant about international affairs. (At his Senate confirmation hearings he did not even know the leaders of Zimbabwe or South Africa.) The project has four components—information sources, political involvements, covert activities, and a quasi-governmental institution. Initially, the CIA and the National Security Planning Group were to be responsible for the covert component, but the CIA was pulled out because people thought its past invidious activities would create a bad public image for Project Democracy. This project will apparently be used by the United States to train young leaders in other countries and to foster the growth of labor unions, political parties, news outlets, businesses, and universities in countries where democracy is not permitted.

The question I put is "Will Project Democracy be used in the Philippines, South Africa, El Salvador, Guatemala, Brazil, Chile, and other oppressive dictatorships that are propped up and often have been installed by the United States?" It is time that neither America nor Russia was allowed to intervene internally or externally in the affairs of any other country. Most Third World countries are struggling for their independence as America once did, and it is absolutely not indicated for the United States to determine the future of any other country in the world. Such behavior openly flouts the principles enunciated in the Declaration of Independence.

Comparison of World Military Spending on Conventional and Nuclear Weapons

Randall Forsberg's analysis of the purposes of military spending shows that only about 20 percent of the U.S. military budget is used for nuclear weaponry—to design, develop, and manufacture the weapons, as well as to field and train men to operate the nuclear forces. Conversely, 80 percent of the U.S. budget is for conventional weapons and for ground troops, naval forces, and tactical air forces. It is thought the same breakdown is true for the Soviet Union.

On a worldwide basis, only about 12 percent of military spending is allocated to the nuclear arms race. Another 10 percent of total global military expenditures are made by developing nations on conventional weapons—countries in Latin America, Africa, the Middle East, South Asia, and the Far East (excluding China and Japan). Eighty percent of world military spending is for conventional weapons and forces by the industrialized nations of the Northern Hemisphere—the European countries, the USSR, China, Japan, and the United States.

The Role of Conventional Weapons and Armed Forces

(1) One purpose of conventional weapons is to deter a conventional war—for instance, between the superpowers in Europe. In addition, as the nuclear disarmament movements grow, there are calls to increase conventional forces in Europe to prevent a *nuclear* war. (The rationale here is to use conventional forces to deter a conventional war that might escalate to a nuclear war.) At the same time, however, nuclear weapons are also being built and deployed in Europe to deter or prevent a *conventional* war from occurring.

(2) Conventional weapons are used by the superpowers for internal repression—for instance, by Russia in Eastern Europe. (There were some past suggestions by Henry Kissinger and others that should Socialist or Communist parties in Italy or France appear to be winning elections, the West should be prepared to use military force to oust them. So the United States has threatened to use conventional forces for the internal repression of its allies.)

(3) Conventional forces are used primarily by the United States but also by the USSR to intervene in conflicts in the Third World for political, economic, or ideological purposes. What is significant about the role of conventional weapons in U.S. national security is that none of these missions has anything to do with defense of the United States. Rather, they are intended to defend U.S. interests abroad. For the United States, the first category is to help its allies; the second is for interference in the affairs of its allies; the third is for pure aggression.

The Role of Nuclear Weapons

(1) Nuclear weapons are intended to deter nuclear attack by either superpower upon the other. Deterrence itself is a vague, esoteric theory, which holds that the possession of nuclear weapons will prevent nuclear war. This argument is frequently presented to me as a reason why war has not occurred in Europe for thirty-seven years. I am often reminded of a patient who appeared in the casualty department of a hospital some twenty years ago. He was an old man who said he had been driving all his life and had never had an accident, but this night he appeared with a broken neck, having had an accident for the first time. Obviously, driving for so many years had not deterred him from having an accident.

(2) Nuclear weapons are intended to back up the use of conventional armed forces in the roles previously described. The United States has used this policy against the Soviet Union for years. Although the nuclear weapon used on Hiroshima was said to have ended the war with Japan, the bomb on Nagasaki was used to intimidate the Soviet Union. It was to show Russia that America had a nuclear monopoly and was prepared to use it if the USSR used its conventional forces in a manner objectionable to the United States. Therefore, right from the start, nuclear policy was inextricably intertwined with conventional war, power politics, and "massive retaliation." That is, Soviet conventional forces were to be deterred by the U.S. nuclear threat to obliterate major Soviet cities—appropriate as long as the United States had a nuclear monopoly.

Even after the Soviets developed the bomb, until the mid-sixties, the United States enjoyed overwhelming nuclear superiority, and so the policy of massive retaliation remained (although the theory of "flexible response" was developed during the Kennedy administration in the Single Integrated Operational Plan [SIOP] of 1963), augmented by a threat to use tactical nuclear weapons first against invading Russian conventional forces in Europe.

America developed its strategic forces between 1960 and 1967, and Russia developed its forces between 1965 and 1971. Therefore, only in the last fifteen years has America become vulnerable to a massive Soviet retaliation in which most U.S. cities could be destroyed within thirty minutes. From 1945 to 1971, America acted as a global nuclear bully, threatening total death and destruction to hundreds of millions of Russian people.

For the next decade, 1971 to 1981, both sides accepted the fact of second-strike "parity"—each side would retain enough nuclear weapons after a first strike against it so that it could obliterate the other side in the second strike.

But the response of the United States to parity has been to try to recover its lost position of nuclear superiority by building and deploying more modern and more accurate new weapons: the MX and Trident II and the Pershing II first-strike missiles. Thus a plan for a "winnable" counterforce first-strike nuclear war was enunciated by the Pentagon in 1982. This policy is overtly crazy because if the United States builds these new weapons, parity will be lost, along with the opportunity to stop the arms race bilaterally through a nuclear weapons freeze. The Russians have frequently stated that they, too, will build such missiles, and the arms race will then career totally out of control.

The rationale for these new nuclear forces is once again to end parity and to reach for U.S. strategic superiority. This will be used to reinforce American use of conventional force overseas to defend U.S. interests. To effectively stop the nuclear arms race and to move rapidly to bilateral nuclear disarmament, several simultaneous steps need to be taken: (1) a nuclear weapons freeze; (2) a nonintervention treaty signed by the superpowers, which will end military intervention in developing countries and in superpower satellites; (3) a reduction in the huge conventional forces of NATO and the Warsaw Pact and in the conventional forces of Japan and China; (4) an end to the massive international arms trade to

Third World countries, which would be destabilizing in itself, even if the superpowers ceased their interventionist tactics; (5) an end to innovation and development of conventional weapons—developments in fighter planes, tanks, ships, and missiles create instability and uncertainty about the future; and (6) at the same time, a move toward rapid bilateral nuclear disarmament.

There would then no longer be a tremendous preponderance of military superiority in the Northern Hemisphere, and tension would decrease throughout the world. Only if the superpowers engage in serious nuclear disarmament will they have any moral authority to police other potential or actual nuclear nations. France has already stated that should the superpowers act in this fashion it would have no rationale to continue its *force de frappe*—now known as *force de dissuasion*.

Eventually, conventional weapons should be used only for national defense, that is, to defend a nation's shores and boundaries, and nuclear weapons will be eliminated.

Even this is not a logical conclusion because wars can no longer be fought. We have opened Pandora's box, and the fissioned atom means that we can fight wars no longer. For example, if World War II had been fought today with conventional weapons, Europe would still be radioactively uninhabitable because of the destruction of the many nuclear reactors that dot its landscape. America is in a similar position with its seventy-three large power reactors plus many military and research reactors and huge vats of radioactive waste scattered ubiquitously across the country.

High Tech: C³I

I have always cringed when people extol the wonders of high technology as if it is and will be the answer to all our needs and dreams. In fact, the most creative research in high technology is conducted by those scientists in universities and weapons labs and industries involved with the military. So extraordinarily sophisticated is this technology nowadays that satellites from space can photograph license plates on earth, with the result that nothing on the earth is actually private anymore. Satellites can also monitor all radio, telephone, and other communications in the Soviet Union and other countries, including Australia; and the whole world is wired up like a ticking time bomb by this extraordinary technology, ready to explode with only a thirty-minute warning. Enormous sums of money are channeled from the government and Pentagon into this high-tech research and development, and many major corporations are involved.

When the President touts the virtues of high tech, it is obvious to me that most people have absolutely no idea what high tech really means and that this new scientific development could instigate the murder of hundreds of millions or billions of human beings.

Another aspect of the high-tech revolution that frightens me is the video-game industry, which has captured and captivated our children. Many of these computer games are nuclear war games that are, in effect, conditioning our offspring from a very early age to the prospect of nuclear war. I can think of no more insidious and invidious influence that could be distorting these lovely innocent and open minds than these genocidal games. They are overtly aggressive and are apparently very attractive to boys of all ages. The primary-school boys say they love playing them, and when they finish, they feel very active and aggressive. Girls, on the other hand, soon tire of them and walk away wondering at the boys' fascination. Recently, I was in a large department store and saw two little boys, aged two and three, amusing themselves while their father purchased some sheets. They were making noises like video games and had already, at these tender ages, been inculcated with the nuclear war mentality. As a pediatrician and teacher, I seriously question the moral integrity of the video-game industry, which is having such an insidious influence on our children.

To illustrate this point, here is some public-relations copy taken from the pamphlet advertising Star Path video games for children.

COMMUNIST MUTANTS FROM SPACE: "Your Mission: Vaporize the mutant warriors before they overrun your home planet. These Commie Mutants are crazy! Wipe out wave after wave of them, and they keep on coming. The more you vaporize, the meaner they get. Well . . . You've got a few tricks up your sleeve, too. The 'Shields' option lets you deflect their bombs with a tug on the joy stick. 'Time Warp' lets you gain back lost ground, when necessary. 'Penetrating Missiles' and 'Guided Missiles' lets you mow them down in style, but the real trick is to keep your planet safe for democracy without using any special features. Up to four can play and the screen keeps track of the highest scores just to make sure the heroes get the recognition they deserve."

KILLER SATELLITES: "Your mission: Zap this orbiting junkyard of satellites before they knock your hometown back to the Stone Age. You're the one defender. Test pilot of the only rocket plane that can intercept and outmaneuver this deadly rain of molten metal. Now you're low on fuel and ammo, but watch out when you land. Touch down in an ocean and you're up the creek. And that leaves the Big Apple a pancake."

These games are not wholly fantasy. The Air Force Space Command has a bill before Congress sponsored by Senator Bill Armstrong and Representative Ken Kramer of Colorado called the People Protection Act.

There are five major provisions: (1) turn the new Air Force Space Command into an overall space command for all armed forces; (2) create an Army Space Command under it for ground-based space weapons; (3) establish a single agency for directed-energy weapons—lasers, microwaves, particle beams, etc.; (4) take military missions of the space shuttle away from NASA's responsibility for exclusive Pentagon control; and (5) order NASA to launch a manned space station as soon as possible (President Reagan suggested this in his 1984 State of the Union address).

The Air Force Command believes war in space is inevitable, that fighting in space will be "the decisive form of military power," and that the United States will win if it hurries. The Soviet Union, in the summer of 1983, suggested negotiating a ban on military force in or from space. The administration has ignored this offer. The Space Command planners want to restore "preatomic notions of military superiority," to "make conflict at the upper levels of military violence [nuclear attack] again thinkable." They think this would be an "invigorating turn of events for the spiritual vitality of the Western democracies."

When President Reagan addressed two thousand high school students in Orlando, Florida, in March 1983, he praised the use of video games for children. He said to a cheering crowd, "Many young people have developed incredible hand-eye-brain coordination playing these games. The air force believes these kids will be outstanding pilots should they fly our jets. Watch a twelve-year-old take evasive action and score multiple hits while playing Space Invaders, and you will appreciate the skills of tomorrow's pilots."

The military have also echoed these sentiments. Not only are our children being brainwashed to accept the concept of nuclear war, but apparently they are being trained to be able to fight one.

The *Star Wars* type of film also reflects the insidious acceptance by society of high-tech war in space—recently advocated by the President of the United States. Such films gross enormous sums of money, and although they are fantasy at this time, the research and development of high-tech weapons is not far behind these fantasies.

I remember when the first space shuttle landed after a successful mission. Thousands of Americans turned out to celebrate its landing, as they once turned out with picnic lunches to gaze at the wonders of atmospheric nuclear explosions. People carried signs reading WE'RE NUMBER ONE AGAIN. The space shuttle has become a largely military operation, so that now one third of all shuttle flights will be funded by the Pentagon and reserved for military measures. It is used to launch antisatellite platforms and other contributions to war in space—which, of course, is internationally banned by the Weapons in Outer Space Treaty signed by the superpowers. The crew from the shuttle will be trained to use wire-cutting pliers to remove a satellite's power cells and render it inoperative. Astronauts could also attach a limpet mine to a satellite's hull and use telemetry to detonate it. During a typical seven-day mission, an American space shuttle could destroy up to twelve Soviet satellites.

According to Dr. George Keyworth, the White House science adviser, the space shuttle will be a necessary element for the transportation and integration of a future space-based ballistic-missile defense system. The potential military functions of the shuttle are: (1) to carry into orbit the Defense Support Program 647 Early Warning Satellites, the U.S. Air Force Defense Satellite Communications System's Phase III Satellites, the Fleet Sat Com Fleet Satellite Communications System Satellites, Defense meteorological satellites, long-wavelength infrared surveillance sensors, and even laser weapons; (2) to provide in-orbit servicing and refurbishment of low-altitude military satellites; and (3) to retrieve defunct but still highly sensitive satellites.

In June 1983, President Reagan previewed a new MGM film called *WarGames*. This film is about an adolescent boy who plugs his home computer into the NORAD system and almost sets off World War III. Reagan was discussing his MX policy with a group of congressmen in the White House following the preview, and suddenly his face lit up, and out of the blue he started describing the movie. One of the congressmen reported later, "I was sitting there so worried about throw-weight, and Reagan suddenly asks us if we have seen *WarGames*. He was in a very good humor. He said, 'I don't understand these computers very well, but this young man obviously did. He had tied into NORAD.' "

In the age of high-tech nuclear war, this lack of knowledge about computers is a most serious admission for the Commander-in-Chief to have voiced. Ultimate authority for the release of nuclear weapons rests with the President. It derives from his constitutional position as Commander-in-Chief in accordance with the Atomic Energy Act of 1947. In practice, this authority is exercised jointly by the President and the Secretary of Defense. They are described as the National Command Authority. The chain of command for the actual execution of nuclear war should go from the NCA through the Chairman of the Joint Chiefs of Staff to the executing commander, as defined in 1971. In operations involving strategic nuclear weapons or in a crisis situation, the President may bypass the Joint Chiefs and perhaps even the senior commanders in the field and communicate directly with the commander on the spot. However, the chain must include the Secretary of Defense and the Chairman of the Joint Chiefs of Staff—an arrangement reconfirmed by Secretary of Defense Schlesinger in the last traumatic days of the Nixon administration to ensure that Nixon could not mobilize any U.S. military forces without the consent of himself and the Chairman of the Joint Chiefs of Staff, General George Brown.

Because the system to control and conduct nuclear war is composed of the most complex technology that man has ever devised, it would seem mandatory that the person in control should have at least a working knowledge of the system.

Caspar Weinberger, Secretary of Defense, displays a similar lack of in-depth knowledge about nuclear weapons and the supportive technology behind them.

The following section outlines the Command, Control, Communications, and Intelligence system (called C^3I), which will determine the future of life on our planet. This system has two functions: *Intelligence:* to assess all aspects of Soviet weapons systems, to monitor a Soviet attack, and to assess Russian damage after a nuclear war; and *Command, Control, and Communications:* to control and communicate with all the U.S. strategic, tactical, and conventional weapons and forces and all the allied forces before, during, and after a war.

Command

In the event of the death of the President and Secretary of Defense, there are well-defined lines of succession to maintain a viable National Command Authority (NCA). From the President, the succession of command follows the constitutional succession of presidential authority: the Vice-President, the Speaker of the House of Representatives, the President Pro Tempore of the Senate, and all the members of the Cabinet (from Secretary of State to Secretary of Education). In the case of the Secretary of Defense, the succession proceeds as follows: Deputy Secretary of Defense, Secretary of the Army, Secretary of the Navy, Secretary of the Air Force, Director of Defense Research and Engineering, Assistant Secretary of Defense, and the General Counsel of the Department of Defense (in order of their length of service as such); the Under Secretaries of the Army, Navy, and Air Force (in order of their length of service as such); and the Assistant Secretaries of the Army, Navy, and Air Force (in order of their length of service as such). The highest-ranking survivor would continue to run the government, approve the victory or surrender terms, and marshal the surviving resources for a post-attack recovery. Apparently, several thousand preselected bureaucrats belong to some thirty federal agencies deemed "essential" and "uninterruptable" and would also probably be necessary for post-attack recovery, according to a series of executive orders dating back to 1969. These include the U.S. Postal Service and the Railroad Retirement Board. This whole effort to ensure the continuity of government (COG) entails saving government officials in the event of nuclear war.

The two agencies responsible for the bulk of COG planning and financing are the Defense Department and the Federal Emergency Management Agency (FEMA), an institution created in 1979 by consolidating several small emergency-related agencies. More taxpayer money is being invested in this effort than in saving the lives of 220 million taxpayers and their families. Apparently, this enterprise has been organized by the Reagan government with little fanfare or debate. The money for this program is allocated under a category called Federal Preparedness—the estimated budget in 1983 was $115 million. In 1981, after President Carter enunciated Presidential Directive 58 ordering redoubled emphasis on the COG program, the budget was only $7 million. Apparently, when interviewed in May 1983, Pentagon spokespeople would not discuss COG or its funding, saying that it is all classified. There is little congressional oversight of COG programs and funding. The Armed Services Committees are involved in the authorization programs, as is HUD. Independent-agency appropriations subcommittees do most of the appropriating. All of this work is done in closed sessions.

Apparently, some of the government officials are to be protected in a series of underground and aboveground shelters, including a massive bunker near Mt. Weather close to Berryville, Virginia, which reportedly has two thousand cots. It is said, however, that none of these installations would survive direct or nearby hits. Most of these sites were built more than twenty years ago.

The question to be asked by society is who gives these government people the authority to decide who gets to live or die in a nuclear war. It seems ironic that those very people who have planned and equipped the nation to fight a nuclear war that could bring about the death of most of the civilians in the society are themselves planning to survive the very war they instigate. Because a full-scale nuclear war could certainly threaten most human life in North America, let alone the world, this type of survival planning by an elite is, in fact, a form of unintended eugenics. Are they then carriers of the genetic material that society would deem suitable to survive—they who induced the murder of hundreds of millions of people? Those are questions that have never been asked and that must be posed in a democratic society.

The National Command Authority and their subordinates would be quickly taken to a secret command post near Washington. In 1954, the command facility was located some distance from Washington at Ft. Ritchie, Maryland, and this reinforced-concrete hardened center is known as the Alternate National Military Command Center (ANMCC). In 1961, Secretary of Defense Robert McNamara decided to convert three special communications KC-135 tanker aircraft to serve as the National Emergency Airborne Command Post (NEACP, pronounced *kneecap*). The old planes have since been replaced by a number of E-4Bs and converted Boeing B-747s. These airborne command posts bear the primary responsibility for providing the link between the NCA and the subordinate commands and strategic forces in nuclear war.

Obviously, neither the White House nor the National Military Command Center (NMCC) in the Pentagon are designated or designed to survive a direct nuclear attack. Any comprehensive Soviet attack would target both these facilities and the underground ANMCC. Therefore, the survival of the NCA is dependent upon its ability to reach the specially equipped plane (NEACP) and be safely airborne by the time the Russian hydrogen bombs hit Washington. Until recently, the NEACP plane was usually based at Andrews Air Force Base in Maryland, ten miles east of the White House, but now it is based at Grissom Air Force Base in Indiana, which will render this whole scenario impossible.

It is usually assumed that a Soviet attack against Washington and the C^3I centers would involve the use of submarine-launched ballistic missiles, which, if launched from offshore submarines, could take only five to ten minutes to hit their targets, but the helicopter ride from the White House to Andrews Air Force Base typically takes eight minutes, and there is not usually a helicopter based at the White House. In addition, it would be several minutes before the President and his military aide could be collected.

It is not certain whether NEACP would be ready to take off. In the winter, Andrews Air Force Base can be covered with snow, and once when Defense Secretary Brown was urgently called back to the White House from the Middle East during the Iranian crisis, it took four hours to clear a runway of snow.

It is likely that any dedicated Soviet attack would include all airports near Washington where a 747 could land or take off, and obviously, NEACP would be of the highest priority in such an event. Dr. William Perry of the Pentagon testified in March 1979: "The availability of this aircraft cannot be unconditionally guaranteed."

It is likely that the continuity of leadership would be difficult to manage because if the President was killed in a nuclear attack on Washington, many of the most important people in the chain of command, who could be at the White House or the Pentagon or in the immediate environs, would probably be killed, too. Those away or on vacation might be impossible to find. Therefore, as Admiral Jerry Miller, former deputy director of the Joint Strategic Target Planning Staff (JSTPS), testified in March 1976, the United States "might have considerable difficulty in executing a retaliatory strike in the event of the death of the President."

Also, the execution of a retaliatory strike is unlikely to involve much control. The new American leader is likely to be ignorant of the arguments or arcane logic of nuclear strategy, and apt to accept "the recommendations" of the military leaders. Political judgments and subtlety about the conduct of the war are unlikely to survive the death of the true national leader, and if he had harbored any private thoughts about not retaliating, these would probably die with him. This death itself would elicit extreme and probably irrational demands for all-out retaliation if, indeed, they had not existed before.

Control

The means by which the NCA and subordinates direct the U.S. Armed Forces are provided by the Worldwide Military Command and Control System (WWMCC, pronounced *wimmex*), which is a network of command posts, computers, and communications links, established in 1962 "to provide the constituted authorities with the information needed for accurate and timely decisions and the reliable communications needed to transmit these decisions to the military forces under all conditions of peace and war."

The number of personnel dedicated to the strategic command and control capability is impossible to estimate precisely, but probably 25,000 to 30,000 people are involved. The budget to support this activity is about $2 billion to $2.5 billion a year.

The WWMCC system currently consists of thirty-five computers at twenty-six command posts around the world. It has six functions:

- Assessment of the situation
- Tactical warning (warning of impending nuclear war)
- Briefing of the NCA, and then selection of options by these leaders
- Execution of a selected option of nuclear war
- Assessment after the attack of strikes and damage in the enemy country
- Termination of a previously transmitted order, that is, stopping the war

Each of these functions requires extensive communication between WWMCC and a wide range of other systems and organizations, including the White House Communications Agency, the NATO Command and Control System, the Tactical Command and Control Systems, and various intelligence collection and assessment systems.

One of the most important components of WWMCC is the National Military Command System (NMCS), which consists of the national-level command centers and the communications facilities linking them to intelligence systems and other subordinate command centers.

The NMCS has three principal components:

The National Military Command Center (NMCC) is located in the Pentagon and occupies 78,000 square feet of the second and third floors. It is the hub of both routine and crisis command capability, including in the event of strategic nuclear war. The "hotline" between Washington and Moscow is housed here, but no special measures have been taken to protect the NMCC, and the House Armed Services Committee concluded in 1977 that "there is little possibility that the NMCC would survive a nuclear attack directed against it."

The Alternate National Military Command Center (ANMCC), located underground at Ft. Ritchie, Maryland, is seventy-five miles from Washington. This center would not survive a "dedicated" nuclear attack, and so a backup for ANMCC has been built at the Federal Civil Defense Administration's main relocation site at Mt. Weather, Virginia, but this facility is no less vulnerable than Ft. Ritchie. All communications from the NMCC to the worldwide forces are routed through the ANMCC to permit spontaneous control at Ft. Ritchie, if necessary—that is, if the Pentagon is destroyed and Ft. Ritchie is not.

The National Emergency Command Post (NECP) consists of several E-4B Advanced Airborne National Command Post aircraft located at Andrews Air Force Base, Maryland, as previously described.

The NMCS is backed by the National Military Command System Support Center, also located in the Pentagon. This center supports the automatic data processing, computer display, and display distribution systems for the operation of the NMCS, and it also prepares and disseminates appraisals and analyses of attack hazards and of the vulnerability of forces and resources on a worldwide basis. This facility is also unprotected against a nuclear attack on the Pentagon.

Surveillance, Warning, and Assessment. Effective and efficient command and control is totally dependent upon surveillance, warning, and assessment systems that provide data and intelligence to the command systems. These systems have various components:

Satellites: The Defense Support Program (DSP) is the most important component of the early-warning system, designed to detect a ballistic-missile attack from the Soviet Union or its submarines. The DSP consists of three Code 647 satellites in geostationary orbit. (That is, the satellite's orbital speed matches the speed of the earth's rotation, allowing it to "hover" over one area of the earth.)

These satellites provide full coverage of all potential areas of ICBM and SLBM launchings. One is stationed over the Eastern Hemisphere to provide first warnings of a Soviet or Chinese missile launch, and two are stationed over the Western Hemisphere to monitor submarine-launched ballistic missiles off the East and West coasts of the United States. These satellites would give a twenty-five- to thirty-minute warning of an ICBM attack and a ten- to fifteen-minute warning of a submarine-launched ballistic-missile attack. These warnings are relayed from satellites to ground stations in Australia and Buckley, Colorado; NORAD; SAC headquarters near Omaha, Nebraska; the NMCC in Washington; and probably the Situation Room in the White House.

The principal mechanism used by these satellites for detecting a missile launch is a 1-meter Schmidt infrared telescope, which can sense the energy emitted by ballistic-missile exhausts during the powered states of the flights. The satellites also carry ultraviolet sensors, which can detect the fluorescence from gases surrounding the boosters or nose cones during ballistic flights.

To complement the infrared and ultraviolet sensors, the 647 satellite also carries a visible-light sensor, a television-camera device that enables observers at ground stations in Australia and the United States to observe the plumes of ICBMs as they are launched and rise above the atmosphere. In addition to the early-warning function, the infrared equipment on the 647 satellite can be used for post-attack intelligence by providing data and information on the types and explosive forces of nuclear weapons (obtained by analyzing the infrared spectrum observed) and by monitoring warhead impact points in Russia or China or elsewhere.

The satellites are also equipped with Vela sensors, which can detect and assess nuclear explosions by monitoring nuclear particles, gamma rays, X rays, and electromagnetic pulses. This equipment is designed to monitor and gather specific data on Soviet, Chinese, and French nuclear tests and to assess damage after nuclear war.

Some of these satellites are also apparently fitted with Signals Intelligence equipment. One satellite is reported to be able "to pick up, record and transmit emanations from all land-based communication systems, including radio and microwave telephonic transmissions. It was also rigged with other varieties of electronic surveillance equipment, which were sensitive enough to do the work of the hundreds of listening posts the U.S. intelligence community had in such places as Turkey, Iran and West Germany." (But it didn't prevent the United States from missing all the clues as to the upcoming revolution in Iran.)

*   *   *

Radar: Verification of a satellite early warning would be provided ten minutes later by (1) the backscatter, over-the-horizon (OTH) radar system (located on the East Coast and at two West Coast sites); (2) the Ballistic Missile Early Warning System (BMEWS) at radar stations in Thule, Greenland; Clear, Alaska; and Fylingdale, England; (3) Enhanced Perimeter Acquisition Raid Characterization Program, the upgraded safeguard anti-ballistic missile radar at Grand Forks, North Dakota; and (4) Cobra Dane, a large-phased radar at Shemya Island, Alaska, near the end of the Aleutian island chain.

These radars can track the missiles and can help predict impact points. To detect submarine-launched ballistic missiles, the early warning DSP satellites in the Western Hemisphere are complemented by radar stations on Cape Cod in Massachusetts, at Beale Air Force Base in California, at Elgin Air Force Base in Florida, and at two others under construction, probably in Georgia and southwest Texas.

Intelligence Monitoring: Some early-warning and attack assessment could be provided by Signals Intelligence sources, which include some 2,000 signals-intercept ground stations around the world, electronic intelligence and communications intelligence satellites in low orbit, and signals intelligence derived from the 647 geostationary satellites. These sources could detect and provide early warning of launch commands for ICBMs in Russia or China, scrambling orders for strategic bombers to take off, or communications related to attack preparations.

Most of these data and intelligence related to early-warning, mid-attack, or post-attack are relayed to NORAD, SAC headquarters, the NMCC in the Pentagon, and the Situation Room in the White House.

Communication Systems

Because of the enormous amount of data and intelligence obtained from the systems that have just been discussed and because this material must be transmitted to the Command and Control Centers, an enormous network of global communications has been established under the Defense Communications Agency (DCA). It is all under the WWMCC system, which integrates some forty-three different communication systems, so that any Emergency Action Message can be sent from the NMCC in the Pentagon to U.S. military forces. The communications network includes underwater cables, land lines, radio systems across the entire radio-frequency spectrum from extra-low-frequency (ELF) to ultra-high-frequency (UHF), and satellite relay systems. Much of this network is part of the Defense Communication Systems (DCS), which includes 600 facilities and more than 50,000 individual circuits (measuring 30 million miles), 5 satellites, and more than 100 satellite ground terminals.

There are essential, minimum required elements of this system that are designed to survive a nuclear attack. It is interesting that although most of the submarines, ICBMs, and bombers could survive a nuclear war, the communications system is obviously very vulnerable because of the cables, radar dishes, aboveground receiving stations, and even the satellites.

One of the systems to be used after most communication methods have been destroyed is the 494-L Emergency Rocket Communication System (ERCS). Apparently, twelve Minuteman missiles are equipped with UHF radio transmitters instead of warheads, and when all other communications with the forces have been destroyed, these missiles are to be launched. During their thirty-minute trajectory they will communicate with the remaining ICBM and SLBM forces (but only if the submarines trail a radio receiver above the water, thus exposing themselves to detection and attack). The only message these radios are programmed to give is to launch everything left. This final backup system is actually placed in the most vulnerable part of the ICBM force, and it has no part to play in a controlled escalation, but only orders a massive last-ditch response.

Operational Control of Strategic Nuclear Weapons. Control of the weapon systems on ICBMs, bombers, and submarines is maintained by a very complex system of technical safeguards, organizations, and operational procedures designed to ensure that a command to launch missiles or bombers will be received, authenticated, and acted upon promptly and responsibly and also to ensure that these forces cannot be launched accidentally or without proper authority.

There are checks and safeguards inherent in every strategic system. Throughout the chain of command, from top to bottom, two or more men are always required to communicate about and cooperate in giving and receiving launching signals, so that no one person alone could launch a nuclear war. There are, however, fallibilities in this system, and a retired admiral recently told me that there is no system so fail-safe that an intelligent person could not bypass it in order to start a nuclear war.

A brief summary of the control system includes:

Long-range strategic bomber force: For this force to go into action, the attack and targeting order from the National Command Authority has to be authenticated by several levels of command at SAC headquarters before being given to the bomber crew. All commands must be positive, and if at any stage of the attack the crew does not receive the appropriate orders, radio signals, or other communications, the crew must return to base. From the beginning of the attack, each part of the operation must be carried out in a carefully controlled way by two men usually working independently of each other.

ICBMs, Minutemen: These missiles are assigned to Strategic Missile Wings made up of Strategic Missile Squadrons, each of which is allocated 50 missiles. The squadrons are then divided into flights of 10 missiles, and each flight is controlled by two Launch Control Facilities manned by two officers working underground. They monitor the day-to-day operational status and security of the 10 missiles, and they will take action if and when they receive a launch order. After they receive the "go-code," the two officers check the validity and authenticity of the message. Following the instructions, they then select the number of missiles to be launched, enter the target selection into the missile computers, and prepare the missiles for launch. To fire, each officer must insert a key into his own launch console. The consoles are separated by several feet, and both keys must be turned simultaneously and held in position for several seconds. Before the missiles can be launched, two other launch-control officers at another launch-control center have to insert their keys as well, and any launch-control center can nullify a launch entered by a single launch-control center acting independently of the squadron.

* * *

Submarine-Launched Ballistic Missiles: The operational control of submarines in the Atlantic is controlled by the Commander-in-Chief at the U.S. Atlantic Command headquartered in northern Virginia. This authority then passes down through the Commander-in-Chief of the U.S. Atlantic Fleet to the Commander of the Submarine Forces, U.S. Atlantic Fleet, for administrative control. The operational control of Pacific submarines is through the Commander-in-Chief, U.S. Pacific Command, in Hawaii. His subordinates are similar to those of the Atlantic Commander.

As with the bombers and ICBMs, two men at each level are required to launch the submarine-launched ballistic missiles. The submarine has a two-man message-verification team which verifies the receipt of a launch message. This team is made up of two commissioned officers. Once a verified message has been received, the captain would then open the lock on a red "fire button." Thus, he would begin a carefully coordinated launch sequence that would involve several different individuals at various stations on the boat. For an SLBM to be launched, four officers in different parts of the submarine have to turn keys or throw switches. The navigation officer has a switch, the captain and launch-control officer have keys, and the missile-launch officer has a trigger. Each of these switches indicates "Ready to Launch" and does not imply permission. But despite all these internal safeguards, if, in time of emergency, the submarine cannot communicate back to NORAD or the NCA, there is no physical reason why a submarine commander could not launch his missiles alone.

Intelligence

Intelligence obtained from satellites and relayed to ground stations is used to identify Russian military movements and production of weapons, to obtain detailed information from observing weapons testing and launch orders, and to observe Russian territory after a nuclear war.

The agencies involved in gathering and interpreting this information are the CIA, the National Security Agency (NSA), and the National Reconnaissance Office (NRO).

The ways in which these agencies sometimes obtain their information are shown in the use and abuse of Australia. Ever since World War II, Australian security agencies have worked and cooperated with British and American security agencies for mostly military purposes. Today, the NSA is the principal U.S. intelligence agency in Australia. It has a larger presence than the CIA, which is also large, and is more important and secretive than the CIA.

The NSA was created by classified executive order, signed by President Truman in 1952, and is an arm of the Defense Department. An electronic spying operation under the direct command of the CIA director, the NSA operates a massive bank of the largest and most advanced computers available to any agency in the world—computers that break codes, direct spy satellites, intercept electronic messages, recognize target words in spoken communications, and store, organize, and index this information. At the heart of this technology are the digital computers made by IBM, RCA Corporation, and Sperry-Rand, underwritten in a major way by the NSA.

Although the Constitution of the United States demands an open government operating according to precise rules of fairness, the NSA is an unexamined entity. Its annual budget and staff far exceed that of the CIA or FBI. There is no specific federal law that defines its obligations and responsibilities. The agency is based at Ft. Meade, about twenty miles northeast of Washington. Because there is tremendous secrecy surrounding the agency and because it operates in a highly technical field, it is free to define its own goals, which are apparently twofold: (1) It aggressively monitors international communications links, searching for "foreign intelligence," intercepting electronic messages and signals generated by radar or missile launchings; and (2) it prevents foreign penetration of links carrying information bearing on "national security."

A recent unpublished analysis by the House Government Operations Committee reports the NSA may have employed 120,000 people in 1976 (the FBI had one employee for every six in the NSA) and operated two thousand overseas listening posts, with an annual expenditure greater than $157 billion.

From 1952 to 1974, the NSA developed files on 75,000 Americans—civil-rights and antiwar activists and congressmen and citizens who lawfully questioned government policy as well as those who threatened national security. The CIA had access to all these files.

In 1975, the Senate Intelligence Committee investigated the NSA and expressed great concern about its activities and the failure of Congress and the federal courts to comprehend these activities. The report said: "The watch-list activities and sophisticated capabilities that they highlight present some of the most crucial privacy issues now facing this nation. Space-age technology has outpaced the law. The secrecy that has surrounded much of the NSA's activities and the lack of Congressional oversight have prevented in the past bringing statutes in line with the NSA's capabilities. Neither the Courts nor the Congress have dealt with the interception of communications using the NSA's highly sensitive and complex technology."

Apparently, by using this highly sophisticated technology for decoding computer-based material, the NSA can investigate data used for statistical purposes, employment records, and credit-card, banking, and other operations essential to American life. Thus, these data bases are "electronic windows" into the most intimate details of people's lives, but no laws define the limits of the NSA power. It is not subject to any congressional review. With billions in federal dollars, the NSA purchases the most sophisticated communications and computer equipment in the world.

Outside the United States, two thousand permanent intercept stations are based in Britain, Australia, Taiwan, Japan, South Korea, Turkey, Morocco, West Germany, Spain, the Azores, Italy, Greece, Cyprus, Diego Garcia, South Africa, Thailand, the Philippines, Norway, and scores of other places.

The bulk of the NSA work is done by its three service components: the Army Security Agency, the U.S. Air Force Security Service, and the U.S. Naval Security Group.

In Australia, the NSA works with the Defense Signals Director of the Australian Department of Defense Signals Internal Organization. The three main sites of operation are at Northwest Cape in Western Australia, Pine Gap in the middle of Australia near Ayers Rock, and Nurrungar in South Australia. The NSA has a facility below the U.S. Embassy in Canberra that is apparently capable of monitoring Australian diplomatic traffic (this activity is internationally illegal). According to a former NSA officer, the NSA facility at the embassy "is a major overseas coordinating center for Pacific and Indian Ocean NSA stations."

In England, the NSA monitors all British communications, including lower-level materials from Whitehall. Two NSA defectors said in September 1960, "The U.S.A. successfully reads secret communications of more than 40 nations, including its own allies"—Britain, Canada, Australia and New Zealand, and the NATO allies.

The CIA and NSA are involved in the DSP-647 early-warning geostationary satellites operating over the Indian Ocean. These satellites relay their messages to Pine Gap, which is the biggest CIA installation in the world except for Langley, Virginia, which, of course, is the CIA headquarters. In fact, when Pine Gap was installed in the sixties, the Australian government was told it was operated by the U.S. Department of Defense. During the mid-seventies when Gough Whitman, the Labor Prime Minister, began to find out that in fact Pine Gap was a massive CIA installation which used the Defense Department as a cover, the CIA organized a campaign that overthrew the Whitman government (the government I helped elect). Victor Marchetti, former executive assistant to the deputy director of the CIA and co-author of the secret Pine Gap Agreement, described this operation as a "mild Chile." Much of the CIA overthrow is described in a book called *The Falcon and the Snowman* and in an Australian documentary film called *Home on the Range*. As an Australian, my reaction to the disclosures was total outrage that the American government should interfere with and overthrow my government.

The CIA program at Pine Gap is called Rhyolite and uses satellites developed by TRW. (The principal contractors who installed Pine Gap were IBM, TRW Systems, Inc., and E Systems, Inc.) The Rhyolite satellites are launched under cover of the DSP-647 program. These satellites are located 35,900 kilometers above Borneo, and they suck up like a vacuum cleaner a wide spectrum of Soviet and Chinese military communications and radar emissions, which they beam back to Pine Gap. They also monitor telemetry data from Soviet ICBM tests, which allows the United States to know exactly what the Russians are doing. These satellites are also capable of monitoring all Australian domestic communications, which apparently they do.

Pine Gap also is the site of a Pyramider project, which allows the CIA to indulge in covert activities—to communicate with foreign agents, with sensing mechanisms placed in strategic locations around the world, and with backup communications for overseas systems. The Pyramider program was supposed to ensure "maximum undetectability." There is some doubt as to whether the Pyramider or a similar type of system is in operation at this time.

One of the stations at Pine Gap receives for, and controls, orbiting photographic-reconnaissance and electronic-intelligence satellites run by the National Reconnaissance Office, established in 1960 as a coordinating office for the U.S. Air Force, CIA, and NSA spy-satellite program. It is run by the Office of the Secretary of the Air Force in the Pentagon. The satellites involved in this spy operation are Big Bird and KH-11, which can take pictures from an altitude of 150 kilometers, with a resolution of about eight inches. A film is sent back to earth in a capsule, or the KH-11 uses "advanced sensor and data transmission techniques" in spy-satellite programs.

U.S. reconnaissance systems, including Big Bird and KH-11, use infrared and multispectral photography that can penetrate buildings and determine what is happening in missile silos, factories (this could be a way to monitor production of nuclear weapons), trains, petroleum plants, etc., by monitoring the difference in temperature between the facility and the surrounding earth.

Big Bird and KH-11 satellites are the chief means used to monitor Soviet compliance with the SALT treaty. They were also used in a large operation by the United States during its involvement in Vietnam to pinpoint targets for the secret bombing of Cambodia, to monitor the outbreak of the Yom Kippur War in 1973, and to detect the Indian nuclear tests in 1974. B. M. Jasini in *Outer Space 14*, stated: "It has been noted that this use of reconnaissance satellites is not the accepted use stipulated in the SALT agreement."

If Australia is being used in this way, almost surely a large number of other nations' sovereign rights are being violated in a similar way by the U.S. military and intelligence operation.

Australia is also used for other U.S. military purposes. For instance, a large facility was built by the U.S. Navy at Northwest Cape in Western Australia in 1967 and is now one of the most important links in the U.S. global defense network. This facility transmits very-low-frequency (VLF) radio waves that can penetrate the ocean layers to a depth of 30 to 50 feet, and the American nuclear submarines that carry nuclear weapons can receive the VLF radio waves while remaining deeper than 50 feet by trailing submerged antennae, attached by wire, which float up to the 50-foot depth.

The Northwest Cape is the largest and most powerful of the three main VLF stations in the U.S. submarine-communications system. It covers the western and southern Pacific and Indian oceans. The others are at Jim Creek, Washington, which covers the eastern and northern Pacific, the Bering Sea, and part of the Atlantic Ocean, and at Cutler, Maine, which covers the North Atlantic, the North Sea, the Arctic, and the Mediterranean.

Classified messages to submarines in the Indian Ocean are sent from Northwest Cape. The submarines enter the Indian Ocean through the Indonesian Straits (Lombok and Ombai-Wetar) under a secret agreement between the U.S. and Indonesian governments. Because of the strategic significance of these straits, and to maintain friendly interests in the area, the United States condoned the Indonesian massacre of approximately 250,000 people in East Timor.

There is also a U.S. high-frequency transmitter at Northwest Cape. It was used by America during the mining of Haiphong and other North Vietnamese harbors in 1972. More recently a new satellite ground station was installed at Northwest Cape without the knowledge of the Australian government and will greatly improve its importance to the U.S. military operation. It will enable Northwest Cape to fully participate in global events in Europe. The facilities will be used by the U.S. Army, Navy, and Air Force. Northwest Cape is also used by the NSA for electronic-intelligence receivers that monitor Soviet naval communications from Vladivostok, Khabarovsk, and other Soviet bases.

For Australian military personnel to have limited use of the Northwest Cape facility, the government must pay the United States $1 million per year.

In October 1973, the Northwest Cape was put on alert, and it was used in communicating a general nuclear alert on October 25 to U.S. military forces in the west Pacific and Indian oceans. The Australian government was not informed.

Of course, Northwest Cape, Pine Gap, and their sister station Nurrungar are obviously vital Soviet nuclear targets.

Australia did not consent to become a nuclear target, and many people in Australia feel that our country has signed a mutual suicide pact with America by allowing some twenty to thirty American military installations into our country. Indeed, it is possible, according to some studies, that Australian cities and major industries are also targeted in the event of nuclear war.

A facility called TRANET in Smithfield, South Australia, is part of an international network used by the U.S. Navy to track its navigational satellites, which were developed to provide the Polaris missile submarines with high-accuracy navigational capabilities. The other purpose of these satellites is to obtain geodetic information, which involves the measurement of the exact size and shape of the earth and the study of variations in the earth's gravitational field. Such geodetic information, together with the extraordinary mapping capabilities of the Big Bird and KH-11 satellites, provides the accuracy required for U.S. missile attacks on "pinpoint targets" like USSR ICBM silos and command and control centers—that is, information needed in preparation for a preemptive first-strike nuclear war, as stated in the Pentagon's Defense Guidance Five-Year Plan.

Another very serious and important U.S. military installation, about which the Australian public knew nothing, is the Omega station in East Gippsland, Victoria. It is part of an international network of eight stations. The others are situated in Argentina, Japan, Liberia, La Réunion (a French island off the eastern coast of Africa), Norway, North Dakota, and Hawaii. These stations emit radio signals independently, each in turn in a precisely timed sequence, and each signal is repeated every ten seconds. Omega then is an all-weather, worldwide, continuous, very-low-frequency radio navigation system for aircraft, surface ships, and submarines. Omega is the only radio navigation aid that can be used by a fully submerged submarine in mid-ocean. The VLF radio waves are received by trailing antennae at a depth of 12 to 30 meters, so the submarine can operate at a depth of 600 meters.

Omega is used by the fleet ballistic-missile submarines, all U.S. Navy surface ships, most U.S. Navy aircraft, most U.S. submarines, many U.S. Air Force planes, and some U.S. Army weapon systems. The companies that have produced U.S. Omega receivers are Northrop, Canadian Marconi, Dynell, Litton Industries, Rockwell, Tracor, Hoffman Electronics, and II Avionics.

The U.S. nuclear-powered hunter-killer attack-submarine fleet uses Omega receivers. These submarines carry a variety of nuclear weapons, two of which are the SUBROC nuclear antisubmarine missile and the Mark 48 antisubmarine torpedo. These submarines are targeted on Russian fleet ballistic-missile submarines, and therefore they are part of the counterforce first-strike scenario. They also threaten Russia's second-strike capabilities and are, therefore, inimical to stable deterrence. The United States has 75 hunter-killer submarines and is building more. As Russia is constrained by the SALT treaty to just 69 strategic nuclear submarines, the Russians obviously must be concerned about the viability of their deterrent force.

Omega is also used by English submarines and by a West German submarine. The whole of the Western world's navy surface fleet is being equipped with Omega receivers to increase the efficiency of the fleet in naval maneuvers, blockading, convoying, searching, patrolling, rendezvousing, and station keeping. Omega is to be used by many of the U.S. Air Force planes, and it was specifically developed to be used as a guidance input for the glide bombs used in the Southeast Asian air war.

Rationale for the C³I System

The C³I system has a force multiplier effect. It has allowed the potential of nuclear weapons to be used more effectively, thereby enhancing their efficiency by a factor of two to four. In some ways, the nuclear weapon force can be made more efficient by retargeting the missiles after either first- or second-strike nuclear war. The intelligence satellites review the Soviet landscape (called post-attack reconnaissance), relay the information back to the central command (if they have survived), who then, from their airborne command post, communicate with missile silos to order retargeting to new areas (if the satellites have survived the EMP from the nuclear attack).

Also, the rapidly advancing technology of the C³I system allows navigational satellites to provide midcourse internal guidance to the SLBMs to make them extremely accurate and thus to bestow upon these once countervalue city-busting missiles a hard-target counterforce potential for a first-strike nuclear war. The new SLBMs that will have this capability will be the Trident II missiles.

Evolution of C^3I and the Strategic Doctrine

(1) The massive preemptive first-strike doctrine of the early fifties, according to which nuclear weapons were to be used against the Soviet nation in retaliation for unwanted Russian conventional moves, required only a minimal command and control system.

(2) The massive retaliation and assured-destruction second-strike doctrine required 400 survivable strategic nuclear weapons to reach the Soviet Union after America was hit by a first strike. It required only that the command and control systems survive to guarantee communication and implementation of the response order for a second strike.

(3) The scenario of flexible response, damage limitation, nuclear war fighting, and controlled escalation was first introduced by Robert McNamara, President Kennedy's Secretary of Defense. This doctrine has evolved and is now very complicated and probably completely unworkable.

The C^3I system must be durable enough to survive successive nuclear strikes over weeks or months. C^3I must continuously allow political decision makers to select targets, determine firing rates, communicate with the "enemy" to clarify "confusing events," and provide for negotiations and the control of escalation. This of course is a fairyland fantasy in the minds of the war planners. During the incredible fear and emotion in the middle of a nuclear war, nothing and nobody would work according to plan.

The C^3I would have to provide reliable warning of each strike on the United States, together with assessment of damage to Russia and subsequent retargeting of missiles on worthwhile Soviet targets so as not to waste any bombs, and it would have to ensure that strike targets of equivalent value to those that have just been hit in America are chosen. Adequate communication between the NCA and the strategic forces must of course survive to ensure that all this happens.

War Termination. A natural corollary of the last doctrine is to maintain the ability to terminate the nuclear war if one so desires. Unfortunately, and amazingly, most of the R & D effort has been focused on the beginning and early phases of nuclear war and is designed to allow the NCA to take the initiative during the beginning buildup of a nuclear war so America can determine the dynamics of the escalation process.

The only way available at the moment to stop a nuclear war is the hotline, but, strangely enough, this has not been protected against nuclear war (or hardened like the missile silos).

Missiles once launched cannot be recalled or aborted, and it is impossible for the NCA to communicate with the SLBM submarines or low-flying B-52s over Soviet territory.

Control of Nuclear War. Much of the technology that has been developed for the C^{3}I system is oversophisticated and unnecessary. But, in a certain way, what has been designed is almost impossible for industry, the military, or politicians to reject. They become captives of the scientific imperative of this new fun technology.

For instance, in March 1974, Secretary of Defense James Schlesinger testified that the new command and control systems necessary to support the "new targeting doctrine" came to $300 million, of which $186.7 million had already been committed. Then on the same day he also asked Congress for total obligational authority (TOA) for $6.646 billion for intelligence and communications for fiscal 1975—all this for probably unnecessary technology.

Inherent in this surprisingly sophisticated technology is a lethal trade-off. Should the safety mechanisms to prevent accidental or inadvertent firings be so strict as to inhibit a "readiness and reliability" in time of emergency? Actually, the military have resisted installing safety devices like self-destruct mechanisms (such as radio antennae on ICBMs and SLBMs) because this would increase the weight of the missiles and would generate reliability problems: The antennae would increase the vulnerability of the missiles to EMP and other nuclear effects. This sort of thinking is not conducive to the safety of the world. The military prefer to cut back on safety measures to make sure that the missiles will work properly when needed. Once the military was deployed by a nation to protect its citizens; now it is more concerned with protecting its missiles.

Another problem with the C^3I system is the command and control centers themselves, which are the most vulnerable points. For instance, if one of the functions of the C^3I is to produce a force-multiplying effect of 20 percent to 30 percent of the strategic force, then the adversary would obviously try to destroy the command, control, and communications centers first. But, since the C^3I produces the force-multiplying effect only as long as the system is functional, there would obviously be overwhelming pressures to use this system before it is attacked in the first strike. The Catch-22 is that the more sophisticated the C^3I system has become in its force-multiplying potential for controlling the timing and limitation of attacks over a protracted period of time, the more pressures are generated for early and massive use of strategic arsenals. Apparently, this scenario is most realistic for Western Europe, where the control systems for tactical nuclear weapons are particularly vulnerable and tenuous.

Inherent Vulnerability of C^3I Systems in Nuclear War. Any scenario for fighting "controlled" nuclear war is dependent upon the invulnerability of the C^3I systems during a nuclear war. The chain of command is only as strong as its weakest link, and this is the communications link with the command posts. Apparently, current U.S. policy calls for the command and control systems to be able to operate for ninety days from the beginning of a strategic nuclear war, plus an additional period during which the C^3I system is meant to support restitution of the residual strategic forces—presumably to be ready to fight another nuclear war.

The most vulnerable parts of the C^3I systems are the radar dishes, cables, microwave towers, radio and radar antennae, the early-warning apparatus and power supply, the VLF and Omega communications systems for the submarines, and the satellite control system. These are called "soft targets," as are cities.

Mechanisms for Damage to the C^3I System

Blast: Extraordinary overpressures, followed by winds exceeding 500 miles per hour, are created by nuclear explosions, which can destroy everything in the vicinity except hardened facilities, and even these are destroyed by direct hits.

Radiation: There are three types that can damage C^3I systems:

(1) Ionization of the atmosphere from a high-altitude explosion can seriously disrupt VLF transmissions, thus destroying communications with the fleet ballistic-missile submarines.

(2) Another effect is called TREE (transient radiation effects on electronics). This is a combination of the deleterious effects of X rays, gamma rays, and neutrons on materials used in electronic systems like radio and radar sets, gyroscopes, inertial guidance devices, and computers. Solid-state systems like diodes, transistors, and integrated circuits, plus vacuum tubes and gas-filled tubes, can be destroyed by these effects.

(3) The effects of EMP (electromagnetic pulse) have been described previously. The most effective collectors of EMP in the C^3I systems are long runs of cable, piping, or conduit, large antennae and their feed cables, guy wires and support lines, overland power and telephone lines, long runs of electical wiring, railroad tracks, aluminum aircraft bodies, computers, power supplies, alarm systems, intercoms, life-support control systems, transistorized receivers and transmitters, base radio stations, and some telephone equipment. Just one bomb exploded 200 miles above the continental United States could probably knock out most of these systems in the United States, Canada, and Mexico. Fewer than five such explosions would blanket the United States with as much as 50,000 to 100,000 volts per meter. The military have attempted to protect this equipment from EMP, but without much success.

Sabotage: Of course, all these systems are vulnerable to willful sabotage. It is impossible to guard thousands of miles of cable, land-lines, antennae, guy wires, towers, etc., from this possibility.

Nonnuclear Smart Weapons: Like the Exocet missile, these weapons could easily destroy antennae farms, satellite ground stations, radar facilities, and field command posts.

Human Error: Controlling a nuclear war would be one of the most complicated operations ever undertaken by government, and one that cannot be exercised beforehand. The slightest breach of discipline or departure from set procedures could be disastrous; yet what would be the psychological state of the humans at the control post just before and during a nuclear exchange? The most important lesson of past conflicts and crises is that command and control procedures never work at the outset, as predicted in manuals, and communication systems and procedures often fail, frequently at the most inappropriate times, because of human error. To control a nuclear war, the entire sequence of events must work to perfection the first time. "The simple human mistake of entering a single erroneous digit into a launch control computer could be catastrophic, since it could spell the difference between the destruction of the intended target—an ICBM silo or a remote oil field refinery and that of the wrong target—Moscow." Such an error induced the aberrant course and subsequent destruction of the KAL passenger jet.

Natural Phenomena: Solar-induced ionospheric disturbances and the aurora borealis can seriously disrupt high-frequency radio communications. Changes in the earth's magnetic fields and bad weather can adversely affect the accuracy of ICBMs. All the talk about accuracy and first strike is seriously challenged by the fact that ICBMs have never been launched over the gravitational fields of the North Pole. These magnetic forces could considerably disrupt the flight path of the missile.

Equipment Failure: The C^3I system frequently breaks down. A typical example is the Honeywell 6000 series of computers, built in 1964, which are still the basis of the WWMCC. One exercise involving these computers, conducted in 1977, showed that when the computers were tested, they worked only 38 percent of the time.

Jamming: Russia and America are involved in jamming each other's radio communications and frequencies of similar wavelengths. This is called electronic warfare.

The Airborne C^3I Systems After a Nuclear War Begins

According to Dr. William Perry of the Pentagon, in June 1979 testimony, "Nearly all of the command and control systems would be lost during a nuclear attack, and we would be totally dependent upon our airborne command and control forces at that time." I have previously described the vulnerability of the National Command Authority, but we are now assuming that the President or his designated surviving deputy reach the airborne command system in time, and that it takes off before the bomb lands. This NEACP plane is designated to fly above the exploding bombs—if, indeed, it can evade high-air bursts of the hydrogen bombs and it is not damaged by EMP, which is very unlikely. It is to maintain communication with the strategic forces, ICBMs, and satellites by trailing two five-mile-long copper wires behind it, which will be VHF antennae, and other sorts of antennae to monitor different frequencies from satellites. Of course, these wires will be damaged by EMP and the other previously described effects.

There is a second set of alternative airborne command and control planes based at Offut Air Force Base near Omaha, and since February 1961, they have maintained constant airborne control for SAC bomber and missile forces. One is always in the air flying eight-hour missions at 26,000 feet in a random pattern, 175,000 square miles around Offut. These planes are directly linked to SAC, NORAD, the NMCC, and the AABNCP. These also trail wire antennae, 2 miles long, behind them. Three of these planes can actually program and launch the Minuteman force from the air.

The navy has an equivalent set of planes called TACAMO (take charge and move out), two squadrons of C-130 planes that provide continuous airborne VLF communications to the fleet ballistic-missile subs. One aircraft is airborne at all times over the Atlantic, and one over the Pacific. They can pass communications only one way, from the NCA to the subs and other strategic forces. These planes use a five-mile-long trailing wire antenna and drogue, and with the plane flying in a continuous tight turn, the antenna hangs vertically and thereby becomes a relatively efficient VLF radiator.

These command planes could remain in the air for only a few days—seventy-two hours at the most, provided they are supplied with refueling planes—until they run out of engine oil and crew fatigue takes over. The TACAMO planes can stay aloft only ten hours since they have no refueling capacity. The question would then be where they would land after they have conducted the nuclear war. Most airports where large jets could land will almost certainly be destroyed because they are targeted.

Satellite-borne radar will soon be able to detect these

planes in flight, and the powerful communications they emit will make them beacons in the sky to smart weapons and also vulnerable to radio interception and direction-finding by signal intelligence sources. Further, a nuclear weapon exploding above or below such a plane would rip off the wings by shock waves while a blast at the same altitude would tear off the vertical tail. A few bombs would destroy all aircraft in the relevant operating areas.

These airborne command and control posts are far less effective and more dangerous than ground posts for executing and monitoring nuclear war. They can give only one-way communications to the ICBM silos, and they have no capability to retarget the missiles (gone then is the theory of protracted, controlled nuclear war and force-multiplying effects). Moreover, one of these planes can alone launch an ICBM, whereas ground control requires backup concurrence by a second facility. Because the commanders are on a kamikaze mission, one recent review concludes: "The predicament of being trapped in an aircraft that cannot return to the ground without inviting destruction almost guarantees that the general will order attacks with everything in his power before landing." The hotline between Washington and Moscow will almost certainly have been destroyed and therefore will not be available to the NEACP plane. Actually, it is at this time, after a nuclear war has started, that the hotline will be most needed.

Vulnerability of Satellite Systems

Satellites and their ground stations are "the most important" of all the systems the United States maintains for early warning of ballistic-missile attack. Both Russian and U.S. satellites are vulnerable to antisatellite warfare by killer satellites, laser destruction, EMP from weapons exploded in space, and destruction of the ground stations by nuclear war. For instance, the early-warning satellites are terribly vulnerable because they depend on only two ground stations— Pine Gap in Australia and Buckley Air Force Base in Colorado. It is said that these ground stations can withstand five pounds per square inch of blast pressure, but an ability to withstand only one to two pounds per square inch is more probable.

In August 1983, the Soviet Union proposed that the

United States and USSR agree to a complete ban on antisatellite weapons (ASAT): The USSR has a rudimentary ASAT system designed fifteen years ago, consisting of space mines, which are clumsy and inefficient and which represent no substantial threat to U.S. satellites. The administration ignored this offer, and in January 1984, it tested an extremely sophisticated ASAT weapon—a rocket fired from an F-15 fighter. This system, if developed, could strike hundreds of targets per twenty-four hours, whereas the current Soviet system would take more than a week to mount a comprehensive attack.

The Hotline (Molink—The Moscow—Washington Hotline)

The original hotline went into service on August 30, 1963. It used to be a radio and cable link that was, in the past, disrupted six times by accident: A thief snipped out a twenty-foot section in Helsinki in 1964; a thunderstorm damaged an integral power station in southern Finland in 1964; a fire in a manhole in Rosedale cut the circuit in two in 1965; a farmer in Finland plowed the cable in two in 1965; a Finnish postal workers' strike disrupted the circuit in 1965; and a Soviet freighter severed the cable when it ran aground in Denmark in 1966. The hotline communicates with a Telex machine in the basement of the Pentagon. The messages come through in Russian and must then be translated into English and relayed to the White House. This is a very clumsy system of communication and open to misinterpretation.

In September 1971, the hotline was converted to a satellite communications system with ground stations in Etam, West Virginia, Fort Detrick, Maryland, Vladimir, and Moscow, but this is probably even more vulnerable to damage in a nuclear war—the ground stations from direct attack and the satellites from EMP, etc.

Communication with Fleet Ballistic-Missile Subs Before and During Nuclear War

The American submarine fleet carries 5,152 bombs, more than half the strategic weapons of the United States. These are invulnerable because the U.S. nuclear submarines are quiet and cannot be tracked by Soviet hunter-killer subs, and they are also very difficult to communicate with. Very-low-frequency sound waves can reach them near the surface of the water with one-way communication to the submarines' commanders, but the very-low-frequency-transmitting ground stations will almost certainly be destroyed early in the war. VLF gives relative navigational accuracy. Satellites can give good navigation, but they transmit in VHF and UHF. VHF can be received only if the submarine projects an antenna above the water for three to four minutes, thereby exposing the position of the sub. Ultra-high-frequency reception requires exposure of a mast-mounted dish antenna, which is even more difficult to camouflage. To bypass these problems, the navy has commenced construction of an extra-low-frequency transmission system. ELF can penetrate several hundred feet through the water. This system consists of 150 miles of antenna cable buried below two fields, one in Michigan and one in Wisconsin. However, this is very inefficient technology. It would take fifteen minutes to transmit a three-letter signal. This system, of course, would be destroyed by a nuclear attack. The navy considers the TACAMO plan the only reliable system for communicating an emergency-action message to the subs; *but,* fourteen backup planes are needed to keep only one continually in the air over the Atlantic or Pacific, and the home-base airfields at Bermuda and Guam are obviously prime targets. Communications could be only one way from the NCA to the submarines, and all methods of communication probably would be destroyed very early in a nuclear war. Therefore, the only real use for the fleet ballistic-missile submarines (the most survivable part of the triad) is for first strike. They cannot be used for controlled or prolonged nuclear war because the commanders won't know the locations of remaining Soviet targets and so will be unable to target their missiles accordingly. Another reason they are not suitable for controlled, graduated response is because although one Trident submarine carries at least 160 bombs, as soon as a couple of missiles have been launched, the position of the submarine becomes known, and it is then vulnerable to attack from antisubmarine warfare.

Pathogenesis:
The Pathological Dynamics of
the Arms Race

From the beginning, the nuclear arms race has been fueled by a mad lust for power in the air force and later in the navy, and by a fascination with scientific, esoteric, and intellectual pursuits, combined with clinical paranoia about the Russians and rapacious greed exhibited by the military industries.

Thinking about possible weapons for World War III, in fact, began four months before Germany was defeated in World War II, when Air Force General Henry Arnold said to his top advisers, "We've got to think of what we'll need twenty years from now. For the past twenty years, we have built and run the Air Force on pilots, but we can't do that anymore." And he went on to say that he envisioned an age in which intercontinental missiles would dominate warfare and the air force would have to change radically to accommodate such new inventions.

Because the air force had played a major role in ending World War II by its massive bombing of Dresden, Berlin, and Tokyo, and by dropping the atomic bombs on Hiroshima and Nagasaki, it became the most powerful service in the military after the war. In those days many people in the air force believed that America should threaten to use massive nuclear retaliation against the Soviet Union in response to any Russian conventional misdemeanor. The Strategic Air Command (SAC) was a fiefdom created after the war as the first nuclear delivery system, and the confidence of its air force leaders in the air offensive increased with the arrival of the atomic bomb. They still believed in bombing the enemy flat, using the biggest bombs they had. In the late forties and early fifties, the air force had a war plan called Sunday Punch that was essentially a swift all-out atomic blow (called spasm) against every target in the Soviet Union. Years later under the Eisenhower administration, John Foster Dulles advocated the same plan, then called Massive Retaliation. The air force policy at that time also called for the use of atomic bombs in local war if the situation dictated it. General Curtis LeMay said in 1956, "I see that the Russians are amassing their planes for an attack. I am going to knock the shit out of them before they take off the ground."

The utility of bombing was, however, severely challenged in a postwar study. But it was the air force's own view of things that prevailed—with effective lobbying from within the air force by General LeMay and in Congress by special friends of the air force, most notably Arizona's Senator Barry Goldwater.

In 1954, a man named Joseph Loftus recommended a counterforce nuclear war, targeting airfields only and not Russian cities, but he realized that the air force and especially SAC were not interested in counterforce but only in mass destruction. The first time Loftus went to SAC headquarters in Omaha he was invited to the house of General Jim Walsh for cocktails. Walsh, while in the middle of a mini-lecture explaining to Loftus how the big bomb was meant for big damage, screamed, "Goddamn it, Loftus, there is only one way to attack the Russians, and that's to rip them hard with everything we have, and"—at this point pounding his fist on top of the Bible—"knock their balls off!"

General Tommy Power, commander of SAC in 1960, exploded after a briefing by Bill Kaufmann about counterforce limited nuclear war, bellowing, "Why do you want us to restrain ourselves? Restraint! Why are you so concerned with saving *their* lives? The whole idea is to kill the bastards! Look, at the end of the war, if there are two Americans and one Russian, we win!"

Because the air force had benefited from the advice of scientists during World War II, it decided that strategies for the next war could best be formulated with the help of a selected group of such specialists. To this end, in December 1945, the air force established the RAND Corporation. The RAND charter read, "Project RAND is a continuing program of scientific study and research on the broad subject of air warfare with the object of recommending to the Air Force preferred methods, techniques, and instrumentalities for this purpose." The scientific expertise represented was very broad and ranged from physicists, engineers, biologists, zoologists, physiologists, chemists, astronomers, and mathematicians to social and political scientists.

Over time, RAND has had an enormous impact on U.S. policy about nuclear weapons and nuclear war. It has largely planned and devised the strategy and doctrine that has been adhered to over the last thirty-eight years, and even now, any new strategic theories are just rehashed RAND doctrines. Most of the language associated with nuclear war was coined in the corridors of RAND—such terms as superpowers, balance of terror, nuclear exchange, first strike, counterforce, nuclear deterrence, and nuclear war fighting.

RAND attracted some of the most brilliant minds of the time, most of whom, unfortunately, became almost completely divorced from reality as they continued day after day trying to devise scenarios that could make nuclear war practical and winnable. They thought of strategies for massive civil defense programs, working with complex mathematical formulas about how many people would survive with adequate protection factors. They talked endlessly about imagined Russian motives and attack scenarios, so much so that their projected fantasies became reality and hard facts in their minds. They had tremendous influence over air force decisions and over official U.S. government policy. Many of the doctrines they formulated and espoused have become so sacred that they are never questioned by the powers that be—the Pentagon, the administration, or Congress. The public has had very little input over the past thirty-eight years into these esoteric, crazy plans because the language devised by RAND used thousands of complex acronyms, which excluded participation by the lay public in the debate. So the public, by default, abrogated their futures and those of their families to people in the nuclear priesthood. However, the situation is beginning to change as some scientists and others have started to translate the esoterica into ordinary English and explain to the people the true meaning of their nation's nuclear strategies.

Many big businessmen were also involved in helping establish the RAND Corporation. They included Donald Douglas of McDonnell Douglas, Henry Ford, Rowan Gaither (a prominent lawyer), Arthur Raymond of TRW, and many others. Many of these men have remained in the defense industry producing weapons to this day.

The first plan for counterforce nuclear war was devised by a RAND strategist named Bernard Brodie in 1951 because he was appalled by the air force's Sunday Punch plan for massive bombing of cities. His plan called for first use of nuclear weapons by America on Russia, but excluded bombing their cities. A small number of nuclear weapons were to be fired on nonurban targets like airports, while the United States maintained a highly protected reserve force of atomic weapons that could then be used as a bargaining lever—an implicit threat to Russia that unless they stopped fighting, America would start destroying their cities one by one. This plan was premature because in 1951 Russia possessed hardly any nuclear weapons and could not possibly have delivered nuclear bombs on America. At this stage, however, the air force and RAND planned to use nuclear weapons on Russia to discipline them for conventional acts of aggression.

From the early days of nuclear weapons, America has reacted as a big global bully; having built the nuclear weapons first, it has always planned to use them if necessary. In fact, since 1945, America has threatened first use of nuclear weapons at least nine times. This policy prevailed both before and after Russia had built enough nuclear weapons to threaten American cities.

(1) In June 1948, at the beginning of the Berlin Blockade, Harry Truman sent nuclear-capable B-29 planes to bases in Britain and Germany. B-29 planes carried only nuclear weapons. These particular planes were not loaded, but the bluff convinced Harry Truman and his aides of the feasibility of the nuclear threat.

(2) In 1950, Truman warned he might use nuclear weapons against the Chinese who surrounded American troops at the Chosin Reservoir during the Korean War. This strategy, of course, would have killed the marines, who actually escaped anyway.

(3) In 1953, Eisenhower secretly threatened China with nuclear weapons, a strategy that forced a settlement of the Korean War.

(4) In 1958, Eisenhower directed the Joint Chiefs to use

nuclear weapons against China if it invaded the island of Quemoy.

(5) In 1961, after the construction of the Berlin Wall, America threatened to use nuclear weapons first if East Germany prevented the crossing of refugees.

(6) In 1962, President Kennedy threatened to use nuclear weapons against Russia unless it removed its missiles from Cuba, and that threat, plus a naval blockade of its ships, persuaded Russia to remove its missiles.

(7) In 1968, America considered using nuclear weapons when marines were surrounded at Khe Sanh, Vietnam, a strategy that would have killed the marines.

(8) Through Henry Kissinger, Nixon threatened from 1969 to 1972 to use nuclear weapons on North Vietnam. Nixon told H. R. Haldemann: "I call it the Madman Theory, Bob. I want the North Vietnamese to believe I've reached the point where I might do *anything* to stop the war."

(9) In 1980, Carter issued a secret Pentagon study that concluded: "To prevail in an Iranian scenario, we might have to threaten or make use of tactical nuclear weapons." This Middle East doctrine is still current U.S. policy, reaffirmed by Reagan in 1981.

On only one of these occasions would the United States have risked starting an all-out nuclear war, and that was during the Cuban missile crisis. All the others involved a huge and powerful nation threatening little countries with the ultimate genocide so America could get its own way. The American Catholic Bishops have condemned this attitude as immoral.

To my knowledge, Russia has made only two similar threats—once in 1956 during the Suez crisis when Russia had no ICBMs, and once during the Bay of Pigs invasion when Russia had four ICBMs—both empty threats.

Hence the use of nuclear blackmail has been a peculiarly American ploy. Nevertheless, even so-called broadminded intellectuals who sat on Reagan's MX commission (the President's Commission on Strategic Forces) in 1983, including Brent Scowcroft, Harold Brown, James Schlesinger, John McCone, and R. James Woolsey, were obsessed in their report with the thought that "if the Russians get ahead of us, they can threaten us or blackmail us." All of these men are highly intelligent, and all would be aware that the Pentagon scientist Richard Delauer had recently reported that America is years ahead of Russia in almost every weapons and technological system. This sort of thinking has been common ever since 1945, when the nuclear strategists in RAND and in the Pentagon began to assume the worst-case analysis of Russia—usually without any concrete knowledge of Russian capabilities but rather involving a psychological projection of America's evolving nuclear capabilities onto the Russians. For instance, the 1960 missile gap was totally fallacious, and all those people who believed in it were acutely embarrassed when the new U.S. satellite discovered that Russia had deployed only four intercontinental ballistic missiles. Such fantasy thinking is still practiced at the highest levels of government, including President Reagan and Defense Secretary Weinberger, and is overt paranoia.

The definition of a paranoid patient is someone who imagines a certain scenario in his or her own mind, decides (with no objective evidence) that this is exactly what someone else is thinking, and then decides to act on that notion. These paranoid delusions projected onto the Russian leaders come straight from the minds of American strategists and leaders, and these ideas probably reflect exactly what the Americans are planning to do themselves and bear little relationship to Soviet strategy or reality. The only way to find out what the Russians are thinking is to talk to them and ask them.

Soviet policy, which has been stated on frequent occasions, is that because nuclear war would be so devastating and suicidal, Russia has pledged not to use nuclear weapons first. But should one tactical nuclear weapon be used against it, Russia will retaliate by launching its whole arsenal. The Russian leaders are so concerned about nuclear war that on several occasions over the last few years Dr. Evgeni Chazov, the cardiologist of Leonid Brezhnev and Yuri Andropov, has appeared on national Soviet TV for one hour to teach the Soviet population about the medical and scientific consequences of nuclear war. On another occasion, three American and three Soviet physicians appeared on national Soviet TV to discuss the same subject for a one-hour period. This broadcast was not censored and was seen by 100 million to 200 million Russian citizens. During it, one of the Americans had the temerity to criticize the Soviet civil-defense system and to say that it would do no good.

Despite these facts, discussions about Soviet nuclear blackmail prevail in administration circles. The arcane logic goes like this: The Russians launch a first strike on U.S. ground-based missiles, destroying the majority. They use two hydrogen bombs per silo, thus killing between 20 million and 50 million Americans. Such an attack still leaves the United States with 5,142 nuclear bombs in the strategic submarines (minus those destroyed in port) and 3,000 in the intercontinental bombers (those that scramble and take off fast enough not to be caught in the attack). The President now faces a dilemma: Should he retaliate with these remaining weapons—which are only accurate enough for soft targets—and destroy the majority of Soviet cities, thus exposing U.S. cities to a similar retaliatory attack with the remaining Soviet weapons, or should the President accede to the Soviet global demands, thus saving American cities?

There are many obvious flaws to this argument:

(1) Do the Russians really think like this, or is this idea a direct projection of paranoid minds?

(2) The Soviet Union cannot be sure that it actually has any first-strike weapons. Its intercontinental ballistic missiles are becoming more accurate, and the size of its bombs is large, but there is no guarantee that they would be accurate enough to hit all the American missile silos.

(3) The U.S. early-warning DSP-647 satellites and radars would detect the attack, and America could well launch its missiles on warning before the Soviet missiles land. The effect would be to launch an all-out nuclear war because the Soviet satellites then would detect the U.S. attack and obviously would launch the rest of their missiles on warning. Launch on warning is not official American policy, but many people assume it would be used during an attack.

(4) The event would trigger the launching of U.S. submarine missiles and strategic bombers. The airplanes would arrive over Soviet territory after it had been devastated and would be used to bomb the few remaining targets—if they could be identified, because the NCA and most communication networks would have been destroyed. (Russia puts a priority on targeting the C^3I centers in America.)

(5) Even if the Russians were mad enough to launch a

first strike at America's land-based missiles, they would obviously understand that America had another 5,000 or so bombs in reserve, invulnerable to a first strike, which could be used to obliterate their own country.

(6) But in fantasy, which it is, just suppose that the Soviet first strike worked. What would Russia do with the terribly radioactive land that is now the conquered U.S.A.? Twenty million to 50 million people would either be vaporized initially or would die weeks, months, or years later from dreadful radiation-induced diseases. What would the Soviets demand for their blackmail? If indeed they wanted Europe or the Persian Gulf instead of radioactive America, there still would be thousands of U.S. bombs available to be used locally in these territories or to destroy military, industrial, and civilian targets in the USSR.

These American strategic thinkers assume that all would be rational and calm, as U.S. leaders sat waiting in their airborne command posts—assuming they reached them in time—willing to absorb a Soviet first strike without launching on warning. This is not a picture of normal human psychological reaction. People do not function like this under moderate stress, let alone the extreme anxiety and utter panic created in a nuclear war. This is particularly so because the Russians are the self-proclaimed enemies of the United States, and in a war, paranoia, self-righteousness, and fear would all interact to create an extraordinary pressure to bomb the enemy into oblivion.

To understand the complicated dynamics of the whole pathological system that has produced and still perpetuates the arms race, it is necessary first to understand the new weapon systems that are about to be built by the Reagan administration. These weapons are extremely dangerous and destabilizing, and they move the probability of nuclear war into a new realm. They are all an integral part of the Pentagon's Five-Year Defense Guidance Plan, which will give America the "capability" to fight and win a protracted nuclear war over a six-month period. The Russians do not have these particular weapons yet, but they have announced that should America proceed with construction and deployment, they will too. This new arsenal will move America away from "parity" with the Soviet Union and thus destroy the opportunity to obtain a freeze because Russia will not negotiate from a position of "inferiority."

The first weapons to be described are the MX missile, Trident II or D-5 missiles, cruise and Pershing II missiles, and B-1 and stealth bombers.

Here is a list of important technical terms used to describe some important functions of these weapons systems:

Throw-weight or *payload:* The weight of the nuclear warhead after the last rocket motor has separated in flight. The Soviets are ahead in throw-weight because the United States miniaturized its bombs and therefore its bombs are smaller and use the available throw-weight more efficiently. Thus the United States is actually ahead in throw-weight, qualitatively speaking.

Readiness: The number of missiles ready to be launched at any one time. The readiness of U.S. strategic forces is 98 percent, while the Soviet readiness is about 75 percent, although this is hard to verify.

Reliability: Percentage of probability that a missile will land in the "right place" after being launched. The reliability of the U.S. missiles is 75 percent to 80 percent; of Soviet missiles, 65 percent to 75 percent.

Yield: The explosive power of a bomb expressed as tons of TNT equivalence—1,000 tons of TNT equivalence equals 1 kiloton. Russian bombs are bigger, as previously explained.

Accuracy: Measured by "circular error probable" (CEP), which represents the radius of a circle, centered on the target, within which half the bombs are expected to land. The other half will land outside this circle. Until recently, Soviet strategic weapons would miss their mark by as much as 0.7 to 2 nautical miles. Some of the newest Soviet missiles have a CEP of 0.25 to 0.3 nautical miles. By contrast, recent improvements in U.S. missiles place them within a 0.12 nautical-mile radius.

MIRVing: Multiple independently targetable reentry vehicle. This system, developed by the United States in the 1960s and deployed in 1970, was not outlawed by the SALT I treaty because only America could MIRV at that time. But the U.S. advantage was short-lived, and the Soviet Union started MIRVing its missiles in 1975. When a nuclear rocket or missile is MIRVed, it carries more than one hydrogen warhead (each of which is called a reentry vehicle or RV).

These separate reentry vehicles are carried on a "bus," which releases the RVs one by one after it makes preselected changes in speed and orientation so that each hydrogen bomb will land very accurately on target.

With increasing accuracy and with many warheads on one missile, it is possible that only a few missiles launched from one side could destroy all the land-based missiles on the other in a surprise preemptive first-strike attack. To expand on this point a little more: Before MIRVed missiles, a preemptive attack (provided each missile was extraordinarily accurate and managed to land on top of an enemy missile silo) would have required one missile for each silo. But now, theoretically, the attacking country need use only a small fraction of its missiles to destroy all the other country's MIRVed ground-based missiles before they are launched, and it will still end up with many missiles to spare. To adequately destroy or kill a reinforced-concrete missile silo with certainty, it is necessary to use two hydrogen-bomb explosions per silo to ensure destruction—one landing above the silo and, exactly seven seconds later, a second landing near it on the ground. The missile itself will not be destroyed but will be damaged sufficiently to prevent it from being fired. Two missiles, each with 10 warheads, could destroy 10 missile silos, each of which theoretically could contain 10 bombs. Thus, the advantage to offense: 10 warheads destroy 100 warheads. Of course, such an attack is suitable only for land-based missiles and cannot be used against submarines loaded with nuclear missiles or even strategic bombers once they have taken off. But this is a very destabilizing technology because each superpower will continue to wonder when the other might attempt a preemptive first strike. For reasons explained previously, it would benefit the United States to do this because 70 percent of Russian strategic weapons are land-based. The USSR would be crazy to contemplate such a suicidal move with at least 3,000 hydrogen bombs in U.S. submarines ready to destroy Russia in retaliation.

The origin of MIRVed warheads is interesting. As the Soviets moved to develop ABMs in the late sixties and early seventies, the U.S. Air Force supported development of separately targetable warhead "decoys" that would confound Soviet anti-ballistic missile (ABM) defenses. Inevitably, someone pointed out that having developed the guidance systems, it would now be easy to put a real warhead on each decoy and significantly increase both yield and threat. Hence MIRVing. Five years later the Soviets also had MIRVed warheads. They were not included in SALT I or II because neither the United States nor the USSR wanted to halt *arms development* but merely to reduce existing *strategic arsenals*, and they did not achieve that.

Lethality: The ability of a weapon to destroy a hard target or reinforced-concrete missile silo. This is a function of yield in megatons to accuracy expressed as CEP. Making the warhead twice as accurate has the same effect as making the bomb eight times more powerful. Lethality also increases in proportion to the number of bombs dropped on a target as well as to the size of the bombs. In practice, the area of blast destruction is increased by increasing the number of bombs and lowering their individual yield. That is, several small bombs with the same aggregate yield are much more effective spread out over the target area than one large warhead. A 1-megaton yield divided into 20- to 50-kiloton bombs has the equivalent destructive power of a 3-megaton bomb.

For example, when the Minuteman II missile was fitted with a single large bomb of 1-megaton yield with a CEP of 0.3 mile, it was given a lethality of 11. But with 3 warheads, each of 170 kilotons, each with a CEP of 0.2 mile, the Minuteman III has a total lethality of 23. By MIRVing and increasing accuracy by one third, the United States more than doubled the lethality of its long-range missiles at the same time that total megatonnage has been reduced from 1 to 0.54.

Today the Minuteman missiles are being fitted with still another warhead, the very accurate Mark 12A. These warheads have a yield of 335 kilotons each and a CEP of 0.1 mile.

The Soviets have many missiles, but very few are extremely accurate. They have 308 SS-18 missiles with 1, 6, or 10 warheads. The largest single warhead is on some 20 or 30 SS-18 missiles. The yield is 20 to 24 megatons. Other SS-18s are MIRVed and may have an accuracy equal to the Minuteman III.

So far, only land-based missiles have been made very accurate. The submarine-based missiles cannot yet be used for missile-destroying first-strike attacks.

Range of ICBMs: The intercontinental rockets have ranges up to 7,000 nautical miles. This, in effect, means that any place on the earth can be hit within approximately thirty minutes by rockets launched from the American or Russian continents. (The South Island of New Zealand would have to be targeted, of course, by the nuclear submarines.)

The MX Missile—Alias "Peacekeeper"

Research for the MX began in 1966 with a $166-million program to define a successor to the Titan and Minuteman missiles, and the actual MX missile program was initiated in 1972. It was decided at that time that the Minuteman ICBM silos would eventually become vulnerable to a Russian first-strike attack, even though the Russians did not even begin MIRVing their missiles until 1975. Without MIRVing and extreme accuracy, no country can attempt a first strike. This was a projected supposition that was almost certainly based on U.S. activity at the time to vastly increase the accuracy of its ICBMs, which it had already MIRVed. In 1977, Donald Rumsfeld, Secretary of Defense, said, "Our calculations indicate that by the early 1980s there could be a substantial reduction in the number of surviving ICBMs should the Soviets apply sufficient numbers of their forces against the U.S. ICBMs in a first strike." Based on these suppositions, he asked Congress for $294 million for MX missile development and testing so that the MX could be operational by 1983—two years ahead of schedule. President Carter originally rejected this proposal, but decided in October 1977 on full-scale development of this missile. He reversed this decision in 1978, but to appease the hawks on the Committee on the Present Danger, so they would agree to SALT II ratification, in 1979 Carter once again supported full-scale development.

Throughout its history, the MX missile has been designed to be a mobile, invulnerable, extremely accurate system, not subject to a hypothetical first-strike attack. Many methods of "basing" the missile have been considered, including missile pods in the bottom of ponds, truck- and rail-borne capsules, carrying the missile around the highways, hiding it in a submarine, or flying it around in an airplane.

The Pentagon describes the MX as an advanced, high-throw-weight, MIRVed ICBM, capable of fulfilling U.S. strategic requirements into the twenty-first century. It is a massively huge missile, weighing 190,000 pounds or 95 tons, 7 feet 8 inches in diameter, and 70 feet 6 inches long. It is a four-stage rocket and will be able to carry a payload of 4.5 tons over a 7,000-mile range. It will carry between 10 and 20 precision-guided hydrogen bombs in its nose cone or bus. It will be fitted with a new guidance system called the Advanced Inertial Reference Sphere (AIRS), so the rocket will be able to reposition itself as it is traveling through space, giving it a CEP of 600 feet. This guidance system will be supplemented by another system called NAVSTAR—a satellite global-positioning system that will lower the target CEP to 300 feet. NAVSTAR is a system of 24 satellites that will give a true position to the missile in three dimensions within 30 feet and an actual velocity within tenths of a foot per second. The missile's navigation computers will be updated as it flies, and corrections will be made by the bus just before each reentry vehicle or hydrogen bomb is released.

The bombs themselves will be fitted with a precision-guided system called a Maneuverable Reentry Vehicle or MARV. This allows the bomb to retarget or correct its trajectory by performing low-altitude maneuvers so it will be even more accurate before striking the target. The yield of each bomb will be about 350 kilotons, about twenty-seven times larger than the Hiroshima bomb. It hardly matters whether the bomb is extremely accurate or not with this sort of yield, except for hitting missile silos, which have been "hardened" by reinforced concrete against hydrogen explosions.

In 1980 and 1981, the air force wanted to base 200 MX missiles in Utah and Nevada on an underground racetrack, shuttling along 1,200 miles of roadway among 4,600 shelters. (The reason for building so many shelters was to increase the number of targets the Russians would have to destroy while keeping the number of missiles within the SALT II limits.) These 200 missiles would carry 2,000 hydrogen bombs and would be hidden in some of these shelters, so the Russians would never know where they were. To conform to SALT II provisions, America would occasionally open the hatch or roof of the shelters to let the Russian satellites detect and count the missiles, then quickly close the lids and as fast as possible move the huge, cumbersome missiles to other shelters. By the time the Russians had a chance to retarget their missiles, the MX missiles would already have been moved. The ranchers and the Mormon Church among others in Utah and Nevada were very upset with this particular plan because it would have destroyed the natural beauty of their states, as well as making them a first-strike target and using up enormous amounts of precious water in order to lay all the concrete.

This system was therefore rejected, but in late 1982 the Reagan administration came up with a new basing mode called Dense Pack, and the President renamed the MX "Peacekeeper." (To call a missile that carries 10 hydrogen bombs, each about twenty-seven times bigger than the Hiroshima bomb, the Peacekeeper is a cynical travesty.) One hundred MX missiles were to be placed very close together over an area of several hundred square miles, so that if the Russians attempted a first strike, the incoming missiles would explode together over a very short period of time within a very small area and blow each other up, or else produce such collateral damage to each other by the enormous quantities of radioactive debris created that they would be unable to damage the MX missiles in their silos, which had been hardened to withstand such an event. This incredible bomb-damaging scenario is called fratricide (killing a brother)!

Congress did not like this basing mode (also, experts didn't think it would work), so it was rejected in November 1982. However, the President, not to be outmaneuvered, created a "bipartisan" commission (the Scowcroft Commission) of old-time professional military people and past secretaries of defense to devise an acceptable basing mode. All these men had spent their lives involved in some aspects of the arms race. This group gave the opinion that MIRVed missiles are destabilizing because they are targets for a first strike (the Russians could destroy lots of bombs with a few missiles), and they are also good for use in a first strike. The commission then recommended that the United States should build 100 MX missiles, containing 1,000 of these first-strike hydrogen warheads, and place them in preexisting Minuteman silos, thus admitting that they are not worried about a Soviet first strike after all or about the "window of vulnerability," which the President's people were fond of discussing.

They also recommended that 1,000 small, single-warhead missiles called Midgetmen should be built to encourage superpower de-MIRVing. These Midgetmen, however, will almost certainly have first-strike accuracy and will be clustered at six to twelve military bases with roads radiating from them. To use the Pentagon's phrase, they "will dash" under nuclear attack out onto these roads. The missile will be based in an armored vehicle called an armadillo, which, under nuclear attack, can go to the side of the road and burrow into the dirt like that animal, and it will have suckers on its feet to hold it firm while hydrogen bombs are exploding all around it. Then it will come out "undamaged" after the nuclear salvo and send off a single very accurate hydrogen bomb toward as yet undetermined targets in Russia.

This commission of seemingly intelligent men thus contradicted itself by recommending construction of the MX missile when it was opposed to MIRV missiles and also produced a bizarre and fantasylike weapon that could only have come from the heads of military and scientific child-adults who are desperate to keep the nuclear arms-race game going. The commission also stated it is afraid of Russian nuclear blackmail, as described previously.

If the Reagan administration has dropped its scare talk of vulnerability, what then does it want the MX missiles for? Obviously, given its characteristics, the MX is an extraordinarily crafted piece of weaponry designed only for first-strike nuclear war. Once the production lines are cranked up, the United States will not want to stop at 100 missiles, but could well build 300, as previously planned. Three hundred missiles will contain 3,000 thermonuclear warheads, enough to destroy all the Russian land-based ICBMs or the majority of its strategic force (two hydrogen bombs per silo; 1,398 Russian missile silos).

The members of Congress were smitten by this very intelligent bipartisan presidentially appointed panel and were further cajoled and seduced by White House dinner invitations, so they voted for the scheme in November 1983. They did not spend the time to analyze and assess this contradiction adequately themselves. One would have to ask: "Are these legislative representatives in Washington to represent the good of their constituents—men, women, and children and the lives of future generations—or have they given up their souls and intellects to be so bedazzled by dinner at the White House and Gold Medal Presidential Commissions?" This all took place at a time when 74 percent to 79 percent of the American people, on a nonpartisan basis, wanted a bilateral nuclear freeze, which would invalidate the MX.

The saga is not over yet. Congress has many more votes coming up to appropriate funds for the development, production, and deployment of the MX; and my sense is that the American people will determine the outcome of this debate and that their wishes will prevail, since this is a democracy.

The MX missile itself is to cost more than $100 billion, and this figure does not include the cost of the bombs—to be built by the Department of Energy. Actually, because of the MX's admitted vulnerability, military planners have discussed the use of anti-ballistic missile systems to defend the MX-converted Minuteman silos. Such a move will openly defy the Anti-Ballistic Missile Treaty signed by Russia and America in 1972 and will cost enormous sums of money. With the MX, the United States will be able to fight a preemptive first-strike nuclear war and will flout the ABM Treaty. The fiscal 1980 Arms Control Impact Statement said, "If the MX were deployed in substantial numbers, the U.S. would have acquired through both the Minuteman and MX programs an apparent capability to destroy most of the Soviet silo-busting, ICBM force in a first strike." This posture will greatly worry the Russian leaders who will have their fingers hovering over the button, wondering when and whether or not the United States is planning to strike first and destroy their missiles, so the Russians will almost inevitably adopt a launch-on-warning policy, bringing us all closer to the brink of annihilation.

In the November 1982 congressional election the MX-missile contractors more than doubled their campaign contributions to members of Congress. Twelve of the thirteen biggest MX contractors had contributed $780,000 to congressional incumbents by July 30, as opposed to two years before when their total contributions were $455,000. The largest Senate recipients were strong MX supporters in tight races—Howard W. Cannon (D-Nev.) received the most, $21,500; Harrison H. Schmitt (R-N.M.), $17,000; Richard G. Lugar (R-Ind.), $12,850; and Henry M. Jackson (D-Wash.), $11,000.

ASSOCIATE CONTRACTOR & LOCATION	CONTRACT DESCRIPTION AND COST (IN MILLIONS OF DOLLARS)
Aerojet Solid Propulsion Co. Sacramento CA	Stage II propulsion system. Received $11.0 of $129.4 Stage II. $8.2
Avco Huntsville AL	Rocket test cell data acquisition and control of testing environment for use in J-4 and J-5 Arnold Engineering Development Center test facilities. Received $2.8 of $7.5
Wilmington MA	Re-entry system integration. Received $0.005 of $3.4 Re-entry system integration. Received $7.7 of $164.3
Boeing Aerospace Seattle WA	Redirection of basing concept from vertical shelter to horizontal multiple protective structure. TTD $0.046 of $3.4 Horizontal basing system. TTD $0.101 of $24.9 Blast and shock test program. $4.5
Draper Laboratories Cambridge MA	Technical support for guidance programs. TTD $0.038 of $16.5
Energy Research Corp. Danbury CT	MX ground power advanced development program.
E-Systems Greenville TX	Conceal locations of MX missiles. $0.396
Furgo National Long Beach CA	Siting and geotechnical investigations. Received $4.6 of $8.3 Acceleration of geotechnical and siting investigations. TTD $0.013 of $5.5
General Electric Philadelphia PA	Adaptation of MARK 12 re-entry vehicle for the MX. Received $5.3 of $69.9
Geodynamics Corp.* Santa Barbara CA	Geodetic and geophysical support. $2.2
GTE-Sylvania Inc. Needham Heights MA	Command, control and communications system. Received $10.0 of $325.5
Henningson Durham & Richardson Santa Barbara CA	Environmental baseline studies and environmental statements. Received $3.3 of $6.9
Hercules Magna UT	Stage III propulsion system. TTD $0.084 of $75.3 Nuclear hardness and survivability. TTD $0.087 of $5.2 Engineering development, late exercise of Option D equitable adjustment. $87.4

Honeywell Inc. Horsham PA	MX ground power advanced development program.
St. Petersburg FL	Specific force integrating receiver. Received $10.0 of $34.0
Karagozian and Case Los Angeles CA	Engineering services.
Logicon San Pedro CA	Software performance analysis and technical evaluation. Received $0.556 of $9.1
Martin Marietta Denver CO	Performance of MX weapon system assembly. Received $15.7 of $321.5 Assembly, test and system support, option changes and additions. TTD $0.402 of $49.9
Vandenberg AFB CA	Launcher studies and analysis for MX weapon system. TTD $0.352 of $3.1

Northrop
    Precision Products Div.
    Norwood MA
	Third generation gyroscope program. Received $7.6 of $36.2

Hawthorne CA	Inertial measurement unit. Received $17.5 of $235.0 Inertial measurement unit changes. $6.7
Olin Stamford CT	Propellants used to support space shuttle. Titan missiles. F-16 aircraft and MX. $40.1
Questron, Inc. La Jolla CA	Hardened electronics analysis.
R.S. Hanson Co., Inc. Spokane WA	Engineering study—construction equipment.

Ralph M. Parsons Co.*
    Pasadena CA and
    Luke AFB AZ
	Buried trench construction. $6.3

Rockwell International **Autonetics Div.** Anaheim CA	Flight computer and integration of components into guidance and control systems. TTD $0.273 of $259.4
Rocketdyne Div. Canoga Park CA	Stage IV propulsion system. TTD $0.203 of $192.8 Redirection of Stage IV. $8.5
Science Applications Inc. La Jolla CA	MX software studies.
Small Business Adminis. Washington DC	MX software studies and analysis program.
Softech, Inc.* Waltham MA	MX JOVIAL compiler. $1.9

Systems, Science and Software* La Jolla CA	Nuclear hardness and survivability studies. $1.5
Systems Technology Laboratory Inc. Arlington VA	MX basing study.
Thiokol Brigham City UT	Stage I propulsion system. Received $13.6 of $136.5 Stage I and ordnance update. $17.9
TRW Redondo Beach CA and Norton AFB CA and Vandenberg AFB CA Redondo Beach CA	Engineering development. TTD $0.033 of $12.1 Systems engineering and technical support. $42.3 Targeting and analysis program for FY80. $5.8 Development of ST/TS of the Advanced ICBM (MC) weapon system.
Ultrasystems, Inc. Irvine CA and Norton AFB CA	Integrated logistics support.
Weidlinger Associates New York NY	Nuclear hardness and survivability analysis.
Westinghouse Electric Corp. Sunnyvale CA	MX Canister. $6.0

SUB-CONTRACTOR & LOCATION	CONTRACT DESCRIPTION AND COST (IN MILLIONS OF DOLLARS)	ASSOCIATE CONTRACTOR
Air Research Manuf. Corp. Phoenix AZ	Build TVA Actuator.	AEROJET-GENERAL CORP.
Brunswick Corp. Lincoln NE	Manufacture Stage II case.	
Alcoa* Cleveland OH 44105	Aluminum forgings.	AVCO
Atlantic Research Corp.* Gainesville VA 22065	Rocket motor.	
Avco Aerostructures, Inc.* Nashville TN 37202	Deployment module structure.	
G & H Technology* Automation Industries, Inc. Santa Monica CA 90404	Separation connector.	

Company	Description	Prime
Grumman Bethpage NY	20 ship sets of titanium shroud components for MX nose cone. $10.0	AVCO
Honeywell Avionics Division* St. Louis Park MN 55416	Automatic test equipment.	AVCO
O.E.A., Inc.* Denver CO 80210	Separation nut/gas generator.	AVCO
Timex* Pittsburgh PA 15230	Shroud structure material.	AVCO
Unidynamics Phoenix, Inc.* Phoenix AZ 85062	Arm/disarm device.	AVCO

Computer Sciences Corp.
  Applied Technology
  Falls Church VA
	MX C3 system.	GTE-SYLVANIA

Hayes International Birmingham AL	MX C3 system.	GTE-SYLVANIA
Norden Systems Norwalk CT	MX C3 system.	GTE-SYLVANIA
Rockwell* Tulsa OK	Interstage integration.	HERCULES
Hydraulic Research Inc.* Valencia CA	Thrust vector actuation.	HERCULES
BDM Albuquerque NM	Preservation and location uncertainty	MARTIN MARIETTA
Cincinnati Electronics Cincinnati OH	Range and safety receivers. $0.940	MARTIN MARIETTA
Endevco San Juan Capistrano CA	Dynamic data measurement system of 750 channels for MX testing.	ROCKWELL ROCKETDYNE AEROJET MFG. CO.
Goodyear Aerospace Co. Litchfield Park AZ	MX transportation and handling equipment.	ROCKWELL ROCKETDYNE AEROJET MFG. CO.
SCI Systems Inc. Huntsville AL	MX multipliers and power supply verifiers.	ROCKWELL ROCKETDYNE AEROJET MFG. CO.
Systems Engineering Labs Ft. Lauderdale FL	Computers for MX program.	ROCKWELL ROCKETDYNE AEROJET MFG. CO.
American Beryllium Sarasota FL	Beryllium spheres for MX guidance system.	NORTHROP
Systems Engineering Labs Ft. Lauderdale FL	Computers for MX program.	NORTHROP

Hamilton Standard Windsor Locks CT	Flight coolant system. $4.5	ROCKWELL AUTONETICS
Honeywell St. Petersburg FL	Main memory sub-system for MX electronics and computer assembly. $12.0	
Systems Engineering Labs Ft. Lauderdale FL	Computers for MX program.	
Yardney Electric Co.* Denver CO	Guidance and control batteries. $1.0	
Aerojet Manufacturing Co. Fullerton CA	Support for Stage IV.	ROCKWELL ROCKETDYNE
Bell Aerospace, Div. of Textron Inc. Buffalo NY	Support for Stage IV.	
Rockwell Int'l Missile Systems Div. Columbus OH	Support for Stage IV.	
OAO Corp. Beltsville MD	Support for MX software studies and analysis program.	SM BUS ADM
Lockheed Missile Systems Co. Sunnyvale CA **Moog** East Aurora NY	MX Ordnance Initiation sets/flight termination ordnance sets. Stage I thrust vector actuation control system.	THIOKOL
Hercules Bacchus UT	Graphite composite launch tube for MX canister.	WEST- ING- HOUSE

(Both Cannon and Schmitt lost; Jackson is now deceased.) In the House, the lineup consisted of Norman D. Dicks (D-Wash.), $11,500; John P. Murtha (D-Pa.), $10,950; and David F. Emery (R-Maine), $10,050. The twelve contractors were: Aerojet, AVCO, Boeing, General Electric, GTE Sylvania, Hercules, Honeywell, Martin Marietta, Northrop, Rockwell Autonetics, Rockwell Rocketdyne, and TRW.

On the day the MX dense pack was defeated in November 1982, I was lobbying around the halls of Congress. The halls were full of Pentagon lobbyists and lobbyists from these companies, but I saw no American people or their children.

The air force planners in their pitch to the public keep pointing out the number of jobs the project will create. If the same amount of money were spent on education, housing, transportation, or day care, many more jobs would be created. There is no doubt that the corporations will make huge profits. As you read the table of corporations that will make large amounts of money on the MX, remember that two thirds of the world's children are malnourished and starving.

Trident II or D-5 Missiles

There has been noisy and anguished debate about the MX missile for some time, but another almost more dangerous missile is being designed and built and funds are being appropriated by Congress with little or no fuss at all. The Trident II or D-5 missile has no basing problems that can ostensibly upset the public or politicians. It is to be placed inside the new noiseless, invulnerable Trident submarines. Each of these submarines will contain 24 Trident II missiles, and each missile can deliver 8 to 10 warheads with a payload of 450 to 475 kilotons—each 35 times bigger than the Hiroshima bomb. Thus, one Trident submarine could destroy many of the major cities in the Northern Hemisphere. This missile may be able to travel 6,000 nautical miles as opposed to the Poseidon missile, which has a range of approximately 2,000 miles. The new Trident I missile, which has already been used to refit 12 of the 31 Poseidon subs, has a maximum range of 4,350 nautical miles.

The navy already owns 31 Poseidon submarines— noiseless, sleek, invulnerable—half of which are at sea at any one time. Why then does it want more and more sophisticated subs? A single Poseidon submarine can already deliver 160 to 224 independently targeted warheads, and there are only 218 cities in the Soviet Union with a population of 100,000 people or more. The Poseidon submarines have a total patrol area of approximately 2.5 million square miles available in the oceans because of the 2,000-nautical-mile-range of the old missiles. Refitting Poseidons with 4,350-mile-range missiles will give the submarines a 12.5 million to 20 million square miles of patrol area. The new Trident subs will also have this capability, or ten times as much ocean in which to hide.

In fact, Deputy Defense Secretary David Packard directed the navy to begin full-scale development of Trident in

September 1971. The navy announced in 1973 that it would base Trident in the Pacific Ocean with a home port along Hood Canal in Puget Sound near Bangor, Washington. Construction of the first submarine began in 1974, and one of the first Tridents was launched in 1981. Archbishop Hunthausen of Seattle has described the Trident submarine as the Auschwitz of Puget Sound.

Each Poseidon submarine displaces 8,250 tons of water when submerged, but a Trident sub will displace 18,700 tons. It will be 560 feet long (or the length of two football fields placed end to end). Plans now call for the navy to build 11 Tridents, but there have been other suggestions that the final construction will be 15 to 20 Trident subs.

The Trident II or D-5 missiles will be capable of striking any point on more than half the earth's surface, and each missile will deliver 8 to 10 super-accurate MIRVed hydrogen bombs, each with a first-strike hard-target counterforce accuracy. These missiles will be guided by the NAVSTAR satellite system. NAVSTAR, as described before, will provide accuracies to the D-5 missiles of within 30 feet in all three dimensions and velocity to within tenths of a foot per second. The missiles' navigation computers will be updated during the coasting-through-space phase, and corrections will be made by the guidance system on the bus just before each hydrogen bomb is released. The CEP will be 300 feet—a first-strike accuracy.

At present, the U.S. Navy is installing an extra-low-frequency (ELF) radio transmitter in Michigan and Wisconsin by laying miles of cable underground. These two facilities would work as one, constantly pumping millions of watts of electricity into the granite bedrock of Lake Superior, forming a giant underground antenna. This electrical energy would radiate a constant signal around the earth and deep into the ocean. ELF would serve as a giant beeper, summoning all the submarines to the surface and, according to Robert Aldrich, former designer engineer at Lockheed who worked on the Trident program, once summoned to the surface, "existing communication systems could give them the fire order."

Until this time, submarine missiles could be used only for a second-strike, soft-target "city-busting" purpose because they lacked the necessary accuracy for "silo-busting" hard-targeted capability. Now these Trident subs can be used for a first-strike "winnable" nuclear war. In fact, the fiscal 1980 Arms Control Impact Statement reported: "The addition of highly accurate Trident II missiles with higher yield warheads would give the U.S. Submarine Launched Ballistic Missile forces a substantial time-urgent hard-target-kill capability for a first strike. The counter-silo capability of a [deleted] KT Trident II missile would exceed that of all currently deployed U.S. ballistic missiles. Moreover, the additional effects of two potential advances (Trident II and MX) in U.S. counter-silo capabilities by the early 1990's could put a large portion of Soviet fixed ICBM silos at risk. This could have significant destabilizing effects."

The reason that the Trident II missiles are even more psychologically destabilizing than the MX missile is because they are invulnerable to attack and are totally hidden from the Russians. Therefore, the Russians will never know where these terribly lethal first-strike missiles are or when they could attack in a first-strike, whereas the Russians will at least be able to watch the MX silos from their satellites. However, the argument of the professional nuclear strategists is that precisely because the Tridents are hidden, they are more stabilizing because the Russians will not be tempted to try to destroy them with their own first strikes. I think from a psychological point of view this argument is back to front and really reflects the actual U.S. thinking about *their* plans for a strike—another example of projection of one's own thinking onto the enemy.

The Cruise Missile

Cruise missiles are small missiles that incorporate a 200-kiloton hydrogen bomb and a small jet engine. They are being developed by the air force for launching from airplanes (air-launched cruise missiles or ALCM) and the navy—sea-launched cruise missiles (SLCM)—and ground-launched cruise missiles (GLCM).

They are directed by an automatic pilot and controlled by an inertial guidance platform, which in turn is operated by a sensor system called TERCOM (terrain contour matching). TERCOM is a brilliant device that can steer cruise missiles to their targets with such accuracy that they have a 100 percent "kill capacity" against military targets that have been hardened to survive nuclear war. TERCOM compares the ground over which it is flying to a map of the terrain, which is stored in its computer. If the missile deviates from its course, a correctional signal is sent by TERCOM to correct the guidance system. Therefore, TERCOM allows the cruise to skim so low over the ground, going over and down hills, across valleys, and around obstacles, that it can evade radar detection and is therefore invisible. It is thought, however, that the cruise missile will be unable to find its way over homogeneous ground that is covered with snow. This is why the U.S. military plans to test the cruise missile over Canadian territory during the winter, in conditions similar to those it would encounter over the Soviet Union.

The cruise missile is very destabilizing for the arms control process. Because it will be only twenty-one feet long, it is extremely small and can be hidden from satellite detection in haylofts, on trucks, and in sheds on the ground. It will also be dual-capable, meaning that it can carry either nuclear or conventional warheads. Therefore, when it is deployed on the ground in the European theater, in the air, or on surface ships and submarines, it will be impossible for the Russians to count how many nuclear cruise missiles America has. Because of their extreme accuracy for hard-target "killing" capacity and because they will be undetectable by radar during flight, Defense Secretary Caspar Weinberger has defined them as strategic weapons, even though they travel at only half the speed of sound and will take several hours to reach their targets. These weapons will destroy the strategic arms control process, which depends upon absolute weapon verification and detection by both sides.

The air-launched cruise missile will be carried by B-52s and B-1 bombers and can also be transported in converted 747 and DC-10 airplanes. The ground-launched cruise missiles have been deployed by the air force in Europe, starting in Britain in December 1983. The plans are eventually to place 464 ground-launched cruise missiles in Belgium, Holland, England, Italy, and West Germany. Ground-launched cruise missiles fired from mobile launchers anywhere in Western Europe will be able to reach much of western Russia with the ability to kill 40 percent of the Soviet population and destroy most of its industry. Because these weapons are terribly destabilizing to the arms control process, there are huge movements in each of these countries to prevent deployment. Ground-launched cruise missiles in Sicily can also be targeted on the Middle East by the United States.

In addition, the air force has planned to place 4,348 air-launched cruise missiles in its airplanes and in December 1982 deployed its first batch of cruise missiles on 16 B-52 airplanes in Rome, New York. The navy also plans to deploy 3,994 sea-launched cruise missiles on some 200 naval vessels—in attack submarines, cruisers, aircraft carriers, and old refurbished battleships. Any surface ship can be equipped to carry this versatile cruise missile. It is not known by either the United States or the USSR how many will carry nuclear and how many conventional weapons. Already, two old battleships have been taken out of mothballs and refitted to carry cruise missiles, and the navy would like to dock one of these ships, the *Iowa*, in an eastern seaboard harbor. It had suggested Boston, New York, or Rhode Island for this purpose but decided on New York after the New England congressional delegation influenced a very close MX vote in the House.

In mid-1983, the military cancelled plans to procure air-launched cruise missiles, and instead announced that it wants to procure "stealth" cruise missiles. Special aeronautical designs that decrease radar visibility and infrared detection, as well as special construction materials in the missile, comprise "stealth" technology.

The Russians are very concerned about this new weapon (they are five years behind in cruise-missile technology) because cruise missiles could approach their homeland from so many different directions that it would be virtually impossible to defend against them. For instance, after cruise missiles are launched from an airplane flying outside Soviet air space, they will be extremely difficult to detect because they fly so low and are so small, and if they are launched in large numbers—one plane launching 20 cruise missiles—the Soviet Union would have to deploy vast numbers of surface-to-air defense systems. As the military says, "Air-launched cruise missiles are expected to dilute Soviet defenses, facilitating their penetration, as well as that of manned bombers."

Apparently, work is also proceeding at the moment on a supersonic or advanced strategic air-launched missile (ASALM), which will be capable of skimming the ground at supersonic speeds over long distances. It will really be nothing more than a cruise missile with supersonic capabilities.

Pershing II

One hundred eight Pershing II missiles began to be deployed in West Germany in December 1983. These are weapons suitable for use in "decapitation," which the Pentagon Defense Guidance Plan describes as strikes at Soviet command centers. This is an extremely accurate missile with a 99 percent probability of destroying a command bunker or missile silo hardened to withstand blast pressures of 2,000 pounds per square inch (psi). President Reagan has said that it is being built to advance "the cause of peace and disarmament." In the gobbledygook of military language, the administration has stated that the Pershing II "should help maintain current damage expectancies in the face of ongoing Warsaw Pact–Soviet Union efforts to harden critical fixed fear targets."

The Pershing II program will cost $2 billion to $8 billion, and the missiles are to be placed on modified trucks called "transporter-erector-launchers" (TEL). The army signed a contract to continue development of the missile before the funds had been approved by Congress.

The missile will be mounted with a single "selectable" nuclear warhead that will permit the yield or power to be adjusted to deal with varying targets. (Yield will be 1 to 20 kilotons; the Hiroshima bomb was 13 kilotons.) The low range will be used to destroy military or command targets and limit "collateral" damage to adjoining civilian areas. That is, it will "limit" the killing of civilians. The Pershing II missile will have unprecedented accuracy and a maneuverable reentry vehicle (MARV). An onboard computer will compare the target terrain to a reference map giving a radar picture of the target area. The maps in cruise and Pershing II missiles were developed by the Defense Mapping Agency from highly sophisticated mapping satellites. (It is said by some arms experts in Washington that the cruise missile will have a 50 percent chance of delivering its hydrogen bomb to within 4 to 6 feet of the target, although others say this is *extremely* optimistic.) Control vanes will then fly the warhead into the target. The CEP is expected to be 120 feet, compared to the

MX CEP of 300 feet. The range of the missile is classified, but it is about 1,100 miles. A modest extension of this range would enable it to reach Moscow, about 1,100 to 1,200 miles from West Germany; and one can assume the locations of the command bunkers are known. The flight time from West Germany to Moscow is very short—about six to eleven minutes. This fact lies at the heart of Soviet fears about the Pershing II. It will theoretically give the United States the capability to disrupt and destroy the Russian National Command Authority, thus immobilizing Soviet ICBM forces until American ICBMs, cruise missiles, and even bombers can get to them and destroy them. Pershing II lies at the heart of the U.S. first-strike counterforce system.

The very short flight time means that by the time the Russian early-warning satellite systems detect the attack, the Soviet command will only have four to six minutes' notice before its command centers are destroyed. The Russians, therefore, have said that should Pershing II be deployed, they will probably use a launch-on-warning system, where computers decide whether to launch nuclear war (four to six minutes is not enough time for human input into the decision loop). This means our world will be technologically out of human control by 1984 and under control by computers, unless we elect politicians in November 1984 who will cease production and deployment of cruise and Pershing II missiles and remove those few already deployed. What an appropriate date for this to happen!

Because of the frightening characteristics of the ground-launched cruise missiles and Pershing II, many European people are determined that they shall not be deployed. America controls the NATO alliance economically with an iron grip, as it does many Western nations. It is a subliminal policy of the United States to threaten trade with its allies if they do not comply with its military wishes. This is almost certainly happening now, for many European leaders are dubious about the deployment of these weapons, as are their people. I was shocked when I visited Europe two years ago to find that NATO was not really our "Western allies" but was, in fact, controlled and run by the U.S. government. Because the Reagan administration recognizes the concern in Europe over deployment, it has cynically mounted a public-relations campaign to convince the European people that ground-

launched cruise missiles and Pershing IIs are good for them.
To this end, Reagan employed Peter Dailey, his 1980-cam-
paign advertising manager, to lead the effort to win backing
for these missiles. William Clark, the President's former National Security Adviser, originally headed a planning group
for this project, which includes Secretary of State George
Shultz, Secretary of Defense Caspar Weinberger, Charles
Wick, director of the U.S. Information Agency, and Peter
McPherson, administrator of the Agency for International
Development. This group is intended to ensure better overall
coordination of public-information policies to combat what
one official called the "Soviet peace offensive," and to react
better to such public-relations problems as the nuclear-freeze
movement at home. NATO instigated its own public-relations
campaign for the missiles in October 1981. What has happened to the world when cynical public-relations firms using
the techniques of modern psychology are hired to convince
people that nuclear weapons are good for them and their
children? This is the antithesis of morality, humanity, or
anything that physicians, scientists, or politicians should stand
for.

The B-1 Bomber

Ever since World War II, the air force has been attached
to its strategic bomber force, even though these planes have
been outdated by the ICBMs, which can reach the Soviet
Union in thirty minutes, while the planes would take twelve
to fourteen hours to reach the same targets. The initial technology of the B-1 was designed in the 1960s, and much of its
updated equipment was borrowed from more recent aircraft.
At best, critics say, the B-1 is a jumble of yesterday's ideas
coupled with military compromises and welded with political
and economic pressures, a flying white elephant that has
stayed airborne through sheer momentum. The full flight test
of the latest version of the B-1 is scheduled for 1985, and if all
goes well, the nation will have an operational fleet of 90
bombers by the end of 1988. However, most people now
agree that the B-1 is a decade late. The new stealth bomber is
threatening the B-1 with sudden and massive obsolescence.
The B-1 is to be used to air-launch cruise missiles outside the

perimeter of the Soviet air-defense mechanisms. This is a very expensive and sophisticated way to launch cruise missiles, and some people say "it is rather like taking the family Ferrari to the corner grocery." Apparently, it is also to be used as a device for signaling U.S. intentions. America and Russia can easily pick up each other's preliminary moves with their sophisticated surveillance systems long before the B-1 has reached the Soviet Union. As one air force officer described it: "Sending a bomber to deliver such a message is rather like hand-delivering a telegram two days after the message has been phoned through." The USSR will have had time before the bomber arrives to launch one or maybe two missile attacks. The B-1 is also to be used to bomb those silos that still contain unfired missiles or to target "cold-launch" silos, which are reloadable after the initial nuclear attack has been launched. In other words, it is to be used for "postattack reconnaissance."

The B-1 is a four-engine, swing-wing bomber roughly the size of a Boeing 707 and two thirds of the size of a B-52. It is designed to fly at both subsonic and supersonic speeds, and its top speed is 2.2 times the speed of sound. Its range is approximately 6,000 miles without refueling, and it can carry twice the payload of the B-52: 32 ALCMs—16 internally, 8 under the wings, and another 8 under the fuselage. It is designed for low-level penetration of enemy air space, 100 to 300 feet above ground (which is below enemy radar), at high subsonic speeds. It is capable of very quick takeoff, but so also is the B-52. With sufficient warning of a nuclear war, both the B-1 and the B-52 forces could survive by taking off early, but without an early warning, both the B-52 and the B-1 forces would be destroyed. Apparently, Soviet defenses against airplanes are becoming increasingly sophisticated, and within a few years the B-1 will be subjected to attack from Soviet air-defense systems as it enters Soviet territory.

Even though the B-1 is an anachronistic airplane at this time, it is a typical example of how the military-industrial complex works, with personal, professional, political, and economic interests of thousands of individuals and institutions in government and the defense industries intertwined to influence American policy in the name of national security. In 1977, President Carter canceled production of the B-1 because he decided it was not needed, but when the Reagan team was elected, it decided to order every weapon on the shelf, including the B-1. It provides a bonanza for the contracting firms: 100 B-1 bombers at a total program cost of $40 billion.

The Stealth Bomber

This will be an even more sophisticated plane than the B-1 for carrying air-launched cruise missiles, although it will still take twelve to fourteen hours to reach the Soviet Union. It will feature the same kind of radar-evading materials as the stealth cruise missiles.

Competition among aerospace companies for the stealth contracts is fierce. Lockheed, Boeing, and General Dynamics want the cruise-missile contract, and Northrop, Lockheed, and Rockwell want the bomber contract. In fact, Lockheed and Rockwell joined forces to try to win the $25 billion contract for stealth aircraft and defeat Northrop. These two companies have already begun designing a stealth version of the B-1 to outmaneuver the Northrop stealth bomber. Northrop then said it would deliver its bomber in 1988, three years earlier than scheduled, to eliminate the need for the Rockwell-Lockheed B-1 stealth.

These last four weapon systems—cruise missiles, precision-guided Pershing II missiles, B-1 and stealth bombers—are to be used to provide the intermediate links in what the Reagan strategists describe as the "seamless web of deterrence"—falling between conventional warfare options and "execution of a single integrated operational plan" (SIOP), that is, full-scale nuclear war.

The sea-launched cruise missiles will not be "dedicated to the SIOP plan" but will be "part of the strategic reserve force and will be available for reconstitution and targeting if necessary during the post-SIOP period," that is, after the nuclear war. According to Admiral Frank B. Kelso, director of the navy's Strategic Submarine Division, the submarine-launched cruise missile will also "be available for selected release in non-SIOP options . . . to provide extremely accurate strikes against theater targets." That is, these submarine-launched cruise missiles could be used as a partial substitute for the ground-launched cruise missiles in a European theater war if the peace movement prevented GLCM deployment in Europe.

The Neutron Bomb or Enhanced Radiation Weapon

This revolting weapon was designed some twenty years ago by a man named Sam Cohen (known as the father of the neutron bomb). It is an ordinary hydrogen bomb, but the external casing is removed—which reduces the blast but allows a huge flux of neutrons to emerge from the explosion. It typically has the explosive force of a 1-kiloton bomb, but a radiation flux of a 10-kiloton bomb. It is to be used against invading Russian tanks on the conventional battlefield. It does not destroy as much property as an ordinary H-bomb (buildings, cathedrals, etc.) because of its decreased blast, but the neutrons can penetrate the tanks and kill the soldiers.

The 97th Congress approved Reagan's decision to stockpile fully assembled "enhanced radiation–reduced blast" weapons for the 8-inch artillery projectile and for the Lance nuclear battlefield missile, and the administration has also approved the development of a third type of neutron bomb for the U.S. arsenal. This particular bomb is a 155-millimeter nuclear artillery projectile that will be ready for deployment by 1986. All three types of neutron bomb are for use in Europe.

The principal material needed for enhanced-radiation warheads is tritium, and because there is a shortage of this radioactive isotope, the government is currently launching a major program to more than double the production of nuclear material. Tritium decays at a rate of 5.5 percent per year, so the neutron bombs will continually need upgrading at periodic intervals.

The government plans to build 800 8-inch neutron shells, 380 Lance neutron warheads, and 1,000 155-millimeter neutron shells. The latter warheads will cost $3 million each, compared to the cost of $24,000 for a conventional Copperhead precision-guided 155-millimeter artillery shell. Together with the cost of increased production of radioactive material, the total expenditure could exceed $5 billion for these neutron weapons.

Also being designed at the moment are an anti-ballistic-missile neutron bomb for the Low-Altitude Air Defense System and an enhanced-radiation design for a new navy surface-to-air nuclear missile. Apparently, enhanced-radiation hydrogen bombs are now gaining favor in the nuclear-design community, encouraged by the Reagan administration's lack of concern for the negative medical implications of these weapons. Neutron bombs are but three of the twenty-five warhead types in the nuclear stockpile, and they will represent a quarter of the nuclear weapons to be produced in the mid-1980s.

The military utility of these weapons is demonstrated by the way in which they kill people. Neutrons can penetrate any sort of structural material, including armored tanks. Neutron bombs are designed to be used against invading Russian tanks in Western Europe.

The medical implications of this radiation are horrendous. The soldiers who are not killed initially by the nuclear blast will receive such high doses of radiation that they will die within forty-eight hours. The symptoms are vomiting, severe headache, high fever, ataxia (inability to walk straight), delirium, stupor, and psychosis; and some hours before death the victims may have a period of lucidity and normality. Those soldiers and civilians who are farther from the very high dose of radiation will die two to three weeks later from acute radiation illness. They may feel normal for the first one to two weeks and then develop lassitude, bleeding spots under the skin and around the teeth from the gums, vomiting and bloody diarrhea, hair loss (alopecia), and eventually die days later of overwhelming septicemia or massive hemorrhage. Those on the periphery of the radiation field, some miles from the epicenter, will receive doses that will increase their risk of developing leukemia five years later or cancer fifteen to fifty years later. Babies and children are ten to twenty times more susceptible to these effects than adults. Obviously, in the European battlefield, civilians will be affected as well as soldiers.

The neutron bomb as a battlefield weapon in Europe is considered by some military people to be more acceptable than an ordinary hydrogen bomb. It therefore blurs the distinction between conventional and nuclear weapons and could thus induce nuclear war. The Russians do not yet have neutron bombs, but in line with their oft-stated policy, they will retaliate massively with their nuclear arsenal should one nuclear weapon be used against them. Thus the neutron bomb is a trip wire between conventional and nuclear war.

New Conventional Weapons (Near-Nuclear)

Conventional bombs that are called "near-nuclear" weapons are now being built. They have the destructive potential of tactical nuclear weapons but without the radiation and fallout. This "revolution" in conventional weapons began during the Vietnam war and is now becoming very fashionable, as popular demand calls for a decrease in nuclear weapons to be balanced by an increase in conventional ones. It has been fascinating for the weapons scientists to work on these new projects and, of course, lucrative for the manufacturers. After the Vietnam war U.S. and European arms firms developed these more sophisticated weapons for European or Middle Eastern battlefields, and their versatility was recently demonstrated by the French-made Exocet missile, which sank the British destroyer in the Falklands. Because the Non-Proliferation Treaty does not apply to conventional weapons, they can and are being sold to countries in the Middle East, Africa, and other volatile Third World areas—for profit, of course.

It is proposed that these weapons will be delivered by Pershing II missiles, Lance missiles, submarine-launched cruise missiles, and possibly Trident II missiles—making it impossible to differentiate nuclear from conventional weapons and thus destroying the prospects for adequate arms-control treaties.

These nonnuclear weapons use clustered warheads incorporating large numbers of individually guided "submunitions" or bomblets that are dispersed over an area of one square mile or one hundred city blocks. Senator Sam Nunn of the Armed Services Committee stated: "They begin to approach the destructive potential of small yield 2- to 3-kiloton battlefield nuclear weapons." The bomblets are capable of seeking out enemy targets and exploding when they are within firing range, using smart technology. To advance the weapon's kill probability, military scientists have developed revolutionary explosives and warhead technologies. The most potent of these

are called "fuel-air explosives" (FAE), which dispense a cloud
of highly volatile fuel (ethylene oxide, propylene oxide, or
propane) that, when ignited, produces a blast so powerful it
can destroy entire city blocks. The Daisy Cutter in Vietnam
was one of these and was described as "the closest thing to a
nuclear bomb." Another is the "vacuum bomb" used by
Israel in Beirut. The Pentagon is now engaged in producing
even more dreadful explosives called "advanced fuel-air
munitions." It is also developing new munitions called self-
forging fragments (SFF), which are composed of discs of
metal that become shaped into conical projectiles by the force
of the explosion and will tear human bodies apart. These
weapons have a kill probability of 100 percent. The Defense
Department recently sent a circular to many U.S. civilian
hospitals, asking them to participate in the Civilian Military
Contingency Hospital System (CMCHS), saying: "Future large-
scale war overseas will probably produce casualties at a higher
rate than any other war in history."

These submunitions are to be loaded onto surface-to-
surface and air-to-surface missiles with advanced guidance
systems that will deliver the weapons deep into "enemy"
territory far behind the front lines. One of these guided
missiles, the Assault-Breaker, is capable of destroying airfields and tank formations and is viewed by the Reagan administration as one of its three top-priority armaments, together
with the MX and the B-1 bomber.

These dreadful weapons will obviously make escalation
to nuclear war *more* likely because the Russians will build
them, too. (They always copy and follow.) Because any future
conventional war in Europe is therefore likely to produce
such high levels of death and destruction, the other side may
feel compelled to retaliate with tactical nuclear weapons,
particularly as there will be no way for the Russians to differentiate between a nuclear or "near-nuclear" Pershing II,
Trident II, cruise, or Lance missile in flight. Many experts
believe these bombs violate the Geneva conventions, which
ban the use of especially cruel and indiscriminate weapons.

The firms manufacturing these weapons are AVCO,
Honeywell, General Dynamics, Vought, Martin Marietta, and
French, British, and West German firms.

Rapid Deployment Force

Since the Middle East oil crisis, the U.S. military has been preparing the Rapid Deployment Force for use not just in the Persian Gulf but in the Middle East, Korea, South Asia, Europe, or anywhere else around the globe. To this end, the Rapid Deployment Force is expanding at every level—the army has gone from three divisions to five; the air force has grown from five tactical air wings to ten; and head-quarters has increased from 260 persons in March 1982 to 960 in January 1983.

These forces are to use conventional, nuclear, chemical, or biological weapons as necessary in what is called the "integrated battlefield." The units are termed "dual-capable" —nuclear or nonnuclear. To this end, a wing of 28 B-52 bombers with refueling and reconnaissance planes has been provided by SAC to the Rapid Deployment Force. It can provide 200 tons of conventional explosives per day or a range of thermonuclear bombs. These B-52s need a forward operating location, and airports are therefore being constructed or expanded by the United States at Diego Garcia in the Indian Ocean, Ras Banas in Egypt, Thamit in Oman, and in Saudi Arabia and Morocco. Also, three carrier battle groups are stationed in the Indian Ocean and eastern Mediterranean and are loaded with hundreds of nuclear weapons of various kinds allocated to the RDF.

To threaten the use of the Rapid Deployment Force in the Persian Gulf is ludicrous, when only 5 percent of total U.S. energy needs and 13 percent of U.S. oil needs come from the Persian Gulf. Moreover, the Soviet Union is a net exporter of oil and does not need the Persian Gulf oil. Even if it did need the oil, its unquestioned need for wheat has not led Moscow to threaten an invasion of Argentina or Sas-katchewan. Undoubtedly, the U.S. emphasis on "security access" to the Persian Gulf is to protect U.S. energy compa-nies in the processing and global marketing of Persian Gulf oil and European access to the oil. To this end, the U.S. military and political leadership may be prepared to start a nuclear war.

The army has prepared for the RDF a new war-fighting doctrine called Air Land Battle. This doctrine promotes small nuclear-equipped forces as a rapidly deployable substitute for larger, conventionally armed forces. It says the U.S. forces should conduct "rapid unpredictable violent attacks," and the doctrine comes close to calling for preemptive nuclear strikes. It also recommends that when using the new near-nuclear weapons, or in fact nuclear weapons, target troops strike seventy-five to one hundred miles inside enemy territory before they even begin to fight so that the radiation and blast effects kill only enemy troops and civilians and do not affect the U.S. forces. The Air Land Battle plan describes the Middle East and Southwest Asia as "a land of turmoil, terror, violence and bloodshed." It says that if nuclear weapons are to be used, they must be used early and in depth. Many of the "battlefield" nuclear weapons recommended are more powerful than the Hiroshima bomb, which was only 13 kilotons. These are from 60 to 400 kilotons, and plans include the use of neutron bombs as well. The commanders are directed to "operate without interruption," even after the enemy launches nuclear or chemical attack, and to fight on even with "contaminated personnel and equipment," despite the "large number of personnel casualties and much damage to equipment, as well as psychological stress on an unprecedented scale." The army is even talking about "pre-clearance" for use of nuclear weapons—making it unnecessary to ask the National Command Authority before it uses such weapons.

The Air Land Battle doctrine and the Rapid Deployment Force have therefore dangerously increased the risk of a nuclear war triggered by first use of nuclear weapons.

America's drive to achieve strategic superiority over, and not parity with, the USSR through the construction of the MX, Trident II, Pershing II and cruise missiles, and the B-1 and stealth bombers has allowed it once again to be in a position where it can potentially intervene anywhere in the world with impunity, while threatening the Soviet Union with a first strike. The theory is that Russia will then not interfere with America's global pursuits.

Why It Is Not Possible to Keep a Nuclear War Limited

The basic tenet of a limited nuclear war is itself crazy, because even with very careful planning, targeting, and execution of a nuclear attack, with the intent to target only military facilities in order to reduce collateral damage (that is, deaths of civilians), is it possible that the attacked country would see as acceptable with such restraints the death of only three million people, as opposed to ten to twenty million people? The response of the attacked country could lead to all-out nuclear war. The whole U.S. Defense Guidance Plan for limited protracted, winnable nuclear war is based on this assumption, whereas the Soviet strategic commentators have *never* seriously considered the possibility of controlled or limited nuclear war. They say any attacks will lead to simultaneous and massive unconstrained attacks upon a wide range of U.S. targets, including the C^3I system.

The most fundamental tenet of Soviet strategic doctrine is to deter nuclear war. They say: "War with the employment of nuclear weapons can undermine the very foundation for the existence of human society and inflict tremendous damage to its progressive development. Therefore, the most important requirement for progress in our time is the prevention of a new world war." To this end, they believe the better their forces are equipped to wage a nuclear war, the more effective they will be as a deterrent to a nuclear attack on the USSR.

For thirty-eight years, the nuclear doctrine of the United States has been to attack the Soviet Union first with nuclear weapons if the United States disapproves of any Soviet-invoked international incident or war. It could do this because until the late sixties, when Russia deployed survivable weapons in large numbers, the United States had the nuclear monopoly. Now there is strategic parity or equality in intercontinental killing power.

The Soviet Targeting Doctrine states that as soon as Russia confirms that a nuclear attack is under way, its bombers and ICBMs will take off even before the U.S. bombs land on their homeland, and they will retaliate with massive blows against U.S. military, economic, industrial, and political administrative resources in order to frustrate and damage U.S. military operations and thus minimize damage to the Soviet Union.

Such a Soviet attack would massively target all C^3I and military installations, which are scattered ubiquitously throughout the continental United States, all government centers and places where political leadership is concentrated, and all major economic and industrial facilities. (Power stations, which obviously include the seventy-three nuclear reactors, are perhaps one of the single most important nonmilitary targets in Soviet war planning.) Targets also include stocks of strategic raw materials, oil refineries and storage sites, metallurgical plants, chemical industries, and transport operations (railroads and yards, bridges, tunnels, ports, and vessels in the water). Urban centers are not to be attacked in pursuit of some arbitrary minimum level of fatalities, but neither are they to be avoided if they are near military, political, or industrial targets.

The Soviets totally reject controlled escalation and limited nuclear war. Of these ideas Georgi Arbatov, head of the U.S.–Canadian Institute, wrote: "In actual fact, these proposals are an attempt to lull public opinion and to make the prospect of nuclear war more accessible, or, if you like, more digestible."

The very idea of introducing "rules of the game" and of artificial limitations by agreement is based on an illusion and is without foundation. It is hard to imagine that nuclear war, if launched, could be held within the framework of the "rules and not grow into general nuclear war." In 1980, Chairman Brezhnev reiterated these sentiments after President Carter released Presidential Directive 59, and these ideas reflect overwhelmingly the bulk of Soviet military literature.

Although the Soviet Union has developed an impressive array of C^3I facilities, these facilities are weakest in the capabilities to control nuclear war fighting, that is, the capacity for timely intelligence, attack characterization, and damage assessment via satellite detection, and retargeting flexibilities.

So what have American scientists and military strategists been up to for the last several decades? They are totally out of touch with reality, desperately dreaming up schemes where they might be able to use their nuclear weapons in some limited way without provoking massive genocide. This is schizoid thinking. (Schizophrenic thought demonstrates a split between perception of reality and reality.)

In any case, reducing the CEP of the Minuteman III from 300 feet to less with a MARVed 12-A warhead of 335 kilotons in order to reduce collateral damage or deaths of people is ludicrous thinking because of the enormous explosive power of the hydrogen bomb it carries. A limited attack on the Soviet oil supply would kill 836,000 to 1.46 million people and injure 2.5 to 3.8 million more. An equivalent Soviet attack on the U.S. petroleum centers could destroy 64 percent of U.S. refining capacity and kill from 3.2 to 5.03 million people.

A Soviet counterforce or first-strike attack against the U.S. ICBM silos would kill from 800,000 to 50 million people. Such an attack would also involve destruction of ballistic-missile submarines, support facilities, C^3I centers, and the 46 SAC bomber bases. A similar U.S. counterforce nuclear war, targeting Russian military facilities only, would cause 2.65 to 27.7 million deaths, but a "comprehensive" U.S. counterattack could well double these numbers.

By way of comparison, all the wars the United States has fought in the last two hundred years have caused fewer than 1.2 million U.S. deaths (World War II, 291,557 deaths; Korea, 33,629; and Vietnam, 46,558). The United States has suffered *no* civilian casualties since the Civil War. Russia lost 20 million people in World War II, not within the first couple of hours but over a four-year period.

But all estimates are fundamentally inaccurate because the official casualty estimates of nuclear war are based only on blast and fallout, while long-term cancer deaths from fallout and deaths from fire, burns, epidemics, starvation, lack of medical care, ozone destruction, cooling of the temperature of the earth, and many other variables are totally excluded. Consequently, the range of death estimates related to counterforce nuclear war could be twenty times larger. In effect, the counterforce attack could well become a countervalue attack, that is, an attack on civilians.

Various U.S. officials have testified that the United States does not target civilian areas but does target "industrial sites which are co-located with population centers." By virtue of associated industrial and military targets, the United States has targeted all of the 200 largest Russian cities and 80 percent of the 886 cities with populations above 25,000. Many of these cities would receive more than 10 hydrogen bombs. Moscow alone would receive 60, and peak over-pressures throughout central Moscow would be so severe (greater than 100 pounds per square inch) that not a building or tree would be left standing.

A U.S. attack using all the Soviet targets included in SIOP, avoiding population centers per se, would kill from 50 to 100 million people and injure 30 million more. It would destroy 70 percent to 90 percent of major Soviet political and leadership facilities, 20 percent to 50 percent of other military targets, and 70 percent to 90 percent of Russian manufacturing capacity.

These numbers are obscene. Nuclear weapons explode with the force of the energy of the stars, and to imagine they can be used in a precise and discriminate fashion is fantasy thinking or mental masturbation.

As the Department of Defense said in a 1974 report to Congress: "The uncertainties in known nuclear phenomena and weapon system performance, let alone those associated with discoveries which may be made at some future date, must certainly raise serious questions as to the predictability and controllability of nuclear warfare."

Despite these facts, the Reagan administration plans to invest $18 billion to provide a C^3I system that could endure a protracted, winnable nuclear war conducted over a six-month period. One observer on the Reagan staff commented sarcastically about this scheme, "We've been working on this C^3I problem for 5 years now and can report that the system might survive 15 minutes of nuclear war."

The Iron Triangle

In my quest to prevent nuclear war, I became curious about the societal processes which sustained and motivated this enormous industry of death. I discovered that the answer lay at the feet of the scientists and the three arms of the "Iron Triangle"—Congress, the Pentagon, and the military-industrial complex. As a physician, I know that no cure can ever be prescribed for a disease unless the cause or etiology of the pathological process is ascertained. What follows is an explanation of the etiology of the arms race disease.

Former General of the Army Omar Bradley once said, "We have grasped the mystery of the atom and rejected the Sermon on the Mount. Ours is a world of nuclear giants and ethical infants. We know more about war than we do about peace. We know more about killing than we do about living."

Somewhere in the last thirty-eight years, the United States of America has lost its direction and its soul. It has appropriated in 1984 approximately $264 billion for the military, which is 7.24 percent of the total gross national product. The administration has requested authority for $305 billion for 1985. In 1983, $30 billion had been taken out of programs to help people: Medicare, legal services, food stamps, school lunches, assistance to low-income families for heating costs, welfare, aid to cities, student loans, Social Security, job opportunities and training, elementary, secondary, and higher education, child-nutrition programs, housing-assistance programs, Aid to Families with Dependent Children, and compensatory education for disadvantaged children. By August 1983, 34.4 million people in the United States were below the poverty line—defined as $9,900 annual income for a family of four.

Instead, President Reagan plans to spend $1.9 billion for 100 MX missiles, $40 billion for 100 B-1 long-range bombers (which will be obsolete by the time they are ready toward the end of the 1980s), $82.7 billion for Trident submarines (total program cost), $2.27 billion for production of 84 FA-18 attack bombers, $11.1 billion for procurement of 525 Patriot missiles (the cost of these weapons for one year), $500 million for 91 Pershing II missiles, and $54 million for nerve gas.

I come from a country, Australia, where our tax dollars are used for the benefit and not the death of society. We have nationalized medicine, where medical insurance is either national or private, according to the patient's preference, and all medical care is subsidized. Tertiary or university education is free; all people are given an adequate old-age pension, so they can maintain their dignity, and poor people are cared for. Australia is a capitalist society, but we care for our people. What has happened to the great United States of America?

I will now quote Dr. Howard Hiatt from the *New England Journal of Medicine*, October 28, 1982:

In 1967, the World Health Organization (WHO) launched a campaign to eradicate smallpox. Ten years later, the world recorded the last case of this disease, which had claimed millions of lives over the century. The cost, which was estimated to have been $300 million, was borne by contributions to the WHO by nations throughout the world. The United States' share averaged $3 million annually—an amount that may be compared with the $130 million that we now save each year by being able to discontinue vaccination, surveillance, and quarantine programs.

This year, the world will spend $650 billion on arms, including $100 billion on nuclear weapons. Third World countries spend more than $100 billion annually on their military activities. A simple calculation indicates that every four hours throughout the year, world arms expenditures are equivalent to the total bill for the ten-year program that eliminated smallpox. The annual contribution by the United

States to the smallpox program was less than what our nation this year is spending every 50 minutes on our military programs.

Total nonmilitary aid from all nations for Third World countries is less than 5 percent of the world's military expenditures. Over half the world's people do not have safe drinking water. This accounts for most serious disease and for large fractions of the deaths in Third World countries. Although provision for safe water would require a major organizational change, access could be provided within a decade for the majority of people now in need, for an estimated cost of $30 billion a year—a large sum, but less than the cost of 17 days of arms production.

Estimates put at almost 2 million the number of people who die each year from measles, polio, tuberculosis, diphtheria, tetanus, and other diseases for which effective vaccines are available. Three million children could be immunized with such vaccines for the price of one modern fighter plane ($20 million).

Eight hundred million people are thought to suffer from malaria, and each year 1 million children die of the disease in Africa alone. The diversion of half a day's military expenditures would finance the whole malaria control program of the WHO. Military expenditures in one hour exceed the total annual budget for all research on malaria and all other tropical diseases.

Between 450 million and 1 billion people have less food than is necessary for basic survival. The United Nations Children's Fund estimated that in 1978 more than 12 million children under the age of five died of hunger and its effects. The supplemental costs of a twenty-year program to provide essential food and to fill health needs in all developing countries have been estimated to be $80 billion. This would be available if all nations were to redirect 12 percent of this year's military spending. One does not have to be a physician to suggest that such a transfer of funds might lead to more world security than the course on which we find ourselves at present.

Subtracting from the federal budget the government's self-funding trust accounts, which are funded separately from income taxes, like Social Security and Medicare, the Defense Department is by far the biggest single spender. After adding defense-related spending in the Department of Energy, Veterans Administration, and National Aeronautics and Space Administration, the Council on Economic Priorities recently reported that the "total military budget" in 1981 used 48 percent of all federal general funds. In 1984 the number is 55 percent. Projecting to 1986, at the end of the proposed Reagan buildup, the "total military budget" would use up fifty-nine cents of every federal dollar.

In the five years from 1984 to 1988, the Reagan administration plans to spend $1.8 trillion (but actually, if hidden costs are included, $2.5 trillion) on "defense." In comparison, America has spent only $1.5 trillion on defense over the last thirty-seven years. When Reagan was elected, the administration, Pentagon, military corporations, and scientists were like little boys let loose in a candy shop. They ordered every single weapon on the shelves—whatever they had ever fancied, needed, or liked. These figures are absolutely obscene. Apart from the fact that two thirds of the world's children are starving and malnourished, this sort of wild spending, using the people's hard-earned tax dollars, will destroy the American economy, which will be bad for America but probably worse for the rest of the world, which depends on the value of the U.S. dollar for economic survival, and on U.S. exports of food, U.S. technology, and the U.S. market.

The military-industrial complex does not stimulate the economy nor does it provide many jobs for the amount of money spent. For every $1 billion spent by the Pentagon in the private sector, 28,000 direct and indirect jobs are created. The same amount of money would create 32,000 jobs if spent for new public transport (which would also save an enormous amount of energy), 57,000 jobs if used for personal consumption, or 71,000 jobs if spent on education. Military spending increases employment in specific highly skilled and a few semiskilled professions in such industries as aircraft production, electronics, and engineering, and skilled and semiskilled metal work. More than 30 percent of the country's mathematicians work somewhere in the military-industrial complex, as do 25 percent of the nation's physicists, 40 percent of the aeroastronautic engineers, and 11 percent of the computer programmers. On the other hand, domestic spending creates jobs in areas of high public interest—medicine, social work, civil engineering, construction, and education. And as the defense sector becomes more capital intensive, fewer and fewer new jobs are created through new defense expenditures.

The military industry also creates dead-end products in economic terms. Huge amounts of money are spent on the most deadly weapons of mass genocide, which, if they function as intended, will never be used. They therefore sit on the shelves, so to speak, and the money is never injected back into the economy to contribute to further economic production. People can't eat bombs, wear them on their heads, or use them for pleasure. Because 7.24 percent of the GNP is spent on the military, America has a declining economy compared to other countries like Japan, which spends 1 percent, and West Germany, which spends 3.5 percent. Their scientists are used to developing wonderful things that people can buy and sell, thus stimulating their economic systems. By comparison, those nations with relatively high military budgets have relatively poor economic performance. Between 1960 and the oil-price shock of 1973, manufacturing productivity growth in most European nations averaged twice the U.S. rates. Japan's growth rate was more than three times higher. Even after the oil crunch caused depressed economic growth in most of the world, many European countries and Japan still have maintained productivity growth two to three times higher than the U.S. rate.

Adam Smith, in his classic eighteenth-century treatise *The Wealth of Nations*, wrote, "The whole Army and Navy are unproductive laborers. They are the servants of the people, and are maintained by a part of the annual product of the industry of other people." In America, 30 percent or more of the country's best engineers work on military projects because these pay better and are more interesting technologically. At present, defense accounts for 10 percent of U.S. manufacturing ouput and 38 percent of its export sales, while Japan is edging America out of the marketing of advanced computer technology, and the European consortium Airbus Industries is challenging Boeing in the world market for the new generation of fuel-efficient jumbo jets.

America was once the most powerful country economically because of its immense natural resources and also because its scientists and technicians used their creativity to develop a great trading nation on the world scene. No longer does America dominate world markets. Furthermore, very little money has been recycled by civilian industry into upkeep of the plants and the factories in the primary industrial area. Hence, the general workmanship of U.S. goods is generally shoddy compared to that of West Germany and Japan.

The dynamics of the pathology of the U.S. arms race has several different sources. It involves the activities of scientists in specialized "think tanks" and at the universities, the Pentagon, the military and related corporations that manufacture weapons, and the Congress. The last three entities are termed the "Iron Triangle."

Before I describe the Iron Triangle, I will enumerate the activities of the scientists, many of whom have spearheaded the arms race since 1945. At that time, the air force, having used the two atomic bombs in Japan, maintained a proprietary right over nuclear weapons and for many years was the strongest force with respect to nuclear weapons in the Pentagon. For twenty years the air force generals were enthusiastic about the first U.S. use of nuclear weapons at a time when Russia possessed very few, if any, nuclear weapons. Their policy was to bomb the Soviet Union flat if it misbehaved on the international scene.

The air force, appreciating the great consultative value of scientists during World War II, also instituted the RAND Corporation in 1945 to advise and formulate policies for a rational use of nuclear weapons. RAND, an air force–sponsored think tank, with its faculty of economists, biologists, engineers, physicists, mathematicians, and others, was really instrumental in leading military thinking into the nuclear area. Herman Kahn, Albert Wohlstetter, Charles Hitch, Alain Enthoven, Daniel Ellsberg, James Schlesinger, Thomas Schelling, William Kauffman, Harold Brown, Bernard Brodie, and others became almost gods to the air force and to the federal politicians at large. Typical of the type of thinking at RAND, in 1960, Kahn wrote a 652-page book called *On Thermonuclear War*. In this book, he noted that while nuclear war would boost the number of children born with genetic defects, 4 percent are born that way anyway. He wrote, "War is a terrible thing, but so is peace. The difference seems, in some respect, to be a quantitative one of degree and standards." He predicted that while human tragedy would increase after nuclear war, "the increase would not preclude normal and happy lives for the majority of survivors and their dependents."

A huge fallout shelter program costing $200 billion over a twenty-year period would save tens of millions of American lives. He thought such a massive civil-defense program was necessary to "enable the U.S. to take a much firmer position" in the Cold War with Russia. He believed that Soviet–American relations would become so tense that it was "perfectly conceivable . . . that the U.S. might have to evacuate 2 or 3 times every decade." He also said that after a nuclear war, "we can imagine a renewed vigor among the population with a zealous, almost religious, dedication to reconstruction, exemplified by a 50–60–hour work week."

In one of Kahn's lectures, he talked about the post-nuclear-war environment in unrealistic, almost surrealistic, terms: "Now, just imagine yourself in a postwar situation. Everybody will have been subjected to extremes of anxiety, unfamiliar environment, strange foods, minimum toilet facilities, inadequate shelters and the like. Under these conditions, some high percentage of the population is going to become nauseated and nausea is very contagious. If one man vomits, everybody vomits. It would not be surprising if almost everybody vomits. Almost everyone is likely to think he has received too much radiation. Morale may be so affected that many survivors may refuse to participate in constructive activities, but would content themselves with sitting down and waiting to die. Some may even become violent and destructive.

"However, the situation will be quite different if radiation meters were distributed. Assume now that a man gets sick from a cause other than radiation. Not believing this, his morale begins to drop. You look at his meter and say, 'You have received only 10 roentgens; why are you vomiting? Pull yourself together and get to work.' "

Kahn fashioned himself as the ultimate defense intellectual: cool, calm, rational, and fearless.

The mathematician James R. Newman wrote in *Scientific American* that Kahn's book was "a moral tract on mass murder; how to plan it, how to commit it, how to get away with it, how to justify it." This prompted Kahn to write a second book, *Thinking About the Unthinkable*, to justify his rational approach to so ghastly a topic.

In fact, most of the scientists at RAND exhibited no moral scruples in their writings or discussions about their systematic plan to murder tens to hundreds of millions of Russian human beings. They spent all their time fascinated with the plans they had devised, drawing graphs, calculating models based on economic principles, and playing never-ending war games. They had an enormous influence on government thinking, and their strategies and terminologies became so sacred that they are still set in stone.

Kahn was most influential in his discussions on nuclear targeting strategy. He argued in the fifties that simply threatening to destroy Soviet cities in response to a Soviet nuclear attack against the United States was not enough to maintain peace. He contended that the Russians could impose "nuclear blackmail" by first destroying the U.S. nuclear arsenal and then threatening to destroy its cities with a protective "reserve force" of missiles if the United States dared to retaliate. (The Russians had four nuclear missiles by 1962.) To prevent being checkmated in this nuclear chess game, Kahn urged the United States to develop a "credible first-strike capacity" to allow the United States to respond to Soviet conventional aggression (an invasion of Western Europe) by knocking out the Russian strategic forces, and also a "tit-for-tat" capability to enable the United States to first use very small nuclear salvos in the event of Soviet aggression of a smaller order.

Later, in the seventies, when administration officials talked about the vulnerability of the U.S. land-based missile arsenal and the possibility that by attacking it, the Soviets could "deter our deterrent," they were only repeating the Kahn scenario devised twenty years earlier. Kahn did not invent the scenario—it arose from RAND discussions in the fifties— but Kahn systematized and popularized it.

In fact, most of the strategic theories used today are just recycled RAND theories developed years ago by those scientists whose professional aim was to develop credible plans to fight a nuclear war with the Russians, often talking about first strike. The trouble was that they could never, despite their toil during all these years, devise a scenario where they could win without the deaths of millions of people. Yet they persisted tenaciously with their theories, and they are still at it today. They spoke and speak in strange esoteric tongues, because the terminology allowed them to contemplate ghastly scenarios without permitting these stark facts to penetrate their emotions and their souls. The trouble is that these people taught everyone else how to practice this scientific psychic numbing by rational elimination of human emotions from the equation of mass genocide. These men were above all rational! What a disservice to humanity they performed!

The Laboratories

The original villains in the cause of the nuclear arms race were the scientists. They were originally authorized by President Roosevelt to design and construct the first atomic bombs, which they did brilliantly. Some of them realized their shocking contribution to the world when they watched Trinity, the first atomic bomb, explode in the Alamogordo desert in July 1945. Others were stricken after Little Boy was used on Hiroshima. Yet others have been waging a losing battle against the continuous growth of the nuclear arsenals ever since—people like Nobel Laureate Hans Bethe, Bernard Feld, and Leo Szilard.

Unfortunately, the forces of evil prevailed over the frail forces of good. After the war, there were still scientists who were committed to building more bombs. Some were motivated by the fascination of the intellectual challenge—as when Oppenheimer called the problem-solving during the Manhattan Project "technically sweet." Other scientists have been known to say that it is terrific fun to design extremely complex weapons of mass genocide. Others were motivated by fear and distrust of the Russians. Of these, some were emigrants from countries overrun by the Soviets. One of these people was Edward Teller, who has spent his life since World War II promoting the construction of more and better nuclear weapons. He was the instigator of the hydrogen bomb and, indeed, destroyed the career and reputation of Oppenheimer, who was opposed to this fearsome weapon because he said it was unnecessary. Teller has been a ruthless advocate of nuclear weapons to be used if necessary against the Russians.

After the war, the Los Alamos Lab in New Mexico,

which built the first three atomic bombs, continued its work; and ten years later, in 1952, Edward Teller helped found a rival lab, Lawrence-Livermore, in Livermore, California.

These two national laboratories are financed and operated by the Department of Energy under the academic sponsorship of the University of California. This convenient arrangement gives them a degree of independence and neutrality. These labs have designed every nuclear weapon in the arsenal of the United States. Los Alamos operates on a $421 million annual budget and has 7,018 employees. Lawrence-Livermore has a $515 million budget with 7,160 employees. The rivalry between the labs is deliberate government policy to encourage design of the best bombs.

Los Alamos has designed two thirds of the weapons in the nuclear stockpile, and its recent products include hydrogen bombs for air- and submarine-launched cruise missiles and the new Pershing II missile. Livermore was an early advocate of new nuclear artillery shells and short-range-missile atomic bombs for the army.

Weapons designed by the labs are fitted with fuses and with firing and safety devices by the Sandia National Laboratory, which is operated for the government by Western Electric. This lab has branches in New Mexico, California, and Nevada and a budget of $738 million and 7,985 employees.

Sometimes the military asks the scientists to design a specific weapon, but usually the labs design the weapons first and present them to the military for approval. They are the brain trust that continuously spews out ideas for hideous new weapons. As Harold Agnew, former director of Los Alamos Lab, said in reference to his sales pitch, "We used to emphasize cost and practicality until we learned that the 'Gee Whiz, Gosh, Tail Fins, and Chrome Approach' is the best way to go with the military." The scientists are attracted by the intellectual challenge, and the military boys are attracted by the new toys.

The scientists often argue hotly about which are the most appropriate weapons to design and build, but never about whether to do it or not. A dissenting physicist, Hugh DeWitt, who works at Livermore, reports that the labs are "repositories of hawkish views of the world, distrust of the Russians, distrust of arms control, faith in the efficacy of high technology to provide protection and strong opposition to any measures that might limit nuclear weapons development."

Lab officials say they have no difficulty attracting young scientists to the labs because they offer these ambitious young people a chance to work with similar people, using excellent equipment such as 13 CRCY-1 computers, the world's most powerful—all terrific fun. As one scientist, Jerry Zonas of Sandia Labs, said, "I believe weapons are necessary and inevitable. . . . I am not afraid of new technology. Technology is not evil." Robert Thorne, deputy director at Los Alamos, adds, "Most of us believe our efforts will lead to a safer world, one in which arms control will play a part. I don't believe we will ever eliminate nuclear weapons. I don't think we would have a safer or better world if they were eliminated." These men live in their ivory towers both of buildings and of mind-set—they are responsible for the weapons, yet they take no responsibility for them, as if the weapons emerged spontaneously and have a life of their own. They also show absolutely no moral compunction for the deadly genocidal monsters they have been and are creating.

Other scientists, like Herbert York, who was the first director of Lawrence-Livermore Labs, have misgivings about their pasts. York described the motivations of his former colleagues: "They derived either their incomes, their profits, or their consultant fees from it, but much more important than money as the motivating force are the individual's own psychic and spiritual needs. The majority of key individual promoters of the arms race derive a very large part of their self-esteem from their participation in what they believe to be an essential—even a holy—cause."

In April 1983, five Nobel Laureates and sixty-five other scientists presented a petition to officials at Los Alamos Lab, where they were gathered for the lab's fortieth anniversary. The petition urged a massive international reduction of nuclear arms and went on to say, "We are appalled at the present level of nuclear armaments of the nations of the world and are profoundly frightened for the future of humanity. . . . The single crucial fact is that the major world powers now possess a sufficiency of nuclear warheads and delivery systems to destroy each other and a significant part of the rest of the world many times over."

But the people working for the labs win out every time

because they have access to classified information and are extremely powerful and influential within government circles. Over the years, these labs have opposed all suggested nuclear arms cutbacks and test-ban treaties. In 1957, Lewis L. Strauss, chairman of the Atomic Energy Commission, and physicists Edward Teller and Ernest O. Lawrence, went to the White House to dissuade President Eisenhower from negotiating a test-ban treaty with the Soviet Union, and they prevailed. The arguments they used were that continued testing was necessary for the development of clean (fallout-free) bombs for battlefield use in Europe, and that the Russians could cheat on any moratorium by testing in underground cavities that would reduce seismic disturbances.

Similar tired old arguments are still being used against a complete test-ban treaty, which the Russians have been ready to sign for several years. In July 1980 they even agreed to on-site inspection. The labs hold out because they want to continue testing bombs of less than 15 kilotons and they also need to test the hydrogen-bomb warheads for the 17,000 additional bombs the administration plans to build in its "modernization" program. The complete test-ban treaty was, in fact, destroyed in the summer of 1978, when Secretary of Energy James R. Schlesinger, Dr. Harold Agnew, director of Los Alamos, and Roger Batzel of Livermore, went to see President Carter. Agnew said later, "No question about it. We influenced Carter with facts, so that he did not introduce the [treaty] which, we subsequently learned, he had planned to do. There is no question in my mind that Roger and I turned Carter around, because we incurred so many enemies from the other side."

Sir Solly Zuckerman, a leading scientific adviser to the British government during the 1960s, wrote about these scientists in his book *Nuclear Illusion and Reality*.

> In the nuclear world today, military chiefs, who by convention are a country's official advisors on national security, as a rule merely serve as the channel through which the men in the laboratories transmit their view. For it is the man in the laboratory, not the soldier or sailor or airman, who at the start proposes that for this or that reason it would be useful to improve an old or devise a new nuclear

warhead; and, if a new warhead, then a new missile; and, given a new missile, a new system within which it has to fit. It is he, the technician, not the Commander in the field, who starts the process of formulating the so-called military need. It is he who has succeeded over the years in equating, and so confusing, nuclear destructive power with military strength, as though the former were the single and sufficient condition of military success. The men in the nuclear laboratories of both sides have succeeded in creating a world with an irrational foundation on which a new set of political realities has, in turn, had to be built. They have become alchemists of our times, working in secret ways that cannot be divulged, casting spells which embrace us all. They may never have been in battle; they may never have experienced the devastation of war, but they know how to devise the means of destruction. The more destructive power there is, so, one must assume, I imagine, the greatest chance of military success.

The nuclear bombs that the labs develop are tested continually in the Nevada desert at the dry Yucca Lake site about seventy miles north of Las Vegas. Each bomb is packed in a box called a "rack" and lowered into a hole ten feet wide and one mile deep. About every three weeks—eighteen times in 1981—a bomb is exploded. As of September 1982, 380 underground tests had been conducted since the signing of the Partial Test Ban Treaty in 1962, and of these, 43 vented radioactive material into the atmosphere. Since fall of 1983 the administration has returned to an earlier policy of announcing nuclear tests only when they are "significant."

Once the bombs have passed the testing stage, work orders are sent from the Department of Energy to the various plants around the United States that produce the component parts of the nuclear weapons. This huge industrial complex, employing 52,000 people in ten states, covers more land area than Delaware and Rhode Island combined, and is an example of part of the Iron Triangle with government working cooperatively with industry. The U.S. government owns the plants, and the big corporations run them. Phillips, Exxon, Atlantic–Richfield, and other energy giants mine the uranium, the basic raw material for the bombs. General Electric makes electrical components and neutron generators at Pinellas, Florida; Rockwell International makes the plutonium bomb triggers at Rocky Flats, Colorado; Bendix Corporation produces electronic components at Kansas City, Missouri; Monsanto works on isotope separation and detonators at Mound Lab, Miamisburg, Ohio; Martin Marietta produces enriched uranium and plutonium at Oak Ridge, Tennessee; DuPont makes plutonium, tritium, and deuterium at its Savannah River plant in Aiken, South Carolina; and Silas Mason puts all the parts together for completion of the bombs at the Pantex plant in Amarillo, Texas. This description, of course, only covers the production of the warheads themselves. They are then put into various delivery systems, that is, into missiles, artillery shells, submarines, airplanes, etc. It takes only 2 percent of the military budget to design and produce new bombs and to maintain about 30,000 bombs.

The push for *Star Wars* weapons came originally from the Lawrence-Livermore Labs. For the last fifteen years, Edward Teller has been encouraging research on defensive weapons systems in the nuclear age, and in the last five years his protégés have been receiving increased funding for this research. Teller calls this defense system the third generation of nuclear weapons—the power of the hydrogen explosion would be focused and narrowed into direct energy through X-ray lasers or some other device.

A protégé of Teller, Lowell Wood, the head of Livermore's top-secret O Group, is a strenuous promoter of this third generation of nuclear weapons. Teller credits Wood for making the breakthrough in X-ray laser technology. Apparently, the R Group at Livermore, headed by Thomas A. Weaver, has had some success testing such a device, called Excalibur, at the Nevada underground test site. Wood is also very enthusiastic about immobilizing the Russian missiles by using directed EMP.

There is a profound split in the scientific community about the efficacy of these systems; most scientists believe they are ridiculous. The most avid proponents are those who work in the weapons labs, and they claim to have all the data and hence discredit anyone who disagrees with them. When Wood briefed Hans Bethe on this defensive system, Bethe told *Time* magazine, "I don't think it can be done. What is worse, it will produce a *Star Wars* if successful." Wood's response was that Bethe had not challenged the basic physics but, rather, the feasibility and wisdom of finally building such a weapon system (the only sane approach, of course).

Outside people are never used to evaluate and assess the lab's scientific work, so there is no adequate debate on whether or not new weapon systems should be built. Hence the genesis of the nuclear arms race is rather like spontaneous combustion. Eisenhower said in his 1961 Farewell Speech, "Yet, in holding scientific research and discovery in respect, as we should, we must also be alert to the equal and opposite danger that public policy could itself become the captive of a scientific-technological elite."

In September 1982, Teller took his case to the White House and briefed President Reagan on his *Star Wars* concept. Reagan was entranced and, without consulting the normal defense and national security channels and without the active participation of top Pentagon or State Department officials, wrote his *Star Wars* speech in longhand. His own White House science advisers had already decided, after a yearlong study, that antimissile defense was not plausible.

In Reagan's *Star Wars* speech (March 1983), contrary to Eisenhower's warning, he offered an epiphany to the powers of scientific technology to heal all problems, even those it had created. The President has admitted that he really does not understand anything about computers or high technology himself. Yet he said, "The vision is that we embark on a program to counter the awesome Soviet missile threat with measures that are defensive. Let us turn to the very strength in technology that spawned our great industrial base, and that has given us the quality of life we enjoy today." His new scheme is likely to cost between $15 and $300 billion.

In other words, the labs and brilliant scientists, who lack objectivity, are powerfully motivated to develop this third generation of nuclear weapons because they recognize that the first-generation A-bombs and second-generation H-bombs have reached a point of diminishing return. So they have convinced a President who is profoundly ignorant about science to sell their new idea. Thus their careers flourish, and Livermore's budget has gone from $320 million in 1979 to $708 million in 1983.

Within a few weeks of the President's speech, the National Security Council produced National Security Decision Directive 85, with the promising title of "Eliminating the Threat from Ballistic Missiles." What started out as an ill-defined gleam in the President's and Edward Teller's eyes had been granted an impressive bureaucratic life-support system. Despite massive skepticism in the scientific and defense communities, in no time at all various scientists, research labs, defense contractors, and other entrepreneurs from the military-industrial complex have begun to scramble to be first in the door with a plan for studying and developing just the right system to zap incoming Russian missiles.

Robert Bowman, former head of the advanced weapons program, said of the various *"Star Wars"* schemes, "All have staggering technical problems. All are likely to cost on the order of a trillion dollars. All violate one or more existing treaties. All are extremely vulnerable. All are subject to a series of countermeasures. All could be made impotent by a series of alternative offensive missiles and therefore would be likely to reignite the numerical arms race in offensive weapons. All would, if they worked, be more effective as part of a first strike than against one. Most important, all would be extremely destabilizing, probably triggering the nuclear war which both sides are trying to prevent."

This is one more example of the scientific imperative in the nuclear arms race—new weapons technology keeps being discovered by scientific breakthroughs, and just when it no longer seems possible, yet another nuclear weapon or defense system is born. It must then be developed, lest the Russians do it first—another example of the clinical paranoia and intellectual line of reasoning used to justify subconscious emotional drives that fuel the arms race.

The Universities

To their discredit and shame, most large universities are involved in the nuclear and conventional arms race. Although the funding was decreased during and for some time after the Vietnam war because of intense student disapproval, there seems no limit now to Department of Defense funding of campus research, while funding for nonmilitary research has been cut to the bone. Budget analyses by the American

Association for the Advancement of Science show military support of universities growing by 7.4 percent in current dollars from fiscal 1983 to fiscal 1984—to $873 million—a cumulative growth of 58 percent since 1981. Most of this money is earmarked by the Pentagon for basic research, but under this delineation are such categories as self-contained munitions, electro-optic countermeasures, and low-speed take-off and landing: This is applied research for killing. University funding by other federal departments has fallen from 1983 to 1984 by 26 percent for Interior, 69.1 percent for Commerce, 6.4 percent for Transportation, 1.5 percent for Energy, and 8.7 percent for Agriculture. In 1982, the Pentagon used 70 percent of the total federal allotment for R & D (if NASA and DOE are included) and funded 13 percent of all university research.

Johns Hopkins, a university founded by a Quaker, receives the largest military research grants in the nation, followed closely by MIT, which received a 25 percent increase from 1979 to 1980. Harvard University received a 245 percent increase during the same period.

At Princeton University in 1981, the volume of military research reached such proportions that more than 160 employees, including the President and the Provost, held security clearances.

The University of Washington Applied Physics Lab, potentially a major center for research on fisheries and oceanography, has become virtually a wholly owned subsidiary of the U.S. Navy.

Some universities have changed the names of labs so that they are not readily identifiable as military. (For example, after University of Wisconsin students blew up the Army Mathematics Research Center in 1960, it was moved to a less obvious spot and renamed the Mathematics Research Center.)

At the University of Michigan, an academic think tank called Willow Run I was moved off campus in the wake of student protest in 1973 and was renamed ERIM (Environmental Research Institute of Michigan). Its research includes more than $5 million per year from defense contracts for work on optics, lasers, electronic-detection instruments, and a guidance system for the cruise missiles.

Many disciplines at universities are involved in military research, and the Pentagon has made it easier for researchers to become involved by a device called Multi-Disciplinary, Multi-Investigator Programs, where researchers from different fields and different institutions work on small parts of a big project. Participants seldom know how their basic research is being used or how it connects with other work. Brian Martin, a mathematician at an Australian university, said, "The chopping up of the learning experience into specialist bits tends to produce scientists who do not question the premise underlying their work."

The Pentagon also jointly sponsors programs with NASA, DOE, and the National Science Foundation, which gives them an air of respectability and at times confuses the source of the funding. For instance, MIT defense-related projects span everything from oceanography to computer science to electronics. A recent graduate, Steve Solnick, said, "I was working on a project for six months before I knew it was funded by the Department of Defense."

By these and other means, the Pentagon is reestablishing full access to the brain power in the nation's scientific community.

This brain drain may hasten the impending U.S. economic catastrophe. The United States now has, superimposed upon the huge fiscal military burden, a sick domestic industrial structure with little R & D, buses that fall apart, and bridges that collapse, while many areas of research are being neglected. Science and technology are desperately needed to solve the world's problems—scarcity of food, minerals, fuel, shelter, clean air, and clean water, among others.

The universities have prostituted themselves, using their skilled personnel to work for death and not for life. Why do they not have the moral integrity and courage to question what they are doing? The beautiful main building at MIT is crowned by the names of history's greatest scientists and thinkers—Archimedes, Socrates, Darwin, Edison, Osler, and many others. What has happened to the long-held tradition of scientists conducting research for the benefit of mankind? I beg my scientific and academic colleagues to rethink their goals in life. Science should not be prostituted on the altar of lucrative grants awarded for thoughtful proposals outlining better ways to kill.

The Iron Triangle

I constantly ride in airplanes with people who work for the military-industrial complex or war industry (euphemistically called the defense industry). I watch over their shoulders as they pore over their graphs and papers illustrating their latest weapon systems, and occasionally I engage them in conversation, if I am not too tired. Almost universally, I find they have never seriously considered the logical conclusion of their work—nuclear war—and to my surprise, I also find that they are very ignorant about the whole panoply of weapon systems this country has or is building, and that they almost always think the Russians are ahead. We often become involved in heated discussions, but usually, in fact, I prevail, and in the end they thank me for having talked to them and promise to read my book *Nuclear Madness*. They admit that they have never really thought about the broader picture before, and they are usually very loving fathers devoted to their children.

To give an example of the pervasiveness of this whole military-industrial complex: My flight had been delayed at Washington National Airport, so I decided to have dinner in the restaurant to fill in time. The waitress seated me at a table with two men, who did not know each other, nor did they know me. Soon they were engaged in conversation about their occupations. It turned out that they both independently made parts for cruise missiles. I did not identify myself and did not participate in the conversation, but was very sociable. The one dominant theme throughout the conversation was the money they were expecting from government contracts.

Another day I was eating in the snack bar in the same airport and overheard a discussion between several men about how they were ripping off the government and how the cousin of one of them had amassed himself a small fortune by making up survival kits for cold-weather climates with cheap materials and selling them at a handsome price to the Pentagon.

Although these illustrations are only anecdotes, they are representative of the feeling I get as I travel east and west, north and south across this great land. Sometimes as I fly, I look down from the plane window on the large and small towns and ponder the ubiquitous military-industrial complex, which has deliberately placed its factories and work places in almost every community in the United States. The problem sometimes seems so immense that I wonder if we have the power to abort this out-of-control death-dealing industry.

The so-called "defense budget" of the United States accounts for about one quarter of all federal spending, and the main reason for this present situation is the enormous pressures created on the government by the defense-contracting industry. With other military spending, this figure is over 40 percent. These huge businesses are run by men with unique access to government because they are captains of industry and because they manufacture weapons that guarantee "national security." These industries practice aggressive public and government relations, and because of their tight relationship to government, they have induced a narrowing of the debate on strategic and foreign policy over the years. These people have worked synergistically with the scientists from RAND, with universities and labs and other Defense Department-related think tanks, and with the armed forces and the Pentagon.

In fact, the whole government policy on weapons development and procurement with its implications for U.S. foreign policy is dominated and controlled by what some political scientists call the Iron Triangle. The three parts of this triangle are:

• Agencies related to defense in the executive branch of the government—the Pentagon, the National Aeronautics and Space Administration, and a Nuclear Weapons Branch of the Department of Energy.
• The key committees of Congress—House and Senate Armed Services committees and Defense Appropriation subcommittees—and the members of Congress from districts and states where the defense industry is concentrated and important.
• Private industry—the corporations, research institutes, laboratories, trade associations, banks, and defense-related trade unions.

There is an incestuous relationship among the three sides of the triangle, with constant interchange of personnel from one to the other and constant communication, socializing, and working together.

Many politicians become handmaidens to this powerful corporate monopoly and have long ago stopped representing their constituents or their children, or they represent only the corporate contractor constituents. They tend to support any big contract that is offered, as long as it supplies jobs and pours money into their districts, instead of examining what the specific contract means for the eventual life and well-being of the citizens. Thus, millions of innocent American people are trapped in jobs orchestrated by big military corporations, where they make weapons or delivery systems of hideous destructive power in order to feed their children, but which might over time induce the death of their children and their environment.

During World War I, business leaders were used by the federal government as wartime production planners for all sections of U.S. industry. During and after World War II, businesspeople were recruited into government as policy makers. Regulatory commissions have for years been known to be staffed by personnel from the industries they regulated. The administration of military spending has also been staffed, especially in wartime, by executives and officials from the defense industry. During the sixties and seventies, major corporations became very adept at influencing government and executive branch policy makers, to affect legislation, administrative decision making, and its regulatory process. Most of the *Fortune* 500 companies now have Washington offices. The staff from these offices make connections between the companies' needs and government requirements. They gather information and exert political pressure; they advise or campaign for company spending; they organize political grass-roots support (workers, communities, and stockholders); and they influence important staff and members of Congress and officials in government agencies, even in the administration itself. These firms work to achieve a high degree of intimacy between the Pentagon and its contractors, which tends to inhibit cost control, and most Department of Defense contracts eventually become cost-plus. In addition, federal procurement policies give many defense contractors much rent-free production space and equipment and interest-free loans for "progress" on work completed by contractors.

Military-related jobs account for a large percentage of the U.S. work force. The Department of Defense maintains a bureaucracy of more than 3 million people, of whom 1 million are civilians who design, produce, use, and repair weapons. Defense contracting also supplied jobs for 1,170,000 scientists, engineers, technicians, and production workers in 1980.

Working in tandem with the scientists and the armed forces are the business interests. In 1983, about 2.9 million American jobs depended on the manufacture of weapons, not counting the jobs of people on active military duty. Of every four dollars the government spends on procurement, the Pentagon spends three. Or, in other words, the jobs of one out of every ten American workers depend directly or indirectly on defense spending. The Pentagon is the largest single purchaser of goods and services in the nation. Defense industries account for 10 percent of all U.S. manufacturing. In certain states, including California, defense-related employment is the largest single source of personal income. In California there are twice as many defense workers as there are farmers.

Business is very cynical about how it obtains government contracts and has become so powerful within the government that, in fact, America does not have a working democracy in the area of defense. It really has become a system of socialism for the rich and capitalism for the poor. There are no moral scruples involved in the methods adopted by the defense industries to achieve their goals—big government contracts. Many big defense corporate chiefs sit on advisory boards to the Department of Defense, Department of Energy, and NASA. They lobby extensively throughout the federal bureaucracy and support politicians financially through their political action committees (PACs). They work hand in hand with the armed forces at the Pentagon; and there is a constant exchange of personnel from DOD, DOE, NASA, and the corporations. They entertain and become best friends with relevant representatives and senators; they use the large banks that fund them and the investment firms that support their activities in deals. They work with huge trade associations that represent their special interests in Washington, and they also practice fraud and allow cost overruns, which cost the

American people billions of dollars over and above the money already legitimately allocated to build these weapons of genocide.

While the scientists continue designing the bombs and delivery and guidance and C^{3}I systems in their labs, business is really the motor that causes the weapons-making system to run.

The cynical, rapacious attitude of the weapons manufacturers is well illustrated by this quote from a *Boston Globe* column in the business section, written by Michael Johnson, a stockbroker and international-relations specialist at Thomson McKinnon Securities, Inc., in Boston: "Cruise missiles, in a sea and air version, will be bought in quantities. They are a truly elegant solution, typical of what America can do if it so desires. If fired from the Sears Tower in Chicago with the pitching mound of Yankee Stadium as a target, the cruise missile would be considered to have missed if it hit home plate! Best bet is to buy the electronic technology which permits this revolutionary accuracy.

"Don't worry too much about the nuclear freeze movement. Their target is to limit what are, in essence, first generation nuclear weapons. Concentrate instead on second- and third-generation systems. Best bets are the component producers of 'Star Wars' weaponry—particle beams, microwave beams, and laser cannons."

In the ten days after the Korean jetliner was shot down, virtually all defense stocks went up on Wall Street. "The nature of the confrontation has focused attention on military technology and the United States military capabilities," said Phillip Brannon, vice-president of defense electronics research for Merrill Lynch. "But more important is that politically it has firmed up Reagan's position in calling for a stronger defense."

There is a story to be told about the corruption and intrigue in the defense industry that is bigger than Watergate ever was. If we are to expose the dynamics of the pathology of our presently terminally ill planet, we must be prepared to examine the Iron Triangle and the military-industrial complex in minute detail. The psychological attitude of the people who run this system is the etiology or cause of the arms race. To understand this pathology, it is important to look at the various ways in which the military-industrial complex operates.

Mr. Wilson Goes to Washington

A wonderful example of the pathogenesis of the Iron Triangle is illustrated by this fictional, but typical, account of a certain corporate official named Jack Wilson. The account comes, with permission, from *The Iron Triangle*, by Gordon Adams.

Jack Wilson, sitting at his desk in San Jose, was a company man. He had started his career with General Electronics International in 1947, after wartime service in the air force. He had had only two brief stints elsewhere. Once, when GEI lost a major contract, he spent two years in Boston with United Electronics. Later, GEI seconded him for three years to the air force at Wright Patterson Air Force Base as a liaison officer on the company's supersonic-swing-wing (RPV) program. Promotions had come steadily—from engineer to production manager, to division chief for missile programs, and now, to corporate vice-president for government relations. With steady raises, increasing corporate perks, and more power, Jack had developed a loyalty, a family feeling about GEI that would never die. He expected to retire, at least as a vice-president, or even, who knows. . . .

Samuel T. ("Chuck") Fuller had to go some day, leaving the president/chief operating officer job open. Chuck, too, had had a full career. In the 1930s, fresh out of Stanford Engineering, he had created a defense electronics firm, ERW, in the suburbs of San Jose—California's famous Silicon Valley. The sudden boom in Pentagon missile spending had made the firm's fortune and Chuck's career. Having engineered ERW's merger with Fargo Electronics, Chuck went to Washington as the second deputy to the Pentagon's Director for Defense Research and Engineering, one of the Pentagon's most powerful jobs. After four years with the administration, Chuck had returned to California and GEI which had by then absorbed ERW/Fargo as part of a corporate diversification program. Chuck rose rapidly to the top and would retire in two years.

A key to promotion, Jack knew, was the procurement of a major Pentagon contract, which would establish him as the heir apparent for the top job.

Yet Jack knew that there was another strong candidate—

and another route. Bruce Collins, the former astronaut and vice-president for commercial markets, had tried to diversify GEI by developing commercial markets. His efforts had succeeded. If DOD contracts were slow in coming, GEI could build its future in commercial aviation.

For Jack, however, there was no choice. GEI's defense programs had been run separately from commercial business since the war. Company management had simply closed them off. Jack couldn't retool as a commercial man overnight.

Things were at a crucial point for GEI's defense work, moreover. Production on the giant Thunderbird ship defense missile for the navy was tailing off. Jack had design crews, researchers, engineers, looking for work. The end of the Thunderbird contract might force the company to lay them off. With any luck—for them—they would go to work for Thor Electron, or Rubicon, or another industry competitor, making the next contract even harder and more expensive for GEI to bid on. It could be worse though. GEI didn't have to worry about maintaining expensive overhead costs. The navy owned the building and machinery at Plant 5803 outside San Jose. GEI simply used it at minimal rent. If the Thunderbird contract ended, GEI could always give the plant back to the navy.

Still Jack needed a better option. With a new contract and a continued flow of defense funds into the company, he wanted to help create a humming production facility.

Jack knew he needed more information. What did the navy think it wanted? What could the company make? He reached for the phone and set up a meeting with George ("Smiley") Cooper, director of GEI's Advanced Research and Development Office, fondly called the "Junk Works" around GEI because it was located next to San Jose's city dump. He sat down with Cooper and went over the projections. They had to know what the navy had up its sleeve, what new missile systems it was thinking about. Cooper knew a lot on this score. For the past ten years, about $15 million a year had flowed into the Junk Works from the Pentagon's Independent Research and Development Program. GEI scientists used the money to fund new weapons research ideas—ideas they could sell back to the Pentagon. As long as the ideas that came back were promising, the Pentagon kept a loose hand on the money reins.

For the past five years, Cooper had also been a member of the Navy Science Board's Advisory Committee on Ship Defense Systems. This committee brought together everybody—navy people, Green Aerospace, Rubicon, the McDavis Group, GEI. Most of the big contractors had a scientist or engineer member of the group, which was designed to pool ideas on ship defense systems. The navy used it as a sounding board, while the industry people used it to get to know each other and the navy and to push new ideas.

Several years ago, Cooper had done a concept paper at the request of the committee chairman. One of his old friends, Deputy Assistant Navy Secretary for R & D Duffy McNee, had taken a real interest in the proposed system: a new, all-weather missile with a 75– 100-mile range, which could carry nuclear or conventional weapons. Just the thing the navy (and GEI) needed, thought Cooper. For three years, he had been using I R & D to develop the concept, and it was near time to move toward real R & D contracts.

There was some risk in pushing this missile, Cooper told Jack. The navy had to be convinced. GEI's competitors, moreover, had seen Cooper's paper and could be working on their own designs. Rubicon Aerospace was said to be forging ahead. On the other hand, a success in pushing this system would make GEI's Missile Division golden for a decade to come. Cooper and Wilson agreed they needed more information on how to sell the navy and on the work of competitors. Cooper went off to call Assistant Secretary McNee.

Jack began sounding out some other key contacts. First, he called Buff Johnson, his deputy and government liaison officer in GEI's Washington office, which had been established ten years ago as a central location to gather information on Pentagon and NASA contracting and to guide GEI's out-of-town staff when they came to Capitol Hill for testimony and meetings with key members of Congress. Buff had many useful sources. Every couple of weeks, he would have lunch (Dutch treat, under the new entertainment guidelines from the Pentagon) with old friends in the navy's Research Office. It had been seven years since he had retired from the staff there, moving immediately to GEI. But he had kept up his contacts.

He had also spent time on the Hill. While contracting for the navy, he had met many of the staff of the House and

Senate Armed Services committees who worked on naval R & D and procurement. He knew that they were important to getting future defense programs funded. His job now was to keep them informed on GEI programs and to keep a close ear to committee attitudes toward the defense budget. Though not officially registered as a lobbyist—the law was very loose—he did a fair amount of lobbyist's work.

Jack asked Buff for information about his Pentagon network. Had he talked recently with McNee or junior civilian and military people? Did he know where future ship missile defense systems were heading? Who was in charge of this work? Were there special advisory groups GEI ought to be in? Buff found the answers—the navy group working on ship defense was impressed with GEI's progress using I R & D money. But there were other competitors in the field, and he did not know how far along they were, or how interested the navy was in their work. Jack urged Buff to pin down more detailed information. He also asked him to do some sleuthing in ADPA. GEI, along with other major defense firms, belonged to the American Defense Preparedness Association, a trade group committed to serving "the defense needs of our nation." Jack asked Buff to attend the next meeting of ADPA's Missiles Committee to determine who among GEI's competitors had drawn a bead on the market.

Jack then focused in on navy research and development. What kind of missile designs could it be sold? He made a call to Tony Lakeland at the Naval Weapons Center at China Lake. Lakeland had been with GEI's Missile Division for five years before moving to China Lake as an R & D program director. Jack suggested they meet for lunch when he came to GEI's China Lake office the following week. He knew that if GEI was to get in on the ground floor, he had to have some influence over the missile specifications the navy would draw up in preparing its request for bids for R & D contract work. The discussion with Tony gave him useful information and even more useful input into navy thinking.

After these preliminary calls Jack started to plan for a Washington trip. He put Buff to work on the schedule after clearing the trip and the program with an enthusiastic President Fuller. A courtesy visit to Deputy Assistant Secretary McNee was in order, which Cooper arranged. Buff set up detailed discussions with McNee's staff. In addition, there were meetings with the ADPA committee secretary and a friendly visit to the Aerospace Industries Association to discuss forthcoming changes in federal procurement policy.

Buff also arranged some meetings with Hill staffers, though it was early in the missile program to think about a congressional focus for GEI's effort. Jack did meet with Congresswoman Claire Sampson from San Jose. GEI had made steady contributions to Sampson's last three campaigns through its Good Government Fund, a political action committee, and Buff had friendly access to Sampson's legislative assistant. As representative from GEI's district and a member of the Defense Appropriations Subcommittee which would consider the money requests for navy missile R & D, Sampson was doubly important to GEI. The Defense Subcommittee was famous on the Hill for going through Pentagon requests with a fine-tooth comb. In his visit, Jack explained that he was on a general information gathering trip and described GEI's current R & D projects, including ship defense missiles. He pointed out to her how much GEI's 16,000 employees in San Jose supported her work and how important it was to the economy of the district that they be fully employed.

Jack took along a young employee of GEI's Washington office, Neil Jones, to meet with the R & D staff of the House and Senate Armed Services committees. Jones was a presidential interchange executive with GEI. He knew missiles inside out and was very familiar with GEI's technical work. He was also intimately familiar with navy thinking, having been on the staff of the Navseasystcom tactical planning group for two years. He talked technical with the R & D staff and made strong arguments for the military need for GEI's missile.

During Jack's visit, the Washington office arranged a reception attended by several top brass and key civilian policy makers, as well as several members of Congress and staffers—a sort of informal, get-acquainted party. It was a quiet, cautious event. Jack could remember the old days before Proxmire had uncovered abuses. GEI used to have a hunting lodge on Wye Island, off the Maryland coast where they had full weekends with top Pentagon and Hill personnel—hunting, playing cards, drinking, and generally socializing. Press revelations and hearings on Thor Electron and Bow-Wing Electronics had changed all that. Now there was only the occasional cocktail party at a trade association meeting, free tickets to a Redskins' game, a lunch here and there, and—a rarity—a plane trip to the coast for a congressman or bureaucrat. The days of big entertainment and favors were gone, at least for now.

Buff called several weeks after Jack's return from Washington. One of McNee's key staffers was working up a draft Request for Proposals (RFP) for ship defense missiles and GEI had to move fast. Jack called Smiley Cooper and urged him to arrange a meeting between the navy staffer and a Junk Works expert to go over GEI's ideas. A quick week-end conference in Washington was arranged and GEI got its input into the RFP.

When the RFP came out, a month later, it took a middle line between GEI and Rubicon and implied that more than one contractor might be funded for designs. Both GEI and Rubicon bid and won contracts.

Jack's work, however, was just beginning; the production contract was no sure thing. Rubicon had a lot of missile experience and equally good contacts with the Pentagon and the Hill. As the design work proceeded, Jack picked up the pace, keeping up with advance information and bringing influence to bear in the Pentagon. The two design contracts were followed by two engineering development contracts and, in turn, two contracts for prototype development. The navy wanted to fly-off the two missiles against each other.

As the competition heated up and the program progressed, it became more visible, more expensive, and more controversial. The wider the circle of people involved, the more Jack had to do.

There were those both in the defense industry and in Congress who opposed a new missile. Thor Electron, which made the current ship defense missile, met regularly with Hill staffers to encourage Congress to accept a more modest program involving a redesign of the current weapon. Congressman Jerry Friedman of Wisconsin worried about the cost of a new missile. Senator Scott Moran from Pennsylvania warned that the Pentagon budget was eating up social funding.

There was also opposition inside the Pentagon. A navy missile program was pushing the projected budget upward. Supporters of existing systems argued that the new expenditure was not needed and updates of current equipment were adequate. Outside the navy, the other services resisted the threat a growing navy missile procurement program posed for growth in their own weapons-buying.

Sometimes Jack felt like a duck stamping out a forest fire. Every time he thought he had one brush fire out, another jumped up a few feet or a few offices away.

Jack mobilized everyone and everything to push through his program. He paid regular visits to Washington, visiting both the Hill and the Pentagon. He brought company specialists with him, who could make convincing technical cases for the GEI design. They met endlessly with navy people, some of whom had worked for GEI, discussing design changes, problems, cost, etc. Jack had two goals: keep the missile in the DOD budget and encourage GEI's design into the winner's seat. He knew that for this to happen, he had to work both the Pentagon and Hill sides of the street.

Mobilizing the staff of GEI's Washington office, Jack and Buff outlined a campaign of visits to critical members of the House and Senate committees, the Armed Services Committees and the Defense Appropriations Subcommittees, and their staffs. They sent their technical people to convince the R & D Subcommittee staff of the vital importance of the program. They reviewed campaign contributions from GEI's Good Government Fund, noting key members to whom contributions had been made. They looked at the pattern of GEI's subcontract awards. For some years the company had tried to be attentive to the economic and political impact of its subcontracts through which it farmed out over 40 percent of its prime contract dollars. The economic argument carried weight in Congress. Several million dollars in subcontracts in a district was hard to argue with. But GEI couldn't make this argument directly. Its motives would be questioned.

Jack commissioned a study by a private economic consulting firm on the regional impact of the program. District-by-district, GEI could then forecast the results, tailoring individual presentations for specific members of Congress.

Special meetings were held with the two California senators and the San Mateo/San Jose members, Congressman Mattini and Congresswoman Sampson. The economic impact of the program would be largest in their districts. Past history had shown that Mattini, who generally took a critical stance on defense spending, had always been willing to go to bat for GEI when jobs in the district were at stake. The California delegation moved into this action, calling on colleagues, sending staff around to encourage other staffers to support the program, and writing the Pentagon.

Congresswoman Sampson was a major leader of this effort. As a member of the House Defense Appropriations Subcommittee, her arguments commanded attention in the Pentagon. The Pentagon and the White House knew that her support was needed for other programs. Trade-off possibilities were endless. With an incumbent President up for reelection, Sampson's arguments about electoral support in her district found receptive listeners among the White House staff.

Turning to the Pentagon, Jack worked on other problems. GEI had to be sure its prototype came within close range of Rubicon in price, performance, and schedule. Buff's office and the California staff pursued contacts and discussions with the navy's technical and contracting people, acquiring up-to-date information on the missile test evaluation. Jack and Buff also marshaled every possible supporter to argue in the Office of the Secretary of Defense that the weapon was necessary. He made several calls to analysts of naval strategy in various universities, one of whom agreed to write an opinion piece on the missile in *The New York Times*, which the policy makers would read.

Jack aimed at other journals, making several phone calls a week to writers for *Aviation Week* and the *U.S. Naval Institute Proceedings*. He offered to provide information on recent developments in GEI's program and arrange visits to the plant for reporters. Several favorable write-ups resulted from these efforts, including a highly detailed, technical piece in *Aviation Week*. Jack mobilized the company's PR people in San Jose who placed GEI's missile in the advertising copy of *Time* and *Business Week*.

Jack moved, too, to bring GEI's local dependents to put pressure on Congress and the executive branch. A company planning committee, Operation Common Good, had drawn up a plan aimed at mobilizing public opinion in San Jose. OCG prepared films and demonstrations for Fourth of July exhibits and American Legion meetings, provided speakers for men's and women's club meetings on the nation's defense and the importance of a well-defended fleet. It sent press releases to local papers in all the key subcontracting locations and arranged for plant visits for important union and local government officials. It organized delegations of local citizens to visit Congress and the White House with statements of support. A nationwide campaign of ads urged readers to write GEI for an "Owner's Manual" for the missile and Jack drafted a letter from President Chuck Fuller to employees, subcontractors, and stockholders, urging them to write to Congress.

Decision time was near, Rubicon Aerospace and GEI kept pushing. White House and Hill pressures won the day over the opposition of the Secretary of Defense: The missile was approved. Now came the question of funding. Jack and Rubicon's lobbyist turned to the Hill, with more visits to key staff, more reminders of campaign contributions and subcontracting benefits. The opponents of the missile lost in the Appropriations Committee, introduced a motion on the floor of the House amending the Defense Appropriations Act, but lost again, 207–142. The arena for the contestants now was moved to the Senate.

Senator Scott Moran from Pennsylvania led an effort in the Senate Appropriations Committee to delay a production decision on the missile until after the presidential campaign. The amendment barely squeaked through the committee, which meant a floor fight. Despite door-to-door lobbying and Pentagon phone calls, the amendment was passed.

The competing contractors united in their efforts to support the program. GEI and Rubicon pulled out all the stops in the Conference Committee, calling members, orchestrating local employee, stockholder, subcontractor, and other grass-roots pressures. Two GEI board members who formerly worked at high levels in the Pentagon made personal calls to several key senators and congressmen. One of them, the chairman of United Western Bank, also made some calls to former colleagues in the Treasury Department, pointing out the importance of funds to California's industrial sector. In response, congressional relations staff at Treasury made contact with key Appropriations Committee members. The battle in conference was won; the amendment was removed; funding was approved.

Jack's attention turned back to the Pentagon and White House. He could not be sure that his missile would win. The two missiles were close in design and performance specifications. GEI had a slight lead in the fast schedule it could promise to the navy, but inside information from GEI's friends in navy R & D suggested that Rubicon might come in with a slightly lower price. He would have to move carefully. In an election year, some pressure had to be directed toward the White House. All avenues would have to be carefully worked.

Jack called Dave Brahman, GEI board member, Harvard graduate, and partner in Shadly, Todd, Millbrook and Coy, one of Washington's leading law firms. In the 1960s he had served as Deputy Secretary of the Army and later put in two years as director of the Defense Intelligence Agency. His Washington network was wide, his reputation as an insider was unbeatable. Brahman gave Jack advice on how to approach the Republican National Committee and the White House in this election year and agreed to pay visits to some old friends on the White House staff to make the case for GEI's bid.

Meanwhile, in Washington Buff Johnson had come close to blowing the contract. In his anxiety to obtain information on the progress of the navy evaluation, he had sent Gene McConnell, former navy engineer and GEI Washington technical specialist, to the navy program office. There, McConnell, who had a high security clearance, examined a memorandum going through the most recent technical discussions of the navy's missile needs. In it he found some valuable information for GEI's final bid. When Buff saw the notes Gene had taken, he could hardly wait to rush to the Telex and send word back to San Jose. A San Jose employee with lower security clearance, not realizing how sensitive the information was, called the navy R & D office to double-check some points, inadvertently revealing the disclosure of classified information. The flap led to the suspension of two R & D office employees and the temporary withdrawal of Gene's and Buff's security clearances. The bad publicity caused new headaches for Jack, as he fought off press inquiries and tried to dissipate the sense that GEI had special inside information.

From his friends at the Aerospace Industries Association, however, Jack had learned some good news. Rubicon was overloaded with missile work and planners in the Office of the Secretary of the Navy, worried about the state of the Navy Industrial Plant Reserve, wanted to keep GEI's technical work force and operating capacity in missiles alive. When a final contract recommendation reached the Secretary of the Navy's desk, this consideration could weigh in GEI's favor.

Turning back to national politics, Jack helped Dave Brahman set up meetings with finance people from the Republican National Committee to let them know about GEI's Good Government Fund contributions to the President's primary campaign. Brahman impressed on the national committee staff that an award in Santa Clara County would produce a good turnout for the President, while an award in Boston (site of Rubicon's plant) would not necessarily counter the natural tendency of that area's electorate to support the President's liberal challenger. Bob Sperling of GEI's Washington counsel, Worthington & Sperling, made several phone calls, reminding Republican Party officials of GEI's past services and support.

Once more Jack organized local groups who would send delegations to Washington. The San Jose delegation included the mayor, two council members, the head of the local Chamber of Commerce, and the local leader of the metalworkers' union, which organized part of GEI's plant. In Washington, they visited Congresswoman Sampson, Congressman Mattini, the chairs of the House and Senate Armed Services committees, and a staffer from the White House, impressing on each the economic and political benefit of a contract award to San Jose. A local San Francisco banker in the delegation paid a special visit to a friend at Treasury, carefully understating, while making clear, GEI's case.

Mattini, the San Mateo County member of Congress, approached the White House with a joint letter, made calls to friends in the Pentagon, urged other members of Congress to support the effort, and inserted pro-GEI material in the *Congressional Record*, which would be reprinted and distributed.

As the pressure built toward a decision and the contract award, Jack received a phone call from an insider in the navy R & D office, who said Rubicon's missile looked like a winner because of its cost advantages. Jack relayed the bad news to Chuck Fuller, who looked over GEI's cost proposal and then asked Jack how the navy intended to write the contract—one contract for all of the missiles or one for a purchase in batches. Could GEI bid low for the first batch, take the loss, and make it up by getting a higher price for subsequent batches? Fuller knew this was a risky strategy—GEI could end up eating the loss as other contractors had in the past. Fuller's staff debated the issue and came up with a marginal price. Buff indicated that his navy sources felt a revised bid could save the day for GEI. The bid was lowered. A week later, to the popping of champagne corks in Washington and San Jose, GEI's Sting-Ray was announced to be the winner.

After a contract award, there are always a few protests. True to form, columnist Bill Sanderson suggested that political favoritism had won the day: President Hardy, wanting to curry the support of Californians for his campaign, had promised the congressional delegation the contract. Jack had already planned his strategy. He and Buff called the White House, prepared a statement that denied any such commitments, and discussed a press release with the PR people at the Office of the Secretary of Defense, pointing out the favorable evaluation of GEI's missile, its performance in the fly-off and the price competitiveness with Rubicon. Gradually the public furor died down.

Once GEI had the production contract for the new Sting-Ray missile, Jack's operation became less central. In San Jose, GEI workers worked side by side with navy engineers and contract managers and an auditor from the Defense Contract Audit Agency (DCAA). This working relationship was made easy by the fact that, over the years, GEI had hired several former employees of the navy and DCAA. They knew the contract guidelines and procurement regulations, knew how to negotiate contract changes, understood the red tape and paperwork, and could help ease the relationship with the navy.

The calm did not last forever. Two years later, as part of a more general investigation into the relationship between contractors and the Pentagon, the Senate Banking Committee held hearings to examine efforts to stimulate grass-roots support for their defense programs. The committee was concerned that the expenditures for such grass-roots lobbying had been charged to contract costs. The Pentagon might be indirectly subsidizing lobbying aimed at Congress. A questionnaire to GEI, among others, asked about their grass-roots lobbying. It was sent straight to Jack Wilson, who immediately got on the phone with the government relations officers of the other companies in the survey to see if they intended to respond. In the end, they all agreed that a failure to respond could lead to a subpoena of data and to negative PR for the companies. As a group, they prepared a general outline for each company to use in its response to the committee, providing a minimum of information, but trying to appear helpful. Further work remained, though, since the committee was bound to proceed to hearings. The committee staff wrote President Fuller asking him to testify. Jack prepared the testimony. He knew that the facts were amply documented by the Defense Contract Audit Agency. He decided, therefore, to come clean and offer to negotiate a payback to the Pentagon. In addition he drafted some possible questions and answers, prepared full data on GEI's many grass-roots efforts for the Sting-Ray, and arranged Fuller's trip to Washington. He made sure that GEI's documentation went in at the last minute, limiting the committee's time for careful perusal. Fuller's testimony went well, and Jack had to respond to only a few follow-up inquiries the president had thought it unwise to answer on the spot. By and large, Jack knew, the publicity from these kinds of hearings had a short shelf-life; in a few months it would be forgotten.

Jack's most important remaining job on the Sting-Ray program was to deal with the press about the increasing cost problem the company faced, as materials became more scarce and management cost control proved inadequate. By now, he knew, much of the public was numb to cost overrun problems. As long as the information could be kept fairly quiet, GEI's image was not likely to suffer.

The Sting-Ray was a success. Jack Wilson had played a key role in bringing a new major contract to GEI.

Two years later President Fuller retired. President Jack Wilson, tanned from the Caribbean holiday that his wife had insisted he take, sat down at his new desk. Zestfully, he leafed through the paper outlining his first item of business: plans for a successor missile to the Sting-Ray.

Washington Offices of the Military Corporations

The multibillion-dollar defense industries use Washington offices and work out of suites in the office buildings of Rosslyn, Virginia, near the Pentagon. A typical Washington office of a large defense contractor employs forty to fifty people. Not all of them lobby Congress, but they do lobby the Pentagon under the guise of marketing or customer service. Of the top ten contractors, the largest offices are run by General Electric, which employs eighty people, and by Rockwell, and the smallest by Grumman, with a staff of twenty-four.

The top ten defense companies with major contracts over $1 billion in 1982 were, in order of size, in billions of dollars:

General Dynamics	$5.9
McDonnell-Douglas	$5.6
United Technologies	$4.2
General Electric	$3.7
Lockheed	$3.5
Boeing	$3.2
Hughes Aircraft	$3.1
Rockwell International	$2.7
Raytheon	$2.3
Martin Marietta	$2.0

(See the chart on pages 190–94 for their products.)

Half of these companies are almost totally dependent on winning military contracts and on selling weapons to foreign countries. These firms also hire ex-congressmen and ex-Pentagon officials who understand the Pentagon and the Hill.

Since 1970, 3,700 people have gone through the revolving door (more than 1,800 from 1979 to 1982 alone). This mechanism produces a great opportunity for conflict of interest, and it perpetuates a cozy, almost incestuous, relationship between the men who buy the weapons and those who sell them. Executives who leave top jobs in industry often end up in top-level posts at the Pentagon and may go back to their old companies later. Two examples of this syndrome are Paul Thayer, the former Deputy Secretary of Defense, who was board chairman of LTV Corporation, a major defense contractor (and who left his job in the Pentagon in January 1984 after having been accused of illegally passing along "insider" stock-trading information to others in 1981 and 1982 when he was chairman of LTV Corporation and director of four other companies), and Richard Delauer, former executive of TRW, Inc., now head of Research and Development for the Pentagon.

Because the military pension system allows military personnel to retire after twenty years of service, many of these men transfer straight to defense corporations, taking their inside knowledge and personal contacts with them to benefit the corporations. (In fiscal 1982, 900,000 people of working age with no disabilities were receiving lavish military pensions. One billion dollars a year could be saved by phasing out the pension system for those among these pensioners who have other jobs.) If a military person who wants to work in a certain industry after leaving the Pentagon makes a particular decision while still there, that can mean hundreds of millions of dollars for a company, and the prospect of future company employment obviously becomes greater. Thomas S. Amlie, who was technical director at the Naval Weapons Center at China Lake, California, and who is now a cost analyst at the Pentagon, said, "The military is a closed society that takes care of its own. If a retired general representing a client goes in to see an old classmate still on active duty, he will get a very attentive hearing. The officers on active duty are also thinking ahead.

"Fighting the system gets one blackballed, and future employment prospects are bleak. In this way, the industry has come to completely control DOD even more than its political appointees."

A typical example is Lieutenant General Kelly Burke, who was the air force's top procurement officer, making yes-no decisions on billions of dollars in business for major defense contractors. When he left in 1983, he teamed up with two of his colleagues, Lieutenant General Thomas Stafford, the former astronaut, who preceded Burke in a top procurement job, and Major General Guy L. Hecker, Jr., who was the top lobbyist for the air force on Capitol Hill. They formed a defense consulting firm called Stafford-Burke and Hecker. Six of the ten biggest defense contractors soon became their clients, being advised how to sell to the Pentagon. This is all legal.

In 1983 it was reported that three Boeing executives had received a total of $400,000 in severance pay when they left the company in 1981 for high-level Defense Department positions in the Reagan administration—the three men were Melvyn R. Paisley, assistant secretary of the navy for research, systems and engineering; T. K. Jones, deputy under secretary of defense for strategic theater nuclear forces; and Herbert A. Reynolds, deputy director of the Defense Department's

Office of Intelligence and Space Policy. This side of the revolving door syndrome gives companies access to the executive branch, where the buying is done.

Other prominent people who have been in and out of the Pentagon are Richard Delauer and John F. Lehman. Delauer is currently Under Secretary of Defense for Research and Engineering. From 1943 to 1958, he was an aeronautical engineer and an officer in the U.S. Navy; 1977 to 1981, Defense Science Board; 1978 to 1981, Naval Research Advisory Committee; 1960 to 1981, employed by TRW, Inc. Lehman was, from 1966 to 1968, in the Air Force Reserve; 1968 to the present, Navy Reserve; 1969 to 1974, national security assistant to Henry A. Kissinger; 1974, delegate to the Vienna arms negotiations; 1975 to 1977, deputy director of the U.S. Arms Control and Disarmament Agency; 1981 to present, Secretary of the Navy; 1977 to 1981, partner, Abington Corporation, defense consulting firm, and consultant to Northrop Corporation, TRW Corporation, and Boeing Company.

People also leave Congress to work for defense industries. An example: When Congressman Richard Ichord left Congress in 1981 after twenty years, he joined former representative Bob Wilson, Republican from California, to form the Washington Industrial Team (WITCO). Their clients have included eleven of the thirteen largest defense contractors, including McDonnell-Douglas, General Dynamics, Boeing, Grumman, Northrop, Raytheon, Westinghouse, United Technologies, General Electric, Rockwell International, and Hughes Aircraft.

At least thirty former congressional staff members, many of whom had key positions with Armed Services or Appropriations committees, work for defense firms. Most earn their living by buttonholing their ex-colleagues on behalf of defense contractors.

This side of the revolving door syndrome obviously gives defense firms entry into the legislative process.

These firms lobby mostly in secret in various ways, and they avoid the press. They wine and dine important senators, representatives, and their staffers at lunches, dinners, receptions, and parties. They give them tickets to football and hockey games, concerts and theater, and play golf with them at the Army–Navy Country Club.

They use PACs to pour money into the campaigns of important House and Senate members, targeting key committee members. For instance, in 1982, the PACs of McDonnell-Douglas and Lockheed Corporation gave money to thirty-six of the thirty-nine members of the House Armed Services Committee who were up for reelection. Recipients included all fourteen members of the subcommittee on procurement. Rockwell, Raytheon Company, and Hughes Aircraft gave to ten members of the House Appropriations Committee.

Nine of the ten leading firms gave more than $1,000 to Representative Joseph Addabbo, Democrat from New York, chairman of the subcommittee on defense. Senator John C. Stennis of Mississippi, the ranking Democrat on the Armed Services Committee, received more than $26,000 from the top ten contractors; and Senator John Tower, Republican from Texas, chairman of the Armed Services Committee, received $13,000 from the top ten in 1981 and 1982.

Powerful House leaders also receive money. Eight of the ten contractors gave $1,000 or more to House Speaker Thomas P. O'Neill, Jr., Democrat from Massachusetts; and Representative James Wright, Democrat from Texas, received contributions from nine of the ten contractors. Representatives from important defense-related districts also received contributions. Altogether the PACs of the ten biggest corporations gave $1.5 million to federal candidates in the 1982 election. This figure does not include individual contributions by officials of the corporations nor does it include money spent on state or local races.

The corporations also gave honoraria for speeches by politicians at company meetings, and some congressmen give services to the PACs.

These contributions do not necessarily buy the weapons, but they certainly help, and they do give access to the congressmen's or senators' offices. They create obligations and friendships, and that is how Washington is run. Also, many representatives of these contractors serve on fund-raising committees for key House or Senate members.

The Washington office is perhaps the most important part of the whole corporate operation. It conducts what is called "government relations," which involves lobbying and working directly with the Pentagon, DOE, and NASA. The staff monitors the relevant issues and attempts to influence legislative, procurement, and appropriations decisions as they rapidly move between the executive and the Congress. The Washington office also coordinates a company's entire political strategy from grass-roots organizing aimed at employees and stockholders in local companies, to campaign contributions to members of Congress, to direct contacts with powerful figures in Washington.

These Washington officers accumulate huge amounts of data on government activity, the status of legislation, and key members of Congress, and on procurement policy decisions in the Pentagon, plans and programs for R & D, new regulatory actions, and federal rulemaking. They then send the relevant information back to the company.

Most of these companies also have direct access to the President's staff at the White House. The congressional staff of 23,000, particularly those of key congressional committees, are extremely important people to influence. The Washington officers work with these people continually.

These officers are also engaged in intense lobbying activities both at the congressional level and at the executive level in the Pentagon. They try to influence decisions at all stages. There is an overlap between actual lobbying and information giving and pressure, and because these latter two activities are not classified as lobbying, an enormous part of corporate-government relations is never known by the general public. As one defense lobbyist for GE said, "Visibility is the last thing I need."

The corporations hire lawyers, public-affairs experts and technicians, and outside lobbyists for the lobbying efforts. In fact, a large part of many legal practices represent the company and its sales, as well as strictly legal matters. There are thousands and thousands of lawyers in Washington greasing the wheels for these corporations.

If the people in America wish to survive and save the world for their children, they must rapidly learn how to use their democracy just as these military corporations do and become more skilled than the corporations.

Insurance Companies, Banks, Auditors, and Finance Companies

Another extremely powerful way in which defense firms exert their influence is through financial institutions. The relationships with banks, auditors, insurance companies, and finance companies are usually vested with confidentiality, so most members of the public know nothing about this aspect of the pathogenesis.

Board members of corporations often have significant ties with the boards of financial institutions and vice versa. If a bank or lending company has lent a firm $1 million, it is then in its best interest to lobby for the firm at local, state, and federal levels. Banks are credited with playing a major role in shaping federal policies. It was said by one bank lobbyist, "The bank lobby can almost certainly stop anything it does not want in Congress." The major government agencies regulating financial matters are often staffed by people who come from or return to the financial world. An informal network links bankers and financial officers to politicians and policy makers, which gives them a major role in national policy making.

Banks supply important services to corporations, including financial and management advice, loans of capital, handling of stocks and bond issues, and management of savings plans and pension funds. Banks may also be important stockholders in corporations.

Military corporations don't regularly disclose which financial institutions they conduct business with, or which ones are large shareholders in the companies. Likewise, investment banks and insurance companies don't provide details on their shareholdings or their role in corporate activities.

Chase Manhattan Bank lends money to Boeing, Grumman, Lockheed, Northrop, United Technologies, and shares a board member with Lockheed. Citicorp lends to Boeing, Grumman, Lockheed, and United Technologies. It shares directors with Boeing, Lockheed, and United Technologies. Other banks in similar positions are Morgan Guaranty, the Bank of New York, Bankers' Trust, Manufacturer's Hanover, Mellon Bank, Fargo, Bank of America, Chemical Bank, Continental Illinois, First National Bank of Boston, and Irving Trust.

When I look at this information, the magnitude of the

problem frightens me. Virtually the whole financial network is heavily involved in the weapons industry and what's more, is working actively to support and represent it. It will take an almighty, highly motivated, well-educated, and incredibly determined movement of good American people to shift the whole society toward the life process and divert these unconscious people away from death and suicide.

Accounting Firms

These firms are also heavily into military corporations. The information they choose to recognize or ignore, in setting accounting standards and auditing a company's books, is obviously of great significance to these huge firms. They also play the role of management adviser. Admiral Hyman Rickover has said of these firms, "Companies have great latitude in how they can account for costs and profits for financial accounting purposes. As a result, the figures are susceptible to manipulations and judgments, which can dramatically change reported profits in all—all within the constraints of the so-called 'generally accepted accounting principles.'"

Some examples of accounting firms that represent big defense industries are Arthur Anderson and Company (General Dynamics and Grumman); Arthur Young and Company (Lockheed); Deloitte, Haskins and Sells (Rockwell International); Ernst and Whinney (McDonnell-Douglas); Price Waterhouse (United Technologies); and Touche Ross and Company (Boeing and Northrop).

A 1976 Senate report on accounting was very critical about the way these firms, as auditors, represented the private over the public interests. "It appears that 'the Big 8' [accounting] firms are more concerned with saving the interests of corporate management who select them and authorize their fees, than with protecting the interests of the public, for whose benefit Congress established the position of Independent Auditor." Frequently, staff from auditing companies go to work for the defense companies they have audited. Pentagon officials do not check the veracity of the audit statements they receive. One said, "We are ordered to take that information at face value. The presumption is that they are not on the take. If they do something wrong, they'll probably be discovered anyway, and is it really worth it to intimidate these guys?"

Connections and Influence of Officers and Board Members

The men at the top of these industries are extremely powerful and very experienced in handling ties to positions of influence, and they usually have had many years of service in the industry or government. Some have ties to financial institutions that handle the corporation's business; some hold memberships on boards of companies that supply goods to or are themselves defense contractors. Many of them serve in positions for important institutions, such as chairman of the Science Board, associate secretary of state for research and development, and counsel to the CIA.

It is very difficult to obtain information about which of these men holds stock in what companies. This obviously will affect the decisions they make.

In 1977, a Senate study discussed the dangers posed by such a concentration of power and information in any segment of the economy. "These patterns of Director interrelationships imply an overwhelming potential for anti-trust abuse and possible conflicts of interest, which could affect prices, supply and competition and impact on the shape and direction of the American economy."

With the defense budget playing a larger and larger role in the expenditures of America, obviously the preceding statement is a very serious warning. Boeing provides an example of interlocking corporate financial and government responsibilities: In 1978, Boeing's president, Malcolm Stamper, was among the fifteen corporate officers receiving the highest salaries in the country. Boeing's directors were board members of other firms, which received $1,034,000 in Department of Defense contracts in fiscal 1979. Most of these companies were suppliers of components and petroleum to Boeing.

Four Boeing directors had outside ties that would encourage contact with government or defense policy makers. Former Defense Secretary Harold Brown, a Boeing director, was president of Cal-Tech, while Harold J. Haynes, chief executive officer of Standard Oil, was a trustee of Cal-Tech. David Packard, deputy secretary of defense from 1969 to 1971, joined the board of Boeing in 1978 and is the chief executive officer of Hewlett-Packard, a major defense contractor. William Reed, a director, was also a member of the President's Council at Cal-Tech when Brown was president, and George Weyerhaeuser was previously a member of the Advisory Council of Stanford Research Institute and of RAND Corporation—both defense contractors.

Trade Associations

Not only do the military companies have their own Washington offices, but they are also represented by trade associations in Washington. These organizations have been established by the defense industries and by the military services specifically to influence buying of weapons. One Pentagon official said of these associations, "As a social unit, they are an incredible force to be reckoned with by the Congress." They overtly encourage increased defense spending, and they foster specific research and developmental projects. They supply information from industry to DOD and NASA and provide information from federal officials to industry. Senator William Proxmire said they serve as a "go-between for ideas and information to flow from the defense industry to the Pentagon."

Most of these trade associations hold at least one convention per year, all of which are attended by many military and civilian DOD personnel, as well as by Pentagon brass. These people mix socially and form valuable contacts at the conventions. Also at these meetings, the associations present a variety of panels and classified briefings and distribute information on upcoming programs, weapons, and policy development. Some people say that these trade associations serve to cement a relationship that is already too close between the buyers and sellers of weapons. Obviously, these associations and the contacts they catalyze totally exclude any opposing views on military affairs, so that the people of the country are not represented in any of these decisions. The trade organizations also publish frequent newsletters filled with advertising and articles on defense procurement policies and weapons development.

Officials of these trade associations regularly testify before Congress and congressional committees on legislative developments that may affect their clients, on specific procurement policies, and on the general level of defense spending. They also work with committees in the Pentagon to influence the Pentagon's attitude toward various weapons systems.

Here are some of the most important trade and service associations:

• *The American Defense Preparedness Association*, with 600 members from defense contractors and 40,000 members from industry, campus, and the Pentagon. It has an annual budget of $3 million and a full-time staff of twenty-seven. This organization includes all the giants in the defense industry, as well as smaller firms. The giants include McDonnell-Douglas, General Dynamics, Boeing, Lockheed, Northrop, Rockwell International, United Technologies, Grumman, Litton, and Martin Marietta. These firms did $1 billion worth of business with the Pentagon in 1982.

• *National Security Industrial Association*, with 313 defense contractors as members.

• *Aerospace Industries Association*. The 47 member companies include most of the aerospace giants like McDonnell-Douglas.

• *The Air Force Association*, with 181,000 individual and 200 corporate members. Approximately 45 percent of its individual members are on active duty with the air force.

• Others include the Association of the U.S. Army, the Shipbuilders Council of America, the Electronic Industries Association, the Society of Naval Architects and Marine Engineers, and the Association of Old Crows, which represents electronic warfare.

The Association of Old Crows publishes the *Electronic Warfare Magazine*, and the association has a membership of 12,000 devoted to electronic warfare. Electronic warfare has become a lucrative business, and in 1982 worldwide sales of such products reached approximately $7 billion. As one Wall Street analyst said, "War is good business again." Electronic warfare involves making the electronic brains that allow missiles to chase after their targets, that render destroyers vulnerable to a single missile, and that can turn an opponent's radar against him by making it a homing path for an enemy projectile. Companies involved in this particular form of horrendous warfare are IBM, RCA, Eaton, TRW, GTE Sylvania, Raytheon, Grumman, Hughes Aircraft, Litton, ITT, Westinghouse, Ford Aerospace, Northrop, Lockheed, Boeing, Hewlett-Packard, Motorola, National Semi-Conductor, Loral Corporation, Watkins-Johnson, Sanders Associates, and E Systems, Inc.

Many electronic firms have experienced dramatic rises in earnings, and their stocks are selling at enormous prices.

The Technical Marketing Society of America held a conference called New Trends in Missiles—Systems and Technology. Under the heading "Technology and Marketing Imperative," the program read, "December 1983 sees the deployment of medium range missiles throughout Europe. Despite Reagan's 'global limit' of warheads concept, tension is on the increase. The international implication on industry is a worldwide missile market in full expansion. Funding in the U.S. alone has soared to $18 billion. Technological advances in electronics, structures and propulsion are creating new opportunities for autonomous/multi-mode guidance advanced seekers and sensors, sophisticated tracking and jamming, more kills per mass, kinetic energy weapons, maneuvering missiles, ducted rockets, etc. At the same time severe customer affordability problems are creating tougher demands than ever on contractors to reduce costs.

"This conference brings together leading experts from government and industry who will discuss new and improved missile programs and systems in all mission areas (strategic, theatre, tactical), plus key technologies for future missile systems: guidance, propulsion, instrumentation and computers. It will provide a unique insight into longterm DOD policy trends, identify and assess emerging programs, and present the state-of-the-art of crucial missile technologies. It is a must for all scientists, engineers, program and marketing managers who need to formulate realistic business targets and high leverage technology investments."

Advertising and Organization at the Grass-Roots Level

The military companies conduct large advertising campaigns in the military press and also in the lay press. I am always appalled when I open the op ed section of *The New York Times* and see a spectacularly beautiful space-age-designed piece of equipment advertised by Northrop, equipment that is part of the guidance system of a MIRVed missile. To quote from one of these ads: "The wonder of the Star Tracker is its ability to focus on the stars during the day. Developed by

Northrop's Electronics Division, the Star Tracker is the eye of an airborne astroinertial guidance system so precise it is called upon to check the accuracy of other advanced navigational instruments. Northrop is a pioneer in astroinertial guidance and has earned the worldwide reputation for leadership in precision navigation." Obviously, most readers of *The New York Times* would not understand what this particular jargon means, but what it does mean, of course, is that this is part of a first-strike missile system, using the stars for navigation. This sort of advertising for genocidal weapons is as if German industry advertised well-designed parts of its gas ovens in the most prestigious pre–World War II German papers, except that a MIRVed missile could burn and vaporize tens of millions of people in the space of thirty minutes.

The military press, which is covered extensively, includes such publications as *Aviation Week*, *National Defense*, *Armed Forces Journal International*, *U.S. Naval Institute Proceedings*, *Army*, and *Air Force Magazine*.

Aviation Week is read by 102,000 subscribers in 132 countries. It often has privileged access to defense information and plays a key role in the nation's public-information wars. It publishes sensitive information with a degree of impunity not available to the lay public. These frequent advance disclosures may change the balance of power in the world, for it is read at the highest levels of government. It keeps the aerospace and defense industries abreast of the latest technical developments, funding, and trends in policy, and it often serves as the industry spokesman to influence policy changes.

The corporations often conduct this advertising in the interests of "national security," and very often the taxpayer is probably subsidizing these costs.

Corporations also lobby and advertise in the localities where their manufacturing facilities are based. If they need specific funding for a new weapons system, they mobilize the local constituency and the workers in their factories to write to their senators and congressmen and even the President himself. One worker in a Rockwell plant, which was organized to send a letter to Representative Les Aspin (D-Wis.), wrote, "I support the bomber project. OK, OK, I'm really a player just working for Rockwell and they told me to write something." It always amazes me when federal representatives receive hundreds or thousands of these letters supporting particular weapon systems and don't seem to see through the obviously orchestrated effort in order to intelligently assess the propaganda exercise.

An excellent example of this grass-roots organizing is the massive lobbying effort carried out by Rockwell International since 1973 in support of the B-1 bomber. This will be described later.

Research and Development

In 1980, over 60 percent of all federal research and development funding went to aerospace and defense programs sponsored by DOD, DOE, and NASA.

The genesis of most weapon systems takes place in the bowels of the military corporations. The government, to a large degree, helps fund this research—and very often the technological inventions become strategic imperatives once the research and development is completed. The R & D starts years before the weapon systems are made public and is conducted in absolute secrecy in the name of national security—which totally excludes public participation or dissenting views. By the time the new invention is announced, it is usually a political *fait accompli*. Typical weapon systems that have emerged from these programs are cruise missiles, stealth technology, high-energy lasers, space-based satellite surveillance systems, precision-guided ammunitions, lightweight fighters, and strategic bombers.

To a considerable degree, this R & D is funded by DOD through the Independent Research and Development (I R & D) and Bid and Proposal (B & P) programs.

I R & D is the research and development conducted by the corporations that is not sponsored by a contract, grant, or other arrangement. It is planned, sponsored, and directed internally by the company as it attempts to produce better products for its customers—who are DOD, NASA, or DOE. B & P describes the company's effort at preparing and submitting proposals to these government departments. Therefore, a contractor who works on future-oriented defense research and who submits proposals for this work is reimbursed by our tax dollars for part of the cost. The exact amount is negotiated by DOD with each contractor and is dependent on the percentage of the company's total DOD contract work. These funds are *not* scrutinized by the Congress; the public has no idea they exist, although they total nearly $1 billion per year. Moreover, I R & D and B & P programs are focused on the larger firms, which ensures an incestuous, concentrated defense industry. Half this total spending annually goes to the ten top DOD contracting companies.

As *The New York Times* noted in 1976 in an article by John Finney, "Today, policy-making circles in the Defense Department are largely populated by business executives in mid-career, passing through the Pentagon on the way to bigger and better jobs in industry. . . . The trend is particularly pronounced in Dr. Currie's Research and Development office, by far the most important office in the Pentagon for industry because it decides which weapons are to be developed. . . . The roster of Deputy Directors is filled with men who used to work for industry and plan to return to it. As in a game of musical chairs, industry executives rotate in and out of what is known to the Pentagon as the 'R & D Cartel.' "

Of course, this enormously important and influential R & D corporate community is the nidus of the pathogenesis. If these people did not do secret research on unbelievably evil killing systems behind closed doors, supported by our tax dollars, the arms race would cease.

This R & D and the Pentagon demand for new weapons and equipment is always justified by potential Soviet weapon systems. The CIA and Defense Intelligence Agency calculate the nature and extent of these potential threats. In the technical areas—for instance, performance of Soviet aircraft and weaponry—most of this evaluation is contracted out to major private defense companies, because they have the scientific expertise to evaluate capabilities of Soviet weapons.

The end result of this activity is, according to a high-ranking Defense Department official, that "the government ends up contracting out to counter an emerging threat to the very people who profit from it." Michael Vahlos, a former CIA analyst, now at Johns Hopkins University Center for Strategic and International Study, said, "Companies that produce the weapons will always inflate the threat to maximize their sales."

Obviously, paranoid thinking about Russian advances and

technology will line the pockets of the avaricious American corporations. This whole dynamic must be stopped by the American people.

Interservice Rivalry

James Fallows, in his book *National Defense*, says the rivalry between the services for appropriations is often more intense than the rivalry and hostility between the superpowers. The latter, of course, is used to justify the former.

Army, navy, air force, and marines are all represented equally on the Joint Chiefs of Staff. The chiefs are supposed to assess military problems and advise the President. But instead of viewing issues in terms of the broad national interest, each chief tends to view himself as the representative of his own branch of the services and to lobby for programs favored by that particular service. The chairman does not have nearly enough power, according to Air Force General David Jones, former Chairman of the Joint Chiefs, to counterbalance the often parochial views of the service chiefs and the civilian defense officials who support them.

In preparing for meetings of the Defense Resources Board, a high-level Pentagon group that is supposed to match available funds with defense requirements, the Chairman of the Joint Chiefs has only five staff members to analyze proposals and collect information, while each service chief has thousands of employees to carry out similar tasks.

Because of the strong parochial interests, there is really no central control at all. Former Navy Under Secretary James Woolsey wrote, "A gaggle of kibbutzes has formed throughout the government on these questions. . . . For years, the only central voice in defense has been provided by the civilian staff of the Secretary of Defense. Lacking military expertise, it has largely failed."

To give an example of the sort of gross waste produced by this interservice rivalry, there are at present all sorts of duplications among the four tactical air forces—one each for the army, navy, air force, and marines—paid for by the taxpayers. For the most part, each of the services flies different aircraft, which means few of the thirty production lines run at economical rates.

Each service has a civilian secretary and a military chief

of staff. Each has its own special think tank (like RAND for the air force), lobbying associations, weapons contractors, and its own military academy. Consequently, each service tends to view the national interest from the vantage of its own special interests and traditions.

These services are united only through the Office of the Secretary of Defense and through the Chairman of the Joint Chiefs of Staff. Both of these positions are relatively weak, and the issues of national defense are now so extremely complicated with all the new technology and incredible numbers and variety of weapons that it becomes extremely difficult for civilian officials to separate service bias from sound analysis (if, indeed, there can be the latter in the nuclear age).

David Jones says that in this sort of atmosphere, "There is good justification for every weapon system. . . . I could develop a rationale for a 700-ship Navy or 10 additional fighter wings. But, that doesn't mean that we ought to do it." Currently, the navy plans to build three additional aircraft carriers, each with 100 fighter planes and scores of support ships.

Corruption and Government Manipulation by Large Defense Corporations

There are several classical weapon systems that have been massaged through Congress by an orchestrated effort conducted over the years by the corporations. They are just prime examples, however, of dynamics that are continually occurring for myriads of weapons.

B-1 Bomber. This anachronistic airplane was first discussed by the Strategic Air Command at Offutt Air Force Base in Nebraska in 1962, just as the last B-52 was built. The air force was impatient to get on to its next generation of planes.

Actually, by the time ICBMs were deployed, there was no need for more planes to carry nuclear weapons because the ICBMs destroy their targets in thirty minutes, whereas these lumbering planes take ten to fourteen hours to reach Russia. Hence, the B-52, B-1, and stealth bomber (if it is ever built) will be used for postattack reconnaissance.

Most of the initial technology of the B-1 was designed in

the sixties, and much of the updated equipment has been borrowed from more modern aircraft. The official cost of each B-1 was $45.5 million, which has since risen to $280 million, the total cost of the program being $20.5 billion. This cost does not include the money the air force has used to study, develop, and promote the new plane since 1962, nor does it include inflation, which the air force estimates will be $10 billion by 1988. This official cost does not cover replenishment of spare parts or the sophisticated ground-support equipment and training devices necessary to use the bombers. It has recently been modified to carry cruise missiles, but the Soviet Union has had twenty-one years to devise adequate air defense against it should it attempt to fly over Soviet air space to drop gravity bombs once it has delivered its cruise missiles. It is anachronistic before it is produced. In 1977, a Pentagon assessment of the B-1 said that for this reason it was unnecessary, and the B-52 would be good "indefinitely." The air force reinforced its case for the B-1 by canceling improvements to the B-52 fleet and exaggerating the cost of maintaining the B-52s.

Despite these obvious flaws and the huge expense, the B-1 program has survived for twenty-one years because of an enormously intricate complex of contractors, subcontractors, and interest groups that have supported it. Even after President Carter decided to cancel the plane in 1977, Congress voted funds to build and test one more plane.

There has been little independent evaluation of the bomber or its mission since it was first proposed. Much of the "outside" analysis of the Soviet weaponry that the B-1 might have to face has been done by direct B-1 contractors or by think tanks, neither of them eager to destroy a bomber that they or their clients were determined to build.

There were early cost overruns on the B-1, which were not quickly corrected and which in some cases were reported to Congress only by independent watchdog agencies. Consequently, in 1974, only four years after the first development contract was signed, the General Accounting Office reported that the air force had reduced the performance requirements for the B-1 by 20 percent for maximum speed, 25 percent for internal missile payload, and 15 percent for takeoff distance.

After Carter canceled the B-1, he allowed Rockwell to continue to receive R & D funds to keep the "bomber option" alive. So Rockwell stored 43,000 pieces of specialized equipment and materials, such as titanium, in air force warehouses at government expense until Reagan gave it the go-ahead again. According to a former Rockwell employee, Bobby Witzezak, Rockwell also shaved costs on the B-1 program, during the years when it received only R & D funds, by charging bomber costs to its space-shuttle contract. In 1982, after a three-year FBI investigation, Rockwell had to pay $500,000 in compensatory damages to the government and spend $1 million for a computerized time-keeping system because of allegations that from 1975 to 1978 it had charged other work to its shuttle contract.

In the mid-seventies, Rockwell spent tens of thousands of dollars on information and lobbying activities and on entertaining influential Pentagon officials at its goose-hunting lodge on Chesapeake Bay near Washington, D.C.

Lobbying in Congress over the years has focused on the idea that the B-1 would provide jobs and incomes to many congressional districts. During the lobbying campaign, the air force teamed up with the United Auto Workers, who were expected to get a big share of the jobs.

Grant Miller, a retired air force colonel who was a chief B-1 lobbyist for a decade, said, "I had a list of every B-1 contract over $10,000, of the location of the contracts state by state, Congressional district and town, and a map showing numbers of dollars and employees. We'd sit down, make assignments, [decide] who we needed to work on. We'd find out who had the most influence with that guy, and we'd get the Air Force Association or somebody to work. It was really an orchestrated effort." This was only a small part of a huge machine that was supporting the B-1 bomber: air force officers whose careers were linked to a successful B-1 program, industry and government researchers and designers, the giant aerospace corporations led by Rockwell, plus all the 5,200 subcontractors spread over forty-eight states, and the politicians in Congress, as well as White House and Pentagon officials. (With so many different subcontractors making different components for the plane, I doubt that the plane will ever function adequately.)

Rockwell's B-1 revenues are predicted to reach $10 billion by 1987 with pretax profit margins at 15 percent.

The subcontractors include most of the heavyweight

contractors: Boeing, TRW, Westinghouse, General Electric, Goodyear, Singer, Sperry, Bendix, Bought, Martin Marietta, Northrop, Litton, IBM, Teledyne, Brunswick, AIL Division of Eaton, United Technologies, Kaman Aerospace, and others. Each of these major subcontractors has a Washington office and its own lobbyists. It can generate powerful coalitions of workers, union leaders, local businessmen, and government officials in home districts to pressure their congressional representatives.

Almost all of the major subcontractors have held seats in the last twenty years on either the Defense Science Board or the Air Force Scientific Advisory Board. These boards help assess the nature of the Soviet threat and help determine what weapons the United States needs in response. For example, Richard Delauer, formerly top executive in TRW, now under secretary of defense for research and engineering, was a member of the Defense Science Board when the B-1 was moving from concept toward production; and Assistant Secretary of Defense Richard M. Paul was a consultant to Boeing. A congressional staff aide, who has studied the B-1 program, said it is a closed club. "A few years after a program like this gets started, there comes the consensus that the airplane absolutely must be built. The consensus is held by the believers. It doesn't matter really whether they're in industry or government or flow back and forth. There are two problems with this: One is that the program picks up tremendous forward momentum and probably nobody can stop it for whatever reason. The second is: Everybody wants his favorite widget built into the airplane, so the performance becomes compromised and the cost goes up." Another former defense official said, "These people aren't disloyal; they just get blinders on and they see in the data what they want to see."

It is widely accepted in congressional and defense-industry circles that companies often choose subcontractors or sites for new plants with politics or political influence in mind.

Rockwell has been extremely successful in spreading its B-1 subcontracts all over the country. This is not efficient, but it creates enormous lobbying power for jobs, money, etc. For example, of the prototype models already manufactured, the engines were made in Lynn, Massachusetts; the fan-blades in Springfield, Ohio; the rudders in Bloomfield, Connecticut; the stabilizers in Baltimore; the actuators in

Kalamazoo, Michigan; the wing-control surfaces in Tulsa; the
tires in Akron; the parachute escape system in Des Plaines,
Illinois; the secondary power subsystem in Melbourne, Florida;
the windshields in Garden Grove, California; the avionics
integration in Seattle; the radar altimeter in Minneapolis; and
the seats in Denver.

In 1973, a list compiled by Rockwell showed B-1 subcontractors beside the names of nearly every member of the
House and Senate Armed Services committees and Appropriations committees. This is the epitome of pork-barrel politics,
for all these congresspeople feel pressured to vote for this
lemon of a plane because of jobs and money in their districts.

Bureaucracy in government, industry, and outside think
tanks is also part of this old boy supportive network: the
analysts who assess the strategic threat, the accounting firms,
the technicians who test the aircraft and equipment, and
thousands of others. A similar story of intrigue, lobbying, and
corruption has supported Lockheed's C-5B transport plane,
which recently won acceptance by Congress, and also the MX
missile.

The Pervasive Geographical Grip of the Military-Industrial Complex

Having examined the dependency of many states upon
the death industry, I feel from time to time that the task
ahead of us is enormous. The situation will be changed only
by massive demands by the people that Congress enact laws
to convert the military-industrial complex of the United States
from industries creating death to those that will sustain the
life process. Such a move will go far toward guaranteeing
everyone on earth the right to life, liberty, and the pursuit of
happiness, free from starvation, illiteracy, overpopulation,
disease, dirty water, and polluted air—and military threat.
This is the change of thinking to which Einstein referred
when he said, "The splitting of the atom changed everything
save man's mode of thinking; thus we drift toward unparalleled catastrophe."

California is just one example of a state that has become
almost totally dependent upon the military-industrial complex.
There are many other such dependencies, including Connecti-

cut, Massachusetts, Florida, and Washington, D.C., and its surrounding suburbs.

California—The Death State. One in eight working Californians is employed directly or indirectly by the military-industrial complex. One in three manufacturing jobs is related to the aerospace industry, and in Los Angeles County, it is one in every two jobs. Almost half these aerospace workers are employed in military projects.

These people often work in beautifully designed, sleek, sanitary buildings, where the stench of death is never present. They are just doing their jobs, working on government or private contracts, making money, worrying about designs and research and fun places to eat and what they did on the weekend. These silver and glass buildings dot the San Diego Freeway in the south and Silicon Valley in the north. In fact, this Californian way of life has become so fashionable that the mores of the Valley Girls have become chic in society.

Twenty-two percent of all U.S. military spending occurs in California, and this may rise to 30 percent with the Reagan buildup. Forty percent of the new strategic systems—such big ticket items as the B-1, MX, stealth bomber, and cruise missiles—are made in California. The military is California's biggest industry. In 1982, $26.3 billion was awarded in contracts to California by the DOD, and this figure was twice the total receipts of the state's farmers.

There are tremendous rivalries among the various California counties for defense dollars, and immigrant workers are attracted to those counties with the biggest defense contracts.

Four California counties, Los Angeles, Santa Clara, San Diego, and Orange, account for 65 percent of every defense dollar spent in California. Many companies are not usually thought of as defense-related. For example, producers of paperboard containers and boxes did 12 percent of their business with DOD; fabricated-rubber companies, 36 percent; screw-machine producers, 70 percent; computing machines, 54 percent; machine-shop jobbing and repair, 78 percent; and photographic equipment, 69 percent.

Yet this dependency on defense, even though it helped California during the recession, may actually cost the state jobs. The California state government estimated in 1981 that over the next five years President Reagan's defense buildup would create 700,000 new jobs for California, but that another million jobs would be lost because of cuts in domestic spending, which had been necessary to finance new military programs.

California's higher-education system provides the necessary scientific and technical pool for growth. Stanford University gives an essential research base, as well as the personnel pool for Silicon Valley in Santa Clara County. The University of California has, since World War II, maintained a large number of contracts with DOD, and the university's regents also manage the only two nuclear-warhead-design labs in the United States—Lawrence-Livermore in Livermore, California, and Los Alamos Scientific Lab in Los Alamos, New Mexico—under a contract with the DOE.

Because of this strong support from the universities, California has always led in the research and development of weapons. One of three federal R & D dollars is spent in California, and it is exactly this R & D that creates the new weapons systems that are manufactured in California.

Washington, D.C. In Washington, D.C., the military firms have metastasized their offices to suburbs surrounding the Pentagon, in Virginia and Maryland. Arranged along the George Washington Parkway and the Capital Beltway, they are nicknamed the Beltway Bandits. Last year the defense-dominated private sector of the Washington area surpassed the federal government as the principal employer in Washington, D.C., and environs.

In the four northern Virginia cities closest to the Pentagon, there are 620 high-tech firms, with 47,000 employees, more than 70 percent of whom work on defense-sponsored projects. Ray F. Mitchell, a senior partner in a thirty-five-attorney Virginia law firm, said, "We are a combination of California's Silicon Valley and Boston's Route 128."

As you fly into National Airport outside Washington, D.C., you pass a complex of new office buildings called Crystal City. Crystal City is so dependent upon defense spending that one of its developers suggested calling it Pentagon II. In just one building, there are nineteen branch offices for top defense companies, including Rockwell International, General Dynamics, and Newport News Shipbuilding. In 1982, these offices did $11 billion in defense-contract work or about 10 percent of the prime defense contracts.

Cost Overruns and Pentagon Waste

The number of major defense contractors is very small, and the top companies overwhelmingly dominate the market. In fiscal 1982, ten companies received more than 31 percent of all prime DOD contracts. With the exception of General Electric, all of these ten previously named companies have the Pentagon as their principal, if not sole, customer. There is rarely any meaningful competition among the defense contractors once a development contract is awarded. About 60 percent of major weapon-system purchases are made on a negotiated, single-source basis. More than 90 percent of all defense-contract dollars are not awarded on the basis of price competition; therefore, there is no incentive to drive down costs. (Including all items from aircraft carriers down to paper clips, the Pentagon spends $500 million a day, and only 6 percent to 7 percent of all prime contracts are bid for in a competitive fashion.) Twenty-five percent of all defense dollars spent on weapons are for contracts awarded on a cost-plus-fee basis, so that the contractor receives all his costs plus a fee—which is usually 5 percent of the contract value. This policy removes the normal market forces that limit costs.

Because the cost-plus contract is so attractive, many corporations indulge in the practice of "buying in." They submit bids that are less than the actual cost of a weapon system so that they can win the initial R & D contract for a weapon system, and they then count on recouping the initial R & D loss when they win the production contract. This dynamic is the principal cause of the cost overruns endemic in the defense industry. Obviously, Congress and the military buyers find the initial low cost estimate to get a new weapon system started very appealing. It also enables military buyers to crowd more weapon systems into a total given budget, and it allows more congressmen to extend Pentagon favors to more constituents.

There are other major areas where defense spending is distorted. About 30 percent of the cost of new weapons is caused by defense contractors' slipshod work, which then has to be redone.

The air force, because of inadequate management or

oversight, may in fact face a $4 billion shortage of spare parts by early 1984. No one is actually held accountable in the air force for coordinating this aspect of management. Here are other examples of exorbitant prices charged to the Pentagon by contractors and subcontractors:

• A Minuteman II machine screw cost $1.08 in 1982 and $36.77 in 1983—an increase of 3,300 percent.
• A circuit-card guidance system assembly cost $234.05 in 1982 and $1,111.75 in 1983.
• A tiny electric connector plug for FB-111 aircraft cost $7.99 in 1982 and $726.86 in 1983.
• Aluminum ladders cost ten times the price they are in a hardware store—$1,676 each instead of $160 each.

The following are other ways in which the Pentagon pours tax money down the drain:

• Some defense contractors attempt to charge to their government contracts nondefense items like office paintings, lavish dinners, tickets to sports events and movie premieres, home swimming pools, and memberships in health clubs.
• The 1982 budget called for $102.1 million to be spent on military bands—a $9 million increase over two years. Only $11 million is to be spent for the National Endowment for the Arts and for local opera, symphonies, chamber orchestras, and other musical programs—a decrease of 12 percent.
• Two billion dollars could be saved by closing unnecessary military bases.
• Four and a half million dollars per year is wasted because enlisted personnel serve as servants to top military officers.
• Navy artists are paid $350,000 to paint portraits for admirals' offices.
• Each year $2 million is spent on government-subsidized meals in Pentagon dining rooms.
• Each year $887,000 goes to promote rifle practice for Boy Scouts, YMCAs, and other youth groups.
• Eight million dollars is spent for stunt shows conducted by the navy's Blue Angels and the Air Force Thunderbirds and $200 million for the planes.
• Bitter interservice rivalry, where each service wants its own planes, missiles, tanks, handguns, or even belt buckles,

is very expensive. Different weapons are developed for the same targets. There are four tactical air forces—one each for the navy, army, air force, and marines—composed for the large part of different planes, made by competing corporations.
• Each year $70 million could be saved by consolidating the transport systems for the different military services.
• Each year $400 million could be saved by unifying vehicle and equipment maintenance facilities under a single manager, and $1 billion per year by consolidating support services on military bases located in the same geographical area. These include property repair and maintenance, police and fire services, laundries, utilities, and trash and sewage disposal. In Sacramento there are seven major military bases within a sixty-mile area, and they all use separate service systems.
• The DOD spends $300 million per year on recreation facilities, such as golf courses, stables, and boating marinas.
• Military personnel can retire after twenty years' service, even those who have sat behind a desk all their lives. Each year $1 billion could be saved by stopping double-dipping, the practice by which a retired military person receives a pension while at the same time working as a government employee. Also, $6.9 billion could be saved by delaying full entitlement until after thirty years of service and by integrating retirement pay with Social Security benefits.
• Contractors had $11.2 billion worth of equipment in 1981 furnished free by the Pentagon.
• The DOD subsidizes foreign governments on weapons, training, and communications to the tune of hundreds of millions of dollars.
• The services now have two to seven and a half times the number of officers per fighting unit as they had in World War II. The number of unnecessary officers in all services could be reduced.

Admiral Hyman Rickover accused several companies of fraud because they submitted cost overrun claims for shipbuilding. For instance, the Electric Boat Division of General Dynamics Corporation submitted $843 million in overrun claims in late-1970. The Navy Claims Settlement Board said they were entitled to only $125 million, but the navy, rather than face extended litigation, paid the company $484 million. Companies involved in similar cases were the Ingalls Shipbuilding Division of Litton Industries, and Newport News Shipbuilding and Dry Dock Company. And as previously mentioned, Rockwell International Corporation diverted bills from fixed-price defense contracts to its more open space-shuttle contracts.

Other corporations are also guilty. For instance, Pratt and Whitney, the largest suppliers of military-aircraft spare parts, increased its prices for some items by 300 percent in one year, and an air force study found that this company was making no "significant efforts to control indirect costs or drive costs downward." Probably, therefore, the current spare-parts shortage is a result of price increases that far outrun the air force's spare-parts budget.

Congress

These problems do not involve just two sides of the Iron Triangle—the military services and the corporations—but also the third side, the politicians. For instance, last year a House Armed Services subcommittee added to the defense budget some $300 million for work at military bases that the Pentagon did not want done. About two thirds of these projects were in congressional districts represented by members of the committee.

Many congressmen demand defense spending for their districts as political spoils. Representative Jack Edwards of Alabama, the senior Republican on the House Appropriations Defense Subcommittee, said, "Control of the system has got to be done by the Pentagon with the support of the White House . . . . We are not prone to making the right decisions." Don't forget these congressmen, even when not swayed by constituent interests, are continually bombarded by lobbyists from defense contractors.

To indicate another sordid side of this story, under a little-noticed government program, inmates at the only federal prison in New England are producing electronic cable assemblies for guided-missile launchers. Defense Department documents show that Federal Prison Industries, Incorporated, in Danbury, Connecticut, received $20.3 million in contracts in 1982 from the army, navy, air force, and Defense Logistics Agency. Most of the money, $17.7 million, came from the army, which placed orders for electronic cable assemblies to be used in guided-missile launchers and guided-missile remote-controlled devices.

In 1981, total gross sales came to $128 million for Federal Prison Industries, which was founded in 1934 and now operates seventy-five plants at almost all the forty-three federal prisons in the United States. Of approximately 7,000 prisoners in the program, about 1,135 work in the electronics division. The military does not inform the prison officials of the use for the electronic cable assemblies. A prison official said the primary purpose of the work is to reduce idleness in prisons and to provide vocational training. "The program is open to all inmates, but we have a requirement for basic adult education." I consider participating in the death-producing program of the federal government a gross exploitation of prisoners.

How Does the System Work in Russia?

Without the enormous drive for profit, what motivates the arms merchants in Russia? In Nikita S. Khrushchev's memoirs, he recounts the meeting between himself and President Eisenhower, which is very revealing about the dynamics of the nuclear pathology in both countries:

> "Tell me, Mr. Khrushchev," Eisenhower asked him, "how do you decide the question of funds for military expenses? Perhaps first I should tell you how it is with us."
>
> "Well, how is it with you?" Khrushchev responded.
>
> "It's like this," said Eisenhower. "My military leaders come to me and say, 'Mr. President, we need such and such a sum for such and such a program.' I say, 'Sorry, we don't have the funds.' They say, 'We have reliable information that the Soviet Union has already allocated funds for their own such programs. Therefore, if we don't get the funds we need, we'll fall behind the Soviet Union.' So, I give in. That's how they wring the money out of me. They keep grabbing for more, and I keep giving it to them. Now tell me, how is it with you?"

"It's just the same," said Khrushchev. "Some people from our Military Department come and say, 'Comrade Khrushchev, look at this. The Americans are developing such and such a system. We could develop the same system, but it would cost such and such.' I tell them there is no money; it's all been allotted already. So they say, 'If we don't get the money we need and if there is a war, then the enemy will have superiority over us.' So we discuss it some more, and I end up by giving them the money they ask for."

"Yes," said Eisenhower, "that's what I thought."

There are, therefore, many similarities in the way the two countries run their arms industries. In both nations, the armed forces are the biggest consumers of manufactured goods and services. More people are employed in military work than in any other occupation, except agriculture, and military research occupies a very high proportion of the scientists and engineers.

Both the Soviet military-industrial complex and the American military-industrial complex operate fairly independently of the civilian economy. Each has an artificial system of competition, and each enjoys a great political influence. Therefore, in both nations, weapons under development acquire a momentum that carries them into production, regardless of their cost, their efficiency, or their compatibility with the objectives of arms control.

As American aircraft designer and defense expert Pierre M. Sprey told a New York business group: "You'll realize that our Defense Department buys weapons by almost the same system the Soviets do. That is, we have a very large State bureaucracy that buys weapons from another State bureaucracy, for in most respects Lockheed, Raytheon, Westinghouse, Boeing and Northrop are extensions of the State."

The main difference is that the United States is able to maintain a consumer society and a military-industrial complex simultaneously, whereas the Soviet Union can maintain only the military-industrial complex successfully, while its consumers languish in long lines waiting to buy basic items. This is because the Russian GNP is half that of the United States, but the Russians nonetheless spend approximately the same amount on arms as the Americans. However, America's ability to compete in consumer goods on the open market with Japan, Germany, and other countries is declining because of the priority given to weapons.

The Soviet Union has integrated its civilian and military production in the same factories, and it would be easy for them to switch from military to civilian production. In addition, its weapons tend to be much simpler than the extremely complex, sophisticated weapons produced by the United States, weapons that fewer and fewer people are adequately trained to operate. There is a Russian saying: "Equipment should be designed by geniuses to be operated by idiots."

Reagan and Weinberger justify their enormous military buildup by saying that the Soviet Union spent 44 percent more on defense in 1981 than did the United States. However, a recent report by the CIA noted that the 4 percent annual growth rate attributed to the Soviet Union's military-industrial complex may be more like 2 percent to 3 percent—and the Pentagon's Defense Intelligence Agency (DIA) has decided to accept the CIA estimate. In fact, according to Franklyn D. Holzman, professor of economics at Tufts University and a Fellow at the Russian Research Center at Harvard University, the NATO spending advantage over the past decade may be at least $600 billion. There is also evidence that the weapons production of the Soviet Union has slowed down since 1977. Senate testimony in 1983 said that Moscow had been producing a decreased number of missiles, planes, ships, and vehicles each year between 1977 and 1981, partly because the cost is too high and because it, too, is now indulging in complex weapons technology.

A stupid propaganda battle has been waged between the superpowers over the last two years. In 1981 on Weinberger's instructions, the Pentagon produced a glossy book called *Soviet Military Power*. It is full of illustrations, photographs, and graphs that describe Russian weapon systems in dramatic and sometimes admiring terms. Less than a year later, Russia responded with its own version, *Whence the Threat to Peace?*, describing American weapons in equally respectful terms. One Soviet expert said facetiously, "It's like Macy's advertising for Gimbels." Each admires and adopts the trends of the other.

Obviously, there is a symbiotic relationship between the U.S. and Russian military-industrial complexes. As the British historian E. P. Thompson said, "The American missiles prop up the Russian missiles and vice versa."

The Terminal Event

The logical consequence of the preparation for nuclear war is nuclear war. The behavior that perpetuates this race to oblivion can only be changed when people actually allow themselves to contemplate the true medical and ecological implications of such an event. Only then will they make a conscious decision to devote their lives, their fortunes, and their sacred honor to save the creation.

As you read this chapter, think of everything you hold most dear in your life—your children, parents, spouse, friends, home, the beauties of nature in the spring as she unfolds the lilacs, dogwood, wisteria, roses, magnolias, and daffodils. Then transpose the following facts into your own life, and make it real for you. After you have read this chapter, you will realize the intellectual and moral imperatives of understanding the dynamics of the arms race in all its manifestations, so that you can take the law into your own hands and use your democracy to save your world.

After the button is pressed (either by accident or by design), the bombs will begin to hit coastal cities about fifteen minutes following launch from nearby Russian submarines and thirty minutes after launch from ICBM silos in Russia. However, unless there has been a series of escalating events in Europe or elsewhere, the advance notice will not exceed five to fifteen minutes, because the satellites and radars take some time to detect the attack and relay the warning via your radio and TV sets. Of course, you may not have the radio or TV on when the attack occurs. You may be at work, or you may be sound asleep, in which case (if you live in a city) you will be instantly annihilated. In its plans for civil defense, the

281

Reagan administration has said that it may attach a special monitor to your radio or TV set, which turns on automatically to give you warning of the impending attack. I'm not sure why you would need this few minutes' warning—perhaps just to say good-bye.

To understand the magnitude of a nuclear war, we must compare the number of available targets to the number of available weapons. America has 12,000 nuclear weapons it can drop on the Soviet Union, 7,292 within thirty minutes or less, and 4,700 over several hours. Russia has 8,000 strategic bombs it can land on America or other countries, 7,673 within thirty minutes or less. Approximately 60 percent of Americans live in an area of 18,000 square miles and could be annihilated with only 300 1-megaton bombs. Consequently, there is an enormous redundancy of nuclear weapons—called overkill—because there really are not enough targets for all these hideous implements of mass destruction. For instance, the United States has a policy of not specifically targeting population areas, only military and industrial facilities. However, because most of these targets are near population areas, current U.S. war plans target all 200 major Soviet cities and 80 percent of the 886 cities with populations above 25,000. Most of these cities would be bombed by more than 10 weapons, and approximately 60 warheads would land on Moscow alone. Not a single tree or building would be left standing. Russia has similar targeting plans for the United States.

The Royal Swedish Academy of Sciences, in *Ambio* magazine, devised a conservative nuclear war plan and examined the medical and ecological consequences of such an event. Because there is such a huge number of bombs, the academy could find appropriate targets for fewer than half the strategic and tactical nuclear weapons expected to be in the arsenals of the superpowers by 1985. Nevertheless, the horrific targeting plan goes like this:

All cities with populations over 100,000 people in the United States, Canada, Western Europe, Eastern Europe, the USSR, Japan, North and South Korea, Vietnam, Australia, South Africa, and Cuba would be targeted. All of the bombs landing on these cities would be ground-burst weapons, producing enormous quantities of fallout. The bombs and yields allocated to each city would be as follows:

a) *Cities with 100,000–1 million people:* 1 megaton (three 300-kiloton warheads, one 100-kiloton warhead)
b) *Cities with 1 million–3 million people:* 3 megatons (three one-megaton warheads)
c) *Cities with 3 million or more people:* 10 megatons (ten 500-megaton, five one-megaton warheads)

And cities with populations greater than 500,000 people would be targeted in China, Southeast Asia (except Vietnam and North and South Korea), India, and Pakistan:

a) *Cities from 500,000–1 million people:* 1 megaton (three 300-kiloton warheads, one 100-kiloton warhead)
b) *Cities with 1 million–3 million people:* 3 megatons (three one-megaton warheads)
c) *Cities with 3 million or more people:* 10 megatons (ten 500-kiloton warheads, five one-megaton warheads)

In addition, all the important industries in these cities not directly destroyed are targeted with air bursts, as are all the energy supplies and the mineral resources of these countries and other areas in both the Northern and Southern hemispheres.

Military targets not close to cities are also targeted with ground bursts. This includes the airfields and ports in both the Northern and Southern hemispheres.

This outline represents a very conservative nuclear war. It is highly likely that if a nuclear war began, eventually, and probably within several days, most of the bombs of the superpowers and of England, France, and China would have been used. These total 50,000.

To give you an idea of the magnitude of the destruction I am describing, let me drop a 20-megaton bomb on a major city—of course, it could be 10 to 60 smaller hydrogen bombs or a MIRVed "footprint," but it is easier to describe the physical effects of a single large bomb. The Russians have some 100 to 200 of these weapons and almost certainly they will be used on large cities, where the leadership resides and the major control and communications centers are located.

The bomb will come in on a missile at treetop level at about 20 times the speed of sound. If it explodes at ground level on a clear day, it will release heat equivalent to that of the sun—several million degrees centigrade—in a fraction of a millionth of a second. It will dig a hole three quarters of a mile wide and 800 feet deep, converting all the people, buildings, and earth and rocks below to radioactive fallout particles, which will be shot up into the atmosphere in the mushroom cloud.

Six miles from the epicenter, every building will be flattened and every person killed. Because the human body is composed mostly of water, when it is exposed to thousands of degrees centigrade, it turns into gas and disappears. There are photographs of shadows of people on pavements in Hiroshima—that is all they left behind them.

Twenty miles from the epicenter, all people will be killed or lethally injured, and most buildings will be destroyed. The injuries will be multiple and will be superimposed one upon the other. People who are beyond the six-mile, 100 percent lethal range but still close in, who happen to glance at the flash, could have their eyes melted. John Hersey's book *Hiroshima* gives a clinical description of this event:

"There were about thirty men . . . all in exactly the same nightmarish state: Their faces were wholly burned; their eye sockets were hollow; the fluid from their melted eyes had run down their cheeks. . . . Their mouths were mere swollen, pus-covered wounds which they could not bear to stretch enough to admit the spout of a teapot. . . ."

Other people were charcoalized from the heat. In a book called *Unforgettable Fire*, Hiroshima survivors drew pictures of scenes they remembered. One was a mother holding her baby, standing on one foot, running; she and her baby had been turned into a charcoal statue.

Hundreds of thousands of injuries will be created by the enormous overpressures, which will create winds of up to 500 miles an hour. A hurricane force wind has a velocity of 74 miles an hour or more. These winds will literally pick people up off the pavement and suck them out of reinforced-concrete buildings, together with the furniture, converting them into missiles traveling at 100 miles an hour.

When they hit the nearest wall or solid object, they will be killed instantly from fractured skulls, brain trauma, fractured longbones, and internal organ injuries. The overpressures also convert bricks, mortar, and other solid objects into missiles traveling at high speeds until they hit the nearest human being. These overpressures enter the respiratory tract and lungs through the nose and mouth and produce acute pneumothorax with rupture of the lungs, with accompanying sudden death. They also rupture the tympanic membranes, or eardrums, causing deafness.

Glass is also very vulnerable to overpressures, and windows are "popcorned," or extruded outward or inward, by these forces before they shatter into millions of sharp pieces of flying glass, which, if traveling at 100 miles an hour, will penetrate human flesh and produce shocking lacerations and hemorrhage. The Pentagon has published a large book called *The Effects of Nuclear War*, in which there are complex equations and formulae calculating how far a piece of glass traveling at 100 miles an hour will penetrate human flesh.

In a major city, the huge buildings will collapse into the streets, taking their occupants with them. People will be crushed, mangled, and trapped under falling debris.

Thirty-five percent of the energy of the bomb is released as heat. This radiant heat will produce hundreds of thousands of severe burns. A patient with extensive burns is one of the most difficult challenges in medicine. Such a person requires intensive medical care day and night for at least six months, elaborate isolation techniques, operations and skin grafts every couple of days, hundreds of units of blood and blood products, antibiotics, analgesics, and sedation. Even after this intensive treatment, the patient often dies or ends up grotesquely deformed. Because of the cost and intensive medical care involved, there are only about one-thousand acute-burn beds in the whole of the United States (a country with the most sophisticated medical technology in the world).

Twenty-six miles from the epicenter, the heat from the explosion is still so intense that dry objects, such as clothes, curtains, upholstery, and dry wood, would spontaneously ignite, with the result that people could become walking, flaming torches. Wooden houses will also burn spontaneously.

Forty miles from the flash, people who reflexly glance at the incredible light will be instantly blinded by burns to the retina or back of the eyes. (Animals 345 miles from the Bikini explosions in the Marshall Islands were found to have focal retinal burns to their eyes.)

Huge fires will begin to burn over the entire area. A

Acute phase

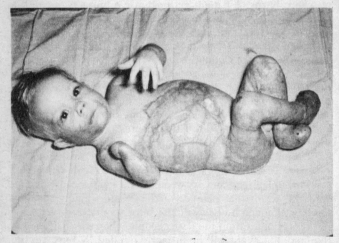

After months of medical treatment and many operations

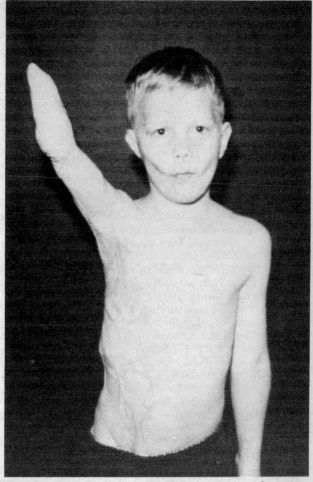

Child growing up minus a hand, and very scarred

typical American city contains five to twenty-five potential ignition points per acre. As the bomb explodes, a huge pressure wave is created, which travels at a speed greater than that of sound. It spreads out from the center of the explosion, followed by winds that transiently exceed 1,000 miles per hour. This wind creates a low-pressure area as it moves upward, and surrounding oxygen-rich air rushes in and feeds the many fires that have been ignited in houses, gasoline tanks, liquid natural gas facilities, oil tanks, and other flammable objects. This fire storm could cover an area with a radius of sixteen to twenty-one miles. Such a fire storm occurred in Hamburg after the firebombing in 1943 and produced temperatures up to 1,472°F. So intense was this heat that days later, as bomb shelters were opened, the fresh air rushing in caused the entire shelter to burst into flames.

A massive conflagration could also occur where all flammable objects ignited and the resultant fires coalesced as they were fanned by the prevailing winds to cover an area of 1,500 to 3,000 square miles. Such a conflagration increases the lethal area of bomb damage by a factor of five. Within this area, of course, fallout shelters would be useless because the fires would suck all the oxygen out of the shelters, which would fill with noxious gases, carbon dioxide, and carbon monoxide, and the occupants would be asphyxiated. The intense blast and heat would convert most shelters into crematoria.

The conservative *Ambio* study determined that in a global nuclear war, of the 1.3 billion urbanized population in the Northern Hemisphere, 750 million people will be killed instantly from blast alone, and a further 340 million will be seriously injured. Within a few minutes, the urban population will be reduced to less than one third, and more than half of the survivors will be injured. These figures do not, of course, include all the other effects of fire, radiation, and thermal burns I have described, let alone the long-term effects on the survivors.

The World Health Organization produced a report in 1983 titled "Effects of Nuclear War on Health and Health Services." They predicted that an all-out nuclear war using the nuclear stockpile of the *Ambio* scenario would result in one billion dead and one billion injured. All of the nations of the world endorsed this report save the U.S. administration and some of its close allies.

Fallout

Much of the targeted city and its people would now be radioactive dust, which would be shot up into the atmosphere and the mushroom cloud. It is difficult to calculate the size of the area that would be covered by lethal fallout because there has never really been a proper ground-burst nuclear test, but one 15-megaton bomb exploded seven feet above the Coral Reef at Bikini atoll caused substantial contamination of an area of 7,000 square miles. A 20-megaton ground-burst explosion over New York, for instance, would probably produce a similar or greater amount of fallout, and if the prevailing wind blew this fallout onto populated areas, it could probably kill about 20 million people—almost 10 percent of the U.S. population.

People die in various ways after exposure to fallout, depending upon the doses of radiation they have received. Radiation is measured in units called rads. The national background level of radiation we all receive every year is 170 millirads (1 millirad equals 1/1000th of a rad). A huge exposure of 5,000 rads or more, as will be received by people closest to the explosion, will produce the *central nervous system syndrome*. The brain cells are severely damaged, and the brain swells inside its fixed box or skull. Because there is no room to accommodate such swelling, symptoms of acute raised intracranial pressure occur—immediate excitability, severe nausea, vomiting, and diarrhea, followed by drowsiness, lethargy, tremors, delirium, frequent seizures, and finally convulsions; prostration and respiratory failure precede death, which occurs within twenty-four to forty-eight hours.

Doses greater than 1,000 rads and less than 5,000 rads will induce death from *gastrointestinal symptoms*. Such high doses of radiation produce death of the cells lining the gut, all the way from the mouth to the anus. The bone marrow that produces white blood cells to fight infection and platelets to induce clotting is also severely damaged by this dose of radiation. Consequently, mouth ulcers, colicky abdominal pain, loss of appetite, nausea and vomiting, and bloody diarrhea all occur within seven to fourteen days. Death is produced by fluid and electrolyte loss, infection, hemorrhage, and starvation.

Doses less than 500 rads are followed immediately by symptoms common to all the other syndromes: nausea, loss of appetite, fatigue, and possibly diarrhea. Fifty percent of patients experience these effects, which subside after several days' duration.

Doses of 200 to 1,000 rads cause bone-marrow death. Fifty percent of people who receive 450 rads will die; the incidence of death decreases below this dose and increases above it. Typical symptoms are immediate vomiting and diarrhea, which subside after six to seven days, followed within three to four weeks by a severe illness. People start to feel tired and weak, notice that their hair is falling out, and they become bald. They develop bloody diarrhea, bleeding under the skin and from the gums, and die from extensive internal hemorrhage and often generalized septicemia or infection.

However, all these radiation syndromes are exacerbated by mechanical injuries and burns. Severe burns lower to 100 rads the dose at which 50 percent of the population dies. Infants, children, and old people are also more sensitive to these lethal effects of radiation than are healthy adults, and 50 percent may die at doses of 200 rads.

Doctors will be killed in higher proportions than the average population because they work and reside in heavily targeted areas. A study done by Physicians for Social Responsibility and published in *The New England Journal of Medicine* in 1962 estimated that after a 20-megaton attack on Boston, there would be one physician for 17,000 injured patients. If that doctor then worked twenty hours a day for eight to fourteen days, he or she could see each patient only once for a ten-minute period (if they could be identified among the debris of the flattened city). This would mean that virtually all the patients would die with such cursory care. Of course, the doctor would be exposing himself or herself to lethal levels of radiation during that initial period. This, in turn, would decrease the number of physicians available to treat people in the coming months and years.

All the people within the bombed areas will die alone, from a combination of trauma, burns, radiation illness, and starvation, often trapped under girders, rafters, and beams in the most intense agony, with no relatives and no help from doctors or health workers even to give them pain-relieving drugs. The federal government has, indeed, stockpiled 70,000 pounds of morphine in case there is a nuclear war. Some officials would like to increase this amount to 100,000 pounds, but the Reagan administration early in 1983 decided to defer the purchase of more morphine to avoid frightening people. This drug is stored in central depots, is certainly not distributed to the few people who know how to use it following a nuclear attack, and will obviously be useless.

After I describe this scenario, many people accuse me of making them feel uncomfortable. I believe it is therapeutic to induce the feeling of severe discomfort in people *before* a nuclear war, so they will be motivated to prevent such an event—the final epidemic of the human race.

You have just read the description of one bomb landing on one city, but there are enough bombs to target all towns and cities with populations down to 10,000 people in both the United States and the USSR. Russia and America also target the energy facilities of the other country, which include the nuclear power plants. Steven Fetter and Kosta Tsipis wrote an article in *Scientific American* describing the consequences of a 1-megaton bomb exploding on a 1,000-megawatt nuclear reactor (standard size). If the radiation in the reactor and the cooling pools containing spent fuel rods were released into the atmosphere, it could contaminate an area the size of West Germany. In fact, the *Ambio* scenario states that an attack just on the numerous nuclear reactors in Western Europe and North America would render these and neighboring countries uninhabitable, by ordinary radiation standards, for years or even decades. If the reprocessing plants (which reprocess spent reactor fuel) and the huge storage tanks containing vast quantities of radioactive waste were also hit, this would greatly increase the radiation dose over many years.

In a full-scale nuclear war, it is probable that the United States would be covered by lethal fallout for the first forty-eight hours, and the subsequent consequences would be so devastating that within thirty days up to ninety percent of Americans could be dead. A similar magnitude of devastation would also be visited upon the Soviet Union, Europe, England, and much of the other territory described in the *Ambio* scenario.

For the survivors in both the targeted and nontargeted countries alike, life would not be worth living. Nikita Khrushchev once said that after a nuclear war, "the living will envy the dead."

Disease

The immediate aftereffects will depend very much on the season. If the holocaust occurs in the summer months, it has been postulated by the U.S. Forest Service that up to 80 percent of the United States could be consumed in fire. Millions upon millions of decaying human and animal bodies will fill the air with the most unbelievable stench, and as they decay, bacteria and viruses will multiply in the dead flesh. The high levels of background radiation will cause mutations in these organisms, so even bacteria that live in harmony with the human body could become more dangerous and virulent. Because birds are very sensitive to radiation, it is possible that most birds in the heavily targeted countries will die. Meanwhile, the insects, which are extremely resistant to high levels of radiation, will multiply prolifically in the absence of their natural predators. Trillions of flies, fleas, lice, and cockroaches will crawl and fly unimpeded over the dead bodies, transmitting disease from the dead to the living. One Hiroshima victim recalled that there were fleas and lice everywhere after the bombs dropped. Rodents will also multiply in these unhygienic conditions. All sewage-disposal and sanitation systems will be destroyed, and the cities of the world will become perfect culture media for pathogens (bacteria, viruses, rodents, and insects).

In 1944 during World War II, the U.S. Army entered Manila and faced the problem of burying 39,000 bodies of Japanese and Filipinos killed during the preceding weeks. It was soon found that American troops were unable to withstand the psychological aspects of this work. "With a few exceptions, nausea, vomiting and loss of appetite occurred within a few days." Local laborers were recruited at double pay to place the dead in large pits; nevertheless, the burial of these 39,000 dead, unhampered by such complications as radioactivity and lack of equipment, required eight weeks.

The unfortunate survivors will be extremely susceptible to contracting disease. A radiation dose as low as 50 rads can diminish the normal functioning of white blood cells, which fight infection. Such a dose will be rapidly accumulated by people who are not in lethal areas of fallout but who are on the periphery or in rural areas. Although the radioactive elements in fallout decay rapidly, even low background levels of radiation emitted from fallout, accumulated on the ground, will quickly add up to a significant dose if people stay outside for many hours.

It is postulated that most supplies of antibiotics and vaccines will have been destroyed, and there will be few if any medical personnel available to treat the survivors.

Susceptibility to infectious disease is further enhanced by a lack of first-class protein, by malnutrition or starvation, and by unsanitary conditions.

It is predicted that epidemics of diseases now controlled by mass-immunization programs will spread among the non-immunized population: diseases such as polio, tetanus, whooping cough, measles, influenza, typhus, smallpox, and diphtheria.

In addition, many diseases that are relatively rare in a pre-attack world will become common, and other diseases common in the Third World countries will spread rapidly in the post-attack developed nations. This is because excellent sanitation and a high standard of living, including immediate therapy with antibiotics, have deprived most people of routine exposure to ordinary diseases and an opportunity to develop appropriate immunities to most of these infections. These diseases include cholera, malaria, plague, rabies, Shigella, typhoid fever, yellow fever, amoebic dysentery, botulism, food poisoning, hepatitis A, meningococcal meningitis, pneumonia, and tuberculosis.

Plague is a good example of a disease with an extremely low incidence in the United States, although it has been responsible for epidemics over the past 3,500 years and in the twentieth century has killed 12 million people. However, it is endemic in wild rodents in eleven western states—more than thirty types of rodents and rabbits have been found to be infected. A nuclear war would create ideal conditions for plague to proliferate. Before a nuclear war, many people are to be evacuated, according to the Federal Emergency Management Agency, to the western states, and they will live in earth-covered shelters, which will provide ideal conditions for transmission of plague from rodents such as rats. Rodents are quite resistant to plague and consequently harbor chronic infection for years. As rodents die from the effects of fallout, starvation, etc., the fleas will leave the bodies in search of other hosts, including man.

It is predicted the rat population in bombed cities will

increase enormously because of the intensely unhygienic conditions. A growth rate of 3 percent to 11 percent per week is expected in the rat population. Rat-transmitted plague is called bubonic plague, with infection and swelling of the lymph glands. Under stressful conditions, this form of the disease can change to a virulent pneumonia called pneumonic plague, which is then highly contagious among human beings. This disease can spread rapidly under conditions of crowding, which will be inevitable in postwar fallout shelters. Some people believe that plague probably represents "the major national threat among the set of vectorborne diseases."

Many of these disease epidemics could be transferred to nontargeted countries by insects, where a highly susceptible population will guarantee widespread contagion.

In Europe, American plans call for the integrated battle-field, which means simultaneous use of conventional, nuclear, chemical, and biological weapons. Therefore, any survivors from a nuclear war on the European battlefield will quickly die from the dreadful effects of these biological and chemical weapons.

Evacuation

The Federal Emergency Management Agency plans to evacuate people from "risk areas" to "host areas," that is, from targeted cities to small country towns and villages. They say they will need three to five days advance notice and they plan eventually to be able to evacuate 250 cities with populations of more than 50,000 people. That is two thirds of the U.S. population or a total of 145 million people.

This apparently will be done at the time of heightened international tension, such as a conflict in the Persian Gulf, Central America, Eastern Europe, or signs that Russia is evacuating her cities. These evacuation plans require eight to ten years to complete at current funding levels, and the sheltering components will require another eight to ten years' planning. Therefore, they will not be complete until the late-1990s, when American demographic patterns will have altered sufficiently to render the plans obsolete. Also, if we have been unsuccessful in arms control and disarmament, Russia will by then have enough bombs to blanket America with blast as well as radiation effects, and thus to render these plans totally irrelevant.

The plans are ludicrous anyway because the Soviet satellites can observe all activities in America and vice versa. If they see that America is evacuating its cities, especially with all the new first-strike weapons sitting on the shelf, the Soviet leaders will naturally conclude that America is preparing for a first-strike nuclear war, at which point they could, in their fear and anxiety, initiate their own first strike against both the military targets, the evacuating populations, and the evacuated cities themselves. Evacuation in this context is an open invitation to nuclear war. Anyway, it is no use evacuating because Russia can see where the people are going and just retarget its weapons. It will know in advance, actually, because these plans are public knowledge. Furthermore, if a government decided to evacuate all these people and no attack occurred, the American people would never participate in such an exercise again.

Apparently Russia has similar evacuation plans which, for the reasons described above, are just as stupid. Furthermore, I have traveled in the Soviet Union, and very few people have cars. The roads are mostly dirt tracks, which are extremely uncomfortable to travel on, and people would be reduced to walking. If either the United States or USSR had to evacuate in the winter, people would find it impossible to dig holes or shelters in the frozen ground, and they would literally freeze to death out in the tundra or U.S. countryside.

FEMA has decided that during this three-to-five day preemptive period before a nuclear war, the evacuating population will remain calm, ordered, and well-behaved. This is a totally unrealistic expectation because I know that I would be in a state of total panic and doom, and there would probably be chaos throughout the land. Nevertheless, we are told to remain calm and not to forget to take our bankbooks, credit cards, insurance policies, and wills, and we must submit change-of-address cards to the post office. We must not take with us drugs or alcohol. As Dr. Herbert Abrams, professor of radiology at Harvard Medical School, has said, that is exactly what he might like to have when he is trapped in a massive traffic jam on the highway waiting to be vaporized. Also, pets are to stay at home with an adequate supply of food and water.

There are actually plans for car breakdowns on the highway. You are to move your car to the side of the road, get out your shovel—which you should remember to take—and dig a large hole and drive the car over the top of the hole. Cover the car and hole with a tarpaulin and hide underneath until the bombs have stopped falling. After some days or weeks, you get out your Geiger counter and measure the ambient radiation levels and, if they are safe, you may leave your shelter!

In most cases, the people in the designated host areas will not have been adequately informed of their roles in the event of nuclear war. They are to hospitably receive thousands or hundreds of thousands of people in their small villages and offer them shelter in their basements. There are plans available to teach people how to make their basements radiationproof. To do this, one piles tons of dirt onto the roof of the basement or the first floor of the house. Unfortunately, earth is extremely heavy, and many floors will collapse under such an enormous weight.

T. K. Jones, who is the under secretary for engineering in the Pentagon, has determined that all people really need to do is dig a hole, cover it with two doors, which presumably they detach from the nearest available house, and pile three feet of dirt on top. T. K. says, "It is the dirt that does it." The question one could logically ask is "Who will put the dirt on top once you have safely entered your hole?"

Fallout Shelters

But realistically, let us talk about fallout shelters after a nuclear war. As previously explained, within targeted areas most people will have been asphyxiated and killed in their fallout shelters. If you live in a rural, nontargeted area and you happen to be awake and listening to your radio or TV and you hear the emergency signal to tell you a nuclear war is about to occur, you will have at the very most fifteen minutes to reach the nearest fallout shelter, if there is one, before the bombs start exploding and releasing their fallout. Once you get into the shelter, you will not be able to reemerge for a period of from three weeks to three months—or even more near highly radioactive cities or areas, depending upon the background radiation levels. In most places where people live and work, typical one-week doses would reach tens of thousands of rads. Here even shelters with high protection factors will not protect people from lethal doses of radiation. (Doses will be lower in some rural areas.)

Conditions in these shelters will be horrendous. They will probably be crowded with adults and children, some of whom have entered after the nuclear war and may have already received a lethal dose of radiation. During the shelter stay, these people will develop vomiting with liquid bloody diarrhea and die down there. Of course, there will be no adequate sanitation, no toilets or sewage system. At best there may be a small chemical unit. People will then have to live with decomposing bodies and revolting sanitary conditions. They cannot go outside or they themselves could be exposed to lethal levels of radiation.

The shelters will have various protection factors (PF), meaning they may be effective at radiation shielding depending upon the thickness of dirt and concrete above them. Despite adequate PFs, they will need to be equipped with air-ventilation facilities that will filter out the alpha- and beta- and gamma-emitting isotopes from the fallout. Otherwise the people will become contaminated inside the shelter by inhalation or ingestion of these radioactive materials—which, incidentally, have no taste or smell and may be invisible or look like dust. These air-filtration systems are not widely developed for commercial sale. Furthermore, the blowers and fans could be rendered inoperable by overpressures of one pound per square inch (which is minimal overpressure created on the very periphery of the area of deleterious effects from a nuclear explosion), and the systems will be blocked by electric power failure. There will be no electric power after a nuclear war because the EMP emitted from the explosions will have rendered all power stations, cables, and electric lines inoperable, apart from the fact that all the power stations are targeted.

If the war occurs during the winter, the people could develop severe hypothermia in the shelters at temperatures of 40°F. or less, and they would freeze to death. In the summer, heat and humidity would become unbearable in the absence of a continuous flow of fresh air. Stagnant, foul-smelling air with crowding, dead bodies, and poor sanitation will encourage the spread of microorganisms. People will be susceptible to disease because the average person needs one gallon of water per day to maintain basic health, but almost certainly the water supply will become sparse or almost nil. Insects will proliferate both inside and outside the shelters. Diseases that thrive in such shelter conditions are meningococcal meningitis and septicemia, influenza and viral respiratory diseases and pneumonia, gastrointestinal disease with vomiting and diarrhea, and hepatitis.

The supply of food almost certainly will be inadequate. It is probable that many people will die without ever emerging from their shelters. A study published in *The Journal of Health Physics* recommended that old people be sent outside as food gatherers, because they would not live long enough to die of leukemia and cancer as a result of their high radiation exposure. Such a scheme, it was claimed, would spare the children and young adults who are very susceptible to the carcinogenic effects of radiation.

Afterward

A colleague of mine had a nightmare recently. She is an Emergency Room physician and she dreamed there had been a nuclear war and Boston had been demolished. She had, however, reached the fallout shelter and remained inside for the adequate period of time until the radiation levels had become relatively safe. She put on her radiation-resistant suit and had her oxygen and food supply strapped to her back, and as she was undoing the hermetically sealed hatches on the shelter, she had two very disturbing thoughts: Her plans were to walk to the west of Massachusetts to find her parents, but she realized there would be no landmarks in Boston, so she would be unable to find her way. Then she thought of the millions of decaying corpses and she realized that as a physician she could not face the devastation. It then became apparent that what she lacked was an adequate supply of sleeping tablets.

What, indeed, will the world be like as the few survivors emerge from their underground graves? There will be millions of decaying human and animal bodies. More than 90 percent of the urban housing will have been destroyed. There will be no available food—no one to transport it, no transportation mechanisms—roads and railways will have been destroyed—and no one to coordinate distribution or even determine the areas of greatest need where the survivors have gathered. Ninety percent of the American fuel supply will have been destroyed since all oil refineries and storage facilities are targeted. If the survivors do obtain any food, it will probably be raw grain, which needs to be processed or cooked before it is edible—but there will be no processing facilities and very few places to cook. Much of this food will already have been contaminated by the fallout.

Many of these people will be severely disturbed psychologically. After Hiroshima and Nagasaki, most of the survivors felt a pervasive sense of guilt that they had survived and their relatives and friends were dead. Many of them still talk about this. It has been estimated that after such a massive disaster, 12 percent to 25 percent of the survivors will develop acute psychoses. (It is well known that people exposed to significant psychological stress will all develop symptoms. The intensity of the stress is more important in determining the nature of these symptoms than is the preexisting personality.) Seventy-five percent would be dazed and stunned and 12 percent to 25 percent of individuals might remain effective. In settings of massive destruction, people become so isolated that psychoses derived from sensory deprivation may occur, and these symptoms will be exacerbated by fatigue and physical trauma. Survivors of the Japanese bombings also experienced pervasive images of the horror and continual fears of the radiation effects, with primal anxieties about cancer and leukemia.

Such severe grief and mental disturbance will persist as they attempt to grow their own food on radioactive land without machinery, fertilizers, or insecticides. Even one year after the nuclear holocaust, the soil may still be so radioactive that continuous exposure during the arduous, primitive food-growing process could expose the people to doses that would give them low sperm counts and anovulatory, disturbed menstrual cycles. Considering the almost troglodyte conditions under which people will have to live, will any of them be able to overcome their grief and severe depression sufficiently to instigate sexual relations to reproduce the species? Fertility will be low and spontaneous abortion and infant mortality will be high. (There will be no medical care available.) People will also be aware that their pervasive exposure to radiation both immediately after the war and chronically thereafter will almost certainly increase their chances of developing leukemia five to ten years later or solid cancers fifteen to fifty years after the initial exposure.

Furthermore, the incidence of genetic diseases will rise over all future generations of humans, animals, and plants. The conservative *Ambio* scenario, which for simplicity used only the accumulated seven-day fallout dose, estimated that such a war would induce 5.4 million to 12.8 million fatal cancers eight to twenty years after the war in the Northern Hemisphere, and within one hundred years, 6.4 million to 16.3 million people in the Northern Hemisphere would suffer genetic defects attributable to their ancestors' exposure in 1985. If these scientists had chosen a twenty-five-year accumulated dose, which, of course, is more realistic, the incidence of cancer and genetic defects would be hugely increased. They also estimated that of those people who do not die from massive exposure to radiation, between 3 and 5 million North Americans are likely to be permanently sterilized by fallout—if, indeed, these people survive the other horrors visited upon them in the aftermath of nuclear war.

When we think of nuclear war, the long-term ecological consequences are probably more important than the acute effects because the state of life on the planet may be permanently altered by such an event. Let us consider the known consequences, but I stress there are many as yet unknown effects which could seriously influence the eventual outcome.

There is only a thirty days' supply of food in the world at any one time, supplied to many Third World nations by Canada, the United States, Argentina, and Australia. Because most of these countries are targeted and because distribution of food depends upon ships, fuel, and people to load, unload, and pilot the ships, and because most of the grain will be destroyed during the war anyway, hundreds of millions of people in the Third World will die from starvation in the first couple of months. There will be total collapse of the international trade and exchange networks. Seven hundred fifty million immediate deaths in the Northern Hemisphere would become 1 billion to 3 billion in tropical regions and in the Southern Hemisphere. (That is three quarters of the earth's population.)

People in the targeted countries will also die from famine because it is possible that most of the crops will have been burned in the continental fires. If the attack occurs in the winter, some people figure that new crops could be planted in the spring. However, it is not easy to estimate how much grain will be left to plant after the war, or where it will be, or who in fact will plant it. Only 6 percent of the U.S. population is currently involved in agriculture, so the majority of the surviving population will have had no experience in farming. Furthermore, these people will have suffered dreadfully during the cold of the winter, living in unheated shelters, exposed to malnutrition, disease, and psychological illness from the loss of their relatives and friends. They will have to hand-till the radioactive land since 99 percent of the U.S. oil-refining capacities will be destroyed, and there won't be fuel to run farm machinery. No fertilizers will be available and no pesticides. Since the insects will have proliferated in the trillions and mutated to become more virile, the crops will almost certainly be failures. If the attack comes in the spring, the tender new shoots will be killed. The attack could destroy 70 percent of the U.S. crop, as well as Soviet and European crops and those of other vulnerable nations. An attack prior to harvest may not induce so much damage— unless the country is covered with fire—but the land may well be too radioactive to harvest.

Crops grown in following years will present other problems—if, indeed, all the seed has not been eaten by the starving survivors. Plants concentrate the radioactive elements that have landed on the soil as fallout. These elements then concentrate even more in a nonuniform fashion in various organs of the human body, exposing people to the threat of cancers years later.

More than 50 percent of the grazing livestock will be killed and more than one quarter of the large farm animals fed on stored food will die immediately. These estimates are based only on blast and fallout effects.

Other long-term ecological effects will ravage the land.

Ozone

In 1975, the National Academy of Sciences conducted a study called "Long-Term Worldwide Effects of Multiple Nuclear Weapons Detonations." They estimated that in a 10,000-megaton nuclear war in the Northern Hemisphere, if many of the weapons exploded were 1-megaton or bigger, 30 percent to 70 percent of the stratospheric ozone layer could be destroyed in the Northern Hemisphere and 20 percent to 40 percent in the Southern Hemisphere. Such big bombs had to be involved because past atmospheric data have shown that nuclear clouds from detonations with yields greater than 1 megaton penetrate into the upper atmosphere or stratosphere. There are approximately 2,800 bombs in the nuclear arsenals of the world today with yields of this size. Both superpowers are moving toward smaller, more accurate bombs, but the old ones will probably still be used in an all-out nuclear war.

These large explosions oxidize vast quantities of nitrogen in the air to form nitrous oxide. Depending on size, altitude, and conditions of the explosion, there would be a release of about 5,000 tons of nitrous oxide per megaton. These nitrous oxides would be injected with the fireball and mushroom cloud into the stratosphere high above the earth, where there is a layer of ozone molecules (each molecule composed of three atoms of oxygen). At ground level this layer would be only 3 millimeters thick at normal temperature and pressure. The nitrous oxide molecules combine chemically with the ozone molecules and destroy them. The lowest levels of ozone after such destruction would occur six months after the war, and the ozone would not be totally replenished for ten years.

The function of the ozone is to protect multicellular organisms from the damaging effects of ultraviolet (UV) light, which is emitted from the sun. Before multicellular organisms were formed, there was no ozone. Then tiny unicellular organisms learned how to create oxygen by metabolizing carbon dioxide through photosynthesis. As the oxygen formed, it rose up into the stratosphere to form the ozone layer. Then, as the lethal levels of UV light at ground level began to diminish, multicellular organisms began to evolve.

Increased UV light will induce a variety of pathological and ecological effects. It is the normal quantity of UV light that induces sunburn at the beach and snowblindness during the winter. However, if the UV light increased dramatically in the Northern Hemisphere, fair-skinned people could develop incapacitating sunburn within ten minutes, and blistering or even lethal third-degree sunburn with thirty to sixty minutes' exposure. Such a hazard would severely restrict outside activity by the survivors. UV radiation could be increased tenfold in the Northern Hemisphere three months after a nuclear war and could be doubled in the Southern Hemisphere for a period of up to two years after the war.

Eyes. UV light is also very damaging to the eyes of humans, animals, birds, and insects. Eyes are very sensitive, precise, highly specialized organs. Several kinds of eye lesion are induced by increased UV light:

• *Photophthalmia* or snowblindness, resulting in the temporary loss of sight for several days. This condition is very disabling and painful. It can be avoided by wearing goggles, but very few people own a set of goggles and those few will almost certainly be destroyed in a nuclear war.

• *Conjunctivitis* or painful red inflammation of the membranes surrounding the cornea.

• *Photokeratitis* or extremely painful and debilitating damage to the cornea (the clear curved plaque that overlies the pupil and iris). Repeated UV injury eventually causes scarring of the cornea and blindness resulting from opaque corneas.

• UV light can also damage the lens and the iris, producing *cataracts* or opaque areas in the lens causing blindness. Among Australian aborigines, who live in intense sunlight for years, significant correlations have been found between cataract prevalence and sunshine, or UV intensity.

Birds, animals, and insects will all be susceptible to these eye injuries, and so will man because, in fact, the use of sunglasses may be counterproductive. Many sunglasses absorb visible light more than UV light. This causes dilatation of the pupils, thus allowing the eyes to absorb greater amounts of dangerous UV light.

If the birds, animals, and insects are blinded over time, much of the ecosystem will collapse: The bees will not be able to fertilize the crops, etc.

Skin. The National Academy of Sciences study also reported that a 50 percent loss in the ozone shield, lasting three years, would increase the incidence of skin cancer and malignant melanoma 3 percent to 30 percent at mid-latitude, the effect of which would persist for forty years. Of course, fair-skinned people will be more susceptible to these effects than dark-skinned people.

UV light induces the production of vitamin D in the skin,

which is a normal, healthy process. However, such an increase in UV light would raise the levels of production of vitamin D in man, animals, and birds, inducing vitamin D toxicity. This can cause kidney and bone damage and even renal failure. The NAS report states, "We do not know whether man and other vertebrate animals could tolerate an increased vitamin D synthesis that might result from a large and rapid increase in UV exposure." They urgently recommended further study of this problem.

Microorganisms. Carl Sagan has stated that recent scientific evidence shows that the single-celled organisms, or bacteria, which live in the soil and upon which all other life depends, are extremely sensitive to the effects of UV light. Because this radiation is so toxic to bacteria, it is used frequently for sterilization of equipment. These microorganisms form the base of the pyramid of life, with man at the apex, and should they be destroyed after a nuclear war, the pyramid of life will collapse.

Plankton and algae. The oceanic web of life depends upon its smallest organisms, which live at the surface of the sea. Recent data show that these single-celled or small multicellular organisms are extremely sensitive to UV light. Some wait until evening hours to divide because their replicating DNA is very much exposed to the lethal effects of UV light during cell division. Some have enzymes by which damage done during the day is repaired at night, and some dive below the surface of the water if the sun appears from behind a cloud. It has been found that if the ozone were decreased by 60 percent this diving organism would be killed mid-dive. The information about this subject is patchy, but it could pose a most serious threat to much of life in the sea and on earth. These life forms produce much of the oxygen which would replenish the ozone layer. Should they be destroyed by the increase in UV light, it is probable that the ozone would never reaccumulate. Crops and plants have also been found to be damaged by UV light. The sensitivity varies according to the species.

Climatic Change

While reduction of the stratospheric ozone layer would allow more heat from the sun to enter the atmosphere, the decreased ozone levels would also prevent much of the heat that is radiated up from the earth from being reflected back to the atmosphere. The combined result of these two dynamics could be a cooling of the earth by 1°F., which would have serious ecological implications. Further, the effect of the subsequent cooling of the upper troposphere and lower stratosphere is likely to be more severe than the cooling at the surface of the earth. This cooling could cause alterations in the cloud cover, which could also influence the climate. These two events, together with the cooling induced by the injection of vast quantities of dust and smoke into the atmosphere, could cool the temperature of the earth by 2°F.

Another scenario, envisioned by *Ambio,* is an all-out nuclear war using hydrogen bombs of a smaller yield than the 1-megaton or more used by the National Academy of Sciences. In this event it is unlikely that significant quantities of nitrogen oxide would initially be injected into the stratosphere to cause the ozone depletion previously described. However, the most significant effect on the atmosphere will occur from the enormous number of huge fires—forests, oil wells, military installations, urban and industrial centers, and gas-production facilities. Such fires would create sufficient quantities of airborne particulate matter in the lower atmosphere, or troposphere, to screen out the sun for weeks or months, thus reducing or even eliminating agricultural crops over large areas of the Northern Hemisphere, so that no food could be grown by the survivors. Dark aerosol deposits would probably kill any plants that did manage to grow.

The vast quantities of nitrogen oxide created from the smaller nuclear explosions and from the fires would cause the rain to become extremely acidic, with a pH of less than 4. It is becoming well known that acid rain kills trees, plants, and aquatic life. Nitrogen oxide in the low-lying troposphere would also induce ozone production. This new tropospheric ozone would cause severe photochemical pollution like that in Los Angeles, which could also severely damage crops.

Thus, the troposphere would become heavily polluted by a toxic dark smog consisting of particulate matter from the fires and aerosolized dirt from the ground-burst nuclear explosions, the nitrogen oxides, and ozone produced by the nitrogen oxides, dioxins, furans, and cyanide.

If this smog induced a reduction of solar penetration to

the earth by a factor of 100, it is quite possible that most of the plants in more than half the Northern Hemisphere oceans would die. Similar darkening of the planet is thought to have occurred 65 million years ago during the Cretaceous-Tertiary boundary era, when a large extraterrestrial body hit the earth and probably caused the widespread and massive extinctions evident in geological history.

But if the ground fires were extremely powerful, the flames could reach up into the stratosphere, carrying nitrogen oxide with them, thus causing further reduction of stratospheric ozone. Another means of upward transport of nitrogen oxide could occur when the heavy, dark, aerosol, low-lying layer was heated by the sun, thus setting up convection currents and wind systems that could transport a large amount of the fire effluents into the stratosphere.

The Nuclear Winter

Since this chapter was written, Carl Sagan, Paul Ehrlich, and their colleagues have published two papers in *Science* that show that the dense cloud of smoke produced by urban fires, forest fires, and burning oil wells could blanket the Northern Hemisphere for many months, causing cooling by 13°F., even in midsummer. This severe temperature change would occur within three to four weeks after a major nuclear exchange, and light from the sun would be reduced to 17 percent of normal. At least a year would be required for light and temperature values to return to normal conditions. The subfreezing dark conditions in the Northern Hemisphere could destroy the biological support systems of civilization, with massive starvation and death from hypothermia and thirst (most fresh water could be frozen to a depth of three feet).

Sagan found that radiation levels would be much higher than previously calculated, as more radioactive nuclear debris remained in the troposphere and fell to the ground as intermediate-term fallout. Thirty percent of the Northern Hemisphere would receive a dose greater than 250 rems (rem is a unit of radiation dosage—Roentgen equivalent man), and 50 percent of northern mid-latitudes would receive a dose greater than 100 rems.

Because of the large temperature gradients at the equator, it is predicted that the smoky cloud would move rapidly down to the Southern Hemisphere, inducing marked cooling and subsequent global disruption of the biosphere.

It is possible, according to the new data, that the population of man could be reduced to prehistoric levels, but the extinction of *Homo sapiens* cannot be excluded. Certainly extinction of a large fraction of the earth's animals, plants, and microorganisms seems inevitable.

These biological effects were calculated from the *Ambio* nuclear-war scenario of a 5,000-megaton exchange, but the threshold for such global cooling was found to be an exchange of only 100 megatons.

Tnus we hold in our hands the ability to destroy most of creation. It could happen any day. We will take with us not only all present earthly life, but all past generations and the magnificent heritage they bequeathed: Beethoven, Mozart, Bach, Rembrandt, Picasso, Dickens, Shakespeare, Gothic cathedrals, beautiful ancient monuments of Europe and Asia. We will also have destroyed most of the germ cells that would have produced all future generations of humans, animals, and plants.

Etiology: Missile Envy and Other Psychopathology

The bombs are not the cause of the problem, but only the symptom of the deranged thought processes of man's mind. To promote the cause of "strength" in the nuclear age by arguing for more bombs is a classic example of prenuclear thinking. Before 1945, it was true that the more conventional weapons the country possessed, the safer it was. Since 1945, any attempt by one country to engineer a superiority in numbers of nuclear weapons has been followed by the other country's matching the numbers games. Thus, as America has led the arms race, so Russia has inevitably and inexorably copied and followed. Ironically, by participating in the crazy logic of nuclear-war-fighting plans and scenarios, America has engineered her own suicide. Before nuclear weapons, the United States was absolutely invulnerable to the threat of military invasion, with two huge oceans to the east and west and two friendly countries to the north and south. Before nuclear weapons, there was never any real attempt to even develop antiaircraft defenses. It is still true that no country could ever hope to invade the United States. But, by following America's lead, Russia could now obliterate this great country in one to two hours.

The truth is that America has placed its destiny in the hands of a few aged, frightened Russian politicians, who are being continuously provoked by the threat of ever more destabilizing weapons and delivery systems and plans to fight and win a protracted nuclear war. When I was in Russia in 1979, our delegation met with high-ranking Soviet officials, including the two diplomats who negotiated SALT II. They were very worried about the threat of nuclear war and terribly concerned about the planned deployment of the ground-launched cruise missiles and Pershing II's in Europe. They talked constantly about World War II and their 20 million dead, and they seemed more frightened of China than of the United States—probably because of their long history of previous invasions by Mongols and Tartars over hundreds of years. They have virtually no important allies in the world, and I think they are acutely aware of the fact that if they invaded Western Europe, most of the people in the Warsaw Pact countries would fight against them. Russia is ringed by countries that harbor American military bases, missiles, nuclear weapons, listening posts, and intelligence systems.

As a physician, I have admitted clinically paranoid and frightened patients into acute medical wards. From long experience, I learned that it is medically contraindicated to threaten a paranoid patient. I abstained from sticking needles into them or hurting them because they might have been provoked to harm themselves or me. Instead, I attempted in a therapeutic way to work within their mental frame of reference, and tried to understand what was really happening in their troubled minds. Such an approach took a lot of courage on my part and also immense patience and love, but it usually paid off. The patients would open up, sharing their troubled thoughts, so I could then engage them in a constructive therapeutic dialogue.

I would, therefore, humbly suggest that it is definitely medically contraindicated to frighten the Russian leaders because if America really provokes their anxieties and fears, they could in their paranoia initiate nuclear war. Americans must also learn to understand that other countries think and feel differently than they do. We must learn to put ourselves in other people's shoes and understand their points of view. For instance, would America tolerate the position it has placed Russia in, as described in previous chapters?

It is also imperative that Americans start to learn about the history and culture of other countries, including the Soviet Union. The behavior of nation states is very much conditioned by their past experiences—the same way that individual human beings are products of their genetic makeup (genotype) and the way their emotional environments have shaped their behavior, particularly during the childhood period. The Russian people and their leaders behave in rigid, uncompromising ways, as they have done for hundreds of years.

They have a proud cultural history of great art, music, and literature—a long history steeped in tradition. But they were a nation of millions of starving serfs, a wealthy middle class, and an extremely rich nobility until the revolution in 1917. Unfortunately, the grand ideals upon which that revolution was based, centered primarily on care for others and the society, collapsed in ruins as Stalin took over the leadership in 1929. This man was an autocratic, paranoid ruler, who once again intimidated the Russian people into a serf-czar mentality.

After years of internal bloodshed and massacres, Stalin's reign of intimidation was replaced by a series of rigid unimaginative leaders, who declined to move far from the authoritarian rules of Stalin—although without the bloodshed. Over the last ten years or so Russia has moderated its behavior toward its citizens. Where once dissidents were killed automatically, they now survive, proclaim their views, and are even permitted to hold interviews with the eager Western press. Jewish emigration fluctuates in a way often related to international pressures and events. However, there is no unemployment problem in the Soviet Union; every person has employment; all have access to free medical care and free education, and the price of food has remained low for twenty years. All citizens are automatically given several weeks' holiday a year, and the standard of living is incomparably higher than in prerevolutionary days when millions of serfs were starving.

Many scholars of present-day Russia are convinced that the leaders are sincere in their attempts to negotiate the control and reduction of nuclear weapons. These scholars are also convinced that if the Soviet leaders felt less intimidated and threatened by the hostile actions and words of the U.S. government, they would feel free to allow increased moderation in their Warsaw Pact countries, to permit more emigration of Jews, and possibly to relax some of the rigid internal restrictions placed upon their own people.

The Tribal Mentality

Why do nations feel obliged to act with such hostility and self-righteousness toward each other? Perhaps the mobilization of people in nation states had its origin in the dynamics of the tribe. Millions of years ago, tribes needed to live together in tightly knit bands which were defensive and aggressive toward any other warring or threatening tribe. Perhaps the tribal mentality was stamped into our genes as a product of evolution and a Darwinian "survival of the fittest" necessity.

However, this tribal mentality, which once guaranteed survival, is anachronistic in the age of mass killing and genocide. Nationalism is just a sophisticated term for tribalism. The same feelings are provoked when the "Star Spangled Banner" is played—pride, unity, comradeship, self-righteousness, and a certain sense that we would fight for the principles enunciated in that song. National anthems and nationalistic songs in most countries in the world evoke similar feelings of tribalism. If Darwin's theory is to prove correct, it is high time for those people who understand that nationalism now means possible extinction of one's own country, as well as the human race, to become leaders among the human family and direct these parochial instincts toward a sense of altruism, pride, compassion, and love for the family of man.

As I work with millions of people, teaching them the medical effects of nuclear war, I find that their instinct for survival overcomes their primitive instinct of nationalism. The instinct for survival is the strongest physiological drive we possess, being more powerful than those for eating or reproduction. When people are faced with imminent prospects of extinction because of their primitive tribalistic drives, they suddenly become transformed as they realize that in order to save themselves and those they love, they must help and love others who are totally alien to them. It seems that these feelings are the real yearnings that each person fundamentally possesses within his or her own soul. We were not put on earth to make ourselves happy. The path to true happiness lies in helping one another.

I have often thought in my more regressive moods that if the Martians invaded earth, all nations would unite in a self-righteous comradeship to do battle with the aliens. Will the alien threat that unites us all today—the omnipresent threat of instant annihilation at any minute, hour, day, month, or year—have the power to save us?

*   *   *

As I discuss the psychiatric aspects of the nuclear arms race, I will divide society into various segments, each of which seems to operate with a separate psychological agenda. Some of the themes I will be discussing I have gleaned from other people's thinking, but many of them are mine and may or may not ultimately prove to be correct.

There is a theory that man is an evolutionary aberrant not designed to survive in the long run. The brain of man developed and evolved in a very short evolutionary time span. In fact, man is a wondrous beast. As soon as he stood on his hind limbs and developed an opposing thumb, which enabled him to hold tools and weapons, he became a threat to other living creatures, including his own species. Certainly, the rapidly developing intellect couched in the huge neocortex of the brain allowed him to indulge in strategic killings of dangerous animals and threatening tribes. It was probably through this process that the brain served man so well, at least until the nuclear age.

It seems that most, if not all, of our emotions still originate in the primitive midbrain, at the base of the brain, while the large cortical lobes of the brain are used to rationalize and justify what our midbrain is telling us to do. There is no person on earth who is totally rational and logical. All human behavior is motivated by our primitive emotional responses and reactions. Many of the emotions have their origins in childhood. We have been conditioned to fear, hate, feel jealous, or to respond in other ways to certain stimuli. For instance, I could meet a woman who, because of the shape of her ears, the tone of her voice, or her powerful personality, reminds me of my dead mother. Without having consciously realized these facts, I may take an immediate dislike to this person whom I hardly know. Obviously, these powerful feelings have absolutely nothing to do with this woman; she simply triggered feelings that I carry around with me all the time. We all have feelings like this every day. We like some people immensely right away or take an immediate dislike to others. It is not difficult to understand these reactions if one takes the time and effort to understand the most important early influences within one's own childhood.

We also tend to project our feelings of inadequacy, fear, or hatred onto other people. For instance, when Ronald Reagan told me during our meeting in the White House that the Russians are evil, godless Communists, and I asked him if he had ever met one and he said no, that is an example of Mr. Reagan projecting his fear and hatred onto the Russians. This nasty side of people is called our dark side. We all have a dark side, which we really do not like to own. We never like to admit that we are haters or we are jealous or we are really a mass of fears and insecurities. It makes us feel much better to dislike other people and blame them for our feelings. How many times have we heard others say, as we say ourselves, "She makes me feel awful" or "He makes me feel frightened?" Nobody can make us feel anything. Each of us is responsible for our own feelings. Other people can trigger these feelings, but we allow ourselves to feel them and they are nobody else's fault.

In a tribal sense, people seem to derive deep feelings of well-being by projecting their fears and hatred in a unified fashion onto a common enemy. This dark side can become evil personified, and Hitler was an absolute master at mobilizing the dark side of the German people, which was projected onto the Communists and the Jews. He was so brilliant at this technique that the Germans unified in their hatred and killed tens of millions of people. This projection of the dark side becomes mass paranoia and mass psychosis.

The American people are taught to dislike and in many instances even hate the Russians. There is a compulsory course taught in the Florida high schools called Americanism vs. Communism (nicknamed AVC by the schoolchildren). In Texas, the children are taught the evils of communism, and other states conduct similar educational campaigns. This sort of childhood conditioning then justifies the projection of the dark side, and nations behave in this way very much as individuals do.

If we are to survive as a species, we must stop this paranoid projection, both in our personal lives and in our collective lives. Therefore, the place to start is in the family and with friends. A good exercise is to pick the person whom you dislike the most in your life, seek them out, and go and talk to them. Discover what they really think of you and tell them honestly what you think of them and why (if you understand your own conditioning), and make friends with them. Nothing is more disarming than making oneself vulnerable by being totally honest. That is what we must do with the

Russians. It is really not too difficult; it certainly takes some courage, but it is eminently rewarding and very satisfying.

Another emotional dynamic that needs to be examined is love. In our society, we are taught that we need love and people should give it to us. In a marriage, unhappiness often eventuates when the partners do not feel that the other really understands or loves them. We need these emotional reinforcements. Actually the contrary dynamic is correct. The only way to true happiness is to give love and have no need. I have found in my marriage that if I blame my husband for my unhappy state and I need his love, I don't get it. But if I abandon my selfish needs and I give him what he needs, making no demands, just loving him, the tables turn and he gives me lots of love (but I have to totally renounce my expectations). In other words, *I* make the first move, and this leads to conflict resolution. The only way a relationship works is for the partners to capitulate on their own wants and desires and to reach out to the other—in other words, to negotiate from the position of so-called weakness and not one of strength. It *always* works. It is frightening to make oneself vulnerable in a conflict situation in a marriage or an intimate relationship. To do this is a sign of real courage and strength. When two wolves are involved in a death struggle, the losing wolf typically recognizes his failure and bares the jugular vein in his neck to his attacking opponent. The other wolf then capitulates and walks off.

The superpowers are married to each other on this planet. They either must live and work together, respecting their differences, or they will die together within an hour or two. In reality, the marriage vow is appropriate for a future life preserving relationship between the United States and the Soviet Union, viz.: for better, for worse, for richer, for poorer, in sickness and in health, forsaking all others, till death do us part, according to God's holy name, I pledge thee my troth. What each superpower must learn is that the true path to conflict resolution is to forget selfish needs and wants, and to pragmatically make the first move. This is negotiating from a position of strength and not weakness. They must learn the true path to conflict resolution. Typically, throughout most U.S.–USSR arms control negotiations, the Americans have made the first move and have taken the initiatives in certain areas, and usually the Russians follow. They are rigid and slow, but they follow. A good example of capitulation and unilateralism was Jack Kennedy's initiative in his American University speech, when he unilaterally stopped testing nuclear weapons. From this initial move, other unilateral moves followed on both sides, and the Russians were so pleased they called this the Policy of Mutual Example.

Men and Women

Men and women are psychologically and physiologically different. Each has a most important role to play in the world, but unfortunately, women play second fiddle on most occasions. In the United States, women won the vote seventy years ago, but they have done virtually nothing with it. If you look at the Congress and the executive branch, there are virtually no women in high office. We have no one to blame but ourselves. For various reasons—feelings of inadequacy, lack of knowledge, lack of energy contingent upon childbirth and child rearing—women have stayed in the background while men have made all significant and major decisions. Now the world is ready to blow up and the women and mothers are worried, but the men still make the decisions.

A man named Mark Gerzon recently wrote a book called *A Choice of Heroes*, in which he examines the state of the world. He determines that it is in a serious dilemma and that certainly in the United States the decisions are made by a small minority—white Anglo-Saxon males, middle-aged and older. Because these people have created such enormous problems, Mr. Gerzon says that we need to examine their psychological pathology. He says that typically these men never show emotion, never admit mistakes, and are very dependent upon others of the same sex for peer-group approval. They are always sure of themselves, are always right, and above all they are always tough and strong. He suggests that in the nuclear age, these men need to redefine strength and courage for themselves, to become men who have the courage to show weaknesses and fallibilities, to show emotion and even to cry when appropriate, and to admit mistakes. It really takes extraordinary strength and inner courage for a man to be able to do this. A weak, unattractive male, on the other hand, is a man who never shows any emotion or even admits to having emotions, who is never fallible and never admits to making a mistake, who hides behind his defense mechanisms and builds missiles. One could call this dynamic a case of acute missile envy. Such men, who in fact hold the reins of power in Washington, in the Iron Triangle, and throughout the land and the world, are anachronistic and dangerous in the nuclear age.

A typical woman is a person who is very much in touch with her feelings, cries when necessary, has a very strong and reliable intuition, which serves her in good stead, and the intuition is almost always accurate. She is not afraid to admit she has made a mistake and is generally interested in life-oriented human dynamics. She innately understands the basic principles of conflict resolution. Most of these women know and understand how to get to a man's deepest emotions: Most men, when in love or infatuated with a woman, will open up and reveal their true feelings, which they would never normally have the courage to do, particularly when dealing with their male colleagues and friends.

Women are nurturers. They are generally born with strong feelings for nurturing of the life process. One reason for this is that their bodies are built anatomically and physiologically to nurture life. Not all women can have babies, nor even desire them, but many have a will to give birth. Whether mothers or not, most women care deeply about the preservation of life. Women are also capable of capitulation and can move into conflict resolution if they make a conscious decision. It is almost always the woman who presents first or who makes the initial move to seek marriage or partner guidance counseling if there are problems in a relationship.

One of the reasons women are so allied to the life process is their hormonal constitution. Let me give a personal example: After I went through pregnancy and the birthing process, I was emotionally and physically engrossed in the babies. I was very frightened lest one of them should have a congenital deformity. I was totally delighted by these perfect little human beings. After the births, if one of the babies cried in another part of the house, I was still so attached to them that my breasts prickled with milk. I have never been so fulfilled in my whole life and because it was the most creative thing I ever did, I would have given birth every year until menopause. I have never felt more nurturing and giving to another human being as in these first few months after pregnancy, and, in fact, for the first time in my life I knew I would give up my own life to save another human being—my baby. To a certain extent, these feelings are induced by the female hormones—estrogen and progesterone, which are secreted in large quantities by the placenta, and probably by the hormone that induces and controls lactation. Indeed, women's psyches are influenced by hormonal levels—varying sometimes in different stages of the menstrual cycle and often influenced by the changes evoked by the contraceptive pill, which can involve depression, loss of libido, and general malaise.

Men, on the other hand, are men because of their hormonal output of androgen. If a male fetus does not have the capacity to respond to male hormones secreted by his testicles, he will develop anatomically into a female. Actually, these women are among the most beautiful, feminine, sexually attractive women because they are incapable of responding physiologically to male hormones. They have a congenital disease called the testicular feminizing syndrome. But if a male has normally functioning androgens, he grows big muscles, a deep voice, secondary sexual characteristics, and body hair. He is typically more psychologically aggressive than women. Some people contend that this is the result of conditioning. I am sure that some aggressive behavior in men is conditioned, but some must also be hormonally controlled. I have observed clinically that when a man develops cirrhosis of the liver, he lacks the ability to metabolize and break down the small quantities of female hormones secreted by his adrenal glands. He becomes both physically and psychologically feminized. He loses his body hair, his testicles atrophy, his skin becomes soft, and he becomes softer and more sensitive psychologically. On the other hand, if a woman is given male hormones because of a medical condition over a prolonged period of time, she will develop big muscles, her body hair will increase, her voice will deepen, and she will become more aggressive psychologically.

Some recent work has shown that little boys under the age of six are more aggressive than girls of the same age. This work could be supported by the experience of teachers in

Educators for Social Responsibility, who observed that primary-school boys become excited when playing video games and, having lost, walk away feeling energetic and aggressively disappointed. Girls will play for a while, but they don't become nearly as emotionally involved as the boys, and they walk away after several games because they are bored.

Some men have recently described to me the fascination that other men and boys have with killing. One man, now a deeply religious person, described to me some of his childhood activities: He used to catch a frog, hold it in the palm of his hand belly-up, and pierce its belly with a very sharp stick. He would then hold it over a fire, turning it slowly on the stick, as it roasted, and he said he had feelings of ecstasy as he watched the frog squirm and burn to death. A French film producer, who used to be a correspondent during the war, interviewed Nazi torturers. He said that initially the cruelty and killing made him physically sick, but he got used to it, and he described an almost orgasmic fascination with killing—almost a feeling of omnipotence.

What is it about their most primitive feelings that makes these men enjoy killing? Is it because women know almost from birth that they can experience the ultimate act of creativity, whereas boys and men lack this potential capacity and replace it with a fascination with control over life and death and a feeling of creative omnipotence? I cannot answer these questions, but maybe the men reading this book will look into their souls and most primitive feelings and urges and examine the validity of these questions.

There is another dynamic operating in the arms race, and that is one of overt sexuality. As I watch adolescent boys and young men in their twenties driving their girl friends around in their souped-up hot rods, it is obvious that these boys are demonstrating their virility as they gun their motors and spin the wheels around corners. I suppose at that age, with life and the whole world ahead of them, these young boys are bursting with energy and their newly discovered sexuality. But I wonder how many of them really ever grow up.

I am reminded of a frequent experience one meets in general practice. Often a young couple, ages seventeen to twenty, come in pregnant. As soon as the girl delivers and becomes a mother, she turns into a woman overnight, emotionally mature and extremely responsible for this new life. Almost always, the boy remains an emotional child and often runs away from his responsibilities by leaving his wife and baby. As I observed many couples, it seemed to me that often these men never mature. They continue to play with dangerous toys—motorbikes, racing cars, weapons, and war—flirting with death.

This experience is confirmed as I travel in planes and stay in hotels. I am surrounded by white-collar corporate men, and I frequently overhear the conversations of those who know each other. These are either very serious business discussions concerned with money or boyish jokes laced with sexual innuendo, at the level of early adolescence. Never do I hear them discussing human relationships or emotional dynamics with each other. Never do I see them developing a real human intimacy as they amuse themselves. On the other hand, I find that women are frequently discussing marriages and human relationships, medical problems, or their children. They are often talking about nurturing subjects.

These hideous weapons of killing and mass genocide may be a symptom of several male emotions: inadequate sexuality and a need to continually prove their virility plus a primitive fascination with killing. I recently watched a filmed launching of an MX missile. It rose slowly out of the ground, surrounded by smoke and flames and elongated into the air—it was indeed a very sexual sight, and when armed with the ten warheads it will explode with the most almighty orgasm. The names that the military uses are laden with psychosexual overtones: missile erector, thrust-to-weight ratio, soft lay down, deep penetration, hard line and soft line. A McDonnell-Douglas advertisement for a new weapons system proudly proclaims that it can "shoot down whatever's up, and blow up whatever's down." Sexual inadequacy in a powerful leader is illustrated by the following example: Hitler once invited a young woman to his room. He stuck out his arm in a Nazi salute and in a booming voice said, "I can hold my arm like that for two solid hours. I never feel tired. . . . My arm is like granite—rigid and unbending, but, Göring can't stand it. He has to drop his arm after half an hour of this salute. He's flabby, but I am hard."

The American missiles are smaller than the Russian

December 27, 1982

Aviation Week
& Space Technology

A McGraw-Hill Publication $5.00

International
Marketing
Directory

Editorial Index 1982

Missile envy

missiles, and this fact is used to good advantage by the generals to persuade Congress that they need more money for more missiles. Boeing constructed a model of the different sizes of missiles and painted the American ones blue and the Russian ones red. The generals take this model to House and Senate hearings and say: "But, Senator, how do you feel when America has these small blue missiles and Russia has these great big red missiles?" They always get what they ask for.

General Patton described war as "the cataclysmic ecstasy of violence." The chairman of the Committee on Public Information during World War I said, "Universal military training means more than national safety and defense. It means national health, national virility. . . . There is not a weakness in American life that it would not strengthen." A Spanish saying goes, "When a nation shows a civilized horror of war, it receives directly the punishment for its mistakes. God changes its sex, despoils it of its common mark of virility, changes it into a feminine nation, and sends conquerors to ravage it of its honor." A quote from Ireland: "Bloodshed is a cleansing and sanctifying rite and the nation which regards it as a final horror has lost its manhood."

The psychologist Carl Jung described two basic psychological principles that govern the behavior of all human beings. They are the anima, or feminine principle, and animus, the masculine principle. Each person has a certain ratio of both operating in the psyche. Let me explain further: Both principles have a positive and negative aspect. The positive anima is the nurturing, caring, loving principle, which women embody and which is also present powerfully in some men. The negative anima is the petulant, bitchy characteristic, best epitomized when a man and a woman have a fight and the man goes away in a huff and won't talk for several days and becomes very petulant. The positive animus is the principle that motivates people to become active in relationships or the world, to take the initiative, and to become a confident, positive, powerful force. Many men embody this principle, but most women have a very undeveloped positive animus, except if they feel their children are threatened. The negative animus is a competitive, egocentric, evil, powerful principle, which can often lead to killing, either in a psychological or physical sense. Many men are also filled and motivated by the principle of negative animus, which, indeed, has the world in its grip. When women attack a man verbally and emotionally, their negative animus is operating.

The challenge that individuals face in the nuclear age because of the survival imperative is to understand the basic principles that underlie and motivate their behavior and to determine how they can induce the atrophy of the negative principles while enhancing the growth of the positive anima and animus. This is, indeed, a challenge. Most men need to learn how to hypertrophy their positive anima and diminish the negative animus, while women on the whole urgently need to enlarge their positive animus and deal with their negative animus. There was one person who probably more than anyone else embodied these positive principles, and that person was Jesus. He was soft and loving, caring and nurturing, but he also had a powerful drive to correct evil and help people do the right things and could sometimes be positively aggressive if the need arose. He expressed righteous indignation and moral outrage when he observed people ill-treating or abusing others, and he uttered some very profound psychological truths. He was probably the most brilliant, well-balanced psychiatrist who ever lived.

Women have a very important role to play in the world today. They must rapidly develop their own power so that they can move out into local, national, and international affairs, taking with them and using their positive animus to save the children of the country and the world. They have learned over the past ten to fifteen years, through the women's liberation movement, that they are as intelligent as men and can be as powerful or more powerful as the occasion arises. They have also developed a confidence in themselves which is delightful to see. The age of women has arrived. If we don't stand up and rapidly become elected to the highest offices in the country and change America's national policies from those of death to those of life, we will all be exterminated. I don't mean that in doing this women should abrogate their positive feminine principle of nurturing, loving, caring, and emotions. (Margaret Thatcher, Golda Meir, and Indira Gandhi became, in fact, men.) I mean they should tenaciously preserve these values but also learn to find and use their incredible power. The positive feminine principle must become the guiding moral principle in world politics.

Women also need to teach men how to get into contact with their emotions. I am married to a very beautiful man, who in the last ten years has learned to recognize and talk about his emotions. But he is still a man and sometimes I am still surprised when I ask him how he felt about a person or a situation and he gives me a chronology of the events and of what occurred. I have to say to him again and several times more, "But I am not interested in how it happened. How did you feel?" I think men have great difficulty in consciously recognizing their feelings and emotions, let alone in talking about them. I think it somehow makes them feel demeaned and probably very vulnerable to have to admit that they feel rejected or hurt or that they are really very competitive and that the last person they spoke with irritated the hell out of them because this person was also competitive.

Through the women's liberation movement, men have indeed become more nurturing and gentle. They have had to stay at home and mind the baby and children and in so doing have become more empathetic with women and the lives women have lived in the past. These men often find they become closer to their children, and they develop tremendous satisfaction when they are involved in the nurturing process. This, of course, usually enhances the relationship between the two parents.

Most of the leaders of American society are married and most of their wives have children and grandchildren. It has been my constant experience that when I speak to a hall full of uninformed people about the medical effects of nuclear war, it is the women who rise up in their seats and who develop a power that they previously lacked. I am sure that I am tapping into the instinct that a woman has to protect her children. The positive animus takes over. But, so often at the end of the lecture, men will come up to me and point out that I did not give the correct number for the cruise missiles or correct some other data or statistics. The women will usually jump down their throats and scream, "That's the sort of thinking that's going to kill us." The men look very shocked and retreat hurt. These men have obviously not let the appalling material I have just presented enter their psyches and have studiously avoided the logical emotional response by clinging to their rational exposition of numbers and tunnel-vision perspective and statistics.

It is true that men on the whole are fascinated with numbers and how things work, and they are very comfortable operating from a rational perspective, ignoring the real emotions that motivate their every action and feeling. That is why it is time for the positive feminine principle in the women and the nurturing, caring men to take over and assume the lead.

I am often accused by men of being too emotional. It is absolutely inappropriate to be unemotional as one contemplates the fiery end of the earth. I often tell these men that if I have two parents in my office and I tell them that their child has leukemia, and neither of them shows any emotional response, I get them a psychiatrist because they urgently need help!

Politicians

An Australian physician who had been living in the United States said to me recently that he found the most powerful country on earth to be like a bullet train, racing very fast down the tracks, but when he got up into the engine, he was shocked to discover that there was no driver.

Most politicians practice prenuclear thinking—they have not taken into their souls the hideous consequences of nuclear war and translated these effects into their own lives. They continually vote for more and more missiles, bombs, ships, planes, satellites, radars, without giving the logical conclusions of their actions a second thought. They have been conditioned to think that more military installations in their districts will create more jobs, and that is better for their reelection prospects.

I took the Physicians for Social Responsibility film *The Last Epidemic* down to Washington to show it to Congress. This is an excellent short film with statements by admirals, ex-CIA officials, and scientists who have been involved in the arms race, and it graphically describes the medical consequences of nuclear war. The room was packed with people, but they were mostly aides and staff people, hardly any of their chiefs. I asked where the senators and representatives

were, and their staff told me they were too busy to attend—
too busy being courted, wined and dined, and cajoled by the
defense contractors and the Pentagon.

These people, mostly men, practice psychic numbing—a
term aptly coined by the psychiatrist Robert Lifton. They
have never morally, ethically, or emotionally contemplated
the logical consequences of their daily actions as they vote to
prepare the earth for a global holocaust. The few politicians
who have seen this film or have been present during a lecture
when a physician presents the medical consequences of nuclear war have almost always had their psychic numbing
shattered. It is easy for a doctor to establish the doctor-
patient relationship with any audience, and to personalize in
a professional way the frightful consequences of nuclear war.
We do this every day with our patients as they present with
serious diseases and must be made aware of the enormous
consequences of their diagnosis. They will then be prepared
to go through the often very unpleasant side effects of their
therapy.

After people have been shocked into reality about their
disease or about their future and the future of their children
in the nuclear age, they will enter the stages of grief. The
first stage is shock and disbelief, which will last for days or
weeks. The whole situation is unreal and will go away. The
next stage is one of deep depression, so profound that they
can lose their appetite and their libido. They lose weight,
wake early in the morning, and have no energy to live a
normal life. This stage may last for months and is followed by
or combined with the stage of anger—railing against God for
the illness of themselves or the planet, against government
authority, etc. The next stage may be bargaining with God—if
they do the right thing, maybe God will let them live. The
final stage of grief is adjustment and acceptance of death or
reality. The patient will then finally be able to die at peace
with himself and his Maker if he has been allowed time to
pass through the other stages of grief.

Similarly, many people when faced with the imminent
prospects of nuclear war will enter this grief process. It is
extremely painful psychologically and most people avoid these
feelings if they possibly can, but only if people will let themselves experience the true gravity of the nuclear peril will
they even be motivated to alleviate the situation. The angry

phase is the most constructive period because anger is a very powerful emotion and can be channeled into constructive areas. When a person is angry, the adrenal glands, which are located just above the kidneys, pump out the hormone adrenaline, which raises the blood-sugar level, pushes up the blood pressure, and turns on the neurons so people become motivated to decide what they have to do to survive. The last stage, acceptance, is also a useful phase, for when people have stopped battling with reality, they have more energy to devote to constructive solutions to their dilemma.

I showed *The Last Epidemic* to the staff at *The Washington Post*. Ben Bradlee gathered his people into a large room, and, before the film began, the defense correspondents and others were arguing about various military strategies and saying "What about the Russians?" I said I would not answer them until they had watched the film. When the lights went on, there was stunned silence in the room. Several of the journalists were in tears, and Ben Bradlee said, "I guess I'm numb." I said, "No you're not. You've entered the first stage of grief." I went on to explain the psychological response that people have to such material. They were fascinated, and later Walter Pincus, the Pentagon correspondent, came up to me and said, "That was the best presentation I ever heard." I was surprised and said, "Why, Walter?" and he explained that he listened to presentations every day about weapons and strategies, professionally produced by the military corporations, but that he had never heard the issue discussed in these terms before. A new facet to the problem had been presented. Emotions are almost never discussed by the people in the media or in the Iron Triangle.

Similarly, it is imperative that our representatives be exposed to the emotional consequences of their actions. The politicians practice old modes of thinking. They believe the more bombs America has, the safer it will be. They don't seem to recognize that more bombs increase the risk and probability of nuclear war simply because, as more people handle the bombs and delivery systems, statistically the chances for risk and error increase.

The total number of nuclear warheads is also a very important factor to consider. As the arsenal increases, the global ecological system becomes more and more threatened.

In fact, more nuclear weapons increase the insecurity of America and the earth.

Sexuality and National Security Politics

Politicians are ultimately interested in power. Power is seductive and corrupting. Seymour Hersh describes in his book *The Price of Power* how decisions were made by Nixon and Kissinger in an arbitrary fashion, often to protect the power and prestige of these two men. The decisions were not based on morality or ethics, but were only to serve their egocentric self-interests.

For instance, they were warned by some officials during the war in Biafra that unless America intervened, within one month 1 million people could be dead. Because Henry Kissinger was having some difficulty with personal relationships in the State Department, nothing was done and hundreds of thousands of people died of starvation in Africa.

The President of the United States has ultimate power and can start a war if he so desires. There are no immediate checks and balances to prevent these decisions being made, and the Nixon White House was run by Nixon and Kissinger alone—two amoral men who were interested only in themselves and their own power.

In his book Hersh discusses the Soviet menace and reports that it was considered "soft" not to be tough on the Russians. These sexual dynamics still prevail in the Reagan administration and the House and Senate.

Lyndon Johnson desperately wanted to be seen as a man, according to the author David Halberstam. "He wanted the respect of men who were tough, real men, and they would turn out to be Hawks." Johnson had two categories: men and boys. The men were "activists-doers who conquered business empires, who acted instead of talked." Boys were "the talkers and the writers and the intellectuals, who sat around thinking and criticizing and doubting instead of doing." Halberstam called Johnson "more than a little insecure." He was acting out his sexual insecurities in the world and in so doing was the catalyst to the deaths of hundreds of thousands of people. Had he had the wisdom and courage to examine his childhood and background and to discover the origin of his insecurities, he could well have become a more whole man whom many millions of people would have perceived as a leader. He would have become a true hero instead of having to leave in disrepute and humiliation. He lacked a well-developed positive anima, and his negative animus was obviously being used to try to compensate for his insecurity to make him feel better. His dark side was projected upon the world.

In *A Choice of Heroes*, Gerzon describes the sexual dynamics in the Johnson administration. "One high-level State Department aide who witnessed many planning sessions recalled how Johnson's decision-makers reenacted this predictable masculine drama. 'I watched the Doves trying to phrase their arguments so as not to look soft,' said James C. Thomson, who now directs the Neiman Foundation at Harvard. 'But, the Doves were intimidated by the brass and the hardliners. Particularly those who had not served in the Armed Forces, such as Humphrey, were vulnerable to the uniform. They never rebut the techno-military 'We've got to be tough' language that the Generals and the Hawks used."

In these tribal power games, the bottom line is always the zero-sum mentality—I win if you lose, and vice versa. There is no middle line or compromise if the masculine ethic is to be preserved. This is the football-game mentality. Boys are taught in school to be intensely aggressive in sports, and the word "kill" is frequently used to drum up the necessary energy to win. If men *have* to prove their masculinity to each other, the safest way to do it is through sports. The ancient tradition of the Olympic games is a healthy, wholesome way for countries to act out their tribal impulses and for men, and indeed women, to prove themselves in competition. I have often thought that the solution to the aggressive needs of the men who control the superpowers would be an annual wrestling match between the Kremlin and the Houses of Congress and the administration and/or the Pentagon. These men could lock each other in intense body-to-body physical combat, which is very exhausting. If necessary, perhaps these matches could be arranged monthly to alleviate the built-up aggressions.

It is always the old men who send the young men off to die in their wars. The tradition is that countries maintain departments of state or departments of foreign affairs full of diplomats who negotiate when difficulties arise between their countries. However, if the negotiations break down, the countries then start killing each other. How primitive! It is never the people who make the decision to kill who get killed. It is the boys who usually don't even know what the dispute is about, let alone understand the intricacies of international politics. The old men act out their fascination with killing, their need to prove their toughness and sexual adequacy by using innocent pawns. This dynamic has been occurring for thousands, if not millions, of years. Now it must stop because any conventional superpower war will most certainly escalate to nuclear war.

How many leaders of the world have ever witnessed the explosion of a hydrogen bomb—felt the heat hundreds of miles away, like a furnace door opening next to their faces, watched the flash through their closed eyes and hands and seen the bones of their hands light up, watched an adjacent battleship rise up in the water like a splinter and disappear? How many of these old men emotionally understand the magnitude of destruction in these small suns? I would venture to say none.

How many leaders of the world have ever watched the miracle of the birth of a baby? How many leaders of the world have helped a child to die and supported the parents in their grief before and forever after? Each life is as precious as any other, and the magnitude of suffering involved in a single death is vast. Yet because these men do not understand these values in their souls, they have produced the lethal equipment and ordered the deaths of hundreds of thousands of people in the past and possibly hundreds of millions in the future.

General Public: Psychic Numbing

Most people were relieved when World War II ended after Hiroshima and Nagasaki and at the same time were shocked by these dreadful new bombs. General fears about nuclear war increased during the era of Dulles brinksmanship in the Eisenhower administration and recrudesced when America and Russia began testing bombs in the atmosphere. Linus Pauling and other scientists and physicians predicted that the high levels of radioactive fallout concentrating in the milk and in children's teeth could increase the incidence of cancer and leukemia in these children many years later. The days of nuclear fallout were followed by the Cuban missile crisis, where nuclear war might have been only hours away. People were so frightened in America that they started building fallout shelters, and the anxieties provoked by the situation induced some to buy guns to defend themselves from their neighbors. This generalized fear helped bring about the Partial Test-Ban Treaty, so that America and Russia could continue nuclear testing, but only underground, thus eliminating atmospheric fallout.

Out of sight is out of mind, and rapidly people's fears of a nuclear war disappeared. The superpowers quietly and efficiently continued testing and increasing their arsenals without any interference from the public or world opinion.

The people of the world lapsed into a state of psychic numbing and pushed the fear of nuclear annihilation into their collective subconscious. Occasionally, if an air-raid siren sounded, some would be reminded of the days when they had practiced air-raid drills in school—by scrambling under desks, hiding in the corridors, or covering their heads with pieces of paper to protect themselves against a nuclear bomb.

When SALT II failed to be ratified by the U.S. Senate, the MX was authorized by President Carter, and Reagan came riding into power on a platform of winnable nuclear war, the old nuclear anxieties began to rear their heads again. The Reagan administration continued making wildly provocative statements about firing nuclear warning shots across the bow of the Soviet Union and having a nuclear war in Europe without pressing a button, and the anxieties mounted. Physicians for Social Responsibility began holding symposia across the country on the medical consequences of nuclear war. These captured the imagination of the media, and once again nuclear war became a prime topic of conversation in many households in America, as well as in Europe and the Soviet Union. Many thousands of people, after becoming aware of the horrific medical effects, were thrown into the grieving process and came out the other end as activists. Millions voted for a nuclear freeze in the 1982 elections, and it passed in eight out of nine states, while 79 percent of people in a March 1983 Harris Poll supported a nuclear freeze.

Most of these people had not really been through the grieving process, however. Although they had become sensitized in a superficial way to the medical dangers of nuclear war, they really had little concept of the magnitude of the arms race even in their own country, let alone in Europe or the world at large.

People avoid facing nuclear reality by several mechanisms:

They practice displacement activity. This dynamic is best illustrated by animal experiments. If you put rats in a cage and threaten them with a lethal situation, they tend to ignore it and run away to another part of the cage and engage in activities that are totally irrelevant to their life-threatening situation. Most people do this every day, as they worry about their work, their families, and become totally engrossed in ordinary, everyday events, thus ignoring the overwhelming danger that hangs over them like a Sword of Damocles every minute of their lives and the lives of their children.

They practice manic denial. Some people deny nuclear reality with such a mania that they indulge in hot tubs, Jacuzzis, fancy cars, gourmet foods, fur coats, and fashionable clothes. In pre–World War II Germany, there was also an atmosphere of manic hedonism, somewhat like the self-oriented, egocentric, pleasure-seeking activities of present-day America and Europe.

Some people are truly ignorant about the imminence of nuclear war. I met a young man, age twenty-one, at a party recently. He was intelligent, but asked me if the bomb dropped on Hiroshima was nuclear and had absolutely no knowledge of the nuclear arms race.

Other people justify the possession of nuclear weapons by saying, "*What about the Russians?*" Some psychiatrists feel that people's fear of nuclear war is projected onto the Russians. This fear is so profound that the Russians become inanimate objects. If they are inanimate beings, we can talk about killing hundreds of millions of people and have no feeling about it. In so doing, we have lost our humanity. This is an extension of the tribal dynamic, where the other tribe is always evil, bad, corrupt, and untrustworthy, but it is overlaid by the profound fear of nuclear war, which obviously threatens to kill not just the other tribe but the home tribe as well.

Another example of denial is exhibited by millions of

fundamentalist Christians, led by Jerry Falwell and others, who believe that the world will be consumed by fire, as in nuclear war, and that one third of men with the mark of God on their foreheads will go straight up to heaven. They call this event *the rapture*, and many of them are actually praying for it to happen. To paraphrase the message carried on some bumper stickers, "I'm praying for the rapture."

Another reason people practice these denial mechanisms is because *everyone is scared of his or her own death* and very few people ever face this reality until a lethal diagnosis has been made. Even then, some people refuse to accept the fact that they are dying.

But to face the death of life on earth is so much more painful than even one's own death. I think I have reached the stage where I could die at peace and accept that reality, and I could even accept the death of one of my children because I know they have to die sometime. What I absolutely cannot accept is the death of life on the planet. We may be the only life in the whole universe, and I used to derive a great sense of emotional security when, as a little girl, I felt certain that if I died, the world would go on.

All these mechanisms are used to avoid the very unpleasant feelings of grief and responsibility. If people are forced to accept reality, they would then also be forced to accept responsibility for their world. This would involve changing the priorities in their lives, so that the exigencies of daily living would become secondary to their need to find solutions to their dangerous dilemma. Why make sure the children clean their teeth, have good nutritious food, or be exposed to a good education when they could be vaporized within the next ten years?

By ignoring the true reality of the imminence of nuclear war we are all practicing passive suicide. When a suicidal patient is seen by a physician, that patient is hospitalized because he or she is mentally sick and needs help. This society is in the grips of a pervasive mental illness, which will lead to its death. Certainly, it takes courage and guts to face the dreadful facts and to accept responsibility as an adult to save the world. But this course of action is very satisfying and the only way parents can ensure a future for their child.

Preventing nuclear war is the ultimate parenting issue, and nothing else matters.

We all behave very much like the Jews in Hitler's Germany after Hitler wrote *Mein Kampf*. They ignored his calculated plans and said "It will never happen to us, because we're Germans." Even when they were being carted off in the cattle trucks, many of them still denied the reality of their situation.

Repression of fear takes more mental energy than accepting the feelings of loss and grief associated with reality. People often tell me that they feel so much more energetic and alive once they have allowed themselves to go through the stages of grief. They become joyous people, who have a sense of mission, and they find with the released energy they are able to achieve the most extraordinary results in society toward ending the nuclear arms race, both at a local and a national level.

It is absolutely inappropriate for anyone to feel psychologically comfortable in this day and age. The physician and writer Lewis Thomas recently gave a speech in which he said that even his attitude toward music has changed since he acknowledged the imminence of nuclear war. He can't listen to beautiful music without feeling an overwhelming sense of grief for the world, a world without Paris and other wonderful cities—a world where the children have no sense of a future. What an absolute tragedy!

Children

Our children are in a terrible dilemma. A survey was conducted by Drs. John Mack and William Beardslee between 1978 and 1981 for the American Task Force on the Psycho-Social Impact of Nuclear Disasters for the American Psychiatric Association. The survey was conducted among one thousand high-school and grammar-school students in Boston. They were asked what they thought about the nuclear age and their future, and the majority of these children said that they felt they had no future. Similar surveys were conducted by the *Houston Post* and by the *Boston Globe*, which produced the same findings.

New Zealand children were surveyed in 1976 and were

found to be very optimistic about their future, but a study in 1982 found a similar feeling of pessimism among New Zealand children. Doctors in Europe report that their children seem to be similarly afflicted.

I have worked with children for years as a pediatrician. My patients are all afflicted with a lethal genetic disease called cystic fibrosis, and they die anytime from birth to the age of thirty. Children are unable to deny harsh realities. They seem to lack the mechanism for repression of unpleasant thoughts, which adults have developed. They are, therefore, extremely vulnerable to fears about nuclear war, the reality of which is apparent to them every day as they watch the TV and read the newspapers. They just have to listen to President Reagan make a speech renaming the MX missile "the Peacekeeper" to realize they are living in an insane world. Children also seem to have an intuitive sixth sense about the truth, which adults usually lack. For instance, some of my young patients have said to me, "I'm going to die tonight," when clinically it was not obvious that they were, and they do. Children are so honest and straightforward that their comments are often disarming to adults, who prefer to dismiss their profound truths as childish thinking and therefore not to be taken seriously. Jesus recognized their simple veracity when he said, "Out of the mouths of babes and sucklings thou hast perfected praise."

Some of the comments that children make about the arms race are so close to the bone that it makes one cringe. For example:

Piper Herman, at Swampscott Junior High School, age twelve, said, her voice trembling, "I just get so scared thinking that tomorrow I might not wake up, and that would just be the end. Because anyone can just push the button. We are studying Russian culture in school; they really are similar. We don't really know that much about what our government is doing, and the people in Russia know even less about what their government is doing."

Karen Zacarias, age twelve, from Swampscott, said, "You know, I feel sorry for the Russians. We both have nuclear bombs, but we are the only country in the whole wide world who has actually dropped one and killed all those people. We're scared of Russia, but they must be superscared of us."

Catherine Rich, age twelve, from Swampscott, said, "I

had nightmares of the bombs slowly floating towards me. I could feel my blood spurting all over the place. But, now it is better knowing it will all be over so fast. I feel scared, but relieved at the same time. It's like having cancer and at least being told you have it."

Susan Sweeney, age seventeen, said, "As for a career, it seems like it is a waste to go to college and to build up a career and then get blown up someday. And, children—I would love to have kids, but I don't want to have them if they have nothing to live for. . . . Everyone's building up these nuclear weapons just to have one more than the other guy. Everyone's power-hungry. It will get to the point where one guy will say: 'You may have more bombs than I, but I am going to get you first.'"

Stacey Sweeney, age fourteen, said, "I think all the leaders in the nation should fight it out in the boxing ring and leave us all out of it. It is really scary."

Susan Sweeney: "What scares me is that President Reagan wants to build up the military. He is trying to say that this way will be more secure, but what he is saying is making me more scared. . . . At least with Carter, the Russians could relax a little. Do we want Brezhnev all jittery?"

Bob Genduso, age fourteen, said, "I don't think one country would ever have the guts to use them. Even if we are the only one that has ever done it, I think the leaders have more sense."

Stacey Sweeney: "But if leaders have so much sense, why have we had so many wars? And didn't they say that World War I would end all wars? Nobody even remembers why that one started, do they?"

Susan Sweeney: "That's what's so scary. I just don't like being kept in the dark. It seems like the whole future of the world is in the hands of about ten people."

Stacey Sweeney: "I have nightmares, not about a nuclear war, but about not being here afterwards. Nothing is in the dream, really like fog. Try to picture nothing. The world is not the way it is meant to be.

"Maybe a million years ago, someone could have done something, but now that all these countries have all these defenses built up ready to fight, it is really too late to do anything. We should be thinking, 'They're people, just like we are.' We should be working together, not against each other."

My own daughter, who is eighteen years old, said to me out of the blue the other day, "Mommy, I don't think I'll ever have any babies." And she loves babies.

We have brought these children into the world where they have no sense of a future. How could we do this to the people we love most in our lives and want the very best for?

Some psychiatrists think that one of the main reasons our children are dropping out, becoming part of the "me now" generation, and are indulging almost universally in drugs and alcohol, is because of this total sense of pessimism about the future.

They feel emotionally and almost physically abandoned by their parents, many of whom are working hard to make sure the children receive good educations, are well-clothed, and are "psychologically secure," while the parents indulge in the societal dynamics of pervasive psychic numbing, furthering their professions and their careers while totally ignoring the fact that their children could be annihilated any day. Some children feel almost desperate in their abandonment. One eighteen-year-old girl approached my husband after he gave a lecture in Florida and said that she and her friends are frantic.

One little boy wrote to President Reagan and said, "President Reagan, you've lived your life. I haven't finished playing yet."

Rachel Bunker, from Framingham High School, wrote a letter to the *Boston Globe* saying, "In the event of nuclear war, the youth of the world has the most to lose. Having no legal power in decisions needed to halt the arms race, we cry out for the right to live our lives in peace without the fear of nuclear annihilation."

These children receive terribly mixed messages from the adults. They are subjected to thousands of hours of television annually, showing the most bloodchilling violence, usually with no human emotions associated with the violence. They have been trained to accept that a violent society is normal, and some children act out the violence in schools, on the streets, and in their homes. There is a coldheartedness about some of these children, which is most distressing. Many of them come from homes with broken marriages; in some areas of the country, like Palo Alto, 70 percent of children in the high schools come from single-parent families. These children have often witnessed little self-discipline in their parents, or from their parents, and have observed less adult discipline in society. So their role models are not those that would predispose them to accept responsibility and self-discipline as adults. They will inevitably grow up psychologically damaged as they inherit a world laced with nuclear weapons ticking like a time bomb ready to explode any day.

When children reach late adolescence—seventeen, eighteen, nineteen—they start to develop psychological defense mechanisms, thus becoming less susceptible to the scary subject of nuclear war. It is interesting that while the primary and secondary school children are acutely aware of the threat of nuclear war, the college-age young adults are almost sublimely unaware of the dangers. Often when I go to colleges to speak, I find it very difficult to arouse the audience to become involved in the subject. Girls clad in designer jeans often get up halfway through the lecture on the medical effects of nuclear war and prance out with smirks on their faces. I appeal to them, saying that this is their world they are inheriting and they have their whole future to look forward to, but they seem strangely unimpressed and uninvolved. Many of my children's friends who are attending college say the apathy is frightening. All their peer group seems to be interested in is graduating and getting good jobs where they will make a lot of money. This attitude has perplexed me for several years, but I think I understand it now. These people were born and grew up after the Partial Test-Ban Treaty went into effect in 1962, during the Vietnam war and Watergate, when nuclear war was never mentioned, and right through the benign seventies. When Reagan was elected and all the talk of nuclear war began again, they had passed the age of susceptibility; they had developed a secure, stable vision of the future and their egos had been formed and were refractory concerning the issue, whereas many older Americans remember the bomb scares and fallout in their youth and are very susceptible to having these old wounds reopened, if they will allow themselves the pain.

It is absolutely amazing that most secondary schools in America still avoid the subject of nuclear war—the single most important issue the children should be discussing. Teachers often feel embarrassed to teach the subject because they have no clearcut answers for the children. It has been the experience of Educators for Social Responsibility that children experience a tremendous sense of relief when adults show concern about their feelings and fears and are prepared to teach and work with them to try to find positive things that children can do to stop and reverse the arms race. Students have actually formed national organizations where they work together to get nuclear war curricula in their schools. They organize petitions and letter-writing drives to the press and the Congress, and they go to Washington to lobby.

Nothing could be more evocative to most caring adults than to see thousands of young children demanding their rights to a future. It brings tears to the eyes.

Physicians and educators and family counselors have found that the only way for parents to give their children some sense of emotional security in the nuclear age is for the parents to take responsibility for their children's future, change the priorities of their lives, and start working to get rid of the bomb. It is an interesting observation that during the adolescent rebellion phase, children whose parents are totally uninvolved in this issue take the weight of the world on their shoulders and bitterly resent the apathy and disinterest displayed by their parents for their future lives, while children whose parents are deeply involved in trying to stop nuclear war rebel against their parents' attending so many meetings and being so interested in such a stupid subject. Our three children have behaved like this, and in a way it has freed them up to go to parties and lead relatively care-free adolescent lives in the nuclear age.

Parents often ask me at meetings if they should discuss nuclear war with their children or what they should do when their child asks if he or she will grow up. My answer always is, "Become more involved in the issue and your child will relax and say, 'Mommy and Daddy are working to fix the situation.'"

As we think about our children, we must remember that they are continually being exposed to the pressures to buy war toys in the toy stores. Many of these war toys simulate nuclear war scenarios and, as with the video games, are conditioning our children to accept the prospects of nuclear war.

Scientists

Having been educated in the scientific discipline of medicine, I have been trained to keep my emotions and biases from entering into my experiments because such bias could influence the data. Similarly, doctors do not let emotions enter into decisions when treating patients. We can be empathetic but not sympathetic; otherwise, we may not be able to bring ourselves to make the necessary coldhearted clinical decisions that will benefit the patients. We must at all times retain our clinical objectivity.

When I graduated in 1961, I thought I knew all there was to be known about medicine. My supreme arrogance and ignorance moderated over the years as I became exposed to the vicissitudes of life, and I have become a much better doctor. As I learned to understand myself and my unconscious conditioning, fears, angers, and insecurities, I could understand my patients' needs far better. The clinical objectivity is now tempered with a deep respect and love for my patients. Most medical care is actually judicious care of the psyche combined with a touch of science when clinically indicated.

Most scientists and doctors are male. The ethic to which they subscribe is a typical male ethic and studiously avoids letting emotion enter their thought processes. It is appropriate that pure science be approached unemotionally, but scientists are in trouble. With unbounded zeal, they have pursued and unlocked the secrets of the universe like little boys let loose in a toy store. They have rarely set foot outside their ivory towers to explain to the general public how these scientific truths can and will be applied to affect the world in which we all live. Most nonscientists remain frighteningly ignorant about the near-fatal state of our planet, and the scientists are rushing ever forward with more technological breakthroughs while remaining invisible to public scrutiny.

A few honorable scientists after World War II realized the magnitude of the dilemma created by the atomic bombs, and these people have worked ever since to try to end the nuclear arms race and to alert the public to its dangers. Unfortunately, they are a tiny minority, and the wealth and power of the corporations and political system back the majority of avid scientists who are wedded to the discovery of ever more frightful ways to wreak havoc on the earth.

As Lord Zuckerman has said, "Scientists are the alchemists of our times. They are the originators of the dreadful secrets whereby man can release the energy of stars on earth. Why are they so blocked and unconscious about their past and why are they still doing it? Why do they see no need to accept responsibility for their actions and to teach the people what they have done to the world?" I think partly that these people know in their souls what they have done and are doing is wrong, but the problems they work on are extremely interesting intellectually. I asked Joe Weitzenbaum, professor of computer science at MIT, why these men work on systems of genocide, and he said, "Do you know why? It's incredible fun." They have an insoluble problem to solve like MIRVing a missile, and they solve it. The intellectual prestige and the approbation from their colleagues must be rewarding. Grants flow in from the Pentagon and corporations, and the scientist is set. His ego is gratified, and he does well financially, which is good for his family. As long as he can avoid thinking about the end result of his work (psychic numbing), he can be emotionally comfortable.

Many scientists who leave military work say that all other jobs are really boring compared with their previous work because the intellectual challenges of the most sophisticated technology ever discovered are exciting.

But there is more to life than intellectual excitement. When people face death at the end of their lives, the most important and significant part of their journey has been their relationship with other people, particularly their families. How will these people die with clear consciences when they realize on their deathbeds that they had played a role in preparing for the deaths of millions of their brothers and sisters, including their families and those they love most?

Robert Lifton describes the process of fascination and near worship that some scientists, military people, politicians, and others have with the nuclear bomb as "nuclearism." The weapons are so dreadful that they must, therefore, be blessed with some innate goodness, and these people worship at the feet of the bombs and deify them.

Many people are frightened of their own deaths, and some people deal with this fear by actually playing with death, as if this activity gives them some power over it. This dynamic is called counterphobic mechanism and may, indeed, be operating in many of these scientists. Certainly, I have always been frightened of death, and one of the reasons I entered medicine was my unconscious need to understand the process of pathological mechanisms and death. So I have indulged in counterphobic thought.

In 1981, I was invited to speak at Sandia Labs in New Mexico. These labs are engaged in the manufacture and design of nuclear weapons and delivery systems. There are thousands of scientists who work at these labs, as well as at Los Alamos Labs some miles away in the hills of New Mexico. However, the suggestion that I also speak at Los Alamos was rejected. The scientists at Sandia met in a large corrugated iron shed, where they gather periodically for lectures. They crowded into this makeshift hall and there was standing room only. I was quite nervous because I knew I was facing a potentially hostile audience. I gave a very careful clinical lecture about the medical and ecological effects of nuclear war, and at the end of this description I begged the scientists to leave their jobs, admitting to them that I knew such a decision would be very difficult.

I took questions, and the first man who stood up said, "You were quoted in the *Boston Globe* as saying that anyone who works for the nuclear industry is either dumb, stupid, or highly compromised." I could feel a rush of feeling in the hall that "at last we've got her." I was very careful and admitted that I had made such a statement and that I was wrong to have said that—in other words, I capitulated totally to my questioners. Deflated, he sat down. Most of the successive questions were hostile, but I was very polite and considerate and the meeting went very well. At the end, the scientists lined up to talk to me, and several of them said, "That was a very good lecture. They needed to hear this," pointing to their colleagues. No one took personal responsibility and accepted the fact that they knew they themselves were in a dilemma. They projected their dilemma onto their colleagues.

It is time that the scientists in the world who are involved in the hideous military arms race face their own consciences and take the initiative to remedy the situation they have created. As the physicians have described the medical effects of nuclear war and the stages of grief consequent to this knowledge, many people who had repressed feelings of grief, fear, and guilt about their previous involvement in the arms race and their true anxieties about the state of the world seem to have been given permission to speak of these fears for the first time. It is becoming acceptable to be against nuclear war, whereas five years ago it was unpatriotic and unacceptable to mention the adverse properties of nuclear weapons.

The scientists have been so brilliant that we now have the technology to solve most problems facing the human race—overpopulation, hunger, energy depletion, polluted air and water, and the myriad medical ailments facing man. If the scientists decided that they would work for the benefit of humanity and not its death, they would earn eternal gratitude from the family of man. Such a challenge is probably the most wonderful and creative project any humane scientist could fulfill. I beg my colleagues to leave the business of death and to exercise their talents to preserve life.

The Military

Many men in the Pentagon do not like nuclear weapons. They know that, with them, they can't fight wars anymore. Some have left, taking their considerable expertise with them to educate the general public about nuclear weapons and nuclear war from a military perspective. Others remain in the services, deeply disturbed about the ever-increasing nuclear stockpile.

The majority of men running the services remain committed to nuclear weapons. They plan and strategize about various ways to fight nuclear war RAND-style, and they have enlarged their list of targets in Russia to 40,000. They have innumerable and integral plans for any international contingency that may arise, and the integrated plan for these strategies is the highly classified secret SIOP or Single Integrated Operational Plan.

I think one way these people compensate for the fact that they really know they can't fight proper wars any longer is to displace this frustration. They indulge in the fascination of and drive to build and experiment with more and more complicated technology and weapons systems, which, of course, are enormously expensive.

So the military forces grow stronger and bigger, not just in the superpowers, but in Europe and in smaller nations all over the world. I think the reason for this absurdity in the face of the anachronism of war is that men have not learned to behave any differently. The whole ethic of masculinity is tied up with being tough and courageous, macho and fearless, and they cling to this behavior by building more weapons with almost frantic desperation.

The military trains its recruits to reject emotion in a cruel and violent way, so it can turn them into professional killers. The drill instructors use the terms "maggot," "faggot," "snuffy," "pussy," or "woman" to knock their men into shape. This talk is demeaning both to women and to the men's own feminine side. They are trying to destroy the feminine principle. The drill instructors are often physically cruel and tough with their recruits and in the past have even killed some young boys in training them.

The result of this training is described in *A Choice of Heroes*. Men in battle develop a tremendous sense of comradeship under the adversity of battle, as they suffer and die next to each other. Only then do these men feel free to cry and show their fear and even to hug and kiss each other to demonstrate their love once they have proven their masculinity. What a tragedy of errors!

Men also love to dress up in uniforms and costumes. They have done this for years. I suppose it could be similar to the female drive to look colorful and attractive. For centuries, men have either strutted around in high heels, lipstick, and wigs or worn gorgeous gowns and cloaks, as in the Elizabethan period, or resorted to extravagant uniforms bedecked with feathers, medals, ribbons, and shiny boots. The uniforms bestow conformity, and conformity is another sign of insecurity. The uniforms reinforce the peer-group pressure to conform to the masculine military ethic.

When my brother, Richard, was a little boy, all he ever drew were big pictures of planes dropping bombs on ships and shooting each other, full of blood and violence. He used to walk around for hours holding an airplane, making loud engine noises and driving us all crazy. Other men recollect in a somewhat embarrassed way their similar childhood memories. I never gave my sons guns; nevertheless, the youngest made his own guns out of sticks and bits of wood and played violent games. Some people say that little boys should be allowed to act out their violent fantasies, so when they grow up they don't need to behave like that anymore. But many men remain intoxicated by violence and potential violence. They watch with fascination the killing power apparent in the speed of military planes, racing cars, and the slow awesome might of Trident submarines. They have been seduced all their lives by the John Wayne image of the tough macho hero who shows no emotions while he kills people and is always right. They have been conditioned to believe that such men are to be emulated.

Many men acting on these impulses were so eager to prove their virility that they faked their ages and signed up in the hundreds of thousands to be slaughtered in the first and second world wars. What a tragedy for these beautiful young lives and for their families! When they actually go to war, as many of them did in Vietnam, they are cruelly disillusioned with the romantic notion of toughness, even though at the time some of them derive a strange pleasure from killing. Many soldiers come home from war psychotic and depressed from their harrowing experiences. All people crack under sufficient stress, and the intense fear of death and the hideous thought of killing—not just other men but also women and children—are often too much for normal men to handle without a severe emotional reaction. They have failed to understand that the image of John Wayne represents an emotional cripple, and they learn a painful lesson about reality and the human brain. War never creates the wonderful John Wayne experiences that men expect. The fantasy is rather like the unreal, old-fashioned love stories where lovemaking never induced pregnancy.

Although society did not welcome the Vietnam soldiers with open arms, it still idolizes veterans of past wars. I have never understood, when I am filling out various application forms, why it is an advantage to be a veteran. This is a glorification of war and killing by a male-dominated society. War is nothing more than institutionalized murder. We say we are a Judeo-Christian society, yet we condone mass murder.

It is said that all wars are fought according to the rules of the last war. American society is still fascinated with prenuclear heroes like John Wayne. Ronald Reagan is to some a prenuclear hero—strangely anachronistic and almost willfully ignorant as he struts the nuclear stage. But he taps into people's tribal archetypal need for masculine heroes who will take care of and protect them. The thinking in America today about strength and toughness and superiority is prenuclear thinking. Together with this tough masculine ethic comes a subliminal fear of war and of being killed. But modern man has even conquered this personal fear of proximal death, of bullets ripping through flesh, and of burned, charred bodies. He has built weapons that can be dropped from on high so the bodies cannot be seen. He relies on buttons that can be pressed from thousands of miles away. He ignores the fact that another button will also be pressed and there will be blood all over America. He feels a primitive need to kill, but also to hide from the actual killing and to block out the reality of it.

I was present at a meeting on the Hill when nuclear war was discussed. The generals and officials were very calm and rational throughout the presentations while numbers and strategies were discussed. After several hours of rational discussion about the prospects of nuclear war, I decided it was time to speak, so I stood up and laid out the clinical details of nuclear war in stark detail. General Daniel Graham, a member of the Committee on the Present Danger, reacted like a cork being taken out of a bottle. He became extremely upset and agitated. General Graham was fine as long as nuclear war was not discussed from a medical or an emotional perspective, but his dark side erupted and was directed at me and toward the Russians, as I explained the clinical details. His hostility was virulent.

Another time I was invited to speak on a Chicago TV program. I thought I would be alone, but at the last minute a retired brigadier general turned up to participate in the discussion. For ten minutes, he talked in a calm, cool, nice way about nuclear war and the possibility of the world being blown up. He also used some factually incorrect information. As the arc lights were turned off at the end, he turned to me and aggressively said, "You should go to Russia." I thought for several seconds and decided to let him see the true fear in my soul, and I said to him, "I fucking want my kids to grow up." Well, he could talk about nuclear war with absolutely no emotion, the deaths of hundreds of millions of human beings, but when a lady said "fuck" to him, he was undone. He went wild and almost physically attacked me. The producer came running out to separate us, and there was nearly a brawl on the floor of the TV studio. This exchange made me realize that a lot of these military characters have an extraordinary amount of anger, which they keep under control at most times, but it is probably this anger and hostility that motivate them in their military careers. I decided then that it was very important to try to uncover these emotions, so we could get to the true etiology of war, and to stop being polite and skating around on the surface of the issue.

On another occasion, I visited SAC headquarters in Omaha, where I was surprised to find that their motto is "Peace Is Our Profession." The SAC Commander-in-Chief, General Bennie L. Davis, discovered that I was about to visit, and he wanted to see me. I was looking forward very much to seeing the Control Center and the B-52s, but they wouldn't let me near any of that stuff. I told them I felt very disappointed and annoyed. Instead, I was given two briefings, one comparing the American and Russian arsenals and pointing out how far behind the United States was on practically all weapons and equipment; the other about the air force's interpretation of the freeze. I felt as if I were back in the Soviet Union, being presented with a whole load of propaganda—simple lies and half-truths. It was humiliating and demeaning for an intelligent person to sit through such obviously fabricated material. As I asked more and more penetrating and difficult questions, more and more officers covered with medals quietly slipped through the door and sat on chairs lining the wall. I felt as if I were being surrounded. I later asked the Methodist minister who had come with me why all the other men had to come in, and he said there was safety in numbers. What an eerie experience!

I was whisked out and taken up to see the general. His room was large, and on several tables there were tall models of missiles. He was a tall, thin, older man who immediately started plying me with veiled, hostile questions. I was very sweet, but gave him as good as he gave and answered his questions with a lot of facts and data. The meeting was only supposed to last fifteen minutes, but he seemed not to want to let me go. I think he thought this woman would be easy to convince, but I was not. Finally, he rather aggressively asked me if I had children, and I told him about my three beautiful children. I then asked him if he had grandchildren. He said,

"Yes," and I said, "How many?" and he said, "Two," and I said, "How old?" and he said something like "Two and six months." Suddenly the atmosphere in the room changed, and I saw by his eyes that I had gotten to his soul. We ended up with a polite shake of the hands. Everyone outside his room apparently had been very worried, wondering what on earth was keeping the general as he talked to this woman. The atmosphere was very tense.

Later I read that he had testified on the Hill and reassured people that American strategy was not now one of mutual assured destruction, but that the policy was now counterforce and war fighting; in other words, winnable nuclear war. I wish I had known that before I had seen him, and I would have moved in even more strongly.

The Industrial Complex

Every Sunday when I open the business section of *The New York Times* and/or the *Boston Globe*, they are full of advertisements for engineers and scientists and computer specialists to work on C^{3}I systems, guidance and delivery systems, satellites, etc. It would appear at a cursory glance that much of the U.S. economy is geared to sophisticated killing techniques.

The corporations operate with a dynamic all their own. Their one motivation is profit, and they will manipulate and do anything—literally anything—to make money. If the managing director or chair of the board of a company does not satisfy the profit motive, he (usually he) is fired. There is absolutely no moral integrity to this whole business, and there is no one person in charge. It is an extremely well-oiled, finely tuned, and very energetic enterprise, which holds the future of America and the world in a viselike, strangling grip. The staff in the large firms have been trained to honor and respect the firm, and there is tremendous peer-group loyalty engendered by the management. Along with this goes conformity, so no one steps out of line, just like a lot of little boys, no one game enough to speak the truth or voice concern or doubt. If they did, they would almost certainly lose their jobs.

I have been on the speaking circuit for many years, but

apart from some Rotary Club luncheons, I have never been asked to speak to any corporations. Corporations are usually a rich source for speaker requests. Obviously, they don't want to expose themselves to the medical messages or they would have to face the psychological and moral consequences of their behavior. They prefer to remain deliberately unconscious, indulging in the practice of psychic numbing.

On the few occasions when my colleagues or I have had the opportunity to confront these people, they always justify their life's work by using the primitive mechanism of blaming the Russians. Projecting the dark side has always been the rationale of the arms race right from the early days of the SAC command and RAND Corporation.

The real motive of the military corporations is greed: to make money in any way possible. The military avenue has proved to be extremely successful for many firms, so it has been refined to such an extent that government appropriations and money are almost self-generating like spontaneous combustion, and the logical conclusion of this very successful financial enterprise will, indeed, be combustion of the world.

In many ways, it seems to me that the deity of America has become money and that the true spiritual concept of God has atrophied on the vine of greed. The vital interests around the world, which the Pentagon vows to protect, are really only vital financial interests for trade or strategic minerals or raw materials. Six percent of the world's population uses 40 percent of the world's natural resources. America has only one vital interest to protect and that is its wonderful, ethical, moral principles, upon which rests the foundation of its society. It is rapidly losing, and indeed has almost lost, these guiding values of its soul, and has replaced them with a rapacious quest for more and more money.

Every year the heads of most of the major corporations and other major national and international political figures gather in a beautiful redwood forest near San Francisco called the Bohemian Grove. Past participants have included Henry Kissinger, Richard Nixon, Gerald Ford, Helmut Schmidt, and many others. The rather extraordinary thing about this elite gathering of some of the most influential people on earth is that women are excluded. Not only are they not permitted to participate in the discussions and lectures, but there are no female waiters or maids, no one of female gender on the property.

There are festivities, as well as serious events, and the gathering always opens with a splendid stage presentation called The Cremation of Care. Men dress up as women in ballet costumes and dance and sing, and there is a large orchestra. Festivities continue throughout the meeting. There is a lot of drinking and male horsing around, and some leave the compound to visit some female people over the road, presumably for the customary sexual activities.

It is obvious that the Bohemian Grove is extremely important for socialization and contact making to foster and improve national and international business relationships. The fact that the participants ostentatiously lock out women indicates that these powerful men are again operating on the masculine principles, excluding and denying their own feminine emotions and values and those of women in general. It is exactly this dynamic that has produced the mess in the world—a world in the grip of the egocentric, power-hungry, selfish, amoral, and killing negative animus. I have publicly criticized the Bohemian Club and the Bohemian Grove in the past, and some of its influential members were very upset with me. So I said, "Well, let me come to the Bohemian Grove and make a presentation about the medical effects of nuclear war," but they would not allow me to come. I believe there should be a public investigation of this situation. We should know exactly what goes on, and it should be opened up to the feminine influences and values. We can't just let the world proceed in this fashion any longer. It is suicidal!

Therapy

As I have written this book, two very obvious conclusions have suddenly dawned upon me:

(1) America must really be planning to strike first in the nuclear war because the counterforce weapons were designed with such extraordinary accuracy simply in order to hit silos full of missiles. If America waited until Russia initiated the nuclear war, all of these new tremendously expensive and sophisticated weapons would be rendered useless because they would hit only empty silos.

(2) Because of the extraordinary vulnerability of the Command, Control, Communications, and Intelligence System, the American arsenal is designed only for first use—not even for a second strike. Most of the C^3I system would be utterly devastated if the Russians strike first. The President and his deputies would be dead. The communication systems to launch the rockets would be destroyed, and the secondary command system would also be destroyed.

What an extraordinary situation! Even Lewis Carroll could not have invented a more fantastic tale.

What are we to do about our terminally ill planet? Ruolph Vircow, a German pathologist who lived in the nineteenth century, said, "Medicine is a social science and politics is medicine writ large."

The only way to prevent nuclear war is to use the democratic system. Many people have lost faith in politics and consider it to be dirty and somewhat beneath them. The American political system as well as most of the democracies in the Western world are wonderful organizations, which, if used effectively in the next several years, can determine the future of the life process.

On the whole, politicians are quite ignorant about the predicted medical and ecological consequences of nuclear war, as well as of the intricacies and implications of all the different weapon systems they continually appropriate money to build. It is urgent that these politicians be educated to understand that we are on the verge of destroying ourselves.

In the past, doctors and medical scientists have educated politicians about the causes of smallpox, malaria, and many other contagious diseases. As a result of this education, elected representatives appropriated money to establish vaccination programs on an international scale to eradicate smallpox. Mass-immunization programs have prevented our children from dying of tetanus, whooping cough, diphtheria, polio, and measles. With scientific and medical advice, the politicians have cleaned up the sewage systems and sterilized the water supplies so that people in Western societies have ceased to die from contagious gastrointestinal diseases. Consequently, the average life expectancy of the population has increased from the forties to the seventies.

A large percentage of the American annual budget is appropriated for the practice of preventive medicine. But we now face the single most important medical catastrophe in history, the final epidemic of the human race. Thus, we must once again demand that our politicians are appropriately educated and become involved in saving our lives.

Prevention of nuclear war is not a radical issue or a Democratic issue. It is a concern that embraces all people of all beliefs, political persuasions, colors, creeds, and races. In fact, it could be said that nuclear war is a Republican issue because it will be bad for business. It also could be acknowledged that prevention of nuclear war is the ultimate patriotic act. Nevertheless, it is an extremely conservative issue because we must conserve life on earth.

Thomas Jefferson said, "An informed democracy will behave in a responsible fashion." It is the responsibility of every American to educate him- or herself about the vast ramifications of the nuclear and conventional arms race, about the military-industrial complex, about past American intervention in other countries, and to keep abreast of present U.S. foreign policies. All this is vital because any superpower confrontation could end in nuclear holocaust.

Understanding this subject is more important than any

other reading you have to do and should become the number-one priority in your life, second only to your family, because such activity might preserve the life of your family.

The next step for you as an informed citizen is to become involved in the education of your friends, relatives, business and professional acquaintances, and to reach out into your local communities to ensure that they, too, understand the gravity of the issue. Learn to use the media in a constructive way. I find if I supplement my local newspaper with daily reading of *The New York Times* I am kept extremely well informed. If you read in the newspapers anything you disagree with, write a letter immediately to the editor. Call the manager of your local TV station or Dan Rather or other national anchorpeople if they are not covering an important story in an adequate way. Organize public meetings in your churches, city halls, movie theaters; promote discussion and controversy everywhere you go, so you will encourage people to start thinking and debating the subject. They will then be stimulated to investigate and to do their own reading.

The 1984 election will be the most important election ever to have occurred in the United States. Because of the precarious state of the arms race, unless we elect a House, Senate, and administration that support and will work for bilateral nuclear disarmament, the world is doomed. Not only must we elect a majority who support these principles, but after the election we must keep Congress on a strait and narrow track, and we must ride them like racehorses, using spurs and whips if necessary. This is because of the extraordinary pressure that the military-industrial complex exerts on the politicians as soon as they arrive in Washington.

The initial urgent step you must take will be to investigate the platform of your incumbent or newly running senators and congressmen and women. Elicit their attitudes toward all aspects of the arms race and foreign policy, and their attitudes toward the Soviet Union. Attend their local meetings as they run for election and ask them intelligent, penetrating questions about the issues that worry you the most. Don't be satisfied with tangential replies. Make sure they answer you in an intelligent fashion. If you disagree with their positions, make it known. Write letters to the newspapers; call the talk-back radio and TV shows; even get on radio and TV yourself. Educate the editorial boards of your local newspaper, TV, and radio stations. Take along a delegation of physicians from your local Physicians for Social Responsibility chapter. Show *The Last Epidemic* and shatter their psychic numbing. If you educate your local media, the job is half done.

Nuclear war must become the number-one issue of the election, and the economy must take second place. What does the economy matter if the world is on the brink of instant annihilation? Prevention of nuclear war must become as sacred as mother's milk or apple pie or Social Security, an issue upon which all politicians vote correctly in order to stay elected, and that includes the President.

If you adequately educate your community, you will find that the politicians will be scrambling to become better educated themselves and that the debate will be lively and stimulating. All incumbents must be answerable for their past voting records. Because the issues are so clear-cut, the best person will surely be elected. This may all sound difficult, but in practice it is easy and very rewarding, although it is obviously hard work. What is a more important issue in which to invest your time and effort?

Let me give you a wonderful example of a success story. Representative Nick Mavroulas, Democrat from Massachusetts, was a hawk and had voted fairly consistently for nuclear weapons. In the winter of 1980, I was invited on a cold night to go to Rockport, Massachusetts, to speak in a small village church about nuclear war. The church was packed and the audience responded enthusiastically. A local woman, Betty Tuttle, who had been looking forward to a peaceful retirement, became very involved and concerned and started a chapter of WAND (Women's Action for Nuclear Disarmament—an organization I had founded several years before). She and other women worked like mad doing all the things I have just suggested, and Mavroulas swung around and started advocating an end to the nuclear arms race and a freeze. Trimarco, the man running against Mavroulas, was a hawk, and he was beaten by several thousand votes after a long, hard race and intensive debate by the electorate. Mavroulas later acknowledged that WAND had been a major factor in his victory, and he is now a leading House opponent of the MX and a proponent of the freeze.

The same community process must occur in the Senate

races and in the presidential race. President Reagan must be challenged on all fronts—his attitude toward the arms race and nuclear war, his policies in Central America and in other countries—and he must *not* be allowed to skate around these subjects and evade the truth. The press has been too lenient with him and has failed to nail him for his obviously inadequate knowledge about the arms race, for his overt distortion of the facts about American and Soviet arsenals, and for his superficial, naïve, and paranoid approach to foreign policy.

Only the people of this nation have the power to alter the political agenda. I have often heard people say that you can't fight City Hall. This is baloney! No matter how much money the corporations pour into the coffers of the politicians via political action committees or individual contributions, it is the people who ultimately have the power to elect or defeat politicians. Here lies the profound strength of the American political system and all other democracies. Don't forget that most elections are won or lost by a few thousand votes.

Only 26 percent of the American public voted for President Reagan. I come from a country where voting is compulsory. If you don't vote, you get fined. So people are obliged to understand who and what they are voting for. I find it extremely worrisome that most Americans don't take the time to vote, let alone become informed about the issues of their nation. At this moment, people are struggling and dying around the world to create their own democracies, yet many Americans who have been given the privilege choose to ignore the enormous responsibility implicit in living in a democracy. Freedom means privilege and privilege means knowledge and responsibility. Freedom does not mean doing what you want to do and to hell with society and everyone else.

At this point in history, the United States has been invested with the responsibility for saving the world. No other country has this opportunity. History has bequeathed the fate of the future of life on earth to the American democracy. Will she react in time or not?

Nineteen eighty-four should see the biggest voter turnout in American history. All unregistered voters should be registered and educated about the fate of the earth and taught about the relationship of their economic and social plight to the enormous expenditures on weapons. The people must take back their democracy and the corporations must learn that the people will decide the fate of their country and the earth. A Harris poll dated January 16, 1984, reported that 63 percent of Americans believe that we will be closer to war by 1986 if Reagan is reelected, and after the President's Grenada speech, 64 percent to 29 percent of women worried that such policies would induce war compared with 49 percent to 48 percent of men. The 1984 election should be guided and determined by the emotions implicit in the positive feminine principle—nurturing, caring, and responsibility toward the life process. The gender gap will loom large and all good-hearted, moral, patriotic Americans will be obliged to participate. (Patriotism is not nationalism; it means love of country, but not to the exclusion of any other country.)

After the 1984 election, the work really begins. Training the elected politicians will really be somewhat like training children. We will have to watch them like hawks. Every vote must be noted, and the electorate will need to know the legislative calendar so they can call or write to their politicians telling them how they must vote. All weapon systems are *verboten*, and the nuclear freeze must be immediate and mandatory.

People must learn to understand how money for weapons is appropriated, which committees on the Hill do what. For instance, all weapons and military systems are determined by two main committees in each house—the Armed Services Committees and the Appropriations Committees. People must get to know which congressmen serve on these committees, who chairs them, and what their electoral districts are. The agendas of these and other relevant committees must become public knowledge and be printed in the newspapers and discussed on the TV news, so that people can lobby frequently at the appropriate times in order to influence the outcome of important votes. People must visit their legislators in large numbers, either in their home districts or on special trips to Washington to ensure that their congresspeople and senators are continually representing the future of their children. The plans for nuclear war are developed in an ethical and scientific vacuum. The medical and ecological data are never considered. The lowest number of weapons for a standard U.S. nuclear attack on the USSR is 2,500, whereas Sagan's new data indicate 1,000 bombs could destroy planetary life. Therefore, the Pentagon and politicians are actively planning for America's suicide. They must be made answerable immediately for this extraordinary irresponsibility.

There will, of course, be stiff competition from the corporations, banks, insurance companies, and Pentagon lobbyists. However, nothing threatens a politician more than a challenge to his or her political survival; hence, the people ultimately hold the power. It will be hard work to ride this new Congress and administration for the four years after the election, but it can and must be done. People will feel proud and will develop confidence in themselves and their country as they demonstrate the positive influence that can be brought to bear on their own government.

All of this may sound unduly optimistic, but it is easy to do and will create a new sense of joy and well-being among the American people. They will have healed their ailing democracy.

If one case of rabies was diagnosed in the city of New York, it would hit the national headlines. The few deaths from cyanide incorporated in Extra-Strength Tylenol became the subject of intense FBI investigations, and there was a fear in the land. It is terribly difficult to make people understand that the threat of nuclear war is just as imminent as taking a capsule laced with cyanide at the height of the scare and much more probable. The media exposure on this overriding issue has been minimal. There is a story in the history of and preparation for nuclear war far bigger than Watergate ever was—the arbitrary decisions, the fraud and corruption, the psychic numbing, the enormous and ubiquitous power and influence of the military-industrial complex, the complicity of the politicians. Yet the majority of the press and TV people who interview me have only a limited, superficial knowledge of this subject, and some are almost totally ignorant.

I find this situation truly appalling. *The New York Times* produces a supplement on homes and furnishings once a week. Why don't they begin to give similar coverage to the vast subject of nuclear war and its preparation? The same could be said for most of the newspapers and TV stations in the country. The *Boston Globe* and the *LA Times* have recently produced excellent supplements on the arms race, but they are the only ones. It should not be a spasmodic response, but weekly. *The New York Times* has thirty sportswriters and only a couple of defense and military affairs correspondents who assiduously cover the stream of information from the Pentagon and administration, but who virtually do not cover counterposing views from many well-informed Americans who want the arms race stopped.

The TV networks are only gradually learning that nuclear war is a subject to be covered. CBS produced an excellent series called *The Defense of America*, but although it was good, it only superficially covered this enormous subject. ABC has made a most provocative and excellent drama about the aftermath of nuclear war called *The Day After*. (In addition, an excellent movie, *WarGames*, depicting the vicissitudes of the NORAD computer systems has been well received by the public.)

Television is an excellent medium and the single most important influence in the country. It could be used as the most wonderful educational tool, but often it is not. It is very difficult to persuade the TV networks to broadcast ads depicting the medical dangers of nuclear war, because they cite the equal-time rule, whereby people from the opposing view will demand a hearing.

Several years ago, I visited the director of advertising at ABC to investigate the possibility of doing some ads using physicians depicting nuclear war as the ultimate medical issue. The ABC attorney came in halfway through the meeting and said in a loud and abrupt way, "What's your bottom line?" I said, "What do you mean?" and he repeated the question. I fumbled around for an answer and finally said, "Nuclear disarmament," and he jumped on me and said, "That's controversial." When I asked him what he meant, he said that Alexander Haig could demand equal time because he believes the only way to prevent nuclear war is to build more bombs. In other words, the adversary to my position would be the government of the United States, which is supposed to be elected to protect the health and well-being of the citizens.

Because the planet is terminally ill, there is an urgency about our work. Traditional arms-control negotiators have in the past sometimes stopped single weapon systems, but on the whole they have just sanctified and justified continuation of the arms race on both sides, becoming themselves its architects. They and their colleagues in the Pentagon and the corporations have also developed an obscure mystical language for the arms race in order to confuse the public. Because of patient demands, physicians have recently learned to demystify the language of medicine so that patients become adequately informed about their illnesses. Similarly, it is time to demystify the arms race. There are no professional "arms controllers." If there were, we surely would have had real arms reductions by this time.

It is also time to change our way of thinking about arms control. I prefer not to use this phrase at all. Let's talk about rapid bilateral nuclear disarmament. It must be rapid because even if we achieve a freeze we still have 50,000 nuclear weapons; even if we move down to 5,000 within five years, that is still ample to kill most people in the world. (Sagan's data imply that 100 megatons could destroy the earth.) Physicians treating a terminally ill patient never compromise. They work on that patient twenty-four hours a day for weeks or months, and occasionally the patient survives. A similar degree of dedication must be shown by the world leaders and their people if we are to save the creation.

After the Pentagon prepared its Five-Year Defense Guidance Plan for protracted winnable nuclear war, I prepared a five-year plan for rapid nuclear disarmament. It has three phases (the last two are adopted from a proposal made by George Kennan):

• A bilateral verifiable freeze on production, deployment, and testing of any more nuclear weapons or delivery systems, to be achieved by the superpowers within one year.
• Fifty percent across-the-board cuts in all nuclear weapons and delivery systems. Each superpower can select which bombs it chooses to discard—to be completed within two years.
• Two thirds cuts in the remainder of nuclear weapons and delivery systems bilaterally—to be completed in two years.

At the end of five years, the United States would have 5,000 bombs and the Soviet Union 3,000. This is still not enough of a reduction, but I would hope that the momentum and goodwill generated would be sufficient by the end of that time to rapidly proceed to zero.

Some people say I am naïve to suggest this time frame and such a severe degree of disarmament. On the contrary, as a physician who has a modicum of comprehension about human behavior, I believe that unless we implement such a plan immediately, it is naïve to suggest that the world will continue unscathed by nuclear holocaust. It is important to define an objective goal. People tend to procrastinate unless they have a defined time limit, and there is no time to waste. Such a proposal is imperative. Only if the superpowers begin to exert nuclear self-discipline will they be in a moral position to exert pressure on other nuclear nations and to lobby to prevent further proliferation of nuclear weapons.

Roger Fisher, a lawyer at Harvard, has suggested a scheme that may help prevent nuclear war. He advises that the codes the President needs to start a nuclear war be buried in the pericardium of the heart of one of the men who normally carries the football (the case containing the nuclear war codes) around behind the President. Should the President decide to start a nuclear war, he would have to slice open the man's chest to retrieve the codes. Apparently, some military people were horrified at this suggestion and said, aghast, "But that would mean killing a man if the President wanted to start a nuclear war."

Conversion from a War Economy to a Peace Economy

After World War II, America took the initiative and quickly converted its economy to peacetime uses. It also behaved in a mature, statesmanlike way on the international scene when it instituted the Marshall Plan, which helped revivify the disastrous economic situations of the European Allies. It also instigated programs that have allowed Japan to develop one of the most successful peacetime economies in the world.

The American corporations that are involved in the arms race are run by very intelligent people who will quickly perceive that the people of America will not allow the war-time economic system to continue to flourish. They will put their heads together and will be motivated to design equipment that will be used to the benefit of people both in the United States and internationally.

The world urgently needs adequate production and equitable distribution of food. It needs vast production of medicines and vaccines and redistribution of medical expertise and medical supplies to the millions of suffering people in the Third World. Adequate distribution of birth control techniques is needed to prevent the global population from growing from 4.5 billion now to 6 billion in 2000. Reforestation of many areas of the world is a mandatory priority, since trees are currently used to provide fuel for the poor countries, and trees recycle carbon dioxide to produce oxygen. The riches of the sea must be equitably distributed among all nations on earth and must not be mined only by those few Western nations that currently possess the technology and expertise to do so. All the world's natural resources must be shared and used for the benefit of the family of man and not hoarded and wasted on production of weapons. Millions of the world's people must be delivered from their situation of illiteracy and poverty—a vicious cycle that perpetuates endemic overpopulation and hunger.

The air and the water of America and large parts of the world are rapidly becoming irretrievably polluted with carcinogenic and mutagenic poisons, produced by industry to make profits. There are 4.5 million known toxic chemicals, and 375,000 new ones are produced annually. Most have never been adequately tested for carcinogenicity, and most are released to the environment, often illegally. Many of these chemicals are by-products of industries that produce plastic throwaway materials that we don't need and the production of which will probably eventually kill many of us. We must reevaluate our whole way of life.

America needs to tighten its belt. My husband and I visited Cuba in November 1979. Before the revolution, malaria, hookworm, tuberculosis, and gastrointestinal diseases were endemic. Cuba now has one of the best medical schemes in the world, so good that Dr. Julius Richmond, President Carter's Surgeon General, visited Cuba to develop ideas for America's health-care system. Prerevolution illiteracy was about 40 percent, and it is now almost negligible. The education programs are excellent. Nevertheless, life is still spare. There is no choice of clothes in the shops—one type of shoe, one type of trousers—and a limited variety of foods. The government has helped its people enormously, and the people are grateful.

We returned to Christmas in America with the stores just dripping with luxury and affluence. We knew then that if America tightened its belt, it could help feed many of the people in the world. Americans do not have a God-given right to be the wealthiest people in the world to the detriment of millions of other people. These poor countries are now developing their own nuclear weapons, and they are justifiably angry. Who will they drop them on?

It is obvious that the global situation is all interconnected and relevant to prevention of nuclear war.

Men are very smart—so smart that they have learned to destroy themselves. They could with a little effort and ingenuity develop a global economic system (excluding the production and sales of weapons) that would benefit the Western corporations, as well as all the countries on earth. For several years, the Third World has been pleading for such a move, but the selfish Western nations have refused to cooperate or contemplate how to alleviate the plight of the poor.

All such a scheme would take is creative initiative with the right motivation. If people see that in the end, they, too, will benefit, as wealth is equitably shared around the world, thus making the world a safer place, they will become enthusiastic about such an endeavor. This is not pie-in-the-sky talk; it is pragmatic and ultimately reasonable and rational. It will only take place if the people in the wealthy Western democracies educate themselves about the plight of mankind and decide for their own well-being that they and their politicians will create the solutions. At the moment, the powerful politicians who met in Williamsburg in 1983 to discuss the global economic crisis behaved like emasculated pawns. They made soothing noises, but did absolutely nothing to change the situation. One of the leading proponents of this negative posture was Ronald Reagan.

Conversion of a corporation from war to peace can be achieved not just by a decision of the corporate heads, but by initiative from the workers. Let me give an example: In England, the Lucas Aerospace Industry made parts for missiles. After many years of making this equipment, the workers finally became concerned about the global implications of their work. They called in some consultants, and they said, "With our technical skills, what can we make that would benefit mankind?" So the consultants designed electric cars, dialysis machines, and mass-transit systems. The workers then took these plans to the management and said, "We are not going to make missiles anymore. We are going to make this equipment." Management was surprised, but was influenced.

Other workers and high technologists are beginning to leave the military industry because of profound moral concern and have formed an organization called High Technologists for Social Responsibility. These people help each other find jobs doing peaceful work. At the moment, however, such jobs are not easy to find. That is why we need to create the political climate that will channel government money into peaceful industry and abolish appropriations for weapons production. It's easy. We the people ultimately control our government through the vote! We own the White House; we own the Pentagon and the Congress. They are our bombs; we paid for them.

Some scientists and their colleagues are also becoming alarmed about the implications of their occupations. I gave a speech at the American Association for the Advancement of Science meeting early in 1982, and a man named Bill Perry, who was the director of public relations for the Lawrence-Livermore Labs, heard me talk. He was taken aback by the information I presented, even though he worked right in the middle of a weapons organization. He spent the next week at the meeting checking around with other scientists to determine if I was a credible spokesperson. Most assured him that I was. He then said to himself, "If only half of what she says is valid, we are in terrible trouble." He contemplated his dilemma for several months and then decided to leave the labs and work for the passage of the nuclear weapons freeze in California. I have rarely seen such an elated man. He addressed a large meeting in the San Francisco Grace Cathedral where he recounted the history of his conversion, and he said, "I feel like a clean man." More people need to open up their souls to the truth and develop the courage to do what Bill Perry did.

Let me now quote two beautiful statements by George Kennan:

We have gone piling weapon upon weapon, missile upon missile, new levels of destructiveness upon old ones. We have done this helplessly, almost involuntarily, like the victims of some sort of hypnotism, like men in a dream, like lemmings heading for the sea, like the children of Hamelin marching blindly behind their Pied Piper, and the result is that today we have achieved, we and the Russians together, in the number of these devices, in their means of delivery, and above all in their destructiveness, levels of redundancy of such grotesque dimensions as to defy rational understanding. . . .

I find the view of the Soviet Union that prevails today in our governmental and journalistic establishments so extreme, so subjective, so far removed from what any sober scrutiny of external reality would reveal, that it is not only ineffective, but dangerous as a guide to political action. This endless series of distortions and oversimplification; this systematic dehumanization of the leadership of another great country; this routine exaggeration of Moscow's military capabilities and of the supposed inequity of its intentions; this daily misrepresentation of the nature and the attitudes of another great people— and a long-suffering people at that, sorely tried by the vicissitudes of this past century . . . this reckless application of the double standard to the judgment of Soviet conduct and our own; this failure to recognize the commonality of many of their problems and ours as we both move inexorably into the modern technological age . . . these, believe me, are not the marks of the maturity and realism one expects of the diplomacy of a great power.

We must reach out to the Russians, who are people like ourselves. I suggest that many Americans visit the Soviet Union as soon as possible, and that we encourage more visits from Soviet delegations. We must demystify the Soviet culture, and they must learn to understand ours. Cultural exchanges and scientific exchanges must increase, and trade between the superpowers must become the utmost priority. Russia for years has been begging to become a major trading partner. Let's do it. Let's move toward them as Richard Nixon once did with that long-hated enemy, Red China. Overnight, China became an ally and a major trading partner. If we did the same thing with Russia, it would cease to be an enemy and the weapons would become anachronistic. It is so simple, obvious, and easy. We must drop our ancient need for a tribal enemy and grow up and become responsible nations.

It is true that we have the secret of atomic energy locked in our brains forever. But this does not mean we can't alter our behavior. Once we practiced slavery, cannibalism, and dueling; as we became more civilized, we learned that these forms of behavior were antithetical to society, so we stopped. Similarly, we can easily stop making nuclear weapons, and we can also stop fighting and killing each other. We must move beyond war, because any small conventional war in the nuclear age could trigger a nuclear war. It was difficult initially to design and construct the weapons, but it would be very easy to dismantle them. It just needs a decision. Disposal of the plutonium will not be easy and safe, and permanent disposal may, indeed, be impossible.

Einstein said we must change the way we think. The answer lies, in fact, in the brilliant psychological teachings of Jesus. If we follow his admonitions and practice what he preached, it will be easy to make friends with Russia.

Ye have heard that it was said by them of old time, Thou shalt not kill; and whosoever shall kill shall be in danger of the judgement: But I say unto you, That everyone who is angry with his brother without a cause shall be in danger of the judgement.

Therefore if you bring thy gift to the altar, and there rememberest that thy brother hath ought against thee, leave there thy gift before the altar, and go thy way; first be reconciled to thy brother, and then come and offer thy gift.

Blessed are the peacemakers: for they shall be called the children of God.

In other words, the anger is the instinct behind the kill. We must stop projecting our anger and dark side out onto others.

Here is another relevant quote:

Why beholdest thou the mote that is in thy brother's eye, but considerest not the beam that is in thine own eye? Or how wilt thou say to thy brother, Let me pull out the mote out of thine eye; and, behold, a beam is in thine own eye? Thou hypocrite, first cast out the beam out of thine own eye; and then shalt thou see clearly to cast out the mote out of thy brother's eye.

This admonition is very relevant for the people of America. They must learn to understand their own past and present history before they can possibly start criticizing that of the Soviet Union.

Ye have heard that it hath been said Thou shalt love thy neighbor and hate thine enemy. But I say unto you, Love your enemies, bless them that curse you, do good to them that hate you, and pray for them that despitefully use you. For if ye love them which love you, what thank have ye? for sinners also love those that love them. And if ye do good to them which do good to you, what thank have ye? for sinners also do even the same.

Ye shall be children of the Most High: For he is kind toward the unthankful and to the evil. He maketh his sun to rise on the evil and on the good, and sendeth rain on the just and on the unjust. Be ye therefore merciful as your Father also is merciful.

Blessed are the merciful: for they shall obtain mercy.

These admonitions are obviously directed in modern times toward the Americans to love the Russians. In other words, we have to learn to love our enemies.

The American Catholic Bishops have written a pastoral letter on nuclear weapons and nuclear war, and they used these teachings of Jesus as a moral foundation. I consider this document to be the single most profound statement ever to be made by the Catholic Church. Other churches and Jewish organizations have made similar statements about the total immorality of the preparation for and probability of nuclear war.

Many people are moving toward this ultimate solution. Journalist Walter Cronkite recently told me that for years he has been in favor of unilateral nuclear disarmament. He thinks that America should totally disarm within ten years and some of the money saved should be used to create satellites and communications systems to educate the people of the world about how to live in peace. The money could also be used for food programs, and to help the industrial conversion process from weapons to peace. He said that he favors passive resistance—that if tens of thousands of people just sat down in front of Russian tanks, what could they do? He said we should make the arms negotiators sit at the table, and stop the clock and lock the door until they achieve appropriate arms reductions.

It is time for people to rise to their full moral and spiritual height, to take the world on their shoulders like Atlas, forgetting all other priorities in their lives, and to say *I* will save the earth. Each person can be as powerful as the most powerful person who ever lived. I have achieved a lot in a foreign country. I am an Australian and a woman, but neither of these factors has been an impediment. Think how much Americans could achieve by using and working through the democracy they have inherited from their forebears. All it takes is willpower and determination.

This quest is a spiritual adventure. It is time for mankind (men and women) to achieve spiritual fulfillment. Each person has a huge amount to offer. Each has a special creativity and potential that can be used—doctors, lawyers, merchants, artists, mothers, women, an endless variety. However, it is imperative that the ego be controlled. Ego needs are enormous and can be extremely destructive when working with others. I have learned in this work that if my ego becomes dominant and I engage in negative thoughts, things always go wrong. If I meditate or pray and decide simply to do what is right—not because it *feels* right but because it *is* right—and I drop my own egocentric needs, things always fall into place in the most amazing way. This takes willpower, but such action is enormously rewarding. As we work with others, we must remember only one thing and that is our final common goal, elimination of nuclear weapons. We don't need our egos fulfilled; we need only to fulfill our destiny on the planet in the twentieth century—to save the world. We must learn to reinforce and support one another. True happiness lies in helping one another. We are all the sons and daughters of God, and under the universal horror of the nuclear Sword of Damocles, we will be united to work together in mutual respect and peace.

No other generation has inherited this enormous responsibility and the privilege of saving all past and all future generations, all animals and all plants. Think of the enormous variety of delicate butterflies; think of the gorgeous birds of the earth, of the endless designs of fish in the sea; think of the beautiful and exotic flowers with their gorgeous and seductive perfumes; think of the proud lions and tigers and of the wondrous prehistoric elephants and hippopotamuses; think of what we are about to destroy.

Rapid nuclear disarmament is the ultimate issue of preventive medicine.

It is the ultimate parenting issue.

It is the ultimate Republican and ultimate Democratic issue.

It is the ultimate patriotic issue.

Above all, it is the ultimate religious issue.

We are the curators of life on earth; we hold it in the palms of our hands. Can we evolve spiritually and emotionally in time to control the overwhelming evil that our advanced and rational intellect has created? We will know the answer to this question in our lifetime. This generation will die having discovered the answer.

Notes

Introduction

Nevil Shute, *On the Beach* (New York: William Morrow and Company, 1957).

Robert Jay Lifton, *Death in Life* (New York: Basic Books, 1983).

David Barash and Judith Eve Lipton, *Stop Nuclear War* (New York: Grove Press, 1982).

Richard Halloran, "Pentagon Draws Up First Strategy for Fighting a Long Nuclear War," *New York Times*, May 30, 1982.

Prognosis: How Long Will the Earth Survive?

Richard Burt, "Carter Said to Back a Plan for Limiting Any Nuclear War," *New York Times*, August 10, 1980.

Center for Defense Information, "Force Level Calculator" (Washington, D.C., 1983).

Center for Defense Information, *Defense Monitor*, Vol. 11, No. 6, 1982.

Robert Aldridge, *The Counterforce Syndrome* (Washington, D.C.: Institute for Policy Studies, 1978).

Richard Halloran, "Pentagon Draws Up First Strategy for Fighting a Long Nuclear War," *New York Times*, May 30, 1982.

Verbal communication with J. Carson Mark, Former Head, Theoretical Division, Los Alamos Scientific Laboratory.

John Bierman, "Nuclear Warning System Rapped," *Boston Globe*, November 10, 1980.

Desmond Ball, *Can Nuclear War Be Controlled?* Adelphi

Papers, No. 196 (London: International Institute of Strategic Studies, 1981).

In Our Defense, film produced by Bill Jersey, Foundation for the Arts of Peace, San Francisco, 1983.

Center for Defense Information, "Cost Defense Guidance Plan," *Defense Monitor*, Vol. 12, No. 2, 1983.

Robert Scheer, *With Enough Shovels* (New York: Random House, 1982).

Roy Gutman, "The Nay-Sayer of Arms Control," *Long Island Newsday*, February 18, 1983.

Text of President Reagan's Address to Parliament on Promoting Democracy, *New York Times*, June 9, 1982.

Laurence Beilenson, *Survival and Peace in the Nuclear Age* (Chicago: Regnery/Gateway, 1980).

Scheer, *With Enough Shovels*.

Steven R. Weisman, "Clark's Move to Interior Makes External Waves," *New York Times*, October 16, 1983.

A.P., *Chicago Sun-Times*, October 29, 1983.

Richard Halloran, "Military Influence Is Seen Expanding," *New York Times*, November 2, 1983.

Arthur Macy Cox, *Russian Roulette* (New York: Times Books, 1982).

Bierman, "Nuclear Warning System Rapped."

David Blundy and John Bierman, "The Computer That Keeps Declaring War," *Times* (London), June 22, 1980.

Cox, *Russian Roulette*.

Jim Bencivenga, "C-Cubed! New U.S. Entrant in Military Technology Race," *Christian Science Monitor*, October 16, 1981.

"Two False Alerts Traced to 46¢ Item," *New York Times*, June 18, 1980.

"Missile Warning Computer Errs Yet Again on Attack by Soviets," *Boston Globe*, June 6, 1980.

"New False Warning of Attack Is Given," *New York Times*, June 9, 1980.

Richard Halloran, "Computer Error Falsely Indicates a Soviet Attack," *New York Times*, June 6, 1980.

Richard Burt, "False Nuclear Alarms Spur Urgent Effort to Find Flaws," *New York Times*, June 30, 1980.

"That Nuclear Alarm Wasn't False," Editorial, *New York Times*, June 30, 1980.

Ball, *Can Nuclear War Be Controlled?*

Christopher Hanson, "Doubts Cast on Security of Military Computers," *Boston Globe*, July 4, 1983.

Bernard Bereanu, "Self-Activation of World Nuclear Weapons Systems," *Journal of Peace Research*, Vol. 20, No. 1, 1983.

William J. Broad, "The Chaos Factor," *Science*, January/February, 1983.

"How Many Bomb Mishaps?" *Christian Science Monitor*, December 26, 1980.

"Summaries of Accidents Involving Nuclear U.S. Weapons, 1950 to 1980," from Department of Defense data, n.d.

David E. Kaplan, "Where the Bombs Are," *New West Magazine*, April, 1981.

Steven Talbot and Jonathan Dann, "Broken Arrows, Broken Sleep," *Los Angeles Times*, March 18, 1981.

Richard Halloran, "U.S. Heightening Defenses Against Nuclear Terrorists," *New York Times*, October 24, 1982.

"If Nuclear Terrorists Ever Threaten, Team Will Respond," *Los Angeles Times*, October 24, 1982.

Ruth Leger Sivard, *World Military and Social Expenditures* (Leesburg, Va.: World Priorities, 1982).

Milton Benjamin, "A U.S. Shift on N-Sale Policy," *Boston Globe*, August 18, 1983.

Edward Markey, *Nuclear Peril* (Cambridge, Mass.: Ballinger, 1982).

Samuel H. Day, Jr., "The Afrikaner Bomb," *Progressive*, September, 1982.

James E. Muller, "An Accidental Nuclear War," *Newsweek*, March 1, 1982.

Verbal communication with Admiral Gene LaRocque, Center for Defense Information, Washington, D.C.

Jerome D. Frank, *Sanity and Survival in the Nuclear Age* (New York: Random House, 1967, 1982).

Ibid.

Case History

William Appleman Williams, *America Confronts a Revolutionary World, 1776 to 1976* (New York: William Morrow and Company, 1976).

Thomas Boylston Adams, "The End of Colonialism," *Boston Globe*, March 13, 1983.

Louis M. Hacker, *The Shaping of the American Tradition* (New York: Columbia University Press, 1947).

Williams, *America Confronts a Revolutionary World*.

George F. Kennan, "America's Unstable Soviet Policy," *Atlantic Monthly*, November, 1982.

Henry Steele Commager, "Outmoded Assumptions," *Atlantic Monthly*, March, 1982.

Ibid.

Ibid.

Kennan, "America's Unstable Soviet Policy."

George F. Kennan, *The Nuclear Delusion* (New York: Pantheon Books, 1982).

Bernard Feld, "Einstein and the Politics of Nuclear Weapons," *Bulletin of the Atomic Scientists*, Vol. 35, March, 1979.

Kennan, *The Nuclear Delusion*.

Barash and Lipton, *Stop Nuclear War*.

Scheer, *With Enough Shovels*.

Kennan, "America's Unstable Foreign Policy."

David Halberstam, *The Powers That Be* (New York: Alfred A. Knopf, 1979).

Peter Goodchild, *J. Robert Oppenheimer: Shatterer of Worlds* (London: British Broadcasting Corporation, 1980, and Boston: Houghton Mifflin Company, 1981).

Kennan, *The Nuclear Delusion*.

Barash and Lipton, *Stop Nuclear War*.

Kennan, *The Nuclear Delusion*.

Frank, *Sanity and Survival in the Nuclear Age*.

Alan Wolfe, *The Rise and Fall of the Soviet Threat* (Washington, D.C.: Institute for Policy Studies, 1979).

Randall Forsberg, "Confining the Military to Defense as a Route to Disarmament," *World Policy Journal*, Vol. 1, No. 2, Winter 1984.

Barash and Lipton, *Stop Nuclear War*.

Ibid.

Forsberg, "Confining the Military to Defense as a Route to Disarmament."

Barash and Lipton, *Stop Nuclear War*.

Solly Zuckerman, *Nuclear Illusion and Reality* (New York: Viking Press, 1982).

James Fallows, *National Defense* (New York: Random House, 1981).

Center for Defense Information, *Defense Monitor*, Vol. 11, No. 6, 1982.

M. R. Montgomery, "The Press and Adolf Hitler," *Boston Globe Magazine*, January 30, 1983.

Halberstam, *The Powers That Be*.

Noam Chomsky and Edward S. Herman, *Political Economy of Human Rights: The Washington Connection and Third-World Fascism* (Montreal: Black Rose Books, 1979, and Boston: South End Press, 1979).

Ibid.

Ibid.

Ibid.

James Bamford, *The Puzzle Palace—A Report on America's Most Secret Agency* (Boston: Houghton Mifflin Company, 1982).

Stephen Schlesinger and Stephen Kinzer, *Bitter Fruit* (New York: Doubleday and Company, 1982).

George H. Crowell, "Central America and the Arms Race" (Paper presented to the Socialism and Economic Justice Subgroups of the Social Ethics Working Group, American Academy of Religion, New York, December 21, 1982).

Stephen Kinzer, "Human Rights Aide Defends U.S. Policy," *New York Times*, January 20, 1983.

James A. Nathan and James K. Oliver, "Conserving Containment," *U.S. Foreign Policy and World Order*, 2nd ed. (Boston: Little, Brown, 1981).

James Garrison, *The Russian Threat* (London: Gateway, 1983).

Gabriel Garcia Marquez, "The Solitude of Latin America," *New York Times*, February 6, 1983.

Juan Mendez, "Reagan's Argentines," *New York Times*, December 22, 1982.

Crowell, "Central America and the Arms Race."

George Crile, "Toppling Managua's Regime," *New York Times*, December 3, 1982.

Walter La Feber, "Making Revolution Opposing Revolution," *New York Times*, July 3, 1983.

Alan Riding, "Violence Rules Central America Despite Pacts and Plans for Peace," *New York Times*, January 23, 1983.

"Central American Politics at a Glance," *New York Times*, December 5, 1982.

"Health and Human Rights in El Salvador, A Report of the Second Public Health Commission to El Salvador" (Boston and New York: Committee for Health Rights in El Salvador, 1983).

Garrison, *The Russian Threat*.

Crowell, "Central America and the Arms Race."

William Shawcross, *Sideshow* (New York: Simon and Schuster, 1979).

Seymour M. Hersh, *The Price of Power* (New York: Summit Books, 1983).

Garrison, *The Russian Threat*.

Ibid.

Walden Bello and Peter Hayes, "Tensions in the North Pacific," *The Nation*, October 1, 1983.

Richard Grimmett, *Trends in Conventional Arms Transfers to the Third World by Major Suppliers, 1974 to 1981* (Washington, D.C.: Congressional Research Service, Library of Congress, 1982).

William Hartung, "Weapons for the World," *Council on Economic Priorities Newsletter*, December-January, 1981–82.

Sivard, *World Military and Social Expenditures*.

Hersh, *The Price of Power*.

Germs of Conflict: The Third World

Cox, *Russian Roulette*.

Ibid.

Ibid.

Ibid.

Scheer, *With Enough Shovels*.

Ibid.

Cox, *Russian Roulette*.

Ibid.

Scheer, *With Enough Shovels*.

Physical Examination

Some of the data cited subsequently in this chapter were updated according to information provided by the Center for Defense Information and are current as of December 1983.

Leslie H. Gelb, "Korean Jet: Points Still to Be Settled," *New York Times*, September 26, 1983.

John F. Burns, "Jet Incident Improves Picture of Russian Military," *New York Times*, September 18, 1983.

David Shribman, "U.S. Experts Say Soviet Didn't See Jet Was Civilian," *New York Times*, October 7, 1983.

"The New Peace Candidate," *Boston Globe*, January 17, 1984.

Richard Halloran, "Spread of Nuclear Arms Is Seen by 2,000," *New York Times*, November 15, 1982.

Robert Scheer, "Teller's Obsession Became Reality in 'Star Wars' Plan," *Los Angeles Times*, July 10, 1983.

William J. Broad, "Rewriting the History of the H-Bomb," *Science*, Vol. 218, No. 4574, November 19, 1982.

Center for Defense Information, "U.S.–Soviet Military Facts," *Defense Monitor*, Vol. 11, No. 6, 1982.

R. Jeffrey Smith, "Soviets Lag in Key Weapons Technology," *Science*, Vol. 219, March 18, 1983.

Center for Defense Information, "U. S.–Soviet Military Facts."

Report of the Secretary-General, United Nations, *Nuclear Weapons* (Brookline, Mass.: Autumn Press, 1980).

Center for Defense Information, "U.S.–Soviet Military Facts."

Ibid.

Barash and Lipton, *Stop Nuclear War*.

William M. Arkin, "Nuclear Security: The Enemy May Be Us," *Bulletin of the Atomic Scientists*, November 1983.

Center for Defense Information, "U.S.–Soviet Military Facts."

Jerome B. Wiesner and Emma Rothschild, "Expand the Arms Talks," *New York Times*, November 11, 1983.

Report of the Secretary-General, *Nuclear Weapons*.

Barash and Lipton, *Stop Nuclear War*.

Center for Defense Information, "U.S.–Soviet Military Facts."

Ibid.

Randall Forsberg, "Confining the Military to Defense as a Route to Disarmament," *World Policy Journal*, Vol. 1, No. 2, Winter 1984.

Ibid.

Ibid.

Ibid.

Roy Gutman, "The Nay-Sayer of Arms Control," *Long Island Newsday*, February 18, 1983.

Forsberg, "Confining the Military to Defense as a Route to Disarmament."

Ibid.

Ibid.

Personal communication with Steven Goose, Fellow, Center for Defense Information, Washington, D.C., 1983.

Walden Bello and Peter Hayes, "Tensions in the North Pacific," *The Nation*, October 1, 1983.

Richard Halloran, "Uncle Sam Pays a High Price for Being in 359 Places at Once," *New York Times*, July 24, 1983.

Ibid.

Clergy and Laity Concerned, "U.S. Bases in the Philippines," *U.S. Bases in the Philippines: Springboards for Intervention, Instruments of Nuclear War;* originally published in *Southeast Asia Chronicle*, special issue on the Philippine Bases, No. 89, May, 1982.

Ibid.

Ibid.

John O. Iatrides, "To Meet Greek Needs," *New York Times*, March 2, 1983.

Philip Taubman, "Role in Panama of U.S. Military Causing Strains," *New York Times*, May 24, 1983.

Desmond Ball, *A Suitable Piece of Real Estate* (Sydney, Australia: Hale and Iremonger, 1980).

Darlene Keju and Giff Johnson, "Kwajalein: Home on the Range," *Pacific Magazine*, November-December, 1982.

Palau, Self-Determination vs. U.S. Military Plans, Publication of Micronesia Support Committee, Honolulu, May, 1983.

Steven R. Weisman, "The Influence of William Clark," *New York Times Magazine*, August 14, 1983.

Jeff Gerth, "Problems Promoting Democracy," *New York Times*, February, 1983.

Forsberg, "Confining the Military to Defense as a Route to Disarmament."

Ibid.

Ibid.

John Noble Wilford, "Mapping in the Space Age," *New York Times Magazine*, June 5, 1983.

"The Super-Charger—Featuring Three New Games," Star Path Corporation, 1982, P.O. Box 209, Santa Clara, Calif.

Flora Lewis, "Lemmings in Space," *New York Times*, January 6, 1984.

Jim Nesbitt, " 'Defender' Ron Scores Zillions With Students," *Orlando Sentinel*, March 9, 1983.

David Hoffman, "Offensive Capability of Shuttle Confirmed by Officials at NASA," *Washington Times*, March 11, 1983.

"Shuttle Needed for Space-Based BMD System," *Aerospace Daily*, Ziff Davis Publishing Company, Washington, D.C., Vol. 121, No. 6, June, 1983.

Thomas Karas, *The New High Ground* (New York: Simon and Schuster, 1983).

Ball, *A Suitable Piece of Real Estate*.

Lou Cannon, "President Goes to the Movies, Skips New Hampshire for NOW," *Washington Post*, June 13, 1983.

In Our Defense, film produced by Bill Jersey.

Ball, *Can Nuclear War Be Controlled?*

Knut Royce, "In Case of N-War, It's Government Officials First," *Seattle Post Intelligence*, May 10, 1983.

Knut Royce, "Destabilization Results When Over-Confidence Pushes Button," *Seattle Post Intelligence*, May 11, 1983.

Ball, *Can Nuclear War Be Controlled?*

Ibid.

Ibid.

Ibid.

Ibid.

Ball, *A Suitable Piece of Real Estate*.

David Burnham, "The Silent Power of the NSA," *New York Times Magazine*, March 27, 1983.

Ball, *A Suitable Piece of Real Estate*.

Robert Lindsey, *The Falcon and the Snowman* (London: Penguin, 1979).

Home on the Range, an Australian documentary film, produced by Gil Scrine, 1982.

Ball, *A Suitable Piece of Real Estate*.

Irving Wallace, David Wallechinsky, and Amy Wallace, "The Forgotten War," *Parade Magazine*, June 12, 1983.

Ball, *A Suitable Piece of Real Estate*.

Ibid.

Ibid.

Ibid.

Ibid.

Pathogenesis: The Pathological Dynamics of the Arms Race

Fred Kaplan, *The Wizards of Armageddon* (New York: Simon and Schuster, 1983).

Ibid.

Ibid.

Jim Calogero, "Conference at MIT Stresses Disarmament," *Boston Globe*, December 5, 1982.

"Standing at the Brink," *Mother Jones*, September-October, 1982.

Daniel Ellsberg, "Call to Meeting," Preface to *Protest and Survive*, edited by E. P. Thompson and Dan Smith (New York: Monthly Review Press, 1982).

Desmond Ball, "International Security, U.S. Strategic Forces: How Would They Be Used?" *Harvard and MIT*, Vol. 7, No. 3, Winter 1982–83, pp. 31–60.

Gregg Herken, *The Winning Weapon: The Atomic Bomb in the Cold War* (New York: Knopf, 1982), pp. 256–74.

Verbal communication with Daniel Ellsberg, December 1983.

Center for Defense Information, "U.S.–Soviet Military Facts."

Barash and Lipton, *Stop Nuclear War*.

Ibid.

Ibid.

Ibid.

Ibid.

Ibid.

Report of the Secretary-General, *Nuclear Weapons*.

Aldridge, *The Counterforce Syndrome*.

Steven Roberts, "Administration Opens a Drive in Congress for MX," *New York Times*, April 21, 1983.

R. Jeffrey Smith, "Soviets Lag in Key Weapons Technology."

Aldridge, *The Counterforce Syndrome*.

Report of the Secretary-General, *Nuclear Weapons*.

Barash and Lipton, *Stop Nuclear War*.

Stansfield Turner, "The 'Folly' of the MX Missile," *New York Times Magazine*, March 13, 1983.

Herbert Scoville, Jr., *MX: Prescription for Disaster* (Cambridge, Mass.: MIT Press, 1981).

Hedrick Smith, "Politically Unprepared: The Administration

Now Seeks to Buy More Time," *New York Times*, December 12, 1982.

Leslie Gelb, "New Deployment Needed, Maybe a New Strategy, Too," *New York Times*, December 12, 1982.

David C. Wright, "Missiles Too Accurate for Our Own Good," *New York Times*, October 8, 1982.

Dale Bumpers, "The MX? No," *New York Times*, October 22, 1982.

"Unguided Missile," *New York Times*, December, 1982.

Charles Mohr, "Pentagon Studies 'Midgetman' Basing," *New York Times*, May 16, 1983.

Charles Mohr, "Fleet of Smaller Missiles to Bolster MX Debated," *New York Times*, March 23, 1983.

"PACs of MX Missile Contractors Doubling Campaign Contributions," *Washington Post*, October 14, 1982.

Aldridge, *The Counterforce Syndrome*.

Report of the Secretary-General, *Nuclear Weapons*.

Barash and Lipton, *Stop Nuclear War*.

STOP Project, "Doomsday in the North Country," *Project ELF*, Summer, 1982.

Barash and Lipton, *Stop Nuclear War*.

Aldridge, *The Counterforce Syndrome*.

Report of the Secretary-General, *Nuclear Weapons*.

Leslie Gelb, "The Cruise Missile," *New York Times*, September 2, 1982.

Center for Defense Information, "The Cruise Missile Era: Opening Pandora's Box," *Defense Monitor*, Vol. 12, 1983.

Charles Mohr, "Cruise Missile Passes Tests, But Its Critics Score, Too," *New York Times*, July 17, 1983.

Charles Mohr, "Pershings Put Moscow on 6-Minute Warning," *New York Times*, February 27, 1983.

Dusko Doder, "Pershing II and Soviet Concern," *Boston Globe*, January 25, 1983.

William Beecher, "Nuclear Jitters in Moscow," *Boston Globe*, November 13, 1981.

Bernard Gwertzman, "Reagan Intensifies Drive to Promote Policies in Europe," *New York Times*, January 20, 1983.

"Britons and U.S. Ad Agency Discuss a Campaign on Arms," *New York Times*, January 31, 1983.

David Wood, "B-1 Symbolizes Power of Military-Industrial Complex," *Los Angeles Times*, July 10, 1983.

Gordon Adams, "The B-1 Bomber: An Analysis of Its Strate-

gic Utility, Cost, Constituency and Economic Impact,"
  Report (New York: Council on Economic Priorities, 1976).
Wood, "B-1 Symbolizes Power of Military-Industrial Complex."
*Countervailing Strategy Demands Revision of Strategic Force
  Acquisition Plans*, Report to the Congress by the Comp-
  troller General of the United States (Gaithersburg, Md.,
  August 5, 1981).
Christopher Paine, "Reagatomics, Or How to Prevail," *Nation*,
  April 9, 1983.
William Arkin, "More Weapons Nobody Wants," *Bulletin of
  the Atomic Scientists*, October, 1982.
Michael Klare, "The Conventional Weapons Fallacy," *Nation*,
  April 9, 1983.
Christopher Paine, "On the Beach: The Rapid Deployment
  Force and the Nuclear Arms Race," *Merip Reports*, No.
  111, January, 1983.
Martha Wenger, "AirLand Battle Doctrine," *Merip Reports*,
  No. 111, January, 1983.
Michael Klare, "An Army in Search of a War," *Progressive*,
  February, 1981.
Ball, *Can Nuclear War Be Controlled?*
Robert Levey, "Support Grows for U.S. School of Peace,"
  Boston Globe, August 4, 1982.

The Iron Triangle

Benjamin Taylor, "Pentagon Seeks $239 Billion to Continue
  Build-Up," *Boston Globe*, February 1, 1983.
Rone Tempest, "U.S. Defense Establishment Wields a Perva-
  sive Power," *Los Angeles Times*, July 10, 1983.
Ibid.
Howard H. Hiatt, "Sounding Board: The Physician and Na-
  tional Security," *New England Journal of Medicine*, Vol.
  307, No. 18, October 28, 1982.
Gordon Adams, "America Held Hostage," *Nuclear Times*,
  April, 1983.
Tempest, "U.S. Defense Establishment Wields a Pervasive
  Power."
Clyde Haberman, "Japan Holds '84 Rise in Arms Spending to
  6.9%," *New York Times*, July 13, 1983.
David Treadwell, "Arms Costs Figure Heavily in Economy,"
  Los Angeles Times, July 10, 1983.

Ibid.

Kaplan, *The Wizards of Armageddon.*

Fred Kaplan, "Herman Kahn: Nuclear Strategist Who Took 'Rational View,' " *Boston Globe,* July 10, 1983.

Orr Kelly and K. M. Chrysler, "While Protestors March, Bomb Business Flourishes," *U.S. News and World Report.*

Ibid.

Ibid.

Herbert York, *Race to Oblivion* (New York: Simon and Schuster, Clarion Books, 1970).

"Frightened for the Future of Humanity," *New York Times,* April 24, 1983.

Robert Scheer, "Teller's Obsession Becomes Reality in 'Star Wars' Plan," *Los Angeles Times,* July 10, 1983.

Ibid.

Zuckerman, *Nuclear Illusion and Reality.*

William J. Broad, "Expanding the Underground A-War," *Science,* Vol. 218, October 22, 1982.

"U.S. Atom Arms Tests at a Post-1970 Record," *New York Times,* October 24, 1982.

Samuel H. Day, "The Nicest People Make the Bomb," *Progressive,* October, 1978.

Scheer, "Teller's Obsession Becomes Reality in 'Star Wars' Plan."

Ibid.

Wayne Biddle, "Publish and Perish Catch in Defense Research," *New York Times,* June 26, 1983.

John Powers, "Pentagon Is Back at School . . . Quietly," *Boston Globe,* September 6, 1981.

Ibid.

Steve Burkholder, "The Pentagon in the Ivory Tower," *Progressive,* June, 1981.

Ibid.

Helen M. Caldicott, *Nuclear Madness* (Brookline, Mass.: Autumn Press, 1979; reprint, with Epilogue, New York: Bantam, 1981).

Gordon Adams, *The Politics of Defense Contracting: The Iron Triangle* (New Brunswick, N.J.: Transaction Books, 1981).

Bob Adams, "Muffled Drums," *St. Louis Post Dispatch,* April 17, 1983.

Tempest, "U.S. Defense Establishment Wields a Pervasive Power."

Michael W. Johnson, "Keeping Up in Weapons," *Boston Globe*, May 9, 1982.

Stephen Daly, "Arms Industry's Hot Stocks," *New York Times*, September 9, 1983.

Adams, *The Politics of Defense Contracting: The Iron Triangle*.

Adams, "Muffled Drums."

Ibid.

John Hanrahan, "Fat City," *Common Cause*, May-June, 1983.

Bob Adams, "Defense 'Revolving Door' Could Lead to Conflict Critics Say," *St. Louis Post Dispatch*, April 19, 1983.

Ibid.

Kenneth B. Noble, "Thayer Quits as Defense Deputy over Expected Charges by S.E.C.," *New York Times*, January 5, 1984.

"Boeing Severance to 3 in Pentagon Under Inquiry," *New York Times*, March 16, 1983.

Adams, "Defense 'Revolving Door' Could Lead to Conflict Critics Say."

"A Revolving Door for Defense Jobs," *Los Angeles Times*, July 10, 1983.

Bob Adams, "Congressmen Who Can Get Helped," *St. Louis Post Dispatch*, April 18, 1983.

Adams, *The Politics of Defense Contracting: The Iron Triangle*.

Ibid.

Ibid.

Ibid.

Ibid.

Bob Adams, "Camaraderie Parlayed into Defense Orders," *St. Louis Post Dispatch*, April 22, 1983.

Adams, *The Politics of Defense Contracting: The Iron Triangle*.

Wood, "B-1 Symbolizes Power of Military-Industrial Complex."

Adams, *The Politics of Defense Contracting: The Iron Triangle*.

Tempest, "U.S. Defense Establishment Wields a Pervasive Power."

David Wood, "Spending Eludes Civilian Control," *Los Angeles Times*, July 10, 1983.

Richard Halloran, "Why the Military Has Four Tactical Air Forces: A Case Study," *New York Times*, June 12, 1983.

Tempest, "U.S. Defense Establishment Wields a Pervasive Power."

Wood, "B-1 Symbolizes Power of Military-Industrial Complex."

Gordon Adams, "The B-1 Bomber: An Analysis of Its Strategic Utility, Cost, Constituency and Economic Impact."

Charles Mohr, "Lockheed's Grip on Washington," *New York Times*, October 17, 1982.

David Shribman, "The MX's Economic Impact," *New York Times*, December 7, 1982.

Robert Scheer, "California Wedded to Military Economy, But Bliss Is Shaky," *Los Angeles Times*, July 10, 1983.

Rone Tempest, " 'Beltway Bandits,' Ring Washington," *Los Angeles Times*, July 10, 1983.

Hanrahan, "Fat City."

Jonathan Alter and Mary Lord, "Cutting Waste at the Pentagon," *Newsweek*, July 11, 1983.

Tempest, "U.S. Defense Establishment Wields a Pervasive Power."

Wood, "Spending Eludes Civilian Control."

"Federal Inmates in Connecticut Making U.S. Missile Parts," *Boston Globe*, May 9, 1983.

Rone Tempest, "Kremlin System Looks Familiar," *Los Angeles Times*, July 10, 1983.

Franklyn D. Holzman, "A Gap? Another?" *New York Times*, March 9, 1983.

Fred Kaplan, "Soviet Arms Budget Stirs Debate in U.S.," *Boston Globe*, February 16, 1983.

The Terminal Event

World Health Organization, *Effects of Nuclear War on Health and Health Services* (Geneva, 1983).

Kevin N. Lewis, "The Prompt and Delayed Effects of Nuclear War," *Scientific American*, Vol. 241, No. 1, July, 1979.

Jonathan Schell, *The Fate of the Earth* (New York: Avon, 1982).

Ball, *Can Nuclear War Be Controlled?*

Ambio: A Journal of the Human Environment, Royal Swedish Academy of Sciences, Pergamon Press, Vol. 11, No. 2–3, 1982.

Frank H. Ervin, John B. Glazier, Saul Aronow, David Nathan, Robert Coleman, Nicholas Avery, Steven Shohet, and Cavin Leeman, "Human and Ecological Effects in Massachusetts of an Assumed Thermonuclear Attack on the United States," *New England Journal of Medicine*, Vol. 266, No. 22, May 31, 1962.

Victor W. Sidel, H. Jack Geiger, and Bernard Lown, "The Physician's Role in the Postattack Period," *New England Journal of Medicine*, Vol. 266, No. 22, May 31, 1962.

Report of the Secretary-General, *Nuclear Weapons*.

John Hersey, *Hiroshima* (New York: Knopf, 1946).

Japan Broadcasting Corp., ed., *Unforgettable Fire* (New York: Pantheon, 1981).

John Constable, "Burn Casualties," in *The Final Epidemic*, edited by Ruth Adams and Susan Cullen (Chicago: Educational Foundation for Nuclear Science, 1981).

Schell, *The Fate of the Earth*.

Ambio, Vol. 11, No. 2–3.

Judith Miller, "U.S. Delays Buying Morphine to Avoid War-Ready Image," *New York Times*, February 14, 1983.

Steven A. Fetter and Kosta Tsipis, "Catastrophic Releases of Radioactivity," *Scientific American*, Vol. 244, No. 4, April, 1981.

Henry Way Kendall, Physicians for Social Responsibility Symposium on the Medical Consequences of Nuclear Weapons and Nuclear War, Harvard Medical School, February, 1980.

Federation of American Scientists, "Effects of Nuclear War," *Public Interest Report*, Vol. 34, No. 2, February, 1981.

Ervin et al., "Human and Ecological Effects"; Sidel et al., "The Physician's Role."

Herbert L. Abrams, "Infection and Communicable Diseases," in *The Final Epidemic*, edited by Ruth Adams and Susan Cullen (Chicago: Educational Foundation for Nuclear Science, 1981).

The Defense of America, CBS series, 1981.

Jennifer Leaning, "Civil Defense in the Nuclear Age" (Cambridge, Mass.: Physicians for Social Responsibility, 1982).

Scheer, *With Enough Shovels*.

K. S. Gant and C. V. Chester, "Minimizing Excess Radiogenic Cancer Deaths After a Nuclear Attack," *Health Physics*, Vol. 41, No. 3, September, 1981.

Assembly of Mathematical and Physical Sciences, National Research Council, *Long-Term Worldwide Effects of Multiple Nuclear Weapons Detonations* (Washington, D.C.: National Academy Press, 1975).

Ibid.

Schell, *The Fate of the Earth*.

Barrie Pittock, "Atmospheric Effects Reappraised," *Australian Physicist*, Vol. 19:189, 1982.

Schell, *The Fate of the Earth*.

R. P. Turco, O. B. Toon, T. P. Ackerman, J. B. Pollack, and Carl Sagan, "Nuclear Winter: Global Consequences of Multiple Nuclear Explosions," *Science*, December 23, 1983.

Paul Ehrlich, John Harte, Mark A. Harwell, Peter H. Raven, Carl Sagan, George M. Woodwell, Joseph Berry, Edward S. Ayensu, Anne H. Ehrlich, Thomas Eisner, Stephen J. Gould, Herbert D. Grover, Rafael Herrera, Robert M. May, Ernst Mayer, Christopher McKay, Harold A. Mooney, Norman Myers, David Pimentel, and John M. Teal, "Long-Term Biological Consequences of Nuclear War," *Science*, December 23, 1983.

Etiology: Missile Envy and Other Pschopathology

Mark Gerzon, *A Choice of Heroes* (Boston: Houghton Mifflin Company, 1982).

Eleanor E. Maccoby and Carol Nagy Jacklin, "Sex Differences in Aggression: A Rejoinder and Reprise," *Child Development*, Vol. 51, No. 4, December, 1980.

Hersh, *The Price of Power*.

David Halberstam, *The Best and the Brightest* (New York: Random House, 1972).

William Beardslee and John E. Mack, "The Impact of Nuclear Developments on Children and Adolescents," *Psychosocial Aspects of Nuclear Developments*, American Psychiatric Association, Task Force Report 20, 1981.

Barbara MacIntosh, "The Nuclear Nightmare," *Houston Post*, December 13–15, 1981.

Olive Evans, "Handling Children's Nuclear-War Fears," *New York Times*, May 27, 1982.

David Arnold, "The Young and Nuclear War—How Exactly Do They Feel?" *Boston Globe*, October 29, 1981.

Peter Pringle and William Arkin, *S. I. O. P.* (London: Sphere Books, 1983; and New York: W. W. Norton, 1983).

Gerzon, *A Choice of Heroes*.

G. William Domhoff, *The Bohemian Grove* (New York: HarperTorch Books, 1974).

Richard Pollak, "Covering the Unthinkable," *Nation*, May 1, 1982.

John E. Mack, "But What About the Russians?" *Harvard Magazine*, March-April, 1982.

Index

accuracy, 10–12, 182
Acheson, Dean, 59
Adams, Gordon, 238–50
Adams, Thomas Boylston, 48
Advanced Inertial Reference
    Sphere (AIRS), 186
advanced strategic air-launched
    missile (ASALM), 199–200
Afghanistan:
    Soviet invasion of, 80, 84,
        100–1
    Soviet military facilities in, 131
    U.S. influence on, 99–100
Africa, East, 133
Agent Orange, 98
Agnew, Harold, 224, 226
aircraft carriers, 129
Air Force, U.S., 220, 266–70
Air Force Space Command,
    U.S., 144
Air Land Battle, 209–10
Alameda Naval Air Station, 38
Allende, Salvador, 86–87
Alternate National Military
    Command Center
    (ANMCC), 31, 149, 151–52
American Revolution, 63
American Security Council, 78–79
Americans for Democratic
    Action (ADA), 21
Amin, Hafizullah, 100
amphibious assault ships, 129–30
Andropov, Yuri, 13, 20
Angola, Soviet military facilities
    in, 131

antiballistic missile (ABM) treaty,
    18, 66, 70, 118, 189
antisatellite warfare, 12
antisatellite weapons (ASAT),
    172
antisubmarine warfare, 12, 128
antisubmarine weapons, 164
antitank weapons, 127
Arbatov, Georgi, 212
Argentina, 40–41, 86, 163
Armed Forces Journal, 22–23
arms control, 25, 124–27
    initiatives needed in, 314–15
Arms Control Impact
    Statement (1980), 189, 197
arms race, 67–70, 308
    children on, 333–36
    MIRVing and, 68–69
    politicians and, 66, 70
Armstrong, Bill, 144
Assault-Breaker missile, 208
Atomic Energy Act (1947), 146
Australia, 134, 157–63, 216
    Northwest Cape facility in,
        161–62
    Pine Gap facility in, 159–61,
        162

B-1 bomber, 202–4, 266–70
B-52 bomber, 11, 121–22,
    266–67
    accidents with, 35–37
    EMP and, 33
Backfire bomber, Soviet, 77,
    121

Ball, Desmond, 24, 27
Ballistic Missile Early Warning System (BMEWS), 154
Barron, John, 20–21
Baruch Plan, 59
Batzel, Roger, 226
Beilenson, Laurence, 26
Bello, Walden, 104–9
Bereanu, Bernard, 32
Bethe, Hans, 118, 223, 228–29
Bethlehem Steel, 50
Bid and Proposal (B&P) program, 263–64
Big Bird satellite, 161
Boeing Corporation, 71
Bohemian Grove, 348–49
bombers, strategic, 121–22, 156
Boston Globe, 75
Bradley, John, 29
Brandt, Willy, 80
Brazil, 85–86
Brezhnev, Leonid, 20, 71, 77
  freeze advocated by, 78, 82
  limited withdrawal and, 82
Broad, William, 34
Brodie, Bernard, 177
broken arrows (accidents with nuclear weapons), 34–37
Brown, Harold, 105, 127, 178
Brownson, Orestes, 46
Brzezinski, Zbigniew, 79, 82
Builddown proposal, 126
Burt, Richard, 10, 79
Bush, George, 18, 72
  on Soviet military buildup, 75
  on winnability, 24
Byrnes, James, 64

C³ (Command, Control and Communication), Soviet, 16, 24
C³I (Command, Control, Communications and Intelligence), U.S., 24, 142, 147–73
  command in, 147–50
  communications systems in, 154–55

continuity of government (COG) and, 148–50
  control in, 150–57
  evolution of, 165
  intelligence in, 157–64
  modernization of, 30
  nuclear war control and, 166–73
  rationale for, 164–65
  Surveillance, Warning, and Assessment in, 152–54
  vulnerability of, 167–73
C-5B transport plane, 270
California, defense work in, 270–72
Cambodia, 98–99
capitalism, 47
Carlucci, Frank, 23, 25
Carter, Jimmy, 9, 22, 83, 92, 178, 226, 267
  arms reduction proposal of, 77
  détente and, 77–78
  international arms sales and, 110–12
  MX missile and, 185
Casey, William, 77
Castle Air Force Base, 38
Castro, Fidel, 87
Center for Defense Information (CDI), 18–19
Central Intelligence Agency (CIA), 80, 97, 135, 138, 157–61
  Afghanistan and, 100–1
  Australian government and, 160
  Latin American operations of, 85–89, 95
  Pine Gap installation of, 159–61
  on Soviet civil defense, 17
  Soviet defense spending estimated by, 18, 72–75, 279
Chiang Kai-shek, 61
Chile, 86–87
China, People's Republic of, 17, 35, 40, 44, 61, 66, 70, 84
  revolution in, 61
  Soviet fear of, 103–5

China, People's Republic of *(cont.)*
  tanks of, 127
  troop strength of, 127
  U.S. military cooperation
    with, 108
Choice of Heroes, A (Gerzon),
    315–16, 328, 343
Church, Frank, 4, 80
circular error probable (CEP),
    defined, 182
civil defense, 17, 74, 221, 281–82,
    293–96
Civil War, U.S., 48–49, 63
Clark, William, 138, 202
Clark Air Force Base, 132–33
Cleveland, Grover, 51
climatic changes, from nuclear
    war, 304–6
Coalition for a Democratic
    Majority, 72
Cobra Dane, 154
Coffin, William Sloane, 3, 7
Cold War, 64–66, 70
Committee on the Present
    Danger, 66, 75–79, 126, 185
computers:
  false alerts from, 14, 28–32
  hackers and, 32
  obsolescence of, 29–30
  randomness inherent in, 32
Congress, U.S., 4, 71, 214
  defense spending and, 276
  MX missile and, 187–94
  neutron bomb and, 205
  see also House of
    Representatives, U.S.;
    Senate, U.S.
Conn, Rachel, 21
Constitution, U.S., 46
continuity of government
    (COG), 148–50
contracting, defense, 236–51
  "buying in" and, 273
  cost overruns in, 275
  cost-plus-fee basis for, 273
  for MX missile, 189–94
  overpricing in, 273–74
  see also military-industrial
    complex, U.S.

conventional forces, 127–30
  potential use of, 128–30
  reduction recommended for,
    141
  role of, 139–40
conventional weapons, 110–12,
    139
  near-nuclear, 207–8
  sophistication of, 112
Cooling, Benjamin Franklin, 51
counterforce (first-strike) war,
    6, 10–15, 25, 62, 69, 165,
    175–77
  accuracy and, 10–12
  fallout from, 14, 213
  psychological problem of, 14
  scenario of, 12, 213
  strategy behind, 11–12
  U.S. arsenal designed for,
    350
  winnability of, 141
countervalue nuclear war, 10, 213
Cox, Arthur Macy, 4
Cronkite, Walter, 366
cruise missile, 4–5, 77, 197–200
  deployment of, 4–5, 82, 116,
    197–99
  detection of, 4–5, 198
  speed of, 11
Cuba, 50, 87–88, 360–61
  Bay of Pigs invasion of, 88
  revolution in, 87–88
  Soviet brigade in, 4, 80
  Soviet military facilities in,
    131
Cuban missile crisis, 3, 67, 178

Dailey, Peter, 202
Daniels, Marta, 3
Daud, Mohammad, 99–100
Davis, Bennie L., 346–47
Day After, The, 357
Day After Trinity, The, 56
Declaration of Independence,
    U.S., 45–47, 138
Defense Communication
    Agency (DCA), 154
Defense Communications
    Systems (DCS), 155

Defense Department, U.S., 9, 12, 214
  continuity of government and, 148
  interservice rivalry in, 265–66
  locations of nuclear weapons and, 37–39
  offensive orientation of, 22
  R&D in, 263–64, 272
  waste in, 273–76
  see also contracting, defense; defense spending, U.S.
Defense Guidance Plans, 12, 16, 108, 181, 200, 211
  Philippines in, 133
  terrorists and, 39–40
Defense Intelligence Agency (DIA), 279
Defense of America, The, 357
defense spending, U.S., 66, 70, 83, 236
  Congress and, 276
  on nuclear vs. conventional weapons, 139
  social spending vs., 215–19
defense spending, worldwide, 216–18, 279–80
  dead-end products from, 219
  economic stimulation from, 218–19
  medical spending vs., 216–18
  no nuclear vs. conventional weapons, 139
Defense Support Program (DSP), 152–53
Delauer, Richard, 119–20, 179, 253, 269
Democratic Party, 10, 66
détente, 66, 70–72, 77–78, 81
deterrence, 140
Dickinson, Daniel S., 48
Dine, Thomas, 27
Dineen, Gerald, 31
dioxin, 98
disarmament, nuclear, 141, 358–59, 365–67
DSP-647 satellite, 152–53, 160, 180

Dubs, Adolph, 100
Dulles, John Foster, 65, 92, 97, 175

early warning system, 28–33
  Ballistic Missile, 154
  EMP and, 33–34
Effects of Nuclear War, The, 285
Egypt, 84
Ehrlich, Paul, 306
Einstein, Albert, 56, 58, 364
Eisenhower, Dwight D., 43, 65, 76, 97, 177, 226, 229, 277–78
election of 1984, U.S., 116–17
electromagnetic pulse (EMP), 32–34, 168
  results of, 34
  satellites and, 33–34
electronic warfare, 169
El Salvador, 88–91, 112
Emergency Rocket Communication System, 494-L (ERCS), 155
Emerson, Ralph Waldo, 46
Energy Department, U.S., 38, 189, 224, 227
Enhanced Perimeter Acquisition Raid Characterization Program, 154
Ethiopia, Soviet military facilities in, 131
Europe:
  détente and, 80–81
  nuclear war in, 23–24, 81–82
  U.S. as viewed in, 63–64
Europe, Eastern, 64
  see also Warsaw Pact nations
Europe, Western:
  productivity growth in, 219
  Soviet Union and, 60, 80–82
  see also North Atlantic Treaty Organization
evacuation, 293, 294–96
Exocet missile, 112, 127, 207

F-16 fighter, 107
fallout, radioactive, 1, 282, 289–93
  from counterforce nuclear war, 14, 213

fallout shelters, 286, 293, 296–98
Fallows, James, 265
Fate of the Earth, The (Schell), 79
Fat Man, 58
fear, projection of, 212–13
Federal Emergency Management Agency (FEMA), 148, 293–96
Federal Preparedness, 148
Federal Prison Industries, Incorporated, 277
first-strike doctrine, *see* counterforce war
flexible response, 9, 141, 165
Ford, Gerald R., 66, 71, 75
Foreign Assistance Act (1961), 134
Forrestal, James, 43
Forsberg, Randall, 128, 139
494-L Emergency Rocket Communication System (ERCS), 155
Fowler, Henry, 76
France, 35, 40, 50, 124, 139, 142
  revolution in, 47
fratricide, missile, 187
freeze, bilateral, 4, 18, 20–21, 78, 126, 141–42, 358
Fresno Air Terminal, 38

Gaither Report, 65
Gale, Roger, 135
Gaylor, Noel, 18
General Accounting Office (GAO), 29–30, 267
George Air Force Base, 38
Germany, Federal Republic of (West), 219, 220
  Ostpolitik and, 80
Germany, Imperial, 50
Germany, Nazi, 55–56, 59, 76
Gerzon, Mark, 315–16, 328, 343
Giller, Edward B., 38
Goldwater, Barry, 29, 175
Graham, Daniel O., 73, 345
Gray, Collin, 26, 77
Great Britain, 35, 40, 50, 101, 124

Greece, 134
Grenada, U.S. invasion of, 115
ground forces, 18, 69, 127
Guatemala, 91–93

Halloran, Richard, 12
Halperin, Martin, 69
Harriman, Averell, 116
Hart, Gary, 29
Hayes, Peter, 104–9
Helsinki Declaration (1975), 102
Hersh, Seymour, 327
Hiatt, Howard, 216–17
High Frontier system, 117–18
Hiroshima, atomic bombing of, 57, 140, 284, 299
Hiroshima (Hersey), 284
Hitler, Adolf, 55–56, 64, 319
Honduras, 95
Hoover, Herbert, 53
Hopkins, Harry, 64
hormones, male vs. female, 317
hotline, 151, 172
House of Representatives, U.S.: Appropriations Committee of, 41–42, 276
  Armed Services Committee of, 148, 276
  Government Operations Committee of, 158
Housing and Urban Development Department (HUD), U.S., 148
Humphrey, Hubert, 65
hydrogen bomb, development of, 61
Hyland, William, 77

Ikle, Fred, 77
Independent Research and Development (IR&D) program, 263–64
India, 35, 40, 84
Institute for Canadian and American Studies, 4
intelligence activities, 134, 153, 154, 157–64

intercontinental ballistic missiles (ICBMs), Soviet, 122–23, 180
  detection of, 152–53
  hardened silos of, 67–68
  liquid fueling for, 20
  missiles (ICBMs), U.S., 123, 156
Intermediate Range Nuclear Forces (INF) talks, 25, 124–25
  Walk in the Woods proposal in, 25
  zero-zero option proposal for, 124–25
International Institute for Strategic Studies, 24
interventionist strategy, U.S., 133
Iran, 2, 41, 97–98
Iranian hostage crisis, 97, 101
Iraq, 84
Iron Triangle, defined, 234
Iron Triangle, The (Adams), 238–50
Israel, 41, 112, 114, 127, 208
Italy, 139

Jackson, Henry "Scoop," 71, 75, 79
Jackson-Vanick amendment, 71
Japan, 50, 107–8, 220
  atomic bombing of, 57–58, 140, 284, 299
  in World War II, 58
Jefferson, Thomas, 46–47
Jesus, 322, 364–65
Johnson, Lyndon B., 65–66, 327–28
Joint Chiefs of Staff (JCS), 146, 265–66
  Chairman of, 28, 265–66
Jones, David, 265–66
Jones, T.K., 17, 27, 74–75, 252, 296
J.P. Morgan and Company, 52
Jung, Carl, 321

Kahn, Herman, 220–22
KC-10 aerial tanker, 122

KC-135 aerial tanker, 122
Kemp, Jeffrey, 76–77
Kennan, George, 62–63, 116, 358, 362–63
Kennedy, John F., 2–3, 65–67, 178
  flexible response and, 141
  "Strategy of Peace" speech of, 2, 20, 315
Keyworth, George, 145
KH-11 satellites, 161–63
Khrushchev, Nikita, 2, 65, 277–78, 291
  Kennedy initiatives and, 2
Kirkland, Lane, 76
Kirkpatrick, Jeane, 77
Kissinger, Henry, 65, 70, 75, 81–82, 87, 98, 135, 139, 178, 253, 327
Kistiakowsky, George, 9
Kohler, Foy D., 73
Korean jetliner incident, 34, 104, 109, 114
Korean War, 62
Kotrady, Konrad, 137
Kramer, Ken, 144
Kristol, Irving, 72
Kupperman, Charles, 25

land-based strategic systems, 5, 19
LaRocque, Gene, 18
laser beams, 117–18, 228–29
Last Epidemic, The, 324–26
Latin America, U.S. intervention in, 85–97
launch-on warning, 123
Lawrence-Livermore laboratory, 224, 228–29
Lebanon, U.S. involvement in, 114–15
Lehman, John, 77, 107, 253
Lehman Doctrine, 107
lethality, defined, 184
Levin, Carl, 119
Lilienthal, David, 59
limited nuclear war, 9, 23, 27, 65, 108–9
  rejection of, 211–14

limited nuclear war *(cont.)*
  results of, 213–14
  Soviets on, 109, 211–12
  winnable, 12–13
Little Boy, 57
Los Alamos laboratory, 56, 223–24
love, as emotional dynamic in society, 314
Low-Altitude Air Defense System, 206
Luce, Henry B., 61

MacArthur, Arthur, 133
MacArthur, Douglas, 20
McCone, John, 178
McNamara, Robert, 13, 149, 165
McPherson, Peter, 202
Mahan, Alfred T., 49
Maneuverable Reentry Vehicle (MARV), 186, 200
Manhattan Project, 56–58
manifest destiny, 48
Mansfield, Mike, 80
Mao Tse-tung, 61
March Air Force Base, 38
Marcos, Ferdinand, 133, 134
Mark-12A warhead, 123, 184
Mark 48 antisubmarine torpedo, 164
Marshall Islands, 135–38
Marshall Plan, 60
massive retaliation (assured destruction) doctrine, 165, 175
Mather Air Force Base, 38
medical effects of nuclear weapons, 284–94
  disease as, 292–94, 298–300
  fallout and, 289–91
  neutron weapons and, 206
  Soviet TV program on, 17–18
  sterilization as, 299–300
  treatment of, 290–91, 293
  unsanitary conditions and, 292–94
  from UV light, 302–4
Mendelson, Everett, 3
Micronesia, 135–38

Middle East, 134
Midgetman missile, 188
military-industrial complex, U.S., 50–53, 59, 233–80
  accounting firms and, 257
  advertising by, 261–63
  conversion of, to peaceful purposes, 359–62
  financial institutions in, 256–57
  geographical distribution of, 270–73
  grass-roots organization by, 262–63
  "incestuous" relationships in, 234–35, 237–41, 251–53, 258–59, 264
  jobs created by, 236
  leading companies in, 251
  lobbying by, 238–55, 258–63, 268–70
  PACs used by, 254
  politicians and, 235, 253–55
  psychology of, 347–49
  Soviet menace and, 66, 69–70
  steel companies and, 51
  trade associations and, 259–61
  Washington offices in, 254–55
  after World War II, 59–61
  see also contracting, defense
Minuteman missile, 11, 184
Minuteman II missile, 123
MIRV (Multiple Independently Targetable Reentry Vehicle), 19, 68–69, 71, 182–84, 187–88
  advantages of, 183
missile gap, 65, 67, 179
Monroe Doctrine, 48–50, 63, 84, 96
Mt. Weather, Va., 152
Moynihan, Daniel Patrick, 72
Mutual and Balanced Force Reduction talks, 80
mutually assured destruction (MAD) doctrine, 10
MX missile, 11–12, 141, 185–95, 270

MX missile *(cont.)*
  basing modes for, 186–88
  contractors for, 189–94
  description of, 186
mycotoxin (yellow rain), 101

Nagasaki, atomic bombing of, 58,
    140, 299
Nation, The, 104–9
National Command Authority
    (NCA), 15, 146–49, 156
  succession and, 147
National Defense (Fallows), 265
National Emergency Airborne
    Command Post (NEACP),
    149, 152, 170–71
nationalism, 310–11
National Military Command
    Center (NMCC), 31, 149,
    151–52
National Military Command
    System, 152
National Reconnaissance Office
    (NRO), 157, 161
National Security Agency (NSA),
    86, 157–61
National Security Council (NSC),
    29
National Security Decision
    Documents, 12, 230
National Security Planning
    Group, 138
national technical means, 5
NAVSTAR, 11, 186, 196
Navy, U.S.:
  antisubmarine warfare system
    of, 128
  Australian facilities of,
    161–63
  in North Pacific, 106–9
  nuclear weapons storage of, 38
  power projection forces of, 129
  pre-World War I buildup of,
    51
  steel industry and, 51
neutron bomb, 81, 205–7
Newman, James R., 221
New York Times, 10, 12, 14, 75,
    79, 93, 264

Nicaragua, 93–97
Nitze, Paul, 25, 73, 75–76, 125
Nixon, Richard M., 20, 66, 87,
    98, 146, 178, 327
nonintervention treaty, proposed,
    141
North American Air Defense
    Command (NORAD), 29,
    31
  EMP and, 33
North Atlantic Treaty
    Organization (NATO),
    60–61
  antitank weapons of, 127
  bombs over troops chosen by,
    62, 69
  defense spending by, 279
  first use doctrine of, 62, 69
  long-range missiles deployed
    by, 5, 81–82
  Pershing II and, 201–2
  tanks of, 127
  troop strength of, 127
  Warsaw Pact balance with,
    16, 18, 74, 127
North Island Naval Air Station,
    38
NSC-68, 76
Nuclear Emergency Search Team
    (NEST), 40
nuclear energy:
  development of, 56–57
  internationalization suggested
    for, 59
Nuclear Illusion and Reality
    (Zuckerman), 226–27
nuclear war:
  control of, 166–73
  conventional forces and, 140–41
  effects of, 281–307
  famine after, 300–1
  media discussion of, 356–57
  warning of, 282
  winnability of, 12–13, 78,
    141, 214
nuclear weapons, 325–27
  accidents with (broken arrows),
    34–37
  blackmail with, 177–81

nuclear weapons *(cont.)*
    defensive measures against, 117–18
    as deterrence, 140
    explosion of, described, 283–86
    lateral proliferation of, 40–41
    location of, 38–39
    military personnel and, 41–42
    miniaturization of, 69
    worldwide distribution of, 117
nuclear winter, 306–7
Nunn, Sam, 207

Omega network, 163–64
on-site inspection, 78
On the Beach (Shute), 1, 15
On Thermonuclear War (Kahn), 220–21
Oppenheimer, Robert, 56–57, 61, 119
Ortega Saavedra, Daniel, 96–97
over-the-horizon (OTH) radar, 154
ozone layer, 301–4
    eyes and, 303
    microorganisms and, 304
    plankton, algae and, 304
    skin and, 303–4

Packard, David, 76, 196
Pahlevi, Mohammed Reza, Shah of Iran, 97, 99
Pakistan, 41
Panama, 49, 52
Pantex, 38
parity, 13, 78
    end of, 141
    second-strike, 141
particle beams, 118
Peace Through Strength, 78
People Protection Act, 144
Percy, Charles, 119
Perle, Richard N., 25, 71, 77, 125
Perry, William, 169, 362
Pershing 1A missile, 123
Pershing II missile, 5–6, 16, 82, 116, 141, 200–2
    targets of, 6
Persian Gulf, 209

Personnel Reliability Program (PRP), U.S., 41
Philippines, U.S. bases in, 132–34
Physicians for Social Responsibility, 8, 79, 290
Pipes, Richard, 25, 72–73, 74, 76
plague, 293–94
Podhoretz, Norman, 72
Poland, 101–2
Policy of Mutual Example, 2, 315
Pol Pot, 98–99
Poseidon missile, 195
Poseidon submarine, 121, 195, 196
Presidential Directive, 9, 10, 58, 148
Presidential Directive, 9–10, 59, 212
Price of Peace and Freedom, The, 78–79
Price of Power, The (Hersh), 327
Project Democracy, 138
psychological effects of nuclear war, 298–99
psychology, 308–49
    anima vs. animus in, 321–23
    of children, 333–38
    of counterforce war, 14
    grief process and, 325
    hormones and, 317
    of men vs. women, 315–23, 349
    military, 342–47
    of military-industrial complex, 347–49
    psychic numbing and, 323–25, 329–33
    of scientists, 339–42
    sexuality and, 318–21, 327–29
    violence and, 317–18
Pyramider project, 160–61

radar, 29–31, 33, 154
RAND Corporation, 175–77, 220–23
range, defined, 185

Rapid Deployment Force, U.S., 115, 133, 209–10
readiness, defined, 182
Reagan, Ronald, 15–21, 66, 114, 144, 361
  age of, 22
  on bilateral freeze, 18, 20–21
  computers and, 146
  Guardian report on, 23
  on limited nuclear war, 23–24, 108
  on Soviets, 16–20, 26–27, 83, 312–13
  on survivability, 24
  on video games, 144
Reagan administration, 12, 124, 282
  builddown proposal of, 126
  defensive measures sought by, 117–18
  European reaction to, 82–83
  INF talks and, 124–25
  international arms sales and, 110–12
  Middle East policy of, 178
  military buildup of, 13, 181, 215–18
  MX missile and, 187–95
  North Pacific and, 104–9
  on Pershing II, 200–2
  START proposals of, 125–26
  Star Wars weapons and, 229
  Team B report and, 75
  treaty talks abandoned by, 21–22
  winnability and, 12–13, 78, 141, 214
Red Square, brides in, 6
reliability, defined, 182
research and development (R&D), 263–64, 272
reserve, strategic, 10
Rhyolite satellite, 160
Rickover, Hyman, 257, 275
Rockwell Corporation, B-1 bomber and, 267–68, 276
Roosevelt, Franklin D., 43, 56, 58
  Soviet Union recognized by, 55

Roosevelt, Theodore, 48, 51–52
Ross, Thomas, 31
Rostow, Eugene V., 25, 60, 72, 75–76
Rumsfeld, Donald, 185
Russia, Imperial, 50, 55
  revolutions in, 53
  see also Soviet Union

Sachs, Alexander, 56
Sadat, Anwar, 20
Sagan, Carl, 14, 304, 306
SALT I, 66, 70–71
  criticism of, 71–72
  MIRVing and, 19, 68–69, 71, 182
  verification and, 5, 161
SALT II, 3, 75–77
  cruise missiles and, 82
  hearings for, 80
  Pershing missiles and, 82
  strategic parity as basis for, 78
  verification and, 5
Sandia National Laboratory, 224, 341
satellites, 142–47, 161–62
  antisatellite weapons (ASAT) and, 12, 172
  EMP and, 32–33
  operation of, 152–53
  strategic weapons detected by, 5, 161
  vulnerability of, 171–72
SAVAK, 97, 99, 100
Scheer, Robert, 22
Schell, Jonathan, 79
Schlesinger, James, 72, 75–76, 146, 178, 226
Schmidt, Helmut, 81
scientists, 70, 223–30
  psychology of, 339–42
  rational approach of, 220–23
Scoville, Herbert, Jr., 75
Scowcroft, Brent, 178
Scrowcroft Commission, 187–88
Seal Beach Naval Weapons Station, 38, 39
second-strike parity, 141
Seiberling, John, 137

self-forging fragments (SFF), 208
Senate, U.S.:
  Armed Services Committee of,
    29, 119, 148
  Foreign Relations Committee
    of, 80, 119
  Intelligence Committee of, 159
Shultz, George, 22, 77, 202
Shute, Nevil, 1, 15
Signals Intelligence sources,
    153
Sihanouk, Prince of Cambodia,
    98
Single Integrated Operational
    Plan (SIOP), 141, 342
SMART weapons, 127
Smith, Adam, 47, 219
Solidarity union, 102
Somoza Debayle, Anastasio, 93
South Africa, 41, 99, 138
South Korea, 41, 107–8
South Yemen, Soviet military
    facilities in, 131
Soviet Military Power (Defense
    Department), 279
Soviet Peace Committee, 3
Soviet Union, 3–7, 10, 54, 70, 84,
    131
  Afghanistan and, 80, 84, 100–1,
    131
  arms control proposals and, 126
  birth of, 53–54
  China feared by, 103–5
  civil defense system of, 17
  defense spending of, 13, 18,
    72–74, 277–80
  foreign military facilities of, 131
  limited nuclear war rejected
    by, 109, 211–12
  North Pacific and, 104–9
  nuclear weapons developed by,
    61–62
  paranoia of, 103–5, 109, 308–10
  power projection capability of,
    129–30
  Reagan on, 16–20, 26–27, 83,
    312–13
  space warfare and, 143–44
  Targeting Doctrine of, 211–12

technology of, 13, 31
  Third World arms sales of, 110,
    112
  U.S. bases around, 62
  U.S. paranoia about, 44–45,
    59–66, 78–83, 178–81, 313,
    363–64
  vs. U.S. capabilities, 119–20
  Western Europe and, 60,
    80–82
  World War II and, 6, 55, 58
  after World War II, 58–61
space, 143–46
  defensive weapons in, 117–18,
    228–30
  see also satellites
space shuttle, 145
Spanish American War, 49
SS-18 missile, 184
SS-20 missile, 16, 81, 124
Stalin, Joseph, 55, 64, 310
Star Path video game, 143–44
START (Strategic Arms
    Reduction Talks), 19, 25,
    125–27
Star Wars weapons, 117–18, 228–30
State Department, U.S., 65, 92
stealth bomber, 204–5
stealth technology, 199
steel companies, U.S., 51
Stillwell, R.G., 77
Stockholm International Peace
    Research Institute, 37, 124
Strategic Air Command (SAC),
    31, 156, 174–75
  nuclear weapons storage by,
    38–39
strategic weapons, 5, 120–23
  cruise missiles as, 5, 126, 198
  operational control of, 155–57
  tactical weapons vs., 124
  U.S. vs. Soviet totals of, 119–21
Subic Naval Base, 132
submarine-launched ballistic
    missile (SLBM), 5, 154
  detection of, 152–53
  land-based weapons vs. 19
  U.S., control system for, 157,
    164–65, 170, 172–73

submarines, 11, 19, 68, 121
  antiship, 128
  NATO vs. Warsaw Pact, 18
  U.S., communication with,
    19, 161–64, 170, 172–73, 196
SUBROC antisubmarine
  missile, 164
"Summary of Navy Nuclear
  Weapons and Incidents," 37
survivability, 24
*Survival and Peace in the Nuclear
  Age* (Beilenson), 26
survivors, life for, 298–301
Sverdlovsk, nuclear accident at,
  3
Swedish Academy of Sciences,
  Royal, 282, 286, 291, 300,
  305, 307
Syria, 114–15, 131
Szilard, Leo, 56, 58

TACAMO plane, 170, 173
tactical nuclear war, 23–25
tactical nuclear weapons, 69,
  123–26
  distribution of, 123–24
Taiwan, 41, 61
tanks, 18
  comparative totals of, 127
targets and targeting, 5, 9, 222
  C³I and, 167–68
  cities as, 10, 213–14, 282–83
  hard vs. soft, 10
  ratio of weapons to, 281–82
Taylor, Maxwell, 65
Taylor, Theodore B., 34, 69
Team A report, 18, 72, 75
Team B report, 18, 72–75, 78
technology, high, 142–43
Teller, Edward, 56, 61, 117,
  223, 226, 228, 229
TERCOM (terrain contour
  matching), 4, 197–98
terrorist attacks, 39–40
test-ban treaty (1963), 2, 3, 65,
  77, 226–27
tests:
  atmospheric, 1
  underground, 3, 227

Thayer, Paul, 251
Thinking About National Security
  (Brown), 105
Third World, 41, 65, 84–113,
  141–42, 360–61
  conventional arms supplied to,
    110–13, 207
  food supply in, 300
  military spending in, 216
  Soviet intervention in,
    99–103, 130
  U.S. intervention in, 84–99,
    103, 130
Thompson, E.P., 280
Throw-weight (payload), defined,
  182
Titan missile, accident with
  (1980), 36
TRANET, 163
TREE (transient radiation
  effects on electronics), 168
Trident I missile, 195
Trident II (D5) missile, 12, 141,
  165, 195–97
Trident submarine, 12, 195–97
Trinity (the Gadget), 56–57
Truman, Harry S., 20, 58, 158,
  177
  Soviet relations and, 64
Tsipis, Kosta, 291
Two China policy, 61
Typhoon class submarine, 19

ultraviolet (UV) light, 302–4
Uncertain Trumpet (Taylor), 65
United Fruit, 91–92
United Nations (UN), 96, 135
  Atomic Energy Commission
    of, 64
United States:
  discrimination in, 46
  expansionist philosophy of,
    47–50
  foreign military facilities of,
    131–38
  French revolution and, 47
  imperialism of, 47
  industrialism in, 49
  productivity growth in, 219

United States *(cont.)*
  quality of work in, 219–20
  religious ethic in, 46
  Russian revolutions and,
    53–54
  as savior of mankind, 46–47
  self-government and, 45–49,
    138
  Soviet capabilities vs., 119–20
  Soviet Union as viewed in,
    44–45, 54–55, 59–66, 178–81,
    313, 363–64
  strategic weapons distribution
    of, 10–11
  Third World arms sales of,
    110–13
  unionism in, 55
United States leadership,
    42–43, 315, 323–29, 351–56
  paranoia of, 178–81
  psychic numbing of, 324–25
  public pressure on, 352–56
  sexual dynamics of, 325–29
universities, in arms race,
    230–32, 272

vacuum bomb, 208
Vance, Cyrus, 79
van Cleave, William R., 73, 77
verification, by satellites, 5, 161
Vessey, John, 119
video games, 143–45, 318
Vietnam, Soviet military facilities
    in, 130
Vietnam War, 3, 66, 98–99, 178
Vladivostok accords, 71, 77
Vogt, John W., Jr., 73

Wade, James P., Jr., 25–26
Wallis, W. Allen, 77
WarGames, 146, 357
Warnke, Paul, 17, 79
Warsaw Pact nations, 59, 62,
    103–4

  NATO balance with, 16, 18, 74,
    127
  Soviet paranoia and, 103–4
  tanks of, 127
  troop strength of, 127
Washington, D.C., 272–73
Wattenberg, Ben, 72
Wealth of Nations (Smith), 47
Weapons in Outer Space Treaty,
    145
Weinberger, Caspar, 12–13, 22,
    108, 119, 147, 198, 202
Weiss, Seymour, 73
Welch, Jasper A., Jr., 73
West, Francis, 109
wheat sales, 2
Whence the Threat to Peace?, 279
White, T.H., 61
Whitman, Gough, 160
Wick, Charles, 138, 202
Wiesner, Jerome, 64
Wilson, Woodrow, 43, 52–54
winnability of nuclear war, 12–13,
    78, 141, 214
Wolfe, Thomas, 73
Wolfowitz, Paul D., 73
Wood, Lowell, 228
Woolsey, R. James, 178, 265
World Health Organization
    (WHO), 137, 216–17, 287
World War II, 55–58, 292
  Soviet losses in, 6, 58
Worldwide Military Command
    and Control System
    (WWMCC), 30, 150–51, 154

X-ray beams, 118, 228–29

yield, 11–12, 182
Yom Kippur War (1973), 127
York, Herbert, 27, 225

Zuckerman, Sir Solly, 70, 226–27,
    340

ABOUT THE AUTHOR

A pediatrician from Australia, DR. HELEN CALDICOTT is a founder and the president emeritus of Physicians for Social Responsibility and a former member of the faculty at Harvard Medical School. Founder of Women's Action for Nuclear Disarmament, she lectures widely on the arms race. She is the star of the Academy Award–winning film *If You Love This Planet*, wife of Dr. William Caldicott, and mother of three children.

BANTAM NEW AGE BOOKS

Bantam New Age Books are for all those interested in reflecting on life today and life as it may be in the future. This important new imprint features stimulating works in fields from biology and psychology to philosophy and the new physics.

☐ 23564	**THE PICKPOCKET AND THE SAINT**		$4.50
	Sheldon B. Kopp		
☐ 14146	**SUPERMIND: THE ULTIMATE ENERGY**		$3.95
	Barbara B. Brown		
☐ 24147	**CREATIVE VISUALIZATION**	Shatki Gawain	$3.95
☐ 22511	**NEW RULES: SEARCHING FOR SELF-FULFILLMENT**		$3.95
	IN A WORLD TURNED UPSIDE DOWN		
	Daniel Yankelovich		
☐ 25223	**STRESS AND THE ART OF BIOFEEDBACK**		$4.95
	Barbara Brown		
☐ 24682	**THE FIRST THREE MINUTES**	Steven Weinberg	$3.95
☐ 20005	**MAGICAL CHILD**	Joseph Chilton Pearce	$3.95
☐ 24283	**MIND AND NATURE:** A Necessary Unity		$4.95
	Gregory Bateson		
☐ 24458	**ZEN/MOTORCYCLE MAINTENANCE**		$4.50
	Robert Pirsig		
☐ 20693	**THE WAY OF THE SHAMAN**	Michael Hamer	$3.95
☐ 24077	**TO HAVE OR TO BE?**	Erich Fromm	$3.95
☐ 24562	**LIVES OF A CELL**	Lewis Thomas	$3.95
☐ 14912	**KISS SLEEPING BEAUTY GOODBYE**		$3.95
	K. Kolbenschlag		

Prices and availability subject to change without notice.

Buy them at your local bookstore or use this handy coupon:

Bantam Books. Inc., Dept NA, 414 East Golf Road. Des Plaines. Ill. 60016

Please send me the books I have checked above. I am enclosing $_____
(please add $1.25 to cover postage and handling). Send check or money order
—no cash or C.O.D.'s please.

Mr/Mrs/Miss _____

Address _____

City _____ State/Zip _____

NA—5/85

Please allow four to six weeks for delivery. This offer expires 11/85.

SPECIAL MONEY SAVING OFFER

Now you can have an up-to-date listing of Bantam's hundreds of titles plus take advantage of our unique and exciting bonus book offer. A special offer which gives you the opportunity to purchase a Bantam book for only 50¢. Here's how!

By ordering any five books at the regular price per order, you can also choose any other single book listed (up to a $4.95 value) for just 50¢. Some restrictions do apply, but for further details why not send for Bantam's listing of titles today!

Just send us your name and address plus 50¢ to defray the postage and handling costs.

IF YOU'VE ENJOYED OTHER BOOKS FROM OUR NEW AGE LIST, WE'RE SURE YOU'LL WANT TO ADD MORE OF THEM TO YOUR COLLECTION